TECHNICAL INNOVATION AND BRITISH I

Technical Innovation and British Economic Performance

Science Policy Research Unit, Sussex

Edited by
Keith Pavitt

M

First published 1980
Reprinted 1981, 1982

Published by
THE MACMILLAN PRESS LTD
London and Basingstoke
Companies and representatives throughout the world

Printed in Hong Kong

British Library Cataloguing in Publication Data

Technical innovation and British economic performance
1. Technological innovations – Economic aspects – Great Britain
I. Pavitt, Keith
338.'06 HC260.T4
ISBN 0 333 26225 5 (hardcover)
ISBN 0 333 33381 0 (paperback)

Contents

Acknowledgements

The research on which this book is based was financed from a number of sources: the Central Electricity Generating Board, the Department of Industry, the Engineering Industry Training Board, the Leverhulme Trust, the National Economic Development Office, the Science Research Council and the Social Science Research Council. We are grateful for the encouragement given to us to write the book by John Ashworth of the Central Policy Review Staff.

The Science Policy Research Unit has benefited from outside contributions in the form of a specific chapter written by Jonathan Aylen of Salford University. At the same time, all authors benefited greatly from critical comments and suggestions by outside readers of early drafts including members of the staff of CPRS, and David Stout and his colleagues at the National Economic Development Office. We owe a particular debt to Daniel Jones, of the Sussex European Research Centre, who gave generously of his time and his ideas in commenting on other people's work; and to George Ray of the National Institute for Economic and Social Research, who made systematic and helpful comments on drafts of each of the chapters. Nevertheless, the authors take full responsibility for the book's contents. Neither its analysis nor its conclusions are those of the UK Government or any other body.

The authors have put up patiently and gracefully with continuing editorial demands for change, and for greater clarity and brevity. A considerable burden has also fallen on to the Unit's secretarial staff, with constant typing, retyping and revision of the various chapters; we are therefore grateful to Vicky Clay, Rosemary Gee, Janet Grundy, Charlotte Huggett, Maureen Kelly, Marjorie Lee, Milena Mackay, Hazel Robards and Sian Thomas. We are also grateful to Philippa Shepherd who did the copy-editing, and to Vivian Johnson who compiled the index.

Finally, we thank Christopher Freeman, Director of the Unit, who originally had the idea to prepare the book, and has given constant support to its preparation throughout; and Austen Albu who, after his retirement from politics, has not only contributed two chapters to this book, but has generously contributed his insights on a subject that – throughout his industrial and political career – he has always believed to be of major importance.

The author and publishers wish to thank the following who have kindly given permission for the use of copyright material: British Gas Corporation for extracts from the figures in the *Annual Reports 1950–1977*, published by HMSO; Cambridge University Press for the tables from *Industrial Growth and World Trade* (1963) by A. Maizels and *The British Machine Tool Industry 1850–1914* (1976) by R. Floud; Concast A.G., Zurich, for the table from *World Survey* (March 1977); the Controller of HMSO for the tables from official publications; Council of Engineering Institutions for the table from *CEI's 1975 Survey of Professional Engineers*; The Daily Telegraph Limited for the table of CEGB cost figures published in the *Daily Telegraph* 31 October 1978; Engineering Employers' Federation for the table in *Graduates in Engineering* (1977); Financial Times Limited for the table from *Financial Times* (17 January 1977); IPC Science and Technology Press Limited for the table from 'Energy use in U.K. Industry' by J. Chesshire and C. Buckley in *Energy Policy*, vol. 4, no. 2 (September 1976); Lloyds Register of Shipping for the table from their published figures; Metal Bulletin for the table from *Iron and Steel Works of the World*, 6th edn (1974) by R. Cordero and R. Serjeantson; The Metals Society for the table from 'Secondary Refining for Electric Steelmaking' by J. C. C. Leach, in *Ironmaking and Steelmaking*, vol. 4, no. 2 (1977); National Coal Board for the extracts from their published figures; Publications Board of the United Nations for the tables from *Growth and Stagnation in the European Economy* by Svennilson; Science Policy Research Unit, The University of Sussex, for the tables from their papers and publications; The Textile Institute for the table from an article by R. Rothwell published in *Textile Institute and Industry* (July 1977).

Every effort has been made to trace all the copyright holders but if any have been inadvertently overlooked the publishers will be pleased to make the necessary arrangement at the first opportunity.

December 1978 K.P.

Notes on the Contributors

A. ALBU, B.Sc. (London); Fellow of Imperial College, FCGI; Honorary Doctorate (Surrey); Associate Fellow, Science Policy Research Unit, University of Sussex.

J. AYLEN, B.A. (Sussex); lecturer in economics, University of Salford.

C. BUCKLEY, B.Sc. (Bath); M.A. (Sussex); British National Oil Corporation; formerly Fellow, Science Policy Research Unit, University of Sussex.

R. DAY, B.Sc. (CNAA); D.Phil. (Sussex); Fellow, Science Policy Research Unit, University of Sussex.

C. FREEMAN, B.Sc. (London); Honorary D. Phil. (Linköping); R. M. Phillips Professor of Science Policy, Associate of the Insitute of Development Studies, and Director of the Science Policy Research Unit, University of Sussex.

J. GARDINER, B.Sc. (Toronto); M.A. (Guelph).

M. KALDOR, B.A. (Oxon); Associate of the Institute for Development Studies, and Fellow of the Science Policy Research Unit, University of Sussex.

K. PAVITT, M.A. (Cantab); Senior Fellow, Science Policy Research Unit, University of Sussex.

M. ROBSON, B.Sc. (Sussex); Research Office, Science Policy Research Unit, University of Sussex.

R. ROTHWELL, B.Sc. Ph.D. (CNAA); Senior Fellow, Science Policy Research Unit, University of Sussex.

H. RUSH, B.A. (SUHY at Stonybrook); M.A. (Sussex); Fellow, Science Policy Research Unit, University of Sussex.

E. SCIBERRAS, B.A.; M.A. (Sydney); D.Phil. (Sussex), Fellow, Science Policy Research Unit, University of Sussex.

P. SENKER, M.A. (Cantab); Senior Fellow, Science Policy Research Unit, University of Sussex.

L. SOETE, Lic Econ; Lic Dev Econ (Ghent); D.Phil (Sussex), Fellow, Institute of Development Studies, and Associate Fellow, Science Policy Research Unit, University of Sussex.

A. SURREY, B.Sc. (London); Senior Fellow, Science Policy Research Unit, University of Sussex.

N. SWORDS-ISHERWOOD, B.Sc. (London); M.A. and D. Phil. (Sussex); Fellow, Science Policy Research Unit, University of Sussex.

J. TOWNSEND, B.A. (Dublin); Fellow, Science Policy Research Unit, University of Sussex.

W. WALKER, B.Sc. (Edinburgh); M.Sc. (Sussex); Research Fellow, Royal Institute of International Affairs, London, and Visiting Fellow, Science Policy Research Unit, University of Sussex.

1 Introduction and Summary

KEITH PAVITT[1]

This book is about technical innovation in industry: the development, commercialisation, adaptation and improvement of products and production processes. Its basic theme is that differences amongst firms and countries in the OECD area in their capacity for technical innovation have a significant influence on international competitiveness, economic growth and living standards. It argues that, for a long time, British industry's performance in technical innovation has on the whole been unsatisfactory in comparison with nearly all its major competitors, and that there are few signs of improvement. For Britain's economic performance and living standards to improve relative to those of other OECD countries will require – among other things – a deliberate policy to deal directly with British deficiencies in technical innovation.

THE ECONOMIC CONTEXT

Lack of technical innovation is not, of course the only thing that is wrong with the British economy, nor can it be isolated from a great deal else that is happening. Beckerman *et al.* (1965), Cairncross (in press, 1979) and others have argued that Britain is in a vicious circle of low economic performance, low expectations, low investment and therefore yet lower performance. The authors of this book believe that making this circle virtuous will require a fundamental transformation of British attitudes, skills and resources committed to technical innovation.

This is now being recognised by some analysts and policy-makers. In a recent book on Britain's industrial problems compiled at the National Institute of Economic and Social Research (Blackaby, in press, 1979), most of the contributors agree that the nub of the British economic problem is the lack of competitiveness and the inefficiency of manufacturing industry, compared to our major competitors, reflected in relatively slow rates of growth of manufacturing output and productivity, and a steadily declining share of world manufacturing exports. Some of the contributors see other manifestations of British economic ills as consequences, rather than causes, of this lack of competitiveness: the loss of manufacturing employment, low investment, 'stop/go' policies restricting aggregate demand as a consequence of recurrent balance of payments crises, the perception of a heavy burden of public expenditure and high personal taxation.

In any event, by the mid-1970s, Britain had lower productivity than most other EEC and OECD countries. In the EEC and OECD industrial leagues, Britain has been relegated to the Second Division. This relegation is not just a matter of national prestige, or of international standing. It reflects the standard and style of living in Britain compared to other industrialised countries, particularly in private consumption and social expenditures. It also has major political and social consequences, particularly in reinforcing defensive and hostile attitudes towards foreigners and minorities. Our concern with higher productivity and competitiveness in British industry is not simply one of growth for growth's sake. Improved industrial performance in Britain is, we believe, a necessary condition for improved quality of life, and for more relaxed and generous attitudes and policies towards the outside world.

British industrial inefficiency is reflected in low labour productivity and low efficiency of investment, both of which could be symptoms of lack of technical innovation in production processes. There are also disquieting but revealing features in the income and price elasticities of demand for British manufacturing exports and imports. The rest of the world's income elasticity of demand for British manufacturing exports has been lower than the British income elasticity of demand for the rest of the world's manufacturing exports (Thirlwall, 1978; Stout, in press, 1979). This means that Britain tends to run into balance of payments crises when the British economy grows, because it does less well than the rest of the world in making and selling the things that people want to buy as they get richer. The ability to sell these things depends not just on their price, since the British problem has persisted in spite of relatively favourable price trends over the past ten years. 'Non-price factors' are now recognised as important in competitiveness but, as Posner and Steer (in press, 1979) stress, they form part of

> . . . a black box whose basic laws are not well understood.

This book peeps into the black box, and tries to understand a little better what is going on inside it. We do not explore all its corners. Labour and capital productivity, as well as non-price competitiveness, are influenced by things other than technical innovation as we have defined it: for example, labour relations (Dore, 1973); company and national provision for changing levels of economic activity (Lossius, 1977); exploitation of available economies of scale (Jones and Prais, 1978). These factors can all be classified as better management and use of existing capacity. Walker argues in Chapter 2, and Rothwell in Chapter 17, that the problems of managing innovation are often more demanding than those of managing existing capacity. However, the problems of innovation cannot be separated from the others. This can be seen most clearly in the shipbuilding industry (Albu, Chapter 11), but it is apparent also in other sectors that we have examined.

SCOPE AND LIMITATIONS

We have tried as best we could, with the resources at our disposal, to meet the dual objectives demanded by the nature of our task, of breadth and generalisation on the one hand, and of depth and detailed understanding on the other. Part I looks at broad subjects that go beyond specific industrial sectors: the historic dimension of British innovative backwardness (Chapter 2); comparisons between Britain and other countries in innovative activities and export performance (Chapter 3); the training, status and use of engineers and of managers (Chapters 4 and 5); and the role of technical change in the defence industries (Chapter 6). Part II (Chapters 7 to 16) is made up of chapters which explore, in more detail in specific sectors, the links between technical innovation and economic performance, as well as the nature and sources of technical innovation, and the factors affecting its rate and direction. Part III consists of chapters that discuss implications for policy in industry and Government (Chapters 17 and 18).

The book has important gaps. Much of the work presented is based on projects and programmes in the Science Policy Research Unit that were initiated for other purposes. We had neither the time nor the resources to initiate a research programme that would have ensured comprehensive and balanced coverage of the problems related to innovation. In Part I, there is no discussion of workers' and trade unions' attitudes and behaviour towards technical innovation, and we have not been able to pursue in any systematic and scholarly way the scattered bits of evidence that Britain's industrial workforce as a whole is under-educated compared to that of other countries, in the same way that Britain's engineers and managers are. Nor have we been able to explore whether the way that British industry is financed hampers innovation, by comparison with other countries.

In Part II of the book, the range of sector studies is uneven. There is no detailed analysis of any branch of the chemical industry (except a bit in the chapter on gas), of durable consumer goods (such as household electrical appliances, radio and TV, automobiles), or of non-durable consumer goods (such as textiles, furniture, clothing, footwear, leather goods, pottery and glass). On the other hand, energy-related industries are well covered (coalmining machinery, heavy electrical equipment, nuclear energy and gas), as are electronics and steel. In addition, there are several chapters on various branches of the engineering industry: textile machinery, coalmining machinery, forklift trucks, shipbuilding and portable power tools. In spite of the apparently varied nature of these product groups, they have common problems that must be taken seriously, given the importance of engineering products for British trade.

Finally, in Part III, there is no systematic and detailed comparison of the place of innovation in British management practice with that in other countries. Nor is the effectiveness of the various Government policies that influence technical innovation systematically assessed.

In spite of these limitations, some clear and, we think, important conclusions do emerge from the book. Sometimes the conclusions corroborate what other writers have said, sometimes they add a further dimension, and sometimes they say something completely different. The rest of this chapter will be spent in summarising these conclusions, and discussing some of their implications.

TECHNICAL INNOVATION: ITS ROLE AND NATURE

The first conclusion is that, in the industrial sectors where most of the OECD manufacturing exports are concentrated, technical innovation is an essential feature in competitiveness, as measured by world export shares. Pavitt and Soete (Chapter 3) show significant statistical associations between countries' level of innovative activities and their world export shares, in most categories of capital goods and chemicals; the associations also exist, weaker but still significant, in durable consumer goods and in iron and steel.

The causal nature of these statistical associations becomes clearer in the chapters studying specific sectors, which often show how successful innovation has led to growing market shares, and lack of innovation to decline and even extinction. In captial goods, a high premium is placed by users on technical quality. Total life-cycle costs of a capital good depend only to some extent on initial purchase price. From relatively mundane products like forklift trucks and portable power tools (Senker, Chapter 9, Waller and Gardiner, Chapter 11), through textile-machinery (Rothwell, Chapter 7) to large-scale heavy electrical equipment (Surrey, Buckley and Robson, Chapter 13), it is rational for users to put a high premium on technical characteristics of performance and reliability, given that the costs to them of poor performance or breakdown are considerable. Similar considerations may also be relevant to durable consumer goods, which can be described as domestic capital goods (Gershuny, 1978).

High technical quality requires strong innovative effort. It may also mean higher costs and prices, as in the case of textile machinery. In the case of micro-electronics, however, Sciberras (Chapter 16) shows how increased performance and reliability have gone hand in hand with rapidly diminishing costs; this is probably why, as Freeman argues in Chapter 18, the implications of innovation in micro-electronics are so important and so widespread.

On the nature of technical innovation, certain common features certainly do emerge. Formal research and development activities have become more important as sources of technical innovation in textile machinery, coalmining machinery (Townsend, Chapter 8) and other sectors of mechanical engineering, with the increasing penetration of chemical, electronics and other technologies into what were previously considered (often wrongly) as traditional and technically stagnant. In nearly all the sectors that we have studied, an in-house R&D capacity has become a prerequisite for successful innovation. Rothwell points out in Chapter 17 that the successful management of technical innovation in all sectors requires balance and integration amongst what are often considered as separate activities in the industrial firm: R&D production, marketing and planning.

However, the nature of innovations varies widely amongst sectors. In iron and steel (Aylen, Chapter 12) and in gas (Rush, Chapter 15) the major innovations have been process innovations, even if they have been provoked by, or resulted in, some changes in the quality of the product. In mechanical engineering, on the other hand, the main focus has been product innovation, even if the implications for production methods must always be taken into account. Economies of scale have been important in iron and steel, and in all other process industries, and learning economies have been important in the production of electronic components. However, Buckley and Day (Chapter 14) suggest that 'learning economies' in nuclear energy might in fact be negative at present. And the chapters on specific sectors show clear differences in the contributions made to innovation by users, by suppliers of equipment and components, and by members of the workforce.

BRITISH PERFORMANCE IN TECHNICAL INNOVATION

Britain's performance as measured by per capita innovative activities and by per capita exports has been well below that of F R Germany, Sweden,

Switzerland and the Netherlands in chemicals and capital goods, well below all these countries and Japan in household durable consumer goods, and well below F R Germany and Sweden in motor vehicles; only in aerospace and other defence-related sectors does Britain do better than these countries. By comparison with other Western European countries and with Japan, Britain's innovative activities are heavily concentrated in nuclear energy, defence and civil aviation. Between 1967 and 1975, the relative British concentration on aerospace and other defence-related sectors actually increased.

Britain was the only major OECD country where industry-financed R&D activities (one measure of innovative activities in industry) decreased absolutely between 1967 and 1975. The decline compared to other OECD countries was very marked, and can be explained mainly by the lower proportion of value added that British industrialists decided to commit to R&D, and not by the relatively low rate of value added growth. The decrease was very strong in mechanical engineering where, as Albu (Chapter 4) and Swords-Isherwood (Chapter 5) show, there has been a particular reluctance to recruit graduate engineers and managers. The chapters dealing with engineering goods often show that British firms have found it very difficult to keep up competitively with the rate of innovation imposed by Germany, Sweden, Switzerland, Netherlands, Japan and the USA.

The low importance given to graduates in engineering and management is not specific to the mechanical engineering sector. Chapters 4 and 5 show that, by comparison with Continental Europe and with the USA, the degree of academic achievement and professional training of British engineers and managers is generally low. Rothwell suggests in Chapter 17 that this is one reason for the inefficiency in the innovation process – in coupling R&D successfully to production and production and marketing – apparent in the 1950s and 1960s in the UK.

In addition to the rapid British decline in innovative activities in mechanical engineering, there has been a decline in electrical and electronic products. Only chemicals has held up reasonably well, particularly agricultural chemicals and pharmaceuticals. It is perhaps significant that graduate scientists and engineers play a relatively strong role in management in the British chemical industry (Chapter 5).

INTERPRETATION

Our findings are consistent with those of historians who have stressed the relative lack of professional and technical competence of British industry in the twentieth century (Allen, 1976; Barnett, 1972; Hobsbawm, 1968; Landes,

1969). They are also consistent with the results of a number of more recent studies. Walker (Chapter 2) shows how British backwardness could be measured before the First World War as differences between Britain and, say, Germany in broad sectors of production: Britain was still producing more textiles, whilst Germany was producing more chemicals and machines. By the 1950s, these broad sectoral differences had disappeared (Panic, 1976). The differences can now be seen within quite narrow product groups. Compared with Germany and other major competitors, Britain is producing unsophisticated machinery and durable consumer goods, requiring relatively few innovative activities, and having relatively low unit values and value to weight ratios (Stout *et al.*, 1977; Saunders (in press, 3 Sept. 1979).[2] However, with increasing wages and income, it is precisely for the more sophisticated goods that the rate of growth of demand often is the highest. As Rothwell shows (Chapter 7), the main reason British textile manufacturers did not buy British textile machines in the 1970s was not their high price, but their technical inferiority compared to those available from Germany, Switzerland, Czechoslovakia and elsewhere. This interpretation is consistent with the statistical evidence, cited earlier, of the importance of non-price factors in competitiveness, and the unfavourable income elasticities of demand for British exports and imports.

However, we must be aware that this interpretation is based on a world in which the dominant features are competition through product and process innovation, for the development and commercialisation of which firms deliberately commit considerable resources. It differs in important respects from the assumptions about industrial behaviour on which policy prescriptions for industrial innovation are often based.

First, it perceives a different causal relationship between national income per head and industrial innovation. It is often assumed that location of innovation is a consequence of differences in levels of wealth: scientific and technical knowledge flow easily across national and firm boundaries, and proximity to richer markets, where demands for new machines and consumer goods first emerge, gives the decisive advantage in innovation (Vernon, 1966). On the whole, the findings of this book support the view that the causality also runs the other way: firms and countries that deliberately and successfully commit more resources to industrial innovation gain a competitive advantage that increases their relative wealth.

Second, the findings of this book suggest that innovation will not follow automatically if volume of investment is right. Certainly, Aylen (Chapter 12) concludes that the rate of innovation in the steel industry depends strongly on the rate of investment; similar patterns can be observed in most process industries, where innovation consists mainly of embodied change in capital equipment to produce a reasonably homogeneous good. However, as Rush (Chapter 15) shows in the case of gas, the choice of the right technique to embody is not always obvious, and the ability to make good choices and subsequent improvements depends on the deliberate development of an in-house technological capability.

Furthermore, in sectors where there is a strong component of product innovation, the assumed causality from investment to innovation may not hold at all. In electronic components, Sciberras (Chapter 16) shows that the rate of product innovation is extremely high, so that opportunities for new application are emerging continuously: in other words, investment opportunities emerge as a consequence of innovation.[3] And even in the apparently more mundane sectors of mechanical engineering that we examined the main feature of competitiveness has been technical superiority; in this case, both high productivity and high investment can be seen as *consequences* of an innovative lead.

Third, the findings of this book show that the nature of decision-making in industry is very different from that described in many economic textbooks, where the industrialist makes an optimal choice based on perfect knowledge of production alternatives, and of factor prices and market demands. Under such circumstances, the decisions of British industrialists to invest less than the Germans in the newer industries before the First World War (Chapter 2) could be seen as a rational response to economic signals, as could the reluctance of British industrialists to employ graduate engineers and managers in the 1930s (Chapter 4), the lack of investment in R&D by the British weaving machinery industry in the 1950s (Chapter 7), and the lack of investment of the British motor-cycle industry in new designs in the face of Japanese competition in the 1960s (Chapter 17).

However, as writers like Nelson and Winter (1974, 1977) and Rosenberg (1976) stress, knowledge of alternatives is imperfect, obtaining it has a cost, and market conditions and technologies are changing continuously. Under such circumstances, Nelson and Winter argue that industrial decisions are seldom optimal: industrialists are trying to do somewhat better than in the past or just to cope. They have a certain discretion in three related activities: first, the process of search for alternatives, to which resources must be committed; second, the process of choice amongst the alternatives, which is inevitably based on imperfect information, does not therefore have a unique outcome, and involves uncertainty; third, a process of adaptation in search, choice and operating procedures, in the light of further information and experience.

With this view of industrial behaviour, Britain's past and present performance is not just an inevitable consequence of perverted market signals. It is the consequence of an accumulation of discretionary decisions reflecting the conservative characteristics and lack of professional competence of British managers, engineers and workers: relatively little search (i.e. innovative) activity, bad choices, and slow adaptation and learning. A revealing example is provided by Aylen (Chapter 12), who argues that the British steel industry initially took the wrong route in oxygen steel-making in the 1960s, in part because it was unwilling to step outside established practices to the same degree as steel industries in other countries.

POLICY IMPLICATIONS

The policy implications of this interpretation are clear. Technical innovation cannot be expected to happen automatically as a consequence of economic growth, since it is one of its fundamental causes. Nor can it be expected that fine tuning of the economic environment will, in and of itself, create the volume of technical innovation necessary for Britain to improve its industrial performance, since the capacity for technical innovation depends in large part on the attitudes and skills of managers, engineers and the workforce. As Freeman contends in Chapter 18, Britain needs an active policy for the supply side of industry.

One of the main problems is the pattern of innovative activities. Britain has almost a dual structure, with a heavy concentration of innovative activities and international comparative advantage in aerospace and other defence-related activities, and relatively small innovative expenditures and poor export performance in many other sectors of the economy. This finding is not strikingly new (see, for example, Maddock, 1975; Peck, 1968; Vig, 1968). What this book shows in addition is that the relative British concentration on aerospace has been increasing in the 1970s; that innovative activities in the 'bread and butter' industries – as Maddock (1975) has called them – have diminished in Britain, whilst increasing in every other major OECD country; and that this matters greatly for Britain's lack of export competitiveness.

Some analysts argue that Britain should build upon and strengthen its existing advantage in aerospace and defence-related activities. M. Kaldor (Chapter 6) suggests that the high level of innovative activities in the defence sector is an integral part of the relative decline in the capacity for civilian innovation in British industry. It is a consequence of the decline, in that defence markets often secure outlets for the production of uncompetitive British firms. It is also a cause, since it concentrates resources and energies on unnecessary technological embellishments, and allows bad habits to persist, such as the neglect of users' needs and market constraints in R&D programmes. These bad habits have extended into British civil aviation programmes, where unbridled technological ambition has often been allied to a lack of commercial realism.

Eads and Nelson (1971) and Jewkes (1972) have made the same arguments about all Government support for large-scale high technology. Gardner (1976) has systematically quantified the poor financial record of British Government support for development projects in civil aviation since the Second World War, and Walker (1976) has pointed out that the smaller and technologically less ambitious projects have on the whole been relatively more successful. Buckley and Day (Chapter 14) show similar tendencies in the British nuclear programme, where big ambitions have foundered because of neglect of engineering factors and of the market. One additional cost emerges from our studies of heavy electrical equipment and of nuclear energy, namely the dependence of industrial companies for development and design capabilities on Government agencies, thereby reducing their capacity to compete successfully on international markets.

M. Kaldor proposes that British defence R&D programmes should be reduced to more modest proportions, and a similar recommendation for greater modesty is implicit in what Buckley and Day say about nuclear energy. But it would be illusory to suppose that a reduction of British resources in high technology would automatically solve the problems of technical innovation in the remaining 'bread and butter' sectors of British industry: Walker (Chapter 2), Pavitt and Soete (Chapter 3), and Albu (Chapter 4) have all shown in different ways how British industry has invested relatively little in skills and in innovative activities over a long period. Reversing this tendency will require active and deliberate policies, both in industry and in Government.

It would also be an illusion to suppose that Britain can compete on the basis of the existing level of innovative activities financed by industry. As a result of British inefficiency in translating the results of R&D into commercial success, and of the recognition that industrial innovation entails the application of quite a lot of old knowledge, it is sometimes argued that Britain needs to concentrate on the application of existing knowledge, and not on R&D and the creation of new knowledge. This is to misunderstand the industrial function of R&D activities, including basic research. R&D activities can be considered as the technical intelligence function of a company or of a country. Most basic research and applied R&D activities not only make fundamental breakthroughs or demonstrate great virtuosity. They receive, transmit, combine, modify and apply knowledge created by others. It would be a grave mistake to think that the UK could find ways of competing with, say, F R Germany and Japan in industrial innovation, whilst at the same time committing markedly fewer resources to basic research and industrial R&D activities.

It is this lack of commitment to innovation as a weapon in the competitive struggle – be it better product design or process improvement – that Rothwell (Chapter 17) sees as one of the most important deficiencies that must be remedied by the management of British industry. It is not simply a matter of committing more resources to innovative activities, although this will often be necessary. The dual structure of innovative activities in Britain has resulted in some serious imbalances in the activities necessary for successful innovation, with too much 'technology push' in the high-technology sectors being mirrored by too little exploitation of scientific and technological opportunities in the 'bread and butter' industries. This same duality may also have impaired the efficiency of development work, with the neglect of engineering principles (such as the importance of full-scale testing) in some high-technology sectors co-existing with ignorance of science-based opportunities (such as the applications of electronics) in some 'bread and butter' industries.

Rothwell also identifies some other specifically British weakness in innovative activities: the inadequacy of market intelligence in many of the world's most important markets; and the poor links that often exist between product design and production engineering, with the result that new British product designs are sometimes unnecessarily difficult and costly to make. Rothwell stresses that the management of innovation is demanding and difficult, requiring a high level of professional and technical competence. It is here that the most important changes in British management will have to take place.

Freeman argues that an active Government policy for industrial innovation will be necessary to supplement the activities of industrial firms. Its main objective should be to close the productivity gap between Britain and its EEC partners by the end of the century, whilst maintaining its external payments in balance. Its strategy to help achieve this objective should be to improve the relative technical quality and international competitiveness of manufacturing and related goods and services.

Freeman stresses the importance of micro-electronics which, given its pervasiveness in all sectors of industry, will be both an opportunity and a means to identify the nature of the problems.

At the same time, strategies will need to be tailored to the specific nature and requirements of different industries. Some of the problems emerge clearly from the chapters on specific sectors. For example, in mechanical engineering (Chapters 7–11), there is the generally low quality of design, the inadequate recognition of the importance of graduate engineers and managers, and the growing need to be able to design and develop total systems within which particular machines operate. In other areas, there are strengths on which Britain can build. The relative dynamism of the chemical industry in general, and gas in particular, coupled with British strength in coal mechanisation, and with large indigenous reserves of coal and of oil and gas, suggest considerable opportunities in future in a whole range of chemical and energy technologies, products and associated consultancy services.

Amongst the policy instruments to support the strategy, the most important should be an increase in the provision of high-quality education and training for all levels of the industrial workforce. As in the past, specific intervention in specific firms and sectors will also be necessary. The particular instrument of Government intervention – be it subsidies, procurement, public ownership or any other policy instrument – should be deployed not in response to dogma or to crises but to support the long-term strategy.

As Freeman points out, an effective strategy requires changes in doctrine, operating procedures and competence in Government as well as industry. An active policy to improve supply conditions for technical innovation has in the past faced scepticism and even hostility from those who believe that only demand management counts, or from those who believe that there is not, and should not be, anything called a science and technology policy. A successful policy requires close and continuous dialogue between those concerned with technology and innovation, and those concerned with more general industrial policy, and not the compartmentalisation that has often prevailed in the past. In1978, there were some welcome signs in the Department of Industry, and in the Government generally, that some of these changes were taking place.

WIDER PERSPECTIVES

As we said in the opening paragraph of this book, its main purpose is to argue that British industry is on the whole backward in technical innovation, that it matters for Britain's economic performance and living standards, and that something must be done about it. We hope that those who are directly concerned with the problem – in industry and in Government, and in the universities – will be influenced, if not entirely convinced, by the evidence and the arguments that we present. But there is a wider problem and a wider audience, namely, the inability of large sectors of the British population to see that the problem exists and is an important one to solve.

Britain's inadequacies in industrial technology have been apparent at least since the beginning of this century. Walker (Chapter 2) argues that, by the end of the Second World War, Britain still had not made the economic and social transformations necessary for a modern system of manufacture. In

1963, Barna could still say:

> The common elements of the advanced industries of this century are that they are based on science rather than craftmanship, that they market their produce rather than sell it to merchants, and that they are managed by professionally qualified teams rather than by amateurs. The long-term problem is how to make Britain catch up with the best practices of other countries. (Barna, 1963).

Walker (Chapter 2) attributes the persistence of the problem to the cushioning effects of the Empire, providing both market outlets for British products unable to compete elsewhere in the world, and financial income to prop up a shaky balance of payments on the current account. These forces were prevalent until the 1950s, but some of the attitudes have remained. In this book, Freeman talks of a 'narrow-minded complacent insularity reflected in an unwillingness to learn from others'; similar comments were being made about the British before 1900 (Landes, 1969). The outcome of the Second World War may have reinforced these tendencies. Many of today's policy-makers – as well as a large part of the general public – lived their most impressionable years at the special time in the late 1940s and 1950s when Britain was undoubtedly one of the world's technological leaders, before the USA went way ahead in the big, defence-related technologies, Germany re-established its historically pre-eminent position, and Japan and France caught up and overtook Britain.

This book shows that, in relation to technical innovation in industry, things have got worse rather than better over the past fifteen years. British innovative activities have diminished absolutely. Japan has joined the USA and Germany as a technically advanced and innovative nation. There is increasing competition from newly industrialising countries in the technically prosaic product ranges on which much of British industry has come to concentrate. Given this situation, and the increasing world pressure on energy and other natural resources, technical innovation will be at least as important in tomorrow's world as today's.

Britain is not well equipped to face this world. To return to the sporting metaphor used at the beginning of this chapter, it is not an innovative First Division country, and the products that it makes will increasingly be challenged by the newly industrialising countries recently promoted from the Third Division. At the same time, too many people in Britain believe that Britain is sitting somewhere near the top of the First Division.

We hope that this book will help shatter that particular illusion. We also hope that it will not be used as a counsel of despair. As various chapters of this book show, some industries and some firms perform strongly by world standards, and others under threat have improved their situation considerably. Improvement and change are possible if the need for them is recognised, and if the directions for improvement and change are indicated. We hope that this book contributes to both these ends.

NOTES

1. I am indebted to William Walker for preliminary reading and analysis for this chapter.
2. As M. Kaldor (Chapter 6) suggests, this is not the case in defence products, where Britain has its comparative advantage in innovation, and where the unit values and value-to-weight ratios of Britain's major weapons systems are higher than their equivalents in other countries. However, Kaldor argues that weapons sophistication often reflects institutional politics rather than value to the user.
3. Similar results are being obtained by Walsh and Townsend (1978) in the chemical industry, especially in the earlier stages of growth of new product areas, such as pharmaceuticals and plastics. The convenient assumption that invention and innovation follow investment and demand stems in part from a perhaps too hasty interpretation of the pioneering work by Schmookler (1966) on the relationship between patterns of invention and of investment in the USA in the nineteenth century. For a recent critical discussion of demand-determined models of technical innovation, see Mowery and Rosenberg (in press, 1979).

REFERENCES

G. Allen, *The British Disease: a Short Essay on the Nation's Lagging Wealth*, Institute of Economic Affairs (London: IEA, 1976).

T. Barna, 'What is Wrong with Britain's Trading Position – High Prices or Lack of Innovation?', *The Times* (London: 12 Aug. 1963).

C. Barnett, *The Collapse of British Power* (London: Eyre Methuen, 1972).

W. Beckerman and associates, *The British Economy in 1975*, NIESR economic and social studies series no. 23 (London: Cambridge University Press, 1965).

F. Blackaby (ed.), *De-industrialisation* (London: Heinemann, in press, 1979).

A. Cairncross, 'What is De-Industrialisation?', in Blackaby (in press, 1979).

R. Dore, *British Factory – Japanese Factory* (London: Allen & Unwin, 1973).

G. Eads and R. Nelson, 'Government Support for Advanced Civilian Technology', *Public Policy, Vol.* 19, no. 3 (1971).

N. Gardner, 'Economics of Launching Aid', in A. Whiting (ed.), *The Economics of Industrial Subsidies* (London: HMSO, 1976).

J. Gershuny, *After Industrial Society* (London: Macmillan, 1978).

E. Hobsbawm, *Industry and Empire* (London: Penguin, 1968).

J. Jewkes, *Government and High Technology*, Institute of Economic Affairs (London: IEA, 1972).

D. Jones and S. Prais, 'Plant Size and Productivity in the Motor Industry: Some International Comparisons', *Oxford Bulletin of Economics and Statistics,* vol. 40 (1978).

D. Landes, *The Unbound Prometheus* (Cambridge: Cambridge University Press, 1969).

T. Lossius, 'ICI's Synthetic Fibres Business: A Case Study of International Efficiency Comparisons', in C. Bowe (ed.), *Industrial Efficiency and the Role of Government* (London: HMSO, 1977).

E. Maddock, 'Science, Technology and Industry', *Proceedings of the Royal Society of London*, vol. 345 (London: Royal Society of London, 1975).

D. Mowery and N. Rosenberg, 'The Influence of Market Demand upon Innovation', *Research Policy*, vol. 8 (in press, 1979).

R. Nelson and S. Winter, 'Neoclassical vs. Evolutionary Theories of Economic Growth', *Economic Journal,* vol. 84 (1974).

R. Nelson and S. Winter, 'In Search of a Useful Theory of Innovation', *Research Policy,* vol. 6 (1977).

M. Panic (ed.), *The UK and West German Manufacturing Industry, 1954–72: A Comparison of Performance and Structure,* National Economic Development Council, Monograph no. 5 (London: NEDC, 1976).

M. Peck, 'Science and Technology', in R. Caves (ed.), *Britain's Economic Prospects* (Washington D.C.: Brookings, 1968).

M. Posner and A. Steer, 'Price Competitiveness and Performance of Manufacturing Industry', in Blackaby (in press, 1979).

N. Rosenberg, *Perspectives on Technology* (Cambridge: Cambridge University Press, 1976).

C. Saunders, *Engineering in Britain, West Germany and France,* Sussex European Research Centre (University of Sussex, in press, 1979).

J. Schmookler, *Invention and Economic Growth* (Cambridge, Mass.: Harvard University Press, 1976).

D. Stout *et al., International Price Competitiveness, Non-Price Factors and Economic Performance,* National Economic Development Office (London: NEDO, 1977).

D. Stout, 'De-industrialisation and Industrial Policy', in Blackaby (in press, 1979).

A. Thirlwall, 'The UK's Economic Problem: A Balance of Payments Constraint?', *National Westminster Bank Quarterly Review* (Feb. 1978).

R. Vernon, 'International Investment and International Trade in the Product Cycle', *Quarterly Journal of Economics,* vol. 80 (1966).

N. Vig, *Science and Technology in British Politics* (Oxford: Pergamon, 1978).

W. Walker, 'Direct Government Aid for Industrial Innovation in the UK' (mimeo), Science Policy Research Unit (University of Sussex, 1976).

V. Walsh and J. Townsend, 'Technological Forecasting and Trends of Innovation in the Chemical Industry' (mimeo), Science Policy Research Unit (University of Sussex).

Part I

2 Britain's Industrial Performance 1850–1950: a Failure to Adjust

W. B. Walker

Britain's relative economic decline has a longer history than is often assumed by contemporary observers. This chapter sketches the main features of Britain's industrial performance between 1850 and 1950, and considers explanations for the decline of economic power over this period offered by certain economic historians. It will be argued that the difficulties Britain has encountered since the Second World War stem in large part from a long-standing failure to adjust to the spread of industrialisation and the emergence of new forms of production.

1850–1914

The period 1850–1914 has a special interest for economic historians as the period during which a number of countries made substantial advances towards industrialisation, offering the first serious challenge to Britain's industrial supremacy. It is also regarded as the time when the first transitions took place in Europe and North America from the early to the modern industrial economy, involving fundamental changes in the methods and the materials of production; in the organisation of labour; in the use of scientific and technical knowledge; in the marketing of produce; in the range of commodities available in the market-place. Some have identified the period as the beginnings of a second industrial revolution, one that had to wait until the era of economic expansion after the Second World War to be fully realised.[1]

The threat to Britain's trading supremacy began to be felt in the 1870s and 1880s. British manufacturers increasingly found themselves facing severe competition in foreign markets, especially from Germany. Between 1870 and 1913, Britain's share of world trade fell from over 40 per cent to 30 per cent, and the growth of industrial output and productivity failed to match that of her major competitors.[2]

Since Germany and the USA started from relatively low levels of industrial activity, it was to be expected that their growth rates would surpass Britain's (for mathematical reasons if no other). But there were signs that falling British trade shares also reflected a general loss of industrial dynamism, in relation to both production and marketing.[3] A declining rate of domestic investment and productivity growth was linked to the exhaustion of technical opportunity in established industries (iron, cotton, railways, etc.), but more importantly to the failure to move resources into areas of production in which demand in the international economy was growing most rapidly.

A shift in the structure of international trade had accompanied the spread of industrialisation. Import substitution curbed the growth of trade in traditional goods (especially textiles) while increasing demand for capital goods; and the market for consumer durable goods grew rapidly with rising income, even if from a low level. This structural change was accentuated by the emergence of a variety of new technologies – agricultural machinery, ball bearings, electrical equipment, chemicals and many others – and by a shift in established industries towards more sophisticated products, for instance the replacement of cast iron by steel.

British manufacturers continued to dominate world markets in textiles and textile machinery, railway engines, heavy engineering and ships, although no longer without challenge from other producers; but they were slow to enter the newer areas of production. The structural backwardness of British manufacturing before the First World War comes over most clearly when comparisons are made with Germany. As Table 2.1 shows, Britain was dominant in coal and cotton, Germany in the new sectors of steel, machinery and chemicals.

Important changes in the nature of factory production accompanied these structural movements. First, the introduction of the 'American system of manufacture' brought a substantial increase in the mechanisation of productive activities (in some sectors amounting to mass-production), especially in the previously artisan-based manufacture of machinery. This involved the introduction of interchangeable part manufacture; the use of specialised production machinery; the further division – and in some cases de-skilling – of factory labour; the deliberate exploitation of mass-markets to maximise volume of output. Where applicable, it also placed an increasing burden on management, requiring greater training and professionalism.

Second, there was a general intensification in the application of scientific and technical analysis and knowledge to product and process design. Most evident in the new chemical, electrical and transport industries, where

TABLE 2.1 Percentage shares of Western European production, 1913

	Coal Production	*Manufactured output*	*Cotton fibre consumption**	*Steel production*	*Machinery production*	*Chemical production*
UK	52	27	43	23	27	19
Germany	34	32	19	46	48	41
Rest of Europe	14	41	38	34	25	40
Total	100	100	100	100	100	100

NOTE
* Proxy for output of cotton goods.

SOURCE
Svennilson, 1954 (table 1).

organised research and development was sustained by flows of knowledge and skills from Higher Education, its effects were discernible in many other areas of production.[4] It can be seen as part of a wider trend involving systematic analysis in the various department of manufacture (finance, marketing, work-flows, etc.) in the interest of raising efficiency.

While there is a danger of exaggerating the impact of these new business practices on late-nineteenth-century manufacture, their influence was undoubtedly more pervasive in the USA and parts of Continental Europe than in the UK. The substantial growth of output and productivity in the industrialising countries entailed more than adapting and extending the industrial practices pioneered in Britain. They involved the adoption of novel forms of production, whether by way of new industries or new business techniques. A key question is therefore why Britain approached them so reluctantly rather than seizing on them as a means of ensuring further economic expansion.

EXPLANATION OF BRITAIN'S PRE-1914 DECLINE

Hobsbawm has written on this period that 'the sudden transformation of the leading and most dynamic industrial economy into the most sluggish and conservative . . . is the crucial question in British economic history' (Hobsbawm, 1969, p. 178). How have historians tried to explain Britain's loss of industrial vitality? We have to examine two interacting sets of explanations, the one proposing that circumstances internal to the British society and economy stood in the way of change, the other that the incentive to innovate and modernise production was lacking.

Economic barriers: disadvantages of being first to industrialise

It has frequently been asserted that Britain's decline – especially in the second half of the nineteenth century – was linked to the social and economic conditions inherited from her early and pioneering industrialisation. There are three main economic strands to this argument. First, a country that had reached an advanced stage of industrialisation had less opportunity for raising productivity by moving labour from agriculture, handicrafts and other relatively unproductive occupations into industrial employment. Second, late-industrialising countries acquired a relatively modern capital stock, a high proportion of which embodied technology of a recent vintage; they also stood to learn from the mistakes of their predecessors. Third, an established capital stock actively inhibited modernisation, the extra costs attached to replacing old investments strengthening the temptation to hang on to and adapt old plant, and to compete on prices that excluded replacement costs. Physical and technical incompatibilities between the new and the old also adversely affected the choice and efficient operation of new equipment.

While these inhibiting factors undoubtedly placed Britain at a disadvantage, most historians accept that the inertia of an ageing capital stock explains neither the extent to which manufacturers clung to their old techniques, nor the slowness with which the newer industries took root. Besides, the disadvantages of early industrialisation have to be weighed against its advantages – a highly developed industrial infrastructure, accumulated practical experience, prior investments in harbours, transport and urban dwellings, an established network of trading outlets in overseas markets.

Social barriers: management and labour

The 'disadvantage of being first' explanation becomes more powerful when extended to include social and institutional factors. For instance, much has been written about the attitudes and behaviour of the moneyed classes in late Victorian England. A century of economic and political leadership had not unnaturally led the Englishman to have an exaggerated opinion of his intellectual and moral qualities.[5] Few believed that the foreigner could seriously challenge Anglo-Saxon domination.

Britain was not the only country to believe in its innate supremacy over other nations. Germans and Americans lived under similar illusions. The important difference was that their belief in national superiority – and destiny – was a goad to industrial expansion, while in Britain it justified complacency and inaction.

Even more serious was the neglect and disregard for industrial management as wealth accumulated and the more privileged sections of society became engrossed in the pursuit of pleasure and aristocratic status. Those with ambition were increasingly seeking careers outside industry – in Government, the professions and the Empire – at a time when the elites in Continental Europe, Japan and the USA were identifying with the goals of industrialisation and were actively pursuing industrial careers of promoting industrial interests from within other institutions.

At the other end of the social spectrum, it has been argued that the growing militancy of the British labour movement, a result of wretched living conditions, long hours of work, blatant social inequalities, and the fear of technological unemployment, impeded industrial modernisation. It has also been suggested that in some industrialising countries (notably Germany) there was less disdain for the lot of the working classes than in Britain, perhaps reflecting the survival of feudal attitudes and relationships. Landes maintains that the Continental European factory owner 'placed himself *in loco parentis*, treated his workers as minors in need of a firm tutorial hand, and felt a certain responsibility for their job security and welfare – always, of course, at the very modest level suitable to their station' (Landes, 1969, p. 191).[6] The establishment of an elementary welfare state was also an integral part of the Bismarckian drive towards national unity, military and economic.

However, if the number of days lost through strikes is accepted as a reliable measure of industrial conflict, many Continental European countries experienced as much conflict as Britain in the years preceding the First World War.[7] Britain also avoided the proletarian uprisings of 1848 and 1871. The extent to which class differences impeded modernisation is therefore debatable. The desire to defend long-established working practices probably acted as a more important barrier to change. There are, for instance, numerous accounts of opposition by artisans to the introduction of interchangeable part manufacture, which was resented both for its tedium and the threat it posed to their livelihoods.[8] The legacy of archaic skills and social relationships – which craft unions and other institutions strove to preserve – increased the inertia of an outdated capital stock, as did a managerial class that had neither the ability nor the motivation to seize the opportunities provided by the newer forms of production.

Institutional barriers: education, the State, and financial institutions

This structural inertia goes a long way to explaining the slow development in Britain of an educational system able to serve the needs of an advanced industrial economy. An industrial society committed to the survival of craft techniques, and suspicious of professionalism in management and other white-collar occupations, exerted little pressure for educational reform.[9]

Whether in management, engineering or on the shop-floor, skills have a dual function in manufacturing: to ensure the efficient day-to-day running of the industrial enterprise; and to bring about useful change, to recognise and react to opportunities or external threats. A lack of appropriate skills thus carries a double penalty: it reduces efficiency and inhibits innovation.

With little formal education beyond the apprenticeship, earlier industrialisation had relied on the wits and enterprise of individual entrepreneurs and the manual skills of artisans. These were to prove increasingly inadequate as the nineteenth century progressed.[10] Advancing mechanisation and the emergence of research-intensive industries raised the demand for and altered the composition of the skills required in manufacturing. Accountants, supervisors and industrial engineers were required to tighten control of costs and work-flows, sales and service personnel to support the rising volume of manufacture and to plan the future development of the firm. Bureaucracy was becoming necessary for efficient production. And on the shop-floor, there was at the same time a gradual de-skilling of manual labour, and a demand for new types of skills. Where semi-skilled labour was being used, literacy and numeracy improved communications and raised efficiency.

Mechanisation in turn placed demands on machine-builders to devise new types of capital goods, and generally to raise the precision and performance of their products. A change was taking place in both the quality and quantity of engineers required in manufacturing, and scientists were beginning to make a significant contribution to production, especially in the newer 'research-intensive' industries.

Whereas Government had long promoted and enforced primary and secondary education in Europe and the USA (in Prussia as early as 1760), only in the last quarter of the nineteenth century did the State intervene in Britain to establish a national public system of education, with primary education becoming compulsory in the 1880, secondary much later.[11] Even then, universal education was instituted reluctancy and with much misgiving over its effects on popular attitudes. It was frequently more repressive than instructive.

Deficiencies were even more apparent in the teaching of scientific and technical subjects. Scotland, the University of London and a handful of technical colleges apart, formal technical education only began in earnest with the founding of the red-brick universities in the 1870s and 1880s. Even then, the technical departments of the new universities suffered from the start from inadequate funds and low prestige. In Britain a stigma was attached to scientific and technical education – or for that matter any formal education with an industrial leaning – in sharp contrast with Europe and North America, where it was in high demand.

At all levels the educational system was therefore ill-prepared for the transition towards the more advanced forms of production that were developing in the nineteenth century. 'The British . . . entered the twentieth century and the age of modern science and technology as a spectacularly ill-educated people' (Hobsbawm, 1969, p. 182). The Germans and Americans gained a decisive advantage from their early investments in education, and from the priority given to scientific and technical training.

The failure of the State to establish an adequate educational system was symptomatic of a wider phenomenon – the distance that separated Government from industrial production. Owing to Britain's historic commitment to *laissez-faire* and Free Trade, there was little interaction between Government and the owners of industry (except regarding conditions at work), and any moves to develop such an interaction were strongly resisted. This contrasted with many of the emerging industrial nations, where it was accepted that the State should pursue an active industrial policy, promoting structural change, ensuring supplies of skilled manpower, developing trading strategies. Similar comments apply to the financial institutions. In Germany and Sweden, for instance, the banks were closely involved in industrial development and management, whereas in Britain domestic industry increasingly took second place in the financial institutions' investment policies.[12] Some have argued that the obligation to promote industrial interests and to take a long-term view of industrial development that was implicit in Continental European banking practices was absent from the British capital market, at a time when the growing scale of industrial undertakings required close ties between industry and the formal banking system; others that the movement of venture capital away from the UK was a response to profitable opportunities overseas and the diminishing return on domestic industrial investment. There is validity in both views.

As the history of industrialisation in the USA demonstrates, State intervention is not an essential precondition for industrial advance – some would even argue that beyond regulating the general economic environment it is more a hindrance than a help. So long as British industry was prosperous and innovative, *laissez-faire* worked well. But when faced with declining competitiveness in domestic and foreign markets, and an apparent failure of the private enterprise system to respond to the external threat, the Government and the financial institutions showed themselves to be powerless and unwilling to embark on the corrective measures that might have slowed, if not altogether halted, industrial decline.

Lack of pressure for change: factor costs and the Empire

There were thus serious internal constraints on economic development in the later nineteenth century. There also appeared to be an absence of external pressure on industry and Government to bring about the required changes.

It has been suggested that the factor proportions facing British industrialists discouraged labour-saving investment and innovation. Habakkuk (1962) has argued that entrepreneurs in the USA showed a greater propensity to develop and adopt more capital-intensive techniques of production than their British counterparts, since labour was more expensive there relative to capital, and its supply scarcer and more inelastic, owing to the high rewards available in North American agriculture.[13]

This neoclassical interpretation has led to a long and contorted academic debate, which we cannot cover adequately in this context.[14] Suffice it to say that the little statistical evidence that exists on factor costs at this time seems to support Habakkuk's contention about US/UK disparities in the first part of the nineteenth century; but his thesis becomes less convincing in relation to the later period when labour scarcity was no longer a problem in the USA. Furthermore, throughout the nineteenth century Britain was richer in capital and had more expensive labour than other European countries, yet it appears that labour-saving techniques were adopted with greater alacrity in Europe than in Britain – certainly in the last half of the century.[15]

There can be no doubt that relative factor costs influence the choice of technique and the direction of technical change. But it is a mistake to assume that this relationship will take on a common form in countries with different historical backgrounds and socio-economic structures. It is to be expected that entrepreneurial perceptions and drives will vary from country to country, as will the anticipated profitability of investing in particular technologies even under conditions of equivalence in relative factor costs. For reasons that have already been outlined – the lack of appropriate skills, the historic legacy of old technologies and working practices, and so on – it can be demonstrated convincingly that the British were less responsive (and effective in their response) to market signals than their American and German counterparts, and that they could expect less return on their investments even when opportunities were recognised.[16]

Imperial expansion provides the most persuasive explanation for the lack of urgency over industrial modernisation in late Victorian and Edwardian Britain. Facing rising tariff barriers and strong competition in Europe and the USA, British manufacturers found a ready and relatively profitable market for their goods in the less developed regions of the world.[17] Throughout the eighteenth and nineteenth centuries a substantial part of Britain's export trade (typically around 50 per cent) had gone to markets outside Europe and the USA, but this proportion rose steeply towards the end of the nineteenth century. Between 1890 and 1913, the value of exports to Europe and the USA grew by 26 per cent, and to the rest of the world by 81 per cent. By 1913 around two-thirds of Britain's exports were going to the semi-industrial and non-industrial regions of the world.[18] This trade was both cause and effect of the flood of venture capital and manpower into these markets.

The move into the Empire inhibited modernisation in two principal ways. Firstly, the cultural, institutional and economic protection prevailing in Empire markets discouraged risk-taking and removed much of the pressure to improve international competitiveness. It delayed the shift out of textiles and other traditional areas of manufacture into the newer industries; and manufacturers could maintain their allegiance to outdated production methods with impunity. Secondly, the Empire reinforced many of the features of British society and institutions that stood in the way of change: it encouraged Englishmen to believe in their everlasting superiority over other races; administering the Empire provided large numbers of remunerative and prestigious jobs for the educated elite; much of the State's energy was channelled into Imperial policy-making; and the City became more and more attuned to seeking profitable opportunities outside the UK, reducing its sensitivity to domestic industrial needs.

1914–1950

With the outbreak of the First World War, the world economy entered an era of violent military conflict and industrial stagnation. In the decades before 1914, the international community was unable – and unwilling – to adjust to the stresses induced by the spread of industrialisation.

It is not easy to assess the effects of the two World Wars on the well-being of the British economy. On the one hand, they had a progressive influence, speeding up the introduction of mass-production techniques (because of the need for standardised armaments), encouraging the expansion of engineering industries, raising the level of scientific research, increasing contact between State and industry. On the other hand, they were destructive of manpower and plant (the latter especially through neglect), led to growing international indebtedness, loss of foreign markets, and advanced industrialisation in countries outside the war zones.

The presence or absence of progressive tendencies in British industry in this period can best be judged by concentrating on the inter-war period. Here we are faced with something of an enigma. In the light of her pre-First World War industrial backwardness, why did Britain survive the ups and downs of the inter-war period better than most other industrial nations? There was no catastrophic inflation, unemployment was high but not unduly so by international standards, and economic growth – slow and intermittent though it was – matched and in some cases surpassed that achieved by other nations.[19] Did this reflect a genuine improvement in industrial competitiveness relative to other countries?

The world economy between the wars was characterised by sluggish growth of output and productivity, high unemployment, unstable prices and profits, and a breakdown of multilateral trading. The general economic climate was hostile to industrial modernisation. In these circumstances, the actions of firms and Governments were largely defensive, aimed at preserving employment and preventing the complete disintegration of the industrial fabric.

The scrapping of excess capacity and other measures designed to 'rationalise' production brought some improvements in efficiency. For a brief period in the 1920s, rationalisation was especially progressive, particularly in Germany where inflation stimulated capital formation and cartels and restrictive practices were encouraged as a means of promoting industrial reconstruction and modernisation. But at other times and in other places rationalisation was predominantly defensive in character, intended to protect ailing industries by regulating prices and restricting competition. This was especially true in Britain, where the trend towards greater industrial concentration was only on occasion accompanied by efforts to improve management, locate production in the most efficient plants, introduce new production techniques or improve product ranges.[20]

These comments apply mainly to the long-established sectors of manufacture. In other areas, the picture was less gloomy, in Britain as in other countries. But for the depressed economic climate, the progress of the newer industries – and of mechanisation in general – would undoubtedly have been more rapid. Nevertheless, the advances were considerable. The shift to more efficient and flexible energy systems (the use of electric power in factories and households, compressed air in mining and construction), combined with the revolution in transport and communications (motor transport, radio, cheap newspapers), led to significant changes in the lifestyles and expectations of the average citizen, and prepared the way for the great increase in output and productivity that occurred after 1950. Throughout the industrial world, the situation was thus one of stagnation and underinvestment in traditional industries, and expansion in a range of new industries and new parts of old industries, but at a rate insufficient to compensate for rising unemployment.

Between the wars, international trading rose to a peak in 1928, collapsed between 1929 and 1933, and staged a recovery between 1933 and 1938, although not exceeding the level reached in 1913. The growth of industrial production in the 1930s was largely due to reflationary Government policies. In contrast to conditions before 1913, international trading stimulated industrial development only to a limited extent.

The fall in Britain's share of world trade between the wars has to be seen in the context of a general shift of economic power away from Europe. The fragmentation and inefficiency that went hand in hand with bilateral trading was especially damaging to European manufacture, as were the dislocations brought about by the First World War and its aftermath. Industrial power shifted towards North America and Asia. The USA overtook Germany and Britain, and Japan emerged as a serious rival in Far Eastern markets.

Britain's backward industrial structure made her particularly vulnerable to industrialisation in the less developed regions, especially when it involved countries that had privileged access to the British market. The loss of supremacy in textile markets provided one reason for the changing structure of British trade in the 1920s and 1930s, the other being the growth of exports from the newer industries – machinery, transport equipment and chemicals.

Some historians have argued that the shift of resources into these areas of production signalled a revival of industrial enterprise (Pollard, 1978). To an extent it clearly did. However, the achievements of the newer British industries appear less impressive when comparisons are made with other industrial nations. In Germany, for instance, the rise of skill-intensive manufacture was even more pronounced, as is apparent in Table 2.2. Furthermore, an exceptionally high proportion of Britain's exports of machinery, transport equipment and chemicals went to markets outside the industrial bloc – the newer industries were even more heavily oriented towards Imperial markets than the traditional (Table 2.3). There was little international competition to test their true efficiency, and many of the features of backwardness that we have associated with the older sectors of manufacture became incorporated in them.

The Empire played a crucial role in sustaining the British economy between the wars (although it was to prove a two-edged sword in the case of textiles). The proportion of Britain's external trade destined for Empire markets reached a peak in the 1930s. Equally important was the part invisible earnings – most of which were linked to Imperial trade and influence – played in preventing serious deterioration in the balance of payments. Since the early days of the industrial revolution, Britain's visible trade had seldom been in surplus. Rising imports had been more than matched by the income from foreign investments, shipping and financial services. With international trade in the doldrums, the Government-led reflation of the domestic economy in the 1930s opened up a yawning gap between exports and imports (Table 2.4), despite terms of trade that had moved sharply in Britain's favour. That balance of payments difficulties did not bring expansion to an abrupt halt (as they repeatedly did after the Second World War) was entirely due to the continuing high level of invisible earnings. In Svennilson's words, 'by the fullest exploitation of its international margin, the United Kingdom managed to mitigate the effects on its expansion of the fall in exports' (Svennilson, 1954, p. 218).

Inevitably, the level of invisible earnings began to fall in the 1930s, owing to the stagnation in international trade, and to the halting of the outward flow of capital which was required to maintain investments. The elimination of Britain's overseas investments reached a climax in the Second World War, when the net disinvestment amounted to £678 million per annum (Deane and

TABLE 2.2 Composition of British and German exports, 1913 and 1938 (%)

		Raw materials and agricultural produce	*Metals*	*Machinery, transport equipment and chemicals*	*Textiles*	*Other*	*Total*
UK	1913	21.0	12.7	16.3	37.0	13.0	100.0
	1938	21.6	11.5	28.6	21.7	16.6	100.0
Germany	1913	29.2	15.9	19.9	13.0	23.0	100.0
	1938	13.4	19.5	40.8	8.3	18.0	100.0

SOURCE
Derived from Svennilson (1954, table A.59).

TABLE 2.3 Percentage of UK exports destined for markets other than the eight leading industrial nations

	Raw Materials and agricultural produce	*Metals*	*Machinery, transport equipment and chemicals*	*Textiles*	*Other*	*Total*
1913	56	79	78	75	72	72
1938	59	92	89	78	79	79

SOURCE
Svennilson, 1954 (table A.65).

Cole, 1967, p. 37). Thus one of the crucial props of the British economy was removed by the events of the 1930s and 1940s.

A FAILURE TO ADJUST

It is clear from recent research that many of the factors that inhibited modernisation in the late nineteenth century survived after 1945: the low status of industrial employment; managerial shortcomings; an inadequate educational system, especially in relation to technical training; conservatism

TABLE 2.4 Percentages by which imports exceeded exports (by value, visible trade)

	1911–13	*1935–38*
UK	+25	+78
France	+26	+57
Germany	+15	–5
Italy	+51	+25
Sweden	+4	+10
Total Europe	+24	+30

SOURCE
Svennilson, 1954 (table 65).

and suspicion of change in the labour movement; adherence to craft techniques; a capital market that is too little concerned with long-term industrial development; a State lacking the apparatus or the political authority to promote industrial modernisation effectively.

The absence of any traumatic shocks to the British economic system explains why so little effort was made to achieve these transformations. The crises that did occur – the wars, and the upheavals in the 1920s and 1930s – were not so damaging as to seriously disturb the social and economic fabric. Nor were they of such a nature as to focus attention on the relative inefficiency of British manufacture, or on the threat that this inefficiency posed to future prosperity. It has been apparent that the Empire was substantially responsible for the avoidance of crises of the severity that afflicted many other industrial economies. By protecting industry and by supplying the income with which to finance the deficit in visible trade, the Empire allowed Britain to maintain her position of power in the world and to hang on to old and cherished traditions, in work as in play. It also fed the illusion that Britain remained a dynamic and superior nation, an illusion that was not diminished by being on the winning side in two World Wars.

With the end of Empire and the lowering of tariff barriers throughout the Western World in the 1950s and 1960s, the shelter was abruptly removed and British industry was exposed to competition from the advanced countries for the first time since the late nineteenth century (a brief period in the 1920s apart). When viewed in this historic context, the post-war decline of Britain as a major trading nation no longer seems surprising. Low investment and productivity, the burden of public spending, rising imports are but symptoms of a more general failure to adjust to a new international order and to the emergence of more efficient business practices, or rather to adjust fast enough to keep pace with rapid changes occurring elsewhere in the world economy.

NOTES

1. See Landes (1969, p. 235).
2. Average annual growth rates of manufacturing production have been estimated at 2.2 per cent for Britain, 3.9 per cent for Germany and 4.9 per cent for the USA (Lewis, 1978, p. 17). Between 1892 and 1913 the annual rates of growth of productivity (measured by net annual real product per employee) were 0.8 per cent for the UK, 2.3 per cent for Germany and 1.4 per cent for the USA (Phelps-Brown, 1971, p. 106).
3. Various historians have pointed to the vigour of German and the lethargy of British salesmanship in the decades before 1913. The British were as quick to accuse the Germans of unethical behaviour as they are the Japanese today (see Hoffmann, 1933).

4. Alfred Marshall wrote in 1919: 'The present age calls increasingly for a new class of improvements of methods and appliances, which cannot be created by a single alert individual. Many of these, by which man's command over nature has been enlarged during the last decades, have been the product of sustained researches by large groups' (Marshall, 1919, p. 96).
5. It was no coincidence that evolutionary theories – biological and social – were first developed in Victorian England. Darwin wrote in 1874: 'I do not think that the Rev. Mr. Zincke takes an exaggerated view when he says "All other series of events – as that which resulted in the culture of mind in Greece, and that which resulted in the empire of Rome – only appear to have purpose and value when viewed in connection with, or rather as subsidiary to . . . the great stream of Anglo-Saxon emigration to the West. . . . We can at least see that a nation which produced during a lengthened period the greatest number of highly intellectual, energetic, brave, patriotic and benevolent men, would generally prevail over less favoured nations." ' This sentiment was by no means untypical of the time (Darwin, 1874, p. 218).
6. There are contemporary accounts to support this view, mostly in relation to Germany. For instance, Siemens offered a package of welfare measures in return for his employees accepting the 'American system of manufacture' in 1867, including reduced hours of work, increased pay and sick benefits (Siemens, 1957). The Secretary of the Amalgamated Engineers also remarked after a visit to Germany in 1898 that he was 'astounded to see how the comfort of the worker was provided for in the way of supply of food and drink, baths, and in some cases, houses. . . . ' (quoted by Phelps-Brown, 1959, p. 75).
7. Between 1900 and 1913, 51 million days' work was lost through strikes in France, 109 million in the UK (of which 40 million were in 1912), 117 million in Germany (Mitchell, 1976, table C.3).
8. For instance, resistance by artisans (backed by their guilds) in the British watch and clock industry seriously impeded the introduction of interchangeable part manufacture (Church, 1975, p. 621).
9. The belated initiative to reform the educational system came from within Government, not industry – in particular from a handful of individuals with connections in high places, of whom Lynn Playfair – chemist, MP and friend of the Prince Consort – was the most important. See Chapters 4 and 5 for detailed analyses of the training of British engineers and managers.
10. An eminent educationist, Sir James Shuttleworth, wrote in 1866 that: 'The inventive power, the practical sagacity, the enterprise, the courage, and the indomitable perseverance of our race, have made all the vast conquests of our commerce, with little aid from general literacy or scientific cultivation. But the future of the nation requires the light and guidance of a generally cultivated and refined mental power.' (Quoted by Ashworth (1960, p. 195).)
11. By 1910, the percentage of children receiving primary education was on a par with the rest of Europe, but secondary education compared unfavour-

ably. Over a million children received secondary education in Germany in 1910, in Britain 180,000 (Mitchell, 1976, Table J.1).

12. 'The Joint Stock Bank in Germany was not merely a credit organisation but a politico-economic instrument. It was an instrument of German power-policy . . . and became an economic expression as typical of German mentality as the large-scale enterprises, trade unions, or cartel-syndicates. These banks created the German Industrial State and developed concurrently with it' (Bruck, 1938, p. 80).
13. Rosenberg has also pointed out that many American machines were designed to make intensive use of abundant natural resources. Where natural resources were becoming scarce in Britain, craftsmen may have stayed with traditional techniques to conserve materials (see Rosenberg, 1976).
14. See, for instance, David (1975).
15. Milward and Saul go as far as to claim that: 'The history of technology in the nineteenth century suggests that in general innovators in all countries tended to adopt the most modern techniques in the capital goods and durable consumer goods industries with only minor modifications . . . the pattern followed the timing of expansion and therefore the availability of the latest technology, not the relative levels of labour costs' (Milward and Saul, 1973, pp. 174–5).
16. See Landes (1969, p. 337) on the lack of entrepreneurial drive in Britain, and Lewis (1978, pp. 123–8) on the low anticipated yield from British investment in new technologies.
17. That tariff barriers were not the only reason for Britain's declining share of European markets may be illustrated by the following table, which compares the shares of France's imports of machine tools (an industry in which Britain had once held the lead) held by Britain, Germany and the USA in 1865 and 1912. Each country faced similar import duties.

Source of imports of machine-tools to France	*1865* %	*1912* %
UK	70	18
USA	0	17
Germany	2	55
Other (mostly Belgium)	28	10
Total	100	100

SOURCE
Floud (1976, Fig. 4.2).

British imports of the newer types of manufactured goods were also rising fast – especially chemicals, dyestuffs and scientific instruments from Germany; motor cars, machinery and electrical equipment from the USA (see Saul, 1960, p. 37).

18. Statistics taken from Mitchell and Deane (1971, Table 12). British and

German exports of manufactured goods to the industrial, semi-industrial and non-industrial regions in 1913 were as follows ($m):

	From	
To	*Germany*	*UK*
Industrial	925	624
Semi-industrial	218	810
Rest	583	526
Total	1726	1960

SOURCE
Maizels (1963), quoted by Lewis (1978, p. 221).

These figures show that the semi-industrial countries (identified by Maizels as Australia, New Zealand, South Africa, India, Argentina, Brazil, Chile, Colombia, Mexico and Turkey – most of which were within the sphere of British imperial influence) were especially important destinations for British exports.

19. The growth of income and output between 1913 and 1938 in the four leading industrial nations was as follows (1913 = 100):

	Manufactured output	*Real national income per capita*
France	119	110
Germany	144	114
UK	139	120
USA	164	123

SOURCE
Svennilson (1954, table 2).

20. For a contemporary discussion of the British and European efforts to rationalise production in the 1920s, see the Balfour Committee (1929).

REFERENCES

W. Ashworth, *An Economic History of England, 1870–1913* (London: Methuen, 1960).

Balfour Committee, *Final Report of the Committee on Industry and Trade* (London: HMSO. 1929) Cmd, 3282.

W. F. Bruck, *Social and Economic History of Germany from William II to Hitler, 1888–1938* (Oxford: Oxford University Press, 1938).

R. A. Church, 'Nineteenth Century Clock Technology in Britain, the United States and Switzerland', *Economic History Review*, vol. 28 (1975) pp. 616–30.

C. Darwin, *The Descent of Man*, 2nd ed. (London: Murray, 1874).
P. A. David, *Technical Choice, Innovation and Economic Growth* (Cambridge: Cambridge University Press, 1975).
P. Deane and G. Cole, *British Economic Growth, 1688–1959* (Cambridge: Cambridge University Press, 1967).
R. Floud, *The British Machine Tool Industry, 1850–1914* (Cambridge: Cambridge University Press, 1976).
H. J. Habakkuk, *American and British Technology in the 19th Century* (Cambridge: Cambridge University Press, 1962).
E. J. Hobsbawm, *Industry and Empire* (London: Penguin, 1969).
R. Hoffman, *Great Britain and the German Trade Rivalry, 1875–1914* (Philadelphia: University of Pennsylvania, 1933).
D. S. Landes, *The Unbound Prometheus* (Cambridge: Cambridge University Press, 1969).
W. Arthur Lewis, *Growth and Fluctuations, 1870–1913* (London: Allen & Unwin, 1978).
A. Maizels, *Industrial Growth and World Trade* (Cambridge: Cambridge University Press, 1963).
A. Marshall, *Industry and Trade* (London: Macmillan, 1919).
A. S. Milward and S. B. Saul, *The Economic Development of Continental Europe, 1780–1870* (London: Allen & Unwin, 1973).
B. R. Mitchell, *European Historical Statistics, 1750–1970* (London: Macmillan, 1976).
B. R. Mitchell and P. Deane, *Abstract of British Historical Statistics* (Cambridge: Cambridge University Press, 1971).
E. H. Phelps-Brown, *The Growth of British Industrial Relations* (London: Macmillan, 1959).
E. H. Phelps-Brown, 'Labour Policies: Productivity, Industrial Relations, Cost Inflation', in A. Cairncross (ed.), *Britain's Economic Prospects Reconsidered*, (London: Allen & Unwin, 1971).
S. Pollard, Letter to *The Times* (26 July 1978).
N. Rosenberg, 'America's Rise to Woodworking Leadership', in *Perspectives on Technology* (Cambridge: Cambridge University Press, 1976).
S. B. Saul, *Studies of British Overseas Trade, 1870–1914* (Liverpool: Liverpool University Press, 1960).
G. Siemens, *The House of Siemens* (Freiburg: Alber, 1957).
I. Svennilson, *Growth and Stagnation in the European Economy* (Geneva: United Nations, 1954).

3 Innovative Activities and Export Shares: some Comparisons between Industries and Countries

Keith Pavitt and Luc Soete[1]

This chapter compares the level, pattern and trend of British innovative activities with those of other countries, and analyses the degree to which national differences in innovative activities are related to one important aspect of national economic performance: shares of world manufacturing exports. We begin by discussing the problems and possibilities of measuring innovative activities.

THE MEASUREMENT OF INNOVATIVE ACTIVITIES

There is no easy or universally accepted method of measuring the innovative activities that contribute to the quality, efficiency and costs of industrial products and production processes (Freeman, 1974). As with the analysis and forecasting of short-term economic activity, or with any other applied social science, we must make do with a number of imperfect measures. The direct measurement of resources devoted to innovative activities, or counts of successful innovations, would be the most satisfactory measures. But there are considerable problems of data collection, of measuring incremental as well as radical innovations, and of defining a satisfactory sample or, indeed, a satisfactory population of innovations. The larger the aggregate of comparison the more these problems grow.

The advantages and disadvantages of using patent and R&D statistics as measures are quite different. Data are easier to collect, and samples and populations are easier to define; indeed, patent offices contain what is probably the most complete, detailed and longest-running record of information on innovative activity in industry. The disadvantage of patent statistics is the suspicion that, even in aggregate, they do not accurately reflect differences in innovative activity between firms, industrial sectors, countries and time-periods; the problem with industrial R&D statistics is that they measure inputs rather than outputs, and do not capture innovative activities taking place outside formal R&D departments.

Over the past ten to fifteen years, statistics on R&D activities have become widely accepted amongst policy-makers and academics as a proxy measure for innovative activities. Recent empirical studies in the USA and Canada have shown that R&D activities are a major component of total innovative activities, accounting for 45 to 60 per cent of average total costs of introducing an innovation, compared to between 30 and 40 per cent of the cost of tooling and manufacturing facilities, and less than 10 per cent each of manufacturing and marketing start-up costs (Mansfield *et al.*, 1971; Stead, 1976). Considerable progress has been made by Governments and by the Organisation for Economic Co-operation and Development (OECD) in collecting R&D data good enough to make international comparisons (OECD, 1978). These OECD statistics are still limited in both time-period and degree of disaggregation.

Recently, there has been renewed interest in the use of patent statistics, because the Office of Technology Assessment and Forecast (OTAF) in the US Department of Commerce has begun to publish US patent data, including the country of origin, of patents granted in the USA for each year since 1883 (OTAF, 1977a); since 1963, this information can be broken down into forty industrial sectors (OTAF, 1977b).

These data open the opportunity for a more detailed and long-term comparison of innovative activities than available R&D statistics allow, provided that patent statistics are a satisfactory proxy measure for innovative activity. The lack of comprehensive statistics on innovation precludes conclusive proof on this point, but we have been able elsewhere (Pavitt, 1978) to show that the statistics on US patenting to a large extent confirm, and to some extent complement, the conclusions that can be reached on the basis of R&D statistics alone. Thus, in making comparisons amongst US firms, there is a significant correlation between patenting and R&D activities, although patenting statistics provide a better measure of innovative activities in small firms, and R&D statistics of those in large firms (Soete, 1978). Comparisons amongst US industrial sectors also show a significant correlation between each sector's share of total industrial R&D, and its share of total industrial patenting, provided that the aerospace and motor vehicle sectors are excluded. In these two sectors, patent statistics appear to underestimate considerably the volume of innovative activities, just as R&D statistics underestimate those

TABLE 3.1 The percentage distribution of industrial R&D and of US patenting amongst

	Total manufacturing				*Chemicals*			*Mechanical*		
	% US patents	*% total ind. R&D*	*% ind. financed R&D*	*% ind. R&D manpower*	*% US patents*	*% total ind. R&D*	*% ind. R&D manpower*	*% US patents*	*% total ind. R&D*	*% ind. R&D manpower*
Belgium	1.2	1.8	2.0	1.9	1.5	3.3	3.2	1.5	1.0	2.4
Canada	5.9	2.2	2.1	2.3	3.0	1.6	1.7	6.2	3.0	2.6
France	10.2	14.1	10.5	12.8	9.9	11.2	10.5	10.9	7.9	7.3
F R Germany	25.8	24.0	22.0	19.6	29.4	28.7	24.4	28.7	35.5	31.8
Italy	3.3	3.4	4.9	4.3	3.9	4.8	4.7	3.4	3.7	3.9
Japan	27.5	26.9	31.1	32.8	26.3	24.2	30.9	29.9	28.1	31.8
Netherlands	2.6	4.6	3.6	2.9	2.1	4.9	4.7	n.a.	n.a.	n.a.
Sweden	4.2	3.2	2.9	2.4	1.4	1.3	1.0	5.5	6.7	4.5
Switzerland	6.2	2.6	2.9	1.9	10.6	5.9	3.5	n.a.	n.a.	n.a.
United Kingdom	13.2	17.4	12.8	19.1	11.9	14.0	15.5	13.8	14.3	15.5
Total	100.0	100.0	100.0	100.0	100.0	100.0	100.0	100.0	100.0	100.0
Correlation coefficient (r)	1.0	+ 0.96	+ 0.97	+ 0.93	1.0	+ 0.97	+ 0.94	1.0	+ 0.97	+ 0.98

NOTES

n.a. = not applicable

Correlation (*r*) between national percentage of US patenting, on the one hand, and various measures of national R&D shares, on the other.

+ = significant at 1% level
++ = significant at 5% level
+++ = significant at 10% level

---

in non-electrical (mechanical) engineering products and in fabricated metal products.

Most important for the purposes of this chapter, international comparisons of patent and R&D statistics point to almost exactly the same conclusions. Table 3.1 compares ten OECD countries' share of industrial R&D in 1975 with their share of US patenting, for manufacturing industry as a whole and for the six broad sectors within manufacturing that the breakdown of the R&D statistics allows. The table shows high significant correlations between the two measures for manufacturing industry as a whole, and for the three sectors in which more than half of industry's innovative activities, however measured, are concentrated: chemical, electrical and electronic, and non-electrical machinery products. These high correlations are not the consequence of population differences amongst countries; when the national shares for total manufacturing in Table 3.1 are normalised for differences in population, the correlation coefficient (*r*) falls to about 0.83, still significant at the 1 per cent level. For metals and for other transport, the correlation selected OECD countries in 1975

Electrical and electronic			*Aerospace*		*Other transport*			*Metals*		
% US patents	*% total ind. R&D*	*% ind. R&D manpower*	*% US patents*	*% total ind. R&D*	*% US patents*	*% total ind. R&D*	*% ind. R&D manpower*	*% US patents*	*% total ind. R&D*	*% ind. R&D manpower*
0.9	2.0	1.6	n.a.	n.a.	0.5	0.1	0.3	1.3	5.3	4.4
4.7	2.9	2.1	4.8	1.7	5.4	0.4	0.6	8.6	4.5	5.2
10.4	20.2	13.5	19.0	29.7	12.8	12.4	14.2	10.6	10.6	10.4
23.9	25.3	22.6	43.5	23.3	31.8	22.0	20.4	26.7	13.3	13.1
2.6	3.3	3.2	n.a.	n.a.	2.1	n.a.	10.2	2.8	3.5	n.a.
36.6	25.3	34.3	n.a.	n.a.	25.8	39.8	48.0	25.2	46.0	48.1
5.0	4.7	2.7	n.a.	n.a.	n.a.	n.a.	n.a.	n.a.	n.a.	n.a.
2.7	3.0	1.8	3.5	2.9	3.4	n.a.	3.8	7.5	5.4	4.9
n.a.	n.a.	n.a.	n.a.	n.a.	n.a.	n.a.	n.a.	n.a.	n.a.	n.a.
13.4	13.3	18.1	28.8	42.4	17.8	11.7	16.5	16.6	12.0	13.6
100.0	100.0	100.0	100.0	100.0	100.0	100.0	100.0	100.0	100.0	100.0
1.0	+ 0.89	+ 0.97	1.0	0.70	1.0	+++ 0.77	++ 0.77	1.0	++ 0.72	+++ 0.70

The categories used for the patent data and the R&D data are not always strictly comparable. They are as follows:

Chemicals For R&D data, ISIC 351–354. For patent data, US SIC 28.
Mechanical For R&D data, ISIC 382 and 385. For patent data, US SIC 35 and 38 (except 3825).
Electrical and Electronic For R&D data. ISIC 383. For patent data, US SIC 36 and 3825.
Aerospace For R&D data, ISIC plus missiles and rockets. For patent data, US SIC 372 and 376.
Other Transport For R&D data, ISIC 384 less 3845. For patent data, US SIC 371, 373–375, 379 less 3795.
Metals For R&D data, ISIC 371, 372 and 381. For patent data, US SIC 33, 34, less 348.

SOURCE
For data on R&D, OECD (1978). For data on US patenting, OTAF (1977b).

coefficients are not as high, and the problems are those of aggregation.[2] For the aerospace sector, the correlation is low, confirming the lack of reliability of the patent measure.

These data suggest that, aerospace apart, statistics on US patenting are at least as reliable indicators of innovative activity as R&D statistics, and they have the advantage of being more disaggregated since 1963, and of going back as far as 1883. Before looking at the actual statistics, two points need to be made: about measurement, and about concepts.

First, in relation to measurement, we have excluded the USA from the analysis of patent statistics (see, for example, Table 3.1). For international comparisons, we assume that each country has the same propensity to patent in the USA in relation to the size of its innovative activities. This is not the case for the patents of US origin, since the quality of domestic patenting is nearly always lower than that undertaken in foreign countries. For other countries, we assume that, given the size and sophistication of the US market, all countries will wish to sell there, and will have an incentive to get patent protection. In fact, Canada has a higher propensity to patent in the USA than other foreign countries, and Japan has a slightly higher propensity.[3]

Second, a conceptual point: we assume that both R&D and patent statistics capture different aspects of the same process of industrial innovation. This is somewhat different from the normal assumption that, since patents by definition involve novelty, and since invention is defined as novelty, patents capture and measure the earlier stages of a process that leads from novelty/ invention, through development, testing and engineering, to full-scale innovation. Such a view of the innovation process neglects the point that the essential objective of the industrial firm is innovation, not invention. Patents can be viewed as one of the means by which entrepreneurs protect their *innovations*, by making it more difficult for potential competitors to copy or imitate. Patenting activity may extend over the whole of the product life-cycle: from protecting the basic invention, through those patents related to product and process engineering, to a myriad of improvement and blocking patents.

Innovative activities clearly involve much more than R&D and patenting activities. As later chapters show, they involve corporate strategy, production and marketing, and they require a whole range of managerial skills and professional competence beyond those of the laboratory and the patenting department. What we have tried to do so far is to establish that R&D and patenting are valid proxy measures of innovative activities. This is important if we are to be able to make meaningful generalisations.

INTERNATIONAL COMPARISONS OF INNOVATIVE ACTIVITY

Long-term trends

Internationally comparable R&D statistics began to be collected only in the 1960s, and are therefore of no help in examining long-term trends. However, the statistical series recently published by OTAF enables us to assess the extent of British innovative activities relative to those of other countries. Figure 3.1 shows trends in US patenting by six countries since the late nineteenth century. Only Canada has had a slower rate of increase than the UK. The relative decline of the UK has been most perceptible in relation to the more recently industrialising countries: Italy and – above all – Japan, whose rate of increase in patenting in the USA since the mid-1960s has been breathtaking. It has also been noticeable in comparison with the older industrialised nations, France and Germany.

Over the whole period, Germany emerges as the country with the highest share of patenting in the USA, in spite of losing the two world wars. In the

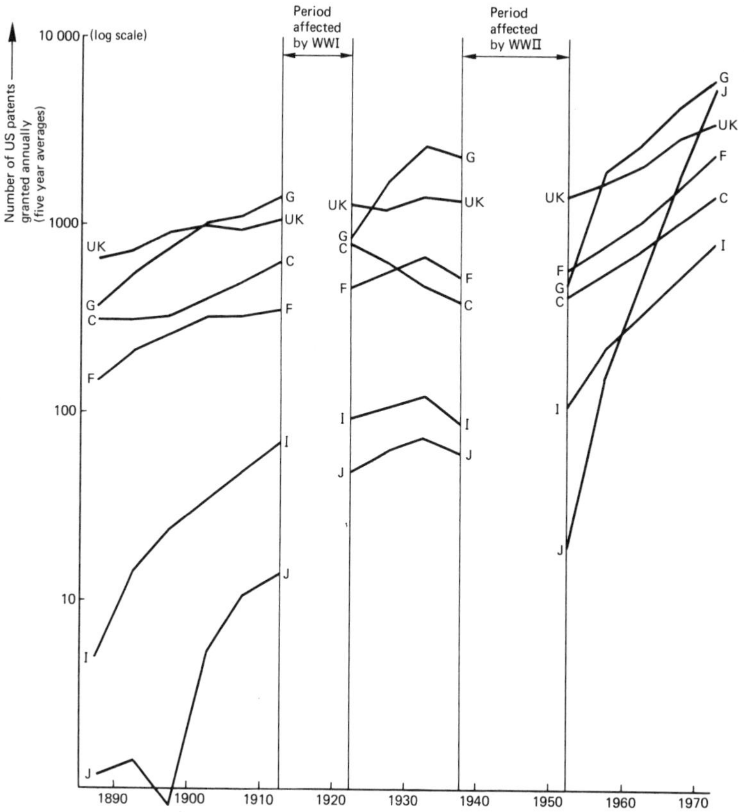

NOTE
C = Canada
F = France
G = Germany
I = Italy
J = Japan
UK = United Kingdom

FIG. 3.1 Long-term trends in US patenting by six countries

SOURCE
OTAF (1977a).

period 1886–90 the ratio of UK to German patenting was 1.6. By 1901–5, it had been reduced roughly to 1.0, and by 1910–15 reached 0.8. After the First World War it went below this ratio by 1926–30 to reach 0.6 in 1936–40. This ratio was reached again by the mid-1960s and by the 1970s was just above 0.5. This pattern of British decline is confirmed by the statistics on R&D expenditure that have been collected by the OECD countries since the 1960s. In 1967, industrial R&D in the UK was roughly at the same level as in F R Germany, and well above France and Japan. By 1975–76 it was not much more than half the German and Japanese levels, and about 20 per cent above the French level.

Patterns of Government expenditure on R&D

A higher percentage of Gross National Product is devoted to Government-financed R&D in the UK than in any other OECD country except the USA: for 1975–76, the percentages were USA – 1.4, UK – 1.3, France – 1.2, F R Germany – 1.2, Netherlands – 0.9, Japan – 0.5, Italy – 0.4, (OECD, in press 1979). Table 3.2 compares the British pattern of Government R&D expenditures with those of the other Common Market countries. It shows the continuing high British expenditure on defence and civil aviation, about 55 per cent of total governmental R&D, compared to 35 per cent in France, just over 10 per cent in F R Germany, and considerably less in all the other EEC countries.[4]

The heavy British expenditure on Government-financed big technologies is reflected very clearly in the patterns of UK patenting in the USA. Over the period 1963 to 1976, the overall UK share of all foreign patenting in the USA was 16.1 per cent, but in aircraft it was 23.4 per cent, in guided weapons and spacecraft 38.1 per cent, and (for the period from 1963 to 1972) in nuclear energy 34.5 per cent. Britain's share of US patenting in these sectors was higher than that of any other foreign country (OTAF, 1973, 1977b).

On the other hand, the proportion of British Government R&D resources spent on basic research ('advance of knowledge') is considerably below that of F R Germany, and only slightly above that of France. Although it is still difficult to make statistical comparisons of basic research, the percentage of Gross National Product spent by the British Government on basic research is well below the equivalent percentages in F R Germany and the Netherlands, and at about the same level as France and Japan (OECD, 1975).

Patterns of innovative activity in industry

The data on R&D expenditure and on US patenting both show essential similarities amongst countries in the patterns of innovative activities within manufacturing industry, namely, a relatively high degree of concentration in electrical and electronic products, chemicals, and non-electrical machinery, with relatively little innovative activity generated in such traditional sectors as textiles and leather goods. However, the data in Table 3.1 confirm the heavy British specialisation in Government-financed big technology. Each

TABLE 3.2 Percentage breakdown of EEC Governments' R & D expenditures, 1973 or 1975

	Belgium	*Denmark*	*France*	*F R Germany*	*Ireland*	*Italy*	*Netherlands*	*UK*
	1973	*1973*	*1975*	*1975*	*1975*	*1975*	*1973*	*1975*
Nuclear Energy (1)	11.5	7.3	7.8	9.4	0	12.3	11.6	6.9
Space (2)	.9	2.6	5.6	4.2	0	8.5	2.8	2.3
Defence (3)	0.4	0.3	29.6	11.0	0	3.4	4.1	46.4
Civil Aviation (8.2.4)	0.2	0	5.1	1.7		0	2.2	8.8
Electronics, Computers, (8.2.3, 9)	1.3	3.1	5.4	2.1	21.9	4.9	0.5	1.1
Other Manufacturing (8, exc. 8.2.3, 8.2.4)	8.6	3.9	3.8	3.6		5.4	4.9	2.5
Advance of Knowledge (11)	54.7	57.4	24.1	51.5	12.5	50.8	49.5	19.9
Other (4, 5, 6, 7, 10)	20.3	20.6	18.6	16.8	65.6	14.7	24.2	12.1
Total	100.0	100.0	100.0	100.0	100.0	100.0	100.0	100.0

NOTE

Numbers in brackets refer to the corresponding EEC nomenclature.

SOURCE

EEC (1974, 1976).

country's sectors of specialisation (or of comparative advantage) can be identified as those where its shares of the ten countries' total of US patents and of R&D are significantly greater than its shares for manufacturing industry as a whole.[5] The R&D shares for the UK confirm what the patent shares indicate, and show a strong pattern of specialisation in the aerospace sector; apart from the USA, only France shows a similar, though weaker, pattern of specialisation. Belgium is specialised in chemicals and metals, F R Germany in chemicals and mechanical engineering, Italy in chemicals, Japan in metals, the Netherlands in electrical and electronic products, Sweden in metals and mechanical engineering, and Switzerland in chemicals.

INNOVATIVE ACTIVITIES AND EXPORT SHARES

The analytical framework

Over the past twenty-five years, economists have renewed their interest in the impact of innovative activities on economic performance. One strand of this interest has been reflected in a large variety of 'growth accounting' exercises showing that only a small part of measured US economic growth since the beginning of the century could be explained by measured increases in labour and capital, and a large part of the unexplained residual was put down to 'technical progress'. Other US studies have shown that 'technical progress' thus defined has been particularly high in sectors with high levels of R&D expenditure, or whose equipment suppliers have high R&D expenditures (Nelson and Winter, 1977). More recently, Schott (1978) has linked British R&D expenditures directly to the technical progress component of a production function. However, in this type of analysis, the problems of measurement and attribution are immense, and the possibilities of disaggregation and international comparison very limited.

On the other hand, the potential for exploring further the links between innovative activities and performance in export markets appears considerable. Since the beginning of the 1960s, innovative activities have become a critical factor in the attempts to explain patterns of international trade, especially the exports of the industrially advanced countries. The so-called 'neo-technology' theories of international trade have been developed to try to explain the apparent contradiction of the 'Leontief paradox', namely, that US exports turned out to be more labour-intensive than US imports, although the prevalent theory of international trade predicted quite the opposite (Leontief, 1953). These theories explain US competitive advantage in terms of a temporary monopoly given by the incorporation of new technology into a product or production process, the process of creating and incorporating the technology being relatively labour-intensive (Posner, 1961; Vernon, 1966).

Apart from industry studies, empirical validation has consisted mainly of exploring the degree to which a country's comparative advantage in exports is correlated with the product group's R&D intensity. Keesing (1967) and Gruber, Mehta and Vernon (1967) have shown that such a correlation is high for the USA. Recent work by Horn (1976), while confirming these results for the USA, shows that the correlation is weaker for F R Germany, valid for Japan only in its trade with less developed countries, and practically non-existent for the UK.

However, these studies suffer from a number of shortcomings. The degree of disaggregation is limited by the R&D statistics. The measures of R&D intensity applicable in the USA are often assumed to apply to other countries. Few have explored the degree to which differences in export performance amongst the industrially advanced countries are related to differences in innovative activities.

We intend here to push such exploration further, on the basis of the US patenting data available for forty industrial branches since 1963 and the corresponding data on the value of exports from the OECD countries.[6] The model that we test is basically Schumpeterian. A relatively high expenditure of resources on innovative activities in a country will result in more competitive products and processes, a relatively high degree of patenting activity in the USA, a relatively strong competitive position, an increase in world market share, and an increase in world export share. If the country is in such a position over a wide range of sectors, its favourable balance of payments will push up its exchange rate and dampen the further expansion of exports, to the extent that price is a significant factor in competitiveness.

The model suggests that, if innovative activities in a sector are significant in international competitiveness, relatively high national levels of patenting in the USA should be associated with relatively high levels of exports, and vice versa. But what should be the precise specification of the regression equation? Regressing absolute US patenting in a sector against absolute exports across countries could be misleading, given that both are co-linear with country population size, and that Japan has about sixteen times more population than Switzerland. Normalising the absolute values by an index reflecting the size of the national industry (for example exports and patents as shares of the industry's sales or employment) is practically impossible, given the available industrial statistics. It is also conceptually questionable, given that in our model a high level of innovative activities will push up income per head and increase domestic sales and employment as well: in other words, the denominator on both sides of the equation will be influenced by the independent variable. For these reasons, we have normalised each country's innovative activities and export values by total population.

There remains the problem of time-lags. If patent statistics are assumed to reflect inventive activity, it is valid to include time-lags in regression equations. However, we have assumed earlier that patenting activity is undertaken to protect innovations, rather than inventions, and takes place over the whole life-cycle of an innovation or family of innovations. Under such circumstances, the search for time-lags is unnecessary, and could even be misleading.[7] As it happens, the results of our regressions are relatively insensitive to the time-lags chosen. We have regressed exports per head in 1974 against patents per head in 1974, in 1969 and in 1964, and the results do not differ significantly. For reasons of statistical convenience, we have chosen to regress exports per head in 1974 against cumulative patents per head for the period from 1963 to 1976.

The statistical results

The results of the regressions are summarised in Table 3.3. Statistically significant relations at the 2 per cent level exist in 23 out of the 40 sectors.

TABLE 3.3 Regression results for 40 industries relating per capita exports to per capita US patents

Industry	*US Standard Industrial Classification*	*Equation t-value b coeff.*	r^2
*I Significant Results**			
Special industrial machinery	355	12.13	.89
Drugs	283	12.12	.89
Metalworking machinery	354	11.99	.88
Engines and turbines (incl. aero)	351	8.40	.79
Instruments	38–3825	8.24	.78
Elec. transmission and distribution equipment	361, 3825	7.88	.77
Ordnance, guided missiles	348, 376, 3795	7.50	.75
Electrical industrial apparatus	362	7.30	.74
Industrial inorganic chemicals	286	5.86	.64
Office and computing machinery	357	5.42	.61
Communications and electronic eq.	366, 367	4.49	.52
Electrical lighting, elec. eq.	364	4.17	.48
Construction machinery	353	4.13	.47

TABLE 3.3 *continued*

	US Standard Industrial Classification	*Equation t-value b coeff.*	r^2
Soaps, cleaning products, etc.	284	4.07	.47
Miscellaneous chemical products	289	3.68	.42
General industrial machinery	356	3.52	.40
Fabricated metal products	34–{3462, 3463}	3.48	.39
Industrial organic chemicals	281	2.92	.31
Motor vehicles	371	2.81	.29
Petroleum products	13, 29	2.79	.29
Railroad eq.	374	2.71	.28
Miscellaneous machinery	359	2.67	.27
Refrigeration and service machinery	358	2.51	.25
II Not-significant Results			
Aircraft	372	2.34	.22
Miscellaneous electrical eq.	369	2.24	.21
Plastic materials	282	2.21	.20
Radio and TV receiving eq.	365	2.20	.23
Electrical household appliances	363	2.16	.20
Rubber products	30	1.82	.15
Farm machinery	352	1.62	.12
Textiles	22	1.59	.12
Misc. transportation eq.	379–3795	1.53	.11
Non-ferrous metal products	333–6, 3398, 3463	1.33	.09
Stone, clay, glass products	32	1.32	.08
Ferrous metal products	331, 332, 3399, 3462	1.30	.08
Agricultural chemicals	287	1.08	.06
Food	20	.99	.05
Motor and bicycles	375	.61	.02
Paints and allied products	285	.52	.01
Ship and boat building	373	.47	.01

NOTE
* Significant at the 2 per cent level.

Regression Equation

$$\frac{X_{ij}}{h_j} = a + b.\frac{P_{ij}}{h_j}, \text{ where}$$

i = industry, j = country, X = exports,
P = US patents, h = population.
Results are for i constant, and varying j.
Regressions include all OECD countries except Iceland, New Zealand and the USA.

SOURCE
Soete (1978).

These include fabricated metal products, scientific instruments, eight out of the nine sectors of non-electrical machinery (farm machinery being the exception), six out of the nine chemical product groups (the others being paints, plastics, and agricultural chemicals), four out of seven of the electrical product groups (the others being radio and TV, electrical household appliances, and miscellaneous electrical equipment), and two out of four of the transport sector other than aircraft.[8]

In none of the traditional materials was there a significant relationship (ferrous and non-ferrous metals; stone, clay, glass and concrete; rubber), nor in the sectors producing non-durable consumer goods (textiles, food products). It could be argued that conventional factor endowments – particularly in low wage rates and in natural advantages – determine export competitiveness in these sectors, and that such factor advantages are also becoming important at the older end of the R&D-intensive industries: paints, plastics, agricultural chemicals, household durable consumer goods.

However, it should be noted that our choice of regression equation and of statistical sample includes biases, some of which serve to augment the degrees of statistical significance, and some to reduce them. The inclusion of OECD countries with a weak industrial base (for example Greece, Ireland, Portugal, Turkey, Yugoslavia) might increase the coefficients of determination (r^2), since in most sectors they tend systematically to have both low exports per

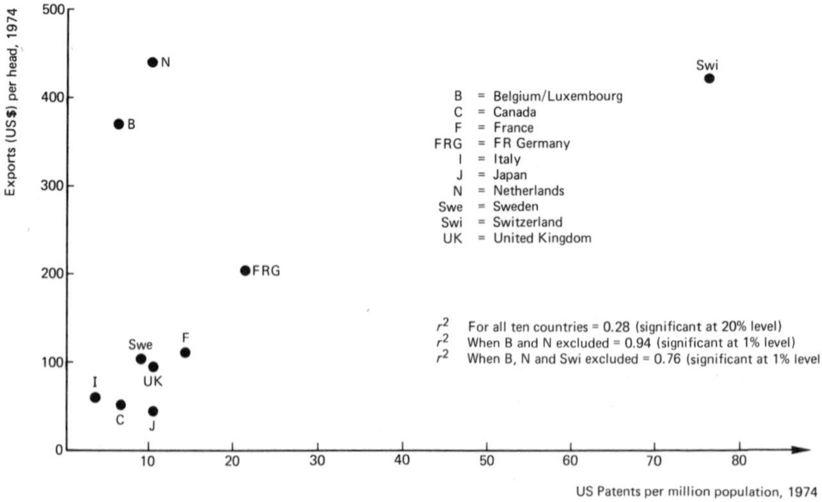

FIG. 3.2 Export performance and US patenting: chemicals (US SIC 28)

SOURCES
OECD (1976), OTAF (1977b)

head and low US patenting per head. In fact, however, their exclusion makes very little difference to the value of the coefficients.

The other sources of bias can be detected in Figures 3.2 to 3.6, which plot, for the ten major OECD countries other than the USA, exports per head (1974) against US patents per head (1974) in some of the major aggregated industries: chemicals, non-electrical machinery, electrical products, electronic products, and motor vehicles. In some cases, the Netherlands or Switzerland dominate the regression line: in a positive sense, when both US patenting and exports per capita are high; and in a negative sense when US

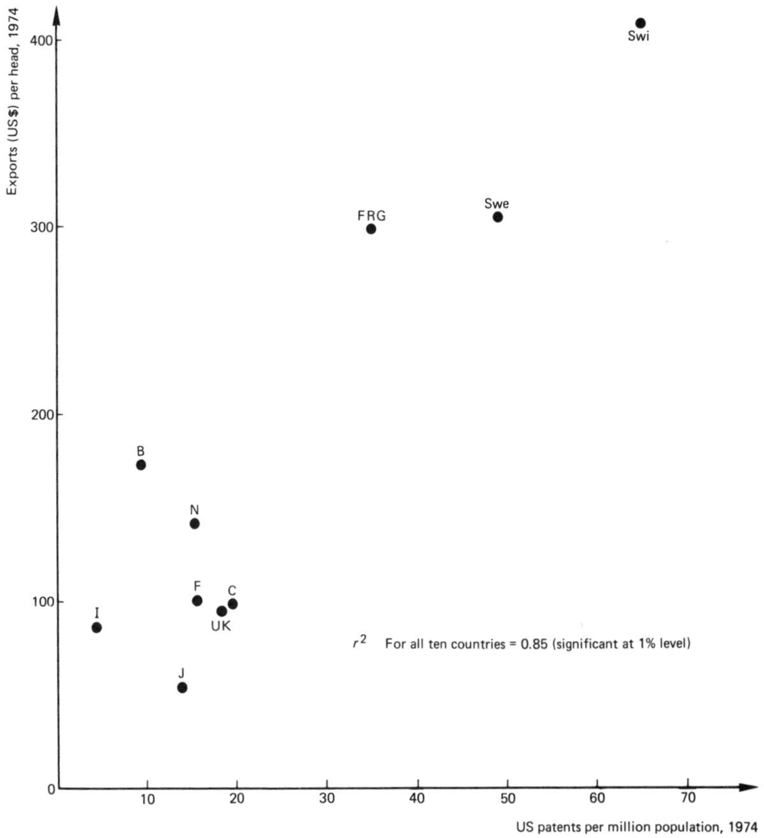

FIG. 3.3 Export performance and US patenting: non electrical machinery (US SIC 35)

SOURCES
OECD (1976); OTAF (1977b).

patenting per capita is high but per capita exports low (often as a result of direct investment abroad by multinational firms based in the Netherlands and Switzerland). We have therefore examined how sensitive the coefficients of determination in Table 3.3 are to the exclusion of the Netherlands and Switzerland, even though the performance of both countries in many sectors may be an exemplar of the importance of innovative activities for international competitiveness.[9]

Figures 3.2 to 3.6 also suggest that the coefficients of determination are significantly influenced in certain sectors by incoming foreign investment, especially in small countries where foreign firms may locate and produce for an international market. Under such circumstances, relatively high per capita exports will be associated with low per capita patenting, and thereby reduce the value of the coefficients. This combination can be seen in the chemical, radio and TV receiving equipment and motor vehicles industries in Belgium/

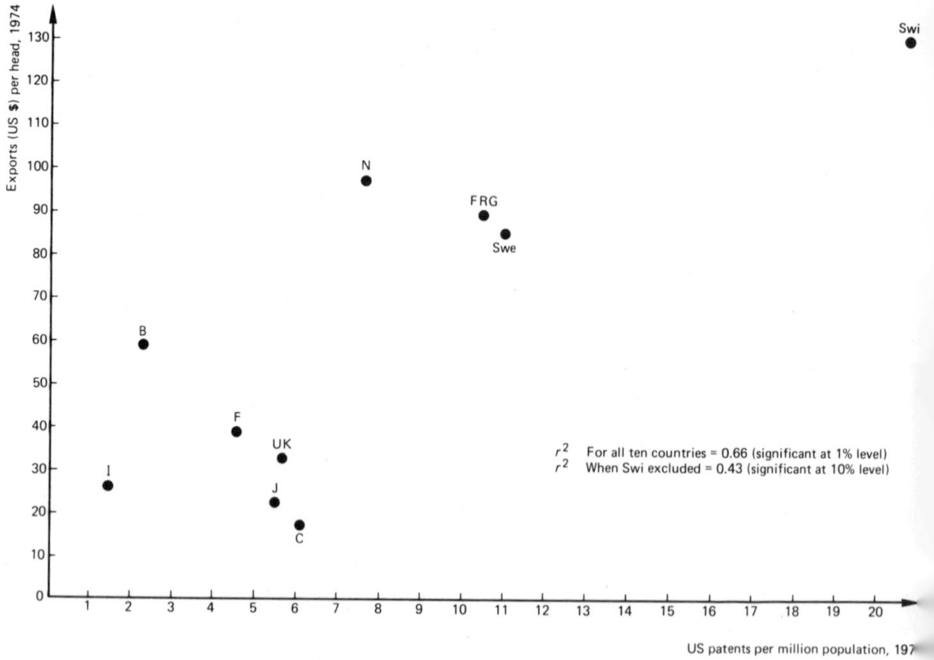

FIG. 3.4 Export performance and US patenting: electrical products (US SIC 361–364, 369, 3825)

SOURCES
OECD (1976); OTAF (1976b).

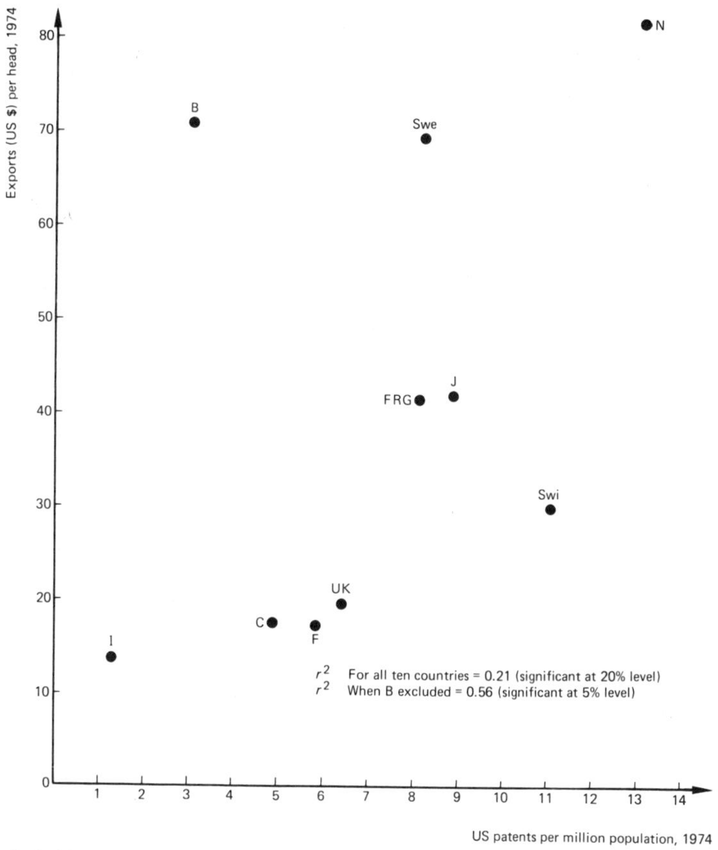

FIG. 3.5 Export performance and US patenting: electronic products (US SIC 365–367)

SOURCES
OECD (1976); OTAF (1977b).

Luxembourg; the chemical industry in the Netherlands; and the motor vehicles industry in Canada. In all these cases, it is plausible to argue that the pattern is caused by direct foreign investment, and in later work we shall explore whether this can be confirmed statistically. In the meantime, we have examined the sensitivity of the regressions to the exclusion of the above countries from the sectors specified.

These sensitivity analyses make virtually no difference to the results in 25 out of the 39 sectors (aircraft being excluded) in which we carried them out. In five sectors they result in a significant decrease in the coefficient of

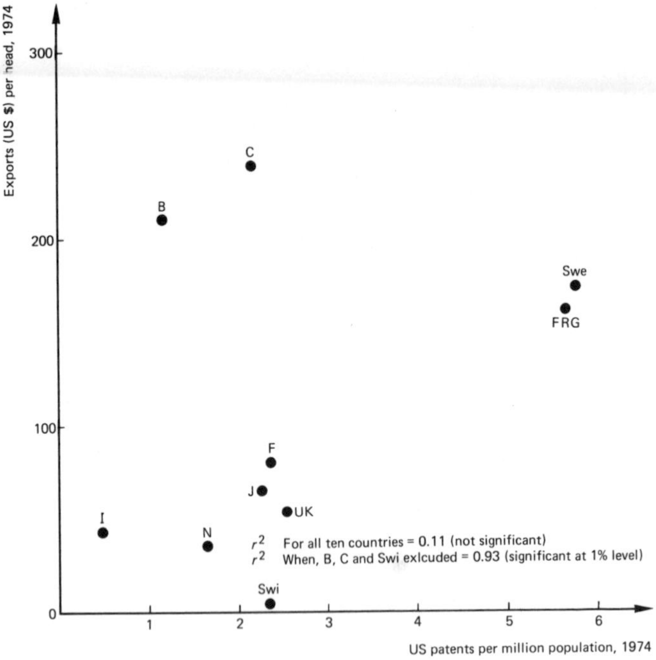

FIG. 3.6 Export performance and US patenting motor vehicles (US SIC: 371)

determination: the elimination of the Netherlands or Switzerland leads to non-significant statistical relations in soaps and cleaning products, petroleum products, scientific instruments, and electrical lighting equipment, and to a considerable reduction in significance in electrical transmission and distribution equipment. At the same time, the analyses lead to a significant increase in the coefficient of determination in nine sectors: two chemical (plastics and industrial organic chemicals), three non-electrical machinery (farm machinery, general industrial machinery, and refrigeration and service machinery), two electrical and electronic (electrical household appliances, radio and TV), motor vehicles, and iron and steel.

Thus, the quality and detail of the US patent statistics have enabled us to identify the impact of innovative activities on export performance with greater precision than Walker (1979) was able to achieve with R&D statistics, although our results do not contradict his. The results of our regressions suggest that the impact is significant in capital goods, most chemicals, and some transport equipment, but not in traditional products or consumer goods. The results of the sensitivity analyses suggest that, for the larger countries at least (France, F R Germany, Italy, Japan and the UK), the impact of innovative activities on exports shares is also significant for durable consumer goods, and for iron and steel.

National strengths and weaknesses in industrial innovation

The data giving exports and US patenting for each country in the forty industrial sectors also enable us to identify some of each country's strengths and weaknesses in industrial innovation. Relative sectoral strength will be reflected in world export shares and US patenting shares both being well above the national average for all manufacturing industry; weakness will be reflected in shares well below the national average. These data enable greater refinement and completion of the analysis of patterns of industrial R&D expenditure, above. They are presented in Table 3.4. They confirm the strong comparative advantage of Britain in sectors closely linked to Government-financed R/D programmes (aircraft and missiles, engines and turbines); they also show Britain's considerable weakness in household durable consumer goods (household electrical appliances, radio and TV). These measures of national comparative advantage do not enable absolute comparisons of performance amongst countries. However, Figures 3.2 to 3.6 show that – in per capita terms – the UK is nowhere near the leading countries in capital goods, chemicals or durable consumer goods. It finds itself generally at the same level as France and Japan, and above Italy. The strong countries are F R Germany and its neighbours Sweden, Switzerland and the Netherlands, and – in electronic products – Japan.

RECENT TRENDS IN BRITISH INNOVATIVE ACTIVITIES

Absolute Decline

We conclude so far that innovative activities are closely associated with export shares in capital goods, chemicals, and durable consumer goods, that the British comparative advantage in innovative activities is in aircraft and other defence-related sectors, and that British innovative activities have declined noticeably compared with those of other countries over the past ten to fifteen years, indeed over the past seventy years. The gap between Britain's innovative activities and those of F R Germany and its neighbours has widened, Japan will soon have left us behind in relative terms, and France will soon have overtaken us. Even more disturbing, the absolute level of resources devoted to innovative activities has gone down sharply since the end of the 1960s.

TABLE 3.4 Some comparative strengths and weaknesses in innovative performances

Country	*Comparative strengths*	*Comparative weaknesses*
Belgium	Ferrous and non-ferrous metals; stone, clay, glass; Chemicals	Transport equipment; Household appliances
France	Railroad equipment; Motor vehicles and Bicycles; Soap and cleaning products	Radio and TV; Household appliances; Machinery
F R Germany	Machinery; Chemicals; Motor vehicles	Petroleum; Food; Ship and boat building; Radio and TV
Italy	Household appliances; Textiles; Chemicals	Radio & TV; Ship and boat building; Electrical transmission and distribution equipment
Japan	Radio and TV; Ferrous metals	Petroleum products; Machinery; Ordnance and missiles
Netherlands	Electrical and electronics; Petroleum; Chemicals	Aircraft and missiles; Transportation equipment
Sweden	Metals and metal products; Household appliances; Motor vehicles; Machinery; Ship and boat building	Chemicals; Petroleum; Textiles; Radio and TV
Switzerland	Drugs; Chemicals	Petroleum; Transportation equipment
United Kingdom	Aircraft and missiles; Engines and turbines; Non-ferrous metals	Household appliances; Radio and TV

SOURCE
OTAF (1977b)

Table 3.5 shows this very clearly. By 1972, employment in manufacturing R&D was 83 per cent of the 1967 level, and by 1975, 81 per cent. Industry-financed R&D declined as a percentage of net output, as did the proportion of US patents of foreign origin from the UK. R&D in motor vehicles and chemicals held up much better than other sectors both in absolute terms and

TABLE 3.5 Trends in UK innovative activities in different industrial sectors

	US Patenting – UK/Non-US (%)			*R&D Manpower (1967 = 100)*				*R&D/Net Output Industry-financed(1) (%)*				*R&D/Net Output Total Financed (%)*			
	1963	*1969*	*1976*	*1967*	*1969*	*1972*	*1975*	*1964*	*1968*	*1972*	*1975*	*1964*	*1968*	*1972*	*1975*
Electrical	21.9	20.5	14.1	100	109	82	82	3.8	7.1	2.9	3.1	4.4	11.1	3.5	3.6
Electronic	28.2	21.0	12.3	100	105	95	88	13.3		12.1	10.1	26.6		20.6	18.8
Mechanical engineering	22.9	20.2	11.0	100	80	53	52	2.7	2.6	2.0	1.9	3.2	3.2	2.1	2.0
Fabricated metal products	25.3	21.4	14.5	n.a.	n.a.	n.a.	n.a.	0.9	0.7	0.6	0.5	1.0	0.8	0.6	0.5
Iron, steel and Non-ferrous metals	17.3	16.3	9.5	n.a.	n.a.	n.a.	n.a.	2.5	1.8	1.5	1.4	2.1	2.0	1.5	1.5
Motor vehicles	25.5	21.1	14.6	100	100	93	102	n.a.	4.7	4.4	5.1	n.a.	4.8	4.4	5.2
Aircraft and missiles	42.1	29.8	18.2	100	90	78	77	4.2	4.9	5.4	5.2	42.7	34.2	34.6	29.0
Chemicals and allied products	16.0	14.6	12.0	100	106	100	98	6.0[2]	5.4[2]	6.4[3]	5.8[3]	6.3[2]	5.8[2]	6.4[3]	6.0[3]
Total Manufacturing Industries	22.0	19.5	12.6	100	97	83	81	2.7	2.6	2.4	2.4	4.4	4.1	3.7	3.5

NOTES
The industrial categories for the patenting data are not strictly comparable to those for the R&D data.
1 'Industry' is taken to include private industry and public corporations
2 Excluding petroleum
3 Including petroleum

SOURCES
OTAF (1977b); UK Government (1967, 1970, 1972, 1976, 1977a – 1977d).

as a percentage of the industries' output; in drugs, paints and agricultural chemicals, the UK even managed to increase its US patent share between 1967 and 1976 (OTAF, 1977b). In all the other major sectors there has been a marked decline in indicators of innovative activity.

In aircraft and missiles, where R&D manpower in 1975 was 77 per cent of the 1967 level, most of the decline resulted from a reduction in Government funding. However, such funding is still very high compared to that of the rest of Western Europe, where the rates of decline of aerospace R&D have been greater. By 1975, Britain was relatively *more* specialised in aerospace R&D than in 1967.

In addition, there has been a reduction of innovative activities since the end of the 1960s in electrical products, in electronic products, and above all, in mechanical engineering. UK electronics declined from 28.3 per cent of all non-US patenting in the USA in 1963 to 12.3 per cent in 1976. Over almost the same period, the percentage of British net output spent on R&D went down from 26.6 to 18.8, mainly as a result of cutbacks in Government R&D expenditures, but also of industry's own funds. In electrical products, the decline resulted mainly from cutbacks in industry's own funds.

In the mechanical engineering industry, R&D manpower almost halved between 1967 and 1975, and the percentage of net output spent on R&D in the industry declined drastically. Some might argue that this trend is not necessarily bad, if it is part of a redeployment of skilled personnel towards other and weaker links in the innovative chain, such as production and marketing. Unfortunately, the official published manpower statistics do not enable us to verify this argument, since they give data for science and engineering employment in manufacturing industry only up to 1971 (UK Government, 1977e). Between 1961 and 1971, the employment of qualified scientists and engineers as a percentage of total manufacturing employment increased steadily from 1.13 to 1.71. The rate of increase was above average in chemical and electronic products, below average in mechanical engineering, and negligible in electrical products.

Since 1971, we have data only for engineers, based on a survey undertaken by the Council of Engineering Institutions. Table 3.6 shows trends in some ways similar to those of the other aspects of innovative activities that we have measured above: a considerable increase between 1966 and 1975 in the proportion of qualified engineers in the chemical industry, a decline since 1971 in the proportion in the electrical and electronics industries, and a steep decline in the proportion in mechanical engineering.[10] If the rate of increase of employment of qualified engineers in all manufacturing industry was the same between 1971 and 1975 as it has been between 1966 and 1971, then the number of qualified engineers in the mechanical engineering sector did

TABLE 3.6 Deployment of qualified engineers in UK manufacturing industry, 1966, 1971 and 1975.

	Percentage of engineers in manufacturing product groups		
	1966	*1971*	*1975*
Chemical and allied industries	13.9	15.0	19.6
Metal manufacture	4.2	3.7	4.2
Mechanical engineering	20.9	18.1	15.7
Electrical machinery	11.8	10.1	7.1
Electronics	16.0	19.7	17.5
Shipbuilding	5.8	5.9	8.4
Aerospace	9.7	8.9	9.9
Vehicle manufacture	4.9	4.7	4.7
Other manufacturing industries	13.0	14.0	13.1
Total	100	100	100

SOURCE
Council of Engineering Institutions (1975).

not increase at all between 1966 and 1975. The reduction of R&D in mechanical engineering has almost certainly not been the result of a redeployment of skilled manpower.

Causes of decline

Some observers see the decline in British innovative activities as a *consequence* of Britain's wider decline: now that Britain is poor, they argue, it can no longer afford large expenditures on innovative activities. This argument is factually wrong. Table 3.7 shows trends in industry-financed R&D activities as a percentage of the domestic product of manufacturing industry for some of the major OECD countries. This percentage has declined considerably since the late 1960s in the UK, whilst it has gone up in Belgium, F R Germany, Japan, Sweden and the USA. By 1975, UK manufacturing industry was spending a smaller percentage of its output on R&D than industry in the USA, Sweden, the Netherlands, probably Japan and certainly in Switzerland, although strictly comparable statistics are not available for the latter. Although the percentage in 1975 was the same in F R Germany as in the UK, this does not capture fully the extent of the innovative effort in the German machinery and metal products sectors.

TABLE 3.7 Trends in OECD countries' expenditures in manufacturing industry as

	R&D financed by manufacturing industry as a percentage of the domestic product of manufacturing industry											
	1964	*1965*	*1966*	*1967*	*1968*	*1969*	*1970*	*1971*	*1972*	*1973*	*1974*	*1975*
Belgium								1.93		2.12		
Canada				1.77		1.65		1.68		1.31		1.47
F R Germany				2.23		2.3		2.6		2.34		2.72
Japan[1]				2.38	2.67	2.7	2.97	3.0	3.13	3.01		
Netherlands						3.53	3.38	3.47	3.52	3.14	3.23	3.55
Sweden				2.74		2.52		3.07		3.02		3.21
United Kingdom[2]	2.82		3.2	3.27	3.16	3.04			2.59			2.74
USA[3]				3.53	3.58	3.77	3.9	3.95	3.80	3.83	4.08	4.15

NOTES

1 Assumes foreign funding is negligible.

2 The UK figures in this table are different in magnitude from those in the last eight columns of Table 3.5 because of differences in the definitions and measurement of net output, and of domestic product of industry.

3 No foreign funding.

Nearly all the decline of British innovative activities relative to those of F R Germany between 1967 and 1975 can be attributed to the diminishing proportion of value added devoted by British industrialists to such activities compared with their German counterparts, and very little to slower growth. Even when compared with Japan, more than half of Britain's relative decline in industrial R&D can be put down to the different allocative decisions of industrialists in Britain and in Japan, and not to Japan's more rapid growth.

What does need explaining is British industry's failure to take advantage of its higher level of R&D activities relative to many of its competitors in the late 1950s and early 1960s (Freeman and Young, 1965). Perhaps much of this lead was a statistical illusion: many countries had only just begun to collect industrial R&D statistics, so that their survey coverage may have been less comprehensive than the longer-standing British surveys. But it is also possible that British innovative activities were inefficient, when compared to those of other countries, so that R&D activities were not effectively translated into competitive and commercially successful products and production processes.

According to Rubenstein *et al.* (1977), British industrialists in the 1970s see the main factor influencing their policies for innovation as the general a percentage of manufacturing domestic product

Total R&D expenditure in manufacture as a percentage of the domestic product of manufacturing industry

1964	*1965*	*1966*	*1967*	*1968*	*1969*	*1970*	*1971*	*1972*	*1973*	*1974*	*1975*
			2.12		1.92		2.18		2.34		
			2.12		2.05		2.13		1.72		1.83
			2.66		2.64		3.02		2.83		3.28
			2.4	2.7	2.72	2.99	3.06	3.2	3.09	3.2	
					3.85	3.73	3.86	3.88	3.48	3.56	3.92
			3.41		2.95		3.58		3.62		3.8
4.64		4.93	5.06	4.99	4.97			4.5			4.56
			7.11	6.92	6.89	6.88	6.69	6.43	6.24	6.42	6.52

SOURCE
OECD (1977b).

economic climate, as reflected in expectations about future growth, and in the pressures on profits from both taxation and foreign competition. Whilst these factors may be at work, they cannot explain everything. Phelps-Brown (1977) has argued that company taxation in the UK is lower than in many other countries. Pratten (1976) has shown that, in equivalent British and Swedish companies, the former employed relatively fewer qualified scientists and engineers, and had a lower level of sophistication of products and production processes. He found that differences in performance could not be explained by differences in taxation or profitability.

One finding by Pratten is confirmed by a comparison of national levels and trends in profitability with national levels and trends in industrial expenditures on R&D activity. International comparisons of profitability pose many conceptual and statistical problems, and the interpretation in Table 3.8 contains a subjective element in the assessment of levels and trends in profitability. It categorises countries according to whether data about them tend to support or to reject hypotheses about the positive relationship between levels or trends in profitability and levels or trends in industrial R&D activities.

TABLE 3.8 Relationships between R&D and profitability in selected OECD countries

		R&D					
		Level			*Trend*		
		Supports	*Rejects*	*Unclear*	*Supports*	*Rejects*	*Unclear*
Profitability	Level	N-lands Japan France	Canada FRG UK Sweden	USA Italy	Japan UK	N-lands Canada FRG Sweden	USA France Italy
	Trend	FRG Japan USA	N-lands UK Canada Italy Sweden	France	FRG Japan UK N-lands	Canada Italy Sweden	USA France

SOURCES
R&D: Table 3.7.
Profit: OECD (1977a), Tables A20 and A21.

None of the possible relationships between profitability and R&D holds for a majority of the nine countries. Only Japan confirms all four positive relationships, given that it has had high and rising R&D expenditures, and a high level and favourable trend in profitability. The experience of the UK industry suggests that a low level and downward trend in profitability could be depressing R&D expenditures. Yet the experience of Canada (high and rising profits, low and falling R&D), and of Sweden (low and falling profits, high and rising R&D) suggests that other factors are also at work.

Even if there were a positive relationship between profitability and R&D, it would still be possible to argue that low profitability is one of the *consequences* of past failure to compete, because of lack of R&D and innovation, rather than a *cause of* lack of innovation; other consequences of such failure could be low expectations about the future and strong pressure of foreign competition. Such competition and low expectations about the future have not stimulated British industry to greater innovative effort; as Table 3.7 shows, quite the opposite has been happening. This is consistent with Walker's argument in Chapter 2 that there has been a long-term tendency in British industry to invest less in innovative activities than our main competitors, whatever the economic circumstances.

In this context, it is perhaps significant that the chemical industry's innovative activities have held up so much better than those of the mechanical engineering sector. The former industry probably sees company-financed innovative activities as an investment for necessary survival and growth, whilst the latter has apparently viewed it as a disposable and peripheral activity. These clear differences might be explained by the degree to which their roots and their attitudes towards professional skills and innovative activities were formed in nineteenth-century Britain. Dealing with this problem will require more than changing the tax system. Some of what we consider to be the deep-seated problems will be discussed in subsequent chapters: the demand for and supply of engineers, the skills and attitudes of management, and the role of defence spending.

NOTES

1. We are greatly indebted to David Critchley, Stuart Gross, Kurt Hoffman and Mick McLean, all of whom contributed significantly to the data-gathering and analysis necessary for the preparation of this chapter. We also benefited considerably from Robert Cahn's and Leslie Cook's critical and constructive comments on an earlier draft.
2. The metals category includes fabricated metal products, where the patent to R&D ratio is relatively very high. The 'other transport' category includes motor vehicles, where the patent to R&D ratio is relatively very low. Thus, differences amongst countries in the relative importance of these two product groups within the wider categories of metals and other transport will lead to differing shares in R&D and in patents in Table 3.1.
3. In 1975, the ratio of Canadian patents in the USA to Canadian international patents (i.e. granted in several countries) was 2.6, for Japan it was 0.85, and for the major W. European countries between 0.4 and 0.57 (OTAF, 1977a, tables A-3 and A-6).
4. In 1977, the UK Government was still supporting civil aviation R&D to a greater extent than all other EEC Governments. In financial terms, the UK accounted for 44 per cent of the total, 15 per cent more than France, and 2.7 times more than F R Germany (Euroforum, 1977).
5. The concept is the same as that of revealed comparative advantage in international trade i.e.

$$Sij/\Sigma_1^i Sij \times \frac{\Sigma_1^i Sij}{\Sigma_1^{ij} Sij},$$

   where Sij is the level of activity of industry i in country j. A figure of more than one shows a comparative advantage, and less than one a comparative disadvantage.

6. The following sectors are not included in the analysis because the data on US patenting is not available: SIC 21: tobacco manufacturers, SIC 23: apparel, SIC 24: lumber and wood products, SIC 25: furniture and fixtures, SIC 26: paper and allied products, SIC 27: printing and publishing, SIC 31: leather and leather products and SIC 39: miscellaneous manufacturing industries.
7. Examples can be found where a major innovation has resulted in a master patent, then exports, and then a cluster of improvement patents. Given the direction of the lag, a statistical analysis could conclude that exports 'caused' technical effort, and it would be wrong.
8. If R&D statistics were used as indicators of innovative activity in aircraft, and if the USA were included, the regression would be highly significant.
9. The high level of Swiss patenting is to be expected in chemical and engineering products, given the proportionately very high level of innovative activities in Swiss industry (OECD, 1977/1978). However, it is also high in such unexpected areas as motor cars, and iron and steel. In iron and steel, this is because all the patents related to oxygen steel-making are registered from Switzerland, not because of Swiss innovative activities. See Chapter 12.
10. The official manpower statistics (UK Government, 1977e) sometimes show distributions of qualified engineers amongst industrial sectors noticeably different from those of the survey of the Council of Engineering Institutions. None the less, the coefficients of correlation between the two distributions are 0.87 for 1966 and 0.83 for 1971, both of which are significant at the 1 per cent level. Furthermore, both distributions show the same trends between 1966 and 1971.

REFERENCES

Council of Engineering Institutions, *The 1975 Survey of Professional* Engineers (London: CEI, 1975).

EEC, *Public Expenditures on Research and Development in the Community Countries: Analysis by Objectives, 1969–1973* (Brussels: EEC, 1974).

EEC, *Le Financement Public de la Recherche et du Developpement dans les Pays de la Communauté, 1974–1975* (Brussels: EEC, 1976).

Euroforum, No. 46/77 (20 December 1977).

C. Freeman, *The Economics of Industrial Innovation* (London: Penguin 1974).

C. Freeman and A. Young, *The Research and Development Effort* (Paris: OECD, 1965).

W. Gruber, D. Mehta and R. Vernon, 'The R and D Factor in International Trade and International Investment of United States Industries', *Journal of Political Economy*, 57 (1967).

E. Horn, *Technologische Neuerungen und internationale Arbeitsteilung,* Die Bundesrepubliek Deutschland im internationalen Vergleich, Kieler Studien *139*b, JCB Mohr (Paul Siebeck) (Tübingen, 1976).

D. Keesing, 'The Impact of Research and Development on United States Trade', *Journal of Political Economy,* vol. 57 (1967).

W. Leontief, 'Domestic Production and Foreign Trade: The American Capital Position Re-examined', *Proceedings of the American Philosophical Society*, vol. 97 (1953).
E. Mansfield *et al., Research and Development in the Modern Corporation* (London: Macmillan, 1971).
National Science Board, *Science Indicators, 1976* (Washington D.C.: 1977).
R. Nelson and S. Winter, 'In Search of a Useful Theory of Innovation', *Research Policy*, vol. 6 (1977).
OECD, *Patterns of Resources devoted to Research and Experimental Development in the OECD Area*, 1963–71 (Paris: OECD, 1975).
OECD, *Commodity Trade Statistics, Series C* (Paris: OECD, 1976).
OECD, *Towards Full Employment and Price Stability* (Paris: OECD, 1977a).
OECD, Information given to the authors by the Science and Technology Indicators Unit (Paris: 1977b).
OECD, *Science Resources Newsletter* (Paris: OECD, 1977/1978).
OECD, *Trends in Industrial R and D in Selected OECD Countries, 1967–75*, mimeo (Paris: OECD, 1978). See also OECD document SPT(78)20, with the same title (1978).
OECD, information given to the authors by the Science and Technology Indicators Unit (Paris: OECD, in press, 1979).
OTAF, *Technology Assessment and Forecast. Early Warning Report of the Office of Technology Assessment and Forecast*, mimeo (US Department of Commerce, Washington D.C.: 1973).
OTAF, *Technology Assessment and Forecast: 7th Report*, mimeo (US Department of Commerce, Washington D.C.: 1977a).
OTAF, 'US Patent Activity in Thirty Nine Standard Industrial Classification Categories', information supplied to the Science Policy Research Unit by the Office of Technology Assessment and Forecast (US Department of Commerce, Washington D.C.: unpublished, 1977b).
K. Pavitt, *Using Patent Statistics in 'Science Indicators': Possibilities and Problems*, a report for the National Science Foundation, mimeo (University of Sussex, Science Policy Research Unit: 1978).
E. Phelps-Brown, 'What is the British Predicament?', *Three Banks Review*, vol. 116 (1977).
M. Posner, 'International Trade and Technical Change', *Oxford Economic Papers*, vol. 13, no. 3, (1961).
C. Pratten, *A Comparison of the Performance of Swedish and UK Companies* (Cambridge: Cambridge University Press, 1976).
A. Rubenstein *et al.*, 'Management Perceptions of Government Incentives to Technological Innovation in England, France, West Germany and Japan', *Research Policy*, vol. 6 (1977).
K. Schott, 'The Relations between Industrial Research and Development and Factor Demands', *Economic Journal*, 88: 349 (1978).
L. Soete, 'Inventive Activity, Industrial Organisation and International Trade', DPhil. thesis, University of Sussex (1978, unpublished).
H. Stead, 'The Costs of Technological Innovation', *Research Policy*, vol. 5 (1976).
UK Government, *Statistics of Science and Technology* (London: HMSO, 1970).

UK Government, *Report on the Census of Production, 1968* (London: HMSO, 1972).
UK Government, *Research and Development Expenditure and Employment,* Studies in Official Statistics, no. 27 (London: HMSO, 1976).
UK Government, 'Industrial Expenditure and Employment on Scientific Research and Development in 1975', *Trade and Industry,* 24 June 1977 (London, 1977a).
UK Government, 'Employment on Scientific Research and Development in Industry in 1975', *Trade and Industry*, 1 July 1977 (London: 1977b).
UK Government, *Report on the Census of Production, 1972* (London: HMSO, 1977c).
UK Government, *Report on the Census of Production, 1975* (London, HMSO, 1977d).
UK Government, *Changes in the Population of Persons with Qualifications in Engineering, Technology and Science, 1959 to 1976* (London: 1977e).
R. Vernon, 'International Investment and International Trade in the Product Cycle', *Quarterly Journal of Economics,* vol. 80 (1966).
W. Walker, *Industrial Innovation and International Trading Performance* (Greenwich, Connecticut: JAI Press, 1979).

4 British Attitudes to Engineering Education: a Historical Perspective

Austen Albu[1]

INTRODUCTION

There is ample evidence of the growing inferiority in numbers and education of British engineers from the middle of the nineteenth century and that the major reason for this has been a lack of demand by British industry for highly qualified staff. What would now be called professional engineers were, until recently, mostly ill-educated and received their training largely by apprenticeship. The only qualification available to the great majority was membership of one of the engineering institutions, in contrast to the degrees or diplomas given after full-time education to Continental European or American engineers. No examination was required for membership until that introduced by the Civils in 1896; a step which was not taken by the Mechanicals and Electricals until 1913. At the end of the nineteenth century it was estimated that Germany had about 30,000 academically trained engineers, with from three to five times as many from the lower-level engineering schools: a total of at least 150,000 (Ludwig, 1974). This was more than the members enrolled on the Technical and Scientific Register of the Ministry of Labour in this country during the Second World War (Board of Education, 1944).

With the exception of the Civils, whose membership included a large number of self-employed consultants, the institutions, most of whose leading members were industrialists, were slow to appreciate the need for full-time higher education and continued to express their view that apprenticeship, with part-time education, was the best training for a professional engineer. The first record of an interest in education by the professional institutions was the Presidential Address to the Civils of John Fowler in 1866, when he referred to the superior mechanical education given in France and Germany but rejoiced in the practical advantage possessed by British engineers. Thirty years later, a committee emphasised for the first time the role of university or college study, with the implication that most of it would be in full-time education (Institution of Civil Engineers, 1906).

In 1882, W. E. Ayrton and John Percy gave a paper on the education of electrical engineers to the Electricals, but in the first ten years of the new century there were only ten references in their proceedings to the subject (Ayrton and Percy 1882, p. 389). One of them was a long paper presented in 1904 by Dr R. Mullineux Walmsley, describing American methods of training engineers, which led to a controversy distinguished by the paucity of contribution by industrialists and the complacency of some of the teachers from technical colleges. The first reference to education in the proceedings of the Mechanicals, whose members were mostly in manufacturing industry, was in 1901 in the Presidential Address of William H. Maw, the American editor of the journal *Engineering*, who became a persistent advocate of engineering education. This was followed by a paper by W. E. Dalby in 1903 (Institution of Mechanical Engineers, 1903, p. 231) after which there were no more than two or three references to the subject until 1939.

Until nearly the end of the century, there had been only four universities in England and Wales and four in Scotland. Engineering schools had developed at Cambridge, London and the Scottish universities, but the numbers graduating from them were very small (Blanchet, 1952; Foden, 1970). During this period the amount and quality of engineering education were substantially increasing on the Continent and in the USA. In 1889 Kaiser Wilhelm II gave the right to the Technischen Hochschulen, founded at the beginning of the nineteenth century, to award the title of Engineer and the Doctorate in Engineering. By 1902 there were 13 institutions teaching engineering and by 1909 there were nearly 11,000 diploma students in the Technischen Hochschulen, while the French had already developed their system of Grandes Ecoles for higher professional education. Higher engineering education thus took place on the Continent in separate institutions and so followed a different pattern from that in Britain. In the United States, in spite of the development of outstanding technical institutions such as the Massachusetts, California and Case Institutes of Technology, engineering was also taught in most of the universities, whose numbers had grown under the terms of the Land Grant Act of 1862.

The beginning of the new century saw the expansion of the civic universities in Britain, mostly based on colleges founded by progressive local businessmen and intended to provide education suitable for industry and commerce. Before the 1902 Education Act, the lack of a public secondary school system and the social and classical bias of the reformed and new 'public' schools, which provided most of the middle-class education, were a serious handicap to the growth of engineering departments in the universities and larger technical colleges (Society for the Promotion of Engineering Education, 1931). In 1897 there was no matriculation examination for students entering University College, London, and very few engineering students would have been able to pass the mathematics examination. Out of more than 200 engineering students entering the Central Technical College annually over the previous five years, about seventy completed the course (Institution of Civil Engineers, 1897). Even by the 1920s the examiners for the Institution of Civil Engineers were reporting very poor results and lack of knowledge of first principles. They put this down to cramming; but it was probably due to the inadequacies of part-time education. By the 1920s the total number of engineering degrees awarded in England and Wales was not much over two hundred, to which should be added a number of college diplomas from institutions teaching at higher levels.

Although the newer and more scientifically based industries began to use more university-trained staff, an increase which accelerated between the wars (Sanderson, 1972), this growth was not typical of most of British industry and certainly not of engineering. During the First World War, the disclosures of weakness in many branches of British industry and the fear of post-war German competition led to a temporary increase of interest in technical education. Chiefly under the influence of their academic members, in 1917 the engineering institutions were instrumental in establishing the Engineering Training Organisation with the object of developing principles for the education of the engineer.

The Organisation conducted a survey by questionnaire among 226 well-known engineering firms on their recruitment policies; of these, 43 had a system of pupillage for those whose training might have included a full-time course at university or college. The fees for pupillage ranged from £50 to £500; several mentioned the desirability of a 'public' school education for their pupils. Sixty-one provided engineering apprenticeships for secondary school boys which were supposed to cover a wide range of practical work and considerable part-time study. The rest did not recruit above the level of a trade apprentice. Only 33 mentioned a degree as a qualification for entry or part of training and only 27 mentioned matriculation or above as a qualification for pupillage.

In spite of the strong support of H. A. L. Fisher, the President of the Board of Education, industry support for the Organisation was poor; only 30 firms out of 246 circularised after the end of the First World War offered to become members (Engineering Training Organisation, 1920). By July 1920 lack of funds led to its collapse and its papers were handed over to the

Federation of British Industries who appeared to have let it quietly die (Institution of Mechanical Engineers, 1918–1920).

AFTER 1918

By comparison with her main industrial rivals, the number of those receiving an advanced full-time technical education in the UK remained very small: in 1908, in the United States it was more than 18,000, in Germany more than 10,000; but in England and Wales only 1632, 20 per cent of whom were under 18 years of age (Roderick and Stephens, 1972, p. 95).

After the war, the Board of Education approached the Institution of Mechanical Engineers for their co-operation, which led in 1920 to the scheme for Ordinary National and Higher National Certificates (ONC, HNC), later extended to other branches of engineering and other subjects. This scheme was fairly successful and its popularity among young engineers forced the institutions to recognise the HNC as an exempting qualification for most of their own examinations. Nevertheless, the numbers did little to bring the number of British engineers with any form of technical education up to that of those elsewhere. By 1938, the number of candidates entered for the ONC (a few of them in chemistry, physics or commerce) had reached 5797, of whom 3313 were successful. At the higher level the number of candidates was 1668, of whom 1137 were successful. By that time the number of those graduating in engineering in the United Kingdom had reached about 1000 a year (Board of Education, 1944). By 1927, 3500 students a year were graduating from Technischen Hochschulen in Germany (Society for the Promotion of Engineering Education, 1931).

The advent of Lord Eustace Percy to the Board of Education, of which he was President from 1925 to 1928, brought a new impetus to the attempts to remedy Britain's weakness in technical education, especially at the higher levels. The report of the Balfour Committee had again drawn attention to the lack of demand by industry for qualified staff (Committee on Trade and Industry, 1927, p. 186).

In 1927 Percy wrote to the President of the Board of Trade with a strong suggestion for an enquiry into the rationalisation of our system of technical education, which he compared unfavourably with what was available overseas. He received a cool reply which implied that British industry was too pre-occupied with its trade worries to have the time to participate in such an activity (Board of Education, 1927).

Percy later appointed a committee under the chairmanship of the distinguished mechanical engineer, Sir Dugald Clark, to examine the provision of education for the engineering industry (Committee on Education for the

Engineering Industry, 1931). The report showed that recruitment from universities and full-time technical colleges was sporadic and individual and often determined by some specific circumstance or requirement. Even more significantly, the bulk of engineering students who entered industry did so in research, teaching, design and sales, rather than production engineering and its management. The committee found that only 28.5 per cent of secondary school pupils entered industrial and agricultural occupations and that there was a prejudice against going into the 'shop'. This was not surprising in view of the almost universal lack of opportunity for training suited to their educational background and capabilities.

The older heavy engineering areas were the most backward. There was fairly general opposition to day-release for education; Rugby, which was the only area to have had experience of compulsory part-time education, alone being in favour. In Sheffield firms with international reputations practically limited new recruitment to elementary schoolboys. Most had no student or premium system and no recruitment of full-time technical college or university-trained men. Such university graduates as were employed were mostly metallurgists and not engineers (Musgrove, 1967). There were, of course, a very few exceptions, such as Metropolitan-Vickers which recruited and trained at its head office up to eighty college-educated men annually.

Meanwhile, the demand for the degrees of London University, awarded after study in the polytechnics and some of the technical colleges, was growing. In 1935/36, of 5353 candidates for degrees of all types at London University 2388 were external students (University Yearbook 1937). A report from the Secretary of the Newcastle upon Tyne branch of the Society of Chemical Industry painted an alarming picture of the attitude of employers to graduates. In electrical engineering, an important local industry, 85 per cent of the students were attached to a local works before entering college and only 20 per cent of these were holding posts in the company five years after graduating (Board of Education, 1935). The Department of Scientific and Industrial Research, in commenting on the report, expressed general agreement, which had also been expressed in their Annual Report for 1930–31 (DSIR, 1930–1931). The problem was to make industry understand that one factor in its troubles was its neglect of science, its failure to employ scientific workers and ensure that it had men of scientific outlook and training in high places.

Meanwhile, the Board of Education continued to take the traditional British market economy view of education, by giving great importance to the attitudes of employers. They noted that

The influence of some of the biggest employers is, however, rather in the

> direction of encouraging part-time attendance at a technical institute with the object of obtaining a degree which they accept as evidence of aptitude and diligence . . . (Board of Education, 1936)

not it will be observed, of technical competence! At about this time an enquiry by the Director of the Careers Advisory Service at Cambridge University as to whether the Nuffield Organisation or the Austin Motor Company would take some of the Universities' graduates received replies that they only recruited to the shop-floor (Hinton, 1976).

No further steps were taken before the outbreak of the Second World War three years later. At that time there were 5288 students in technological departments in the universities of Great Britain and the annual number of graduations had reached about 800 in England and Wales, more than half of which appear to have been at pass or ordinary level. The total number of engineers qualifying annually in England and Wales by degree, HNC or membership examination of a recognised professional institution, according to speciality, is shown in Table 4.1.

TABLE 4.1 Engineers qualifying in England and Wales annually according to speciality (1939)

	Civil	*Elect.*	*Mech.*	*Naval Arch.*	*Other*	*Total*
Universities	330	190	150	7	70	797
Other	13	600	680	3	130	1563
						2310

SOURCE

Interdepartmental Standing Committee on Further Education and Training, 1944; and Percy Committee, 1950.

The Scottish Office estimated an annual output of 250 qualified engineers a year.

In Germany the enrolment of matriculated students in the Technischen Hochschulen (THS) had reached 23,280 by 1927; 3500 were graduating a year, over a thousand of them in mechanical engineering (Society for the Promotion of Engineering Education, 1931). An extremely important development in Germany was the growth of the Ingenieurschulen (IS), now Fachhochschulen, in which a three-year full-time education combined with practical training was given to students who qualified for entry without the *Abitur* of a *Gymnasium*, many of whom had started as craft apprentices.

By 1930, in what is today the Federal Republic of Germany there were at least 460,000 engineers, of whom 100,000 had no formal education and the remainder were roughly in the proportion of one Diplomate from a THS to four graduates from an IS (Ludwig, 1974, p. 19). The nearest British comparison for numbers, not levels of education, were those enrolled at the end of the war on the Central Technical and Scientific Register of the Ministry of Labour and National Service. They were: civil engineers, 13,370; electrical, 36,170; and mechanical, 60,910. There were of course others, but the total of professional engineers qualified to the current standards can hardly have exceeded 120,000.

During the war the annual number of engineering graduates and HNC awards in Britain rose substantially, reaching approximately 3000 by 1943. By 1947/48 the number of graduates had risen to 2300 (Payne, 1960, p. 176) and by 1949 the number of HNC and HND awards to 4528 (Ministry of Education). On the other hand, under the National Socialist regime in pre-war Germany the number of matriculated students in the Technischen Hochschuler fell to 10,308 in 1938 and 5609 in 1941 and the numbers in the Ingenieurschulen from nearly 25,000 in 1928 to just over 14,000 in 1938 (Ludwig, 1974, pp. 276 and 278). On this basis the number of those obtaining diplomas at the end of the Second World War would have fallen to less than 1000 and, for the first time, the number of engineers being produced from university institutions in the UK would have been more than the number in Germany.

Meanwhile the sights of the professional institutions appear to have been rising, as demonstrated by their critical comments on the Government's White Paper on Educational Reconstruction published in July 1943 (Institution of Mechanical Engineers, 1943). The institutions were not the only source of pressure on the Board of Education. The Association of Teachers in Technical Colleges had long been active, and during 1943 a campaign was started to give Bradford Technical College the status of a university. In view of all these pressures the Board recommended to R. A. Butler, the President, who agreed, that a committee of enquiry would be useful and that Percy should be chairman.

At the first meeting of the committee, Sir Lawrence Bragg, Cavendish Professor of Experimental Physics Cambridge University expressed the view that the

> task of the university was to train the mind, while that of the technical high school was to train the student for a specific job.

There was

> a real need to provide a large army of scientific workers who could help the scientists produced by the universities. (Board of Education, 1944)

This view of the respective parts played by scientists and engineers in the generation of technological innovation was to bedevil British policy for the next twenty years. At the second meeting Dr Charles Snow and Professor Wardlaw, giving evidence for the Ministry of Labour and National Service, referred to a drift away from mechanical and electrical engineering (in other words from industry) and to the relatively higher qualification of civil engineers. The Institution of Mechanical Engineers said that before the war nearly all the mechanical engineering graduates had gone either to ICI or Metropolitan-Vickers. In the previous year, 750 Associate Members had been elected, of whom 235 had degrees and 266 HNCs.

The Institution of Production Engineers, originally dominated by machine-tool makers, said that the HNC man was preferred in industry and that the full-time technical courses were not popular. Universities did not produce the type of engineer likely to succeed in production work. Perhaps the best comment on this evidence was that of Dr Abbott, Staff Inspector for Engineering, who said that Dresden's Technische Hochschule produced six to eight machine-tool experts a year at the highest level and that there was no equivalent in this country. We had been unable to satisfy a request from the Viceroy to provide educational facilities in machine-tool design for Indian graduates with works experience. The industry believed that practical training in the workshop was essential to the training of men for high administrative positions and that the industry's practice was to encourage night school training; it would be an advantage if a limited number of men with university degrees were taken into the industry and trained with a view to filling the higher executive posts (Board of Education, PRO ED 46/268). Twenty-five years later, it was reported that 90 machine-tool firms employing 30,000 people had a total of only 25 graduates and that their proportion of qualified drawing office personnel was less than half that in Germany or Switzerland (Board of Trade, 1960).

In their report, the Percy Committee (1945) said that the war-time output of 3000 qualified engineers should be maintained for at least ten years; of these, the universities of England and Wales could produce 1200, leaving the technical colleges to produce the balance. They thought, however, that these figures might be an underestimate and recommended an energetic programme of expansion (Percy Committee, 1945). The committee was not, however, concerned only with numbers but also with quality. It reported a demand for men fitted for executive responsibility and capable not only of research but of applying the results of research for development – a demand which was not being met. It therefore recommended the selection of a strictly limited number of technical colleges in which there should be developed technological courses of a standard comparable with that of university degree courses. It also considered the question of recruitment. Secondary education tended to direct boys of first-rate ability away from industry; it therefore advocated scholarships for technology students and the adjustment of National Certificate courses to make the ONC a suitable qualification for university entry, so that those who entered industry straight from school could re-enter the educational system at a later age.

An important contribution to the discussion was an article written in 1950 by the Engineering Director of ICI, Sir Ewart Smith (Smith, 1950). He demonstrated a strong correlation between the increase in productivity in the UK and USA since 1880 and in the number of technical degrees obtained by men in the two countries. During the inter-war period the number of degrees in technology per 10,000 of the population had increased in the UK from 0.16 to 0.18 per annum, whereas in the USA first degrees in engineering alone grew from 0.7 to 1.05. By 1949 the number of higher degrees in engineering in the USA was nearly equal to the number of first degrees in all forms of technology in the UK.

Early in the 1950s, Winston Churchill, by that time Prime Minister, became alarmed at the scale of Russian technical education, and this no doubt inspired the Government in December 1954 to announce plans for a major expansion of Imperial College, of Manchester College of Technology (now the University of Manchester Institute of Technology) and of the Royal Technical College, Glasgow (now Strathclyde University) as well as the engineering departments of the Universities of Birmingham and Leeds. The Government found it necessary to break the previously assumed constitutional relationship, whereby the University Grants Committee acted independently as the agent for the distribution of Government finance for the universities. In this case the decisions were undoubtedly made by the Government and the UGC accepted them.

In February 1956, the Government at last produced a White Paper (Ministry of Education, 1956) which contained a carefully argued and detailed case for a complete change in the method of providing technical education at all levels. For the first time the Ministry of Education had brought within a single compass the role of all the institutions, from universities to schools, which contributed to technical education and announced Government plans that affected them. The paper pointed out that, although the number of university students in science and technology had doubled between 1939 and 1955, there were still insufficient by comparison with out competitors abroad or with the needs of our own industry and our responsibilities to under-developed countries in the Commonwealth and elsewhere. It quoted figures to show that the UK produced in 1954 57 graduates in engineering and applied sciences per million population compared with 70 in France, 86 in West Germany, 82 in Switzerland and 30 in Italy. The Soviet Union claimed to be producing nearly 300. Figures were not available for the second level of education for most countries, but 8100 HNCs were awarded annually in the UK while the Soviet Union produced 70,000 lower-grade engineers.

The paper spelt out the proposals for what were now to be called Colleges of Advanced Technology. It also recognised the need to increase the training of technicians and craftsmen and announced a substantial programme of investment in technical colleges. As a whole, the White Paper was as strong a statement of intention to intervene in the administration of education, and especially of technical and further education, as had come from any Government and its influence was to lead to radical changes in the next few years. The colleges which achieved the status of CATs seized their opportunities and became increasingly independent in the choice of subjects which they offered for study, most of them branching out into management or the social sciences. They were, therefore, prepared in 1963 when the Committee on Higher Education, under the chairmanship of Lord Robbins, enunciated a set of guiding principles which were to lead to an explosion in University numbers.

So, in less than ten years, what had been local authority technical colleges grew into fully fledged universities, many of them later to move to new buildings on new sites. There was a tendency to try to move too rapidly from the colleges' original purpose and method: the education of applied scientists and technologists by the sandwich system. The latter became increasingly difficult as the student numbers grew and industry became reluctant to increase the number it would accept for the periods of industrial training, although several of the colleges made great efforts to maintain the system after they became universities (Ministry of Education, 1956).

These changes did not, however, mean the end of advanced education in technical colleges. In 1965, strong Government support was announced for the development of the local authority colleges as the basis for a vocationally oriented, non-university degree-giving sector. In 1966, a White Paper was published which proposed the formation of a limited number of 'polytechnics' which might combine existing colleges in different fields and provide education both at degree and sub-degree level in both full-time and part-time courses.

RECENT TRENDS

It will already have become apparent that systematic and detailed comparisons amongst countries in the output and employment of engineers are difficult, given institutional and quality differences amongst countries, and the difficulties of data collection. Such a comparison by the OECD was published in 1970, based on data for the early to mid-1960s and its findings relevant to this subject are summarised in Table 4.2 (OECD, 1970). The difficulties of interpretation are clearly apparent from the figures: the much greater range of quality covered by the definition 'graduate' in the USA than in Western Europe; the qualifications provided for engineers outside university-level education; inadequate systematic coverage for all countries.

In spite of these limitations, the data show some clear differences between the UK, on the one hand, and the USA and other countries in Western Europe, on the other. The British lack of commitment to graduate education for engineers (and for managers) was still apparent in the early 1960s in patterns of employment. The UK appeared not noticeably different from other countries in the total number of graduates in the labour force (line 1) or in the total number of university-trained scientists and engineers, taken together (line 2). The differences do, however, become striking when one concentrates more specifically on engineers and managers. The percentage of qualified engineers (university and non-university) in the labour force in the UK was well below that in F R Germany and the Netherlands, and was not much above the percentages of university-trained engineers alone in Belgium, France and Sweden (line 3). Moreover, the percentage of all graduates in engineering and management jobs was lower in the UK than in other countries for which data were available (lines 4 and 5). Figures for Germany were not available but were certainly much higher (see Chapter 10). As a consequence, the percentage of all engineering and management jobs held by graduates was also lower than in other countries (lines 6 and 7); the difference was particularly striking in engineering jobs, even when those qualified outside the university route are included.

At the same time, the effort made in the UK after the Second World War to increase the number of qualified engineers is also apparent: as a proportion of the age group from 20 to 24, the number of engineers qualifying in the UK through universities and elsewhere compared favourably with other countries (line 8). Since then, the strong emphasis given to engineering education in the UK has continued. As Table 4.3 shows, by the mid-1970s the number of engineers qualifying annually compared favourably overall with France, West Germany and the USA. From 1963/64 to 1975/76, there was nearly a doubling of first degrees in technology from British universities, a 60 per cent

TABLE 4.2 Output and employment of qualified engineers in the early 1960s in selected countries

	UK	*Belgium*	*FRG*	*France*	*Italy*	*Neth.*	*Sweden*	*USA*
1. University graduates as % of the labour force	2.8	2.3	3.1	2.7	2.2	1.4	2.1	7.6
2. Qualified scientists and engineers as % of the labour force	1.04	n.a.	1.45	n.a.	n.a.	1.4	n.a.	n.a.
Science and engineering graduates as % of the labour force	0.7	0.6	0.65	0.7	0.65	0.4	0.7	1.8
3. Qualified engineers as % of the labour force	0.58	n.a.	1.23	n.a.	n.a.	1.29	n.a.	n.a.
Graduates only	n.a.	0.43	0.40	0.55	0.28	0.28	0.59	1.05

4. % of all graduates in engineering jobs	7.0	n.a.	9.1	17.4	n.a.	10.9	n.a.	8.2
5. % of all graduates in management jobs	6.3	n.a.	n.a.	14.3	n.a.	14.8	13.2	12.8
6. % of engineering jobs held by								
(*a*) Qualified engineers	29.3	n.a.	n.a.	n.a.	n.a.	81.1	n.a.	n.a.
(*b*) Graduates	17.7	n.a.	n.a.	54.3	n.a.	62.8	n.a.	54.5
7. Graduates in technology as % of 20–24 age group	0.79	0.57	0.46	1.24	0.33	0.38	0.80	1.48

NOTES

The figures for qualified scientists and engineers include those for graduates. The UK figure for graduates is for 75% of persons who completed their education aged 20 or more. Non-university qualifications include those of the professional institutions and HNC in the UK and those of the Ingenieurschulen and similar institutions in other countries. Engineers jobs (line 4) are defined as ISCO Occupation Group 00 (engineers, architects and surveyors). Managers (line 5) defined as ISCO Occupation Group 1 (Administrative, executive and managerial workers).

SOURCE

OECD (1970).

TABLE 4.3 Number of engineers qualifying annually

	University or equivalent	*Non-university*
USA (1976)[a]	37,970[1]	25,089[2]
France (1975)[b]	11,205[3]	12,778[4]
West Germany (1976)[c]	3,960[5]	11,830[6]
GB (1976)[d]	11,025[7]	6,594[8]
Japan (1973)[e]	62,961	8.235[9]

NOTE

[1] First degrees in Engineering: [2] Two-year degrees in Engineering and Industrial Technology: [3] Diplomates of Grandes Ecoles: [4]Diplomats of Instituts Universitaires (1973): [5]Diplomates of THS excluding architects: [6] Graduates of IS (1970) (15,700 in 1973): [7] University and Polytechnic First Degrees: [8] HNC and HND (of which 1,803 full-time HND): [9] Short University course

SOURCES

[a] Engineers Joint Council, New York.
[b] Engineers training in France: Service Scientifique Ambassade de France à Londres; Service des Etudes Informatiques et Statistiques, Secretariat de l'Etat aux Universitaires.
[c] Statistisches Bundesamt, Bundesrepublik Deutschland.
[d] DES Statistics. University and Polytechnic include some London external degrees obtained by part-time education.
[e] Japanese Ministry of Education: Report on Education (1974)

increase from French Grandes Ecoles, and a slight fall in German THS Diplomates. On the other hand, there had been a dramatic fall in the output from British non-university courses, owing to the changes in qualifying requirements of the professional institutions, a fall after substantial growth in German Ingenieurschulen graduates, and a trebling at the sub-university level in France, mainly from the Instituts Universitaires founded in 1965 (Table 4.3).

This increase in the education of qualified engineers in Britain has had at least two positive and measurable effects. First it led to the increase in the employment of qualified engineers in British manufacturing industry from 64,100 in 1966 to 88,400 in 1971 (Department of Industry, 1977). Second, Table 4.4 shows that it has resulted in an increase in the level of qualifications of the supply of engineers. Nevertheless, from the vantage point of the late 1970s, it is clear that a number of problems remain.

TABLE 4.4 Annual supply of engineers and technologists (1000s)

	Total	*University and CNAA First Degrees*	*Percentage*
1961	9072	4431	49
1971	14562	10235	70
1975	11426	10373	90

SOURCE

Department of Industry (1977).

The first is the educational content and balance between university and non-university engineers. Table 4.3 shows that the numbers of non-university trained engineers in the UK now compare unfavourably with those of most other countries. It is difficult to compare the value of the different sub-university courses; but there can be little doubt that the full-time courses are more valuable than the part-time, even with day release.

Second, the numerical output from the educational system is not by itself a measure of the employment of qualified engineers in industry. One important factor in the 1970s is the number of foreign students graduating, most of whom return to their own countries. The proportion of foreign students admitted to first-degree courses in engineering and technology in the UK has been rising rapidly: 1974 – 19 per cent, 1975 – 23 per cent, 1976 – 29 per cent, although the proportion graduating has only reached 13 per cent. This compares with about 9 per cent of foreign THS diplomates and 6 per cent of IS graduates in Germany in 1976. Their number on British postgraduate courses is probably over 50 per cent (British Association, 1977; Statistisches Bundesamt, 1977). Furthermore, out of the approximately 11,000 engineering students graduating in the year 1976, only some 6100 entered employment in the UK, approximately 5000 of them in industry (Central Services Unit for University Careers and Appointment Services).

Third, there is a clear relationship between the demand by employers for engineers and the numbers who will choose to enter the profession; a decline in recruitment will reflect itself in the applications for admission to university engineering courses. This is what happened from 1972 to 1975 when the numbers of applications from home students fell from about 15,000 to 12,700 and of admissions from 9400 to 8000. Since then there has been a substantial increase, with admissions in 1976 rising to nearly 9000 and applications to nearly 16,000 in 1977, although the proportion of foreign students remains high (EITB and UCCA *Annual Reports*). Unfilled places will lead, in some universities, to lower standards of entry. Evidence given to the Select Committee on Science and Technology showed that, in the years 1973–75, 42 per cent of applicants accepted for engineering and technology courses at universities had worse than the equivalent of 3 Cs at A Level in their school certificates, which was considerably worse than those in other faculties.

Fourth, there is the possibility of a serious imbalance amongst the various sectors of manufacturing industry in the recruitment of qualified engineers. Chapter 3 has already described the relatively low rate of recruitment of qualified engineers in the mechanical engineering sector in the 1960s, and the rapid relative decline in the 1970s, in spite of the evident deficiencies of innovative performance in this sector. Figures published by the Engineering Employers Federation of the numbers of qualified personnel actually employed in different countries (Table 4.5) may not be strictly comparable and they are not confined to engineers only, but they show a substantial difference between the UK and other countries.

TABLE 4.5 Percentage of total workforce in the metal manufacturing industries represented by qualified engineers and scientists in 1974

Sweden	6.6
West Germany	5.7
France	5.3
UK	1.8

SOURCE

Engineering Employers Federation (1977).

'OBS, SALARIES AND STATUS

If salaries are a measure of the value employers put on graduate engineers there is ample evidence that it is lower in the UK than in other countries. In mid-career their salary differentials compared with industrial workers, as shown in Table 4.6, are still smaller than in other European countries,

TABLE 4.6 Ratio of gross pay of professional engineers to blue collar workers 1967

UK	*Sweden*	*France*	*West Germany*
2.46	4.02	5.03	2.75

SOURCE

Fores (1971)

although not much more so than in Germany. As we shall see in Chapter 5, the low status of the British engineer is confirmed by the relatively small number of top managerial jobs held by comparison with those in other countries.

There is also some evidence that British engineers have been paid relatively less than their colleagues in public administration or exercising other functions in industry when compared with other countries (Fores, 1973). International comparisons must be seen in relation to the generally lower professional and managerial salaries in the UK, and there are signs that, with the growth of university education for engineers in the UK, their salaries are rising.

Low status is accorded to engineers by British society. Compared with the elites from the French Grandes Ecoles, moving easily between top posts in public administration and industry, or the diplomates from the Swedish Technical High Schools, British engineers come low in the pecking order. A recent enquiry (Palmer *et al.*, 1977) by questionnaire of sixth-formers taking A level mathematics in fifty secondary schools produced a not unrealistic assessment of the position of the British engineer. To questions as to which of twenty-two occupations was (1) highest paid, (2) had the highest prestige and (3) required the highest intelligence, they put the civil engineer in positions 12, 12 and 11 but the mechanical engineer 17, 18 and 14. In an earlier study, which recorded the opinions of senior school children in Britain, France and Germany, the engineer did not appear in the first six occupations chosen by British children for pay, prestige or intelligence, while in France he was chosen in each list and in Germany for pay and intelligence (Hutchings, 1963a). An American survey in 1977 put engineers fifth, in judging that they had very great or considerable prestige. Only scientists, doctors, ministers and lawyers came ahead of them (Louis Harris and Associates, 1977).

CONCLUSIONS

It has been the historical lack of demand by the engineering and allied industries that has been the main cause of the low level of status, pay and, in particular, education of British engineers. At the same time, engineering has been taught not so much as a vocational subject but as an academic one. Courses have been short and the completion of professional training has been left to industrial employers.

The professional engineering institutions were slow to accept the necessity for full-time education and they have insisted that the practical training of the engineer was their responsibility, although they in fact had no means of ensuring that it was available and properly carried out. The growth of full-time engineering education has reduced the importance of institutional membership to the progressive employer, who is becoming more concerned with the quality of an applicant's degree or diploma and with his own assessment of the experience the applicant has had.

The engineer will have the status of his perceived importance to industry and society will accept the judgement of those who employ him. If British industry does not recognise the danger of failure to maintain a technically competitive world stance, then it will not employ and adequately reward the best-qualified men and women the educational system can provide. Salaries are not the whole problem. If there is to be a steady flow of new entrants to engineering education, there must be a regular rate of industrial recruitment whatever the short-term economic prospects.

The criticism frequently heard of the quality of university graduates probably owes less to their intrinsic merits or demerits than to other factors. The long experience of recruiting through shop-floor apprenticeship, topped up with part-time technical education, has not prepared many employers for the management of young engineers who, however inexperienced, have acquired a lot of knowledge and expect to be treated as professionals (Jahoda, 1963). In addition, international comparisons suggest that we could do with fewer honours graduates taking broader and longer courses and many more practically trained engineers, albeit with full-time education. There are signs that in the United States, to whose system of engineering education the British is now closest, there are similar doubts, with suggestions of a Master's degree for the top professionals and a more practical degree for the majority (American Society for Engineering Education, 1977).

The changes that are required are substantial and involve the universities and polytechnics, industry and the institutions. The institutions should give up their claim to responsibility for qualification and their attempts to monitor the practical training of the individual engineer. No degree would be awarded until the required practical training had been satisfactorily completed. It would then follow that the responsibility for monitoring an individual's training would become that of the students' teachers and industry should accept their right to do so, whether the student is undergoing pre-academic training, sandwich training or postgraduate training (British Association, 1977).

Industry should accept the responsibility, at present accepted by a minority of firms, for the practical side of an engineer's training and should co-operate, possibly through the Engineering Industry Training Board, with the institutions and the educational establishments in determining the nature and content of academic courses and of practical training. Day release for all apprentices and learners should be a statutory requirement, ensuring that all likely to qualify for higher education through the ONC route get the best opportunity to do so.

This essay has mainly dealt with the education of what are generally called professional engineers; but there is considerable evidence that a great part of our industrial labour force, in spite of the Industrial Training Act of 1963, is still worse educated and trained than that of our main competitors. Only well-trained technicians, craftsmen and operatives can get the best out of sophisticated equipment. A competitive technically advanced industry is only as strong as the pyramid of skills which support it.

NOTES

1. In preparing this chapter I was greatly helped by the librarians or archivists of a number of organisations, particularly Mr R. T. Everett, lately Chief Librarian of the Institution of Mechanical Engineers. I am also grateful to the Federation des Associations et Sociétés Françaises d'Ingenieurs Diplômés, the Comité d'Etudes sur les Formations d'Ingenieurs, the Statistischesamt of the F R Germany, Ing. I. Hillmer of the Verein Deutscher Ingenieure, Dr Geer of Gesamtmetall, and the Engineering Manpower Commission of the United States Engineering Joint Council.

REFERENCES

American Society for Engineering Education, 'BE or BE Technology', *Engineering Education* (May 1977).

W. E. Ayrton and John Percy, 'The Technical Education of an Electrical Engineer', *Journal of the Institution of Electrical Engineers,* XI (1882).

J. Blanchet, 'Technical Education in the late 19th Century' (unpublished thesis, Oxford University, 1952).

Board of Education, Papers, PRO ED 24/1875 (5 October 1927).

Board of Education, Papers, PRO ED 46/120 (1935).
Board of Education, Papers, PRO ED 46/291 8829 (1936).
Board of Education, Papers of the Committee on Higher Technological Education, PRO ED 46/295 (1944).
Board of Trade, *The Machine Tool Industry* (London: HMSO, 1960).
British Association, *Education, Engineers and Manufacturing Industry, a Report to the British Association Co-ordinating Group* (1977).
Central Services Unit for University Careers and Appointment Services (Manchester), *University Graduates 1976: Some Details of First Destination and Employment* and *Polytechnic First Degree and HND Students 1976: Some Details of First Distinction and Employment of Students Awarded First Degrees and Higher National Diplomas* (Manchester: CSU, UCAS, 1976).
Committee on Education for the Engineering Industry, *Education for the Engineering Industry* (London: HMSO, 1931).
Committee on Further Education and Training, Second Report (December 1944) in Percy Committee (1944).
Committee on Trade and Industry, *Factors in Industrial and Commercial Efficiency*, Report (London: HMSO, 1927).
Department of Industry, *Changes in the Population of Persons with Qualifications in Engineering Technology and Science 1959–1976*, Studies in Technological Manpower, No. 6 (London: HMSO, 1977).
Department of Scientific and Industrial Research, *Annual Report 1930–1931* (London: HMSO, 1931).
Engineering Employers Federation, *Graduates in Engineering* (London: EEF, 1977).
Engineering Industry Training Board and UCCA Reports.
Engineering Training Organisation, *Schemes and Facilities for Engineering Training and First Report of the Executive, 1920*, bound papers in Institution of Mechanical Engineers Library (1920).
F. Foden, *Philip Magnus, Victorian Educational Pioneer* (London; Valentine Mitchell, 1970).
M. Fores, 'The Professional Engineer in Western Europe', *The Professional Engineer* (Nov. 1971).
M. Fores, 'Engineering and the British Economic Problem', *The Professional Engineer* (July 1973).
Louis Harris and Associates, *Survey, October 8th–16th 1977*, reported in *Public Opinion*, Washington D.C. (March/April 1978).
Lord Hinton, Information supplied to the author (1976).
D. W. Hutchings, *Technology and the Sixth Form Boy*, Oxford University Department of Education (1963a), quoted in 'The Engineer in Western Europe', M. Fores and N. Bongers, unpublished memorandum.
Institution of Civil Engineers, *Report of the Committee on Examinations* (London: ICE, 1897).
Institution of Civil Engineers, *Report of the Committee Appointed on 24th November 1903 to consider and report to the Council upon the subject of the Best Methods of Education and Training for all Classes of Engineers* (London: ICE, 1906).

Institution of Mechanical Engineers, Minutes of Institution of Mechanical Engineers (1918–20).
Institution of Mechanical Engineers, *Proceedings*, vol. 64 (Apr. 1903).
Institution of Mechanical Engineers, 'The White Paper on "Educational Reconstruction" and its Impact on Training for Mechanical Engineering', *Proceedings of the Institution of Mechanical Engineers,* vol. 149 (London: IME, 1943).
Marie Jahoda, *The Education of Technologists* (London: Tavistock Publications, 1963).
K.-D. Ludwig, *Technik und Ingenieure im Dritten Reich* (Dusseldorf: Droste, 1974).
Ministry of Education Statistics.
Ministry of Education, *Technical Education*, Cmd 9703 (London: HMSO, Feb. 1956).
P. W. Musgrove, *Technical Change, the Labour Force and Education: a Study of the British and German Iron and Steel Industries 1860–1964* (Oxford: Pergamon, 1967).
OECD, *Gaps in Technology*, Comparison in Member Countries in Education, R&D, Technological Innovation and International Economic Exchanges, Table 1 (Paris: OECD, 1970).
P. J. Palmer, V. F. Bignell and J. C. Levy, *The Education of Graduate Mechanical Engineers, A Survey of Viewpoints* (London: The City University, 1976).
G. L. Payne, *Britain's Scientific and Technical Manpower* (London: Cambridge University, 1960).
Percy Committee, *Higher Technological Education: Report of a Special Committee Appointed in April 1944* (London: HMSO, 1945).
G. W. Roderick and M. D. Stephens, *Scientific and Technical Education in 19th Century England* (Newton Abbot: David & Charles, 1972).
Michael Sanderson, *The Universities and British Industry 1850–1970* (London: Routledge, 1972).
Sir Ewart Smith, 'The Critical Importance of Higher Technological Education in Relation to Productivity', *The Advancement of Science*, VII: 27 (Dec. 1950).
Society for the Promotion of Engineering Education, *Report of the Investigation of Engineering Education 1923–1929* (Pittsburgh, Pennsylvania: 1931).
Statistisches Bundesamt, *Prufungen and Hochschulen 1973 bis 1976 Bildung und Kultur* (Wiesbaden: Statistisches Bundesamt, 1977).
University Yearbook (1937).
R. M. Walmsley, *Transatlantic Engineering Schools and Engineering, Proceedings of the Institution of Electrical Engineers,* XXXIII (London: IEE, 1904).

5 British Management Compared

Nuala Swords–Isherwood

This chapter argues that the educational background of the average British manager is inferior to that of his equivalent in other major industrial countries, and that there is ground for believing that British managers may be less likely to be educationally and professionally competent. Throughout, we shall be talking about averages: clearly there are many managers and management teams of very high quality in Britain.

INTERNATIONAL COMPARISONS OF MANAGERS

Many of the data on managers are less than adequate because of age, the lack of inter-industry comparisons, the lack of standardisation of methodology and the lack of attempt to take account of the varied character of management tasks and managers. The largest survey undertaken to establish British managers' social and educational background was that undertaken in 1956 for the Acton Society Trust. This was based on information collected from more than 10,000 individuals in 51 large enterprises. About one-fifth of the main sample (3327 people) were graduates (Acton Society Trust, 1956). An increase in the number of formal and professional qualifications was noted, though these qualifications, then as now, were often obtained by part-time study; the preponderance of part-time study is one of the most significant and enduring contrasts with managers in other countries.

Nearly one-fifth of the sample had been to fee-paying schools; it was suggested that, as opportunities in other fields such as the foreign service or the church were reduced, less prestigious industrial careers would become more attractive to the privately educated, and so this high representation would continue. Various factors were found to be closely associated with advancement. In descending order of importance, they were possession of an arts degree from Oxford or Cambridge, attendance at a major fee-paying school, possession of non-technical qualifications (the classic example being accountancy), to have had a first job as a management trainee, to have an arts degree from a non-Oxbridge university (polytechnic degrees had not started then), to have a higher degree, a science degree, to have attended a lesser fee-paying school, a grammar school, to have a technical qualification, and to have had a first job in a technical or senior clerical area.

These are the only available data based on a national sample. The picture presented by other studies discussed here is remarkably similar, and recent evidence suggests that a mix of élite, academically specialised, non-technical education, and the right social background remain the sure road to success in British management.

The importance attached to the ideal type 'academic generalist', or the relative lack of importance given to technical qualifications, is peculiar to the British and US approach to management. Although in both countries large numbers of engineering and science graduates enter industry and achieve eminent positions, there is still a strong presumption that scientific or technical training is in some way narrow and does not fit a person to take general and far-sighted decisions. It is less difficult, apparently, for the non-technically educated person to take sensible decisions in a technically sophisticated industry without technical knowledge.

In Britain and the USA the liberal arts graduate is a favoured potential business leader. Technical expertise or excellence in engineering are not rated nearly as highly as elsewhere. 'Actually the complexities of business are such that someone who understands history, literature and philosophy, who is in a position to do some disciplined thinking, has the type of mind that will ultimately succeed [in business].' (Cables 1955)

Though educational levels are higher among managers and the study of business management more widespread than in Britain, the USA is the country most similar to Britain in the disciplines studied and the overall approach to the management task. It is the closest model but perhaps not the one we should choose to follow. There is evidence that business studies for those without industrial experience is less likely to be of value than a higher level of technical expertise.

The majority of German managers have a post-school education and the level of education and size of firm tend to be related. In the large organisations, between 75 and 90 per cent of top management will be graduates. Formal qualifications are still gaining in importance, and the more prestigious the qualification the better the chances of promotion. About 36 per cent of German managers are university engineering graduates, with law and business economics as the next most important subjects. At the moment, the importance and balance of subjects is altering. Some suggest that engineering, although still the primary route into management, is declining in importance, that engineers are under-represented in the top echelons in proportion to their total numbers, and that business economics is gaining in importance. These changes are, however, hotly disputed. Law, though still important and related to social class, is fading in prestige.

Owner-managers tend to be less well qualified. 'It appears as if formal qualifications are a career prerequisite for managers in employee positions while they are considered a dispensable luxury for owner-managers' (May 1974). It must be remembered that this means less well qualified *vis-à-vis* other German managers, and not the average British manager. German managers favour recruitment and promotion from within the enterprise, and tend to stay within a particular industrial sector. They show little interest in further training, particularly in subjects related to management. This attitude is changing, however, and must be seen in the context of the entirely different system in Germany.

In engineering, the stronghold in Britain of the part-time qualification, the contrast with the German situation is most marked. A study by Hutton, Lawrence and Smith, in 1971, of 1006 qualified German engineers found that 508 held a Dipl. Ing. qualification and 498 an Ing. grad. qualification, all obtained by means of full-time study. The sample was, of course, of engineers and not managers and of the qualified rather than those without qualification. Systems of part-time education in Germany are at once better and more systematically organised and less relied on to produce management talent. In France, the system of education which prepares future managers is at its most elitist and therefore part-time education is of little importance.

Research carried out in 1977 by P. A. Lawrence in a wide range of manufacturing companies confirmed the importance of the engineer in German management and the preference for graduates in subjects of immediate relevance to industry, i.e. engineering, law and business economics. It was found that qualified engineers

> are not exclusively concentrated in R&D, design, production, work planning, testing and technical staff bureaux. . . . engineers are also to be found in administrative jobs in education and training divisions, in personnel, costing, sales, occasionally in finance where they have additional non-technical qualifications, and also in central planning departments concerned with re-organisation. (Lawrence, 1977)

In Germany, there seems to be no feeling that engineering is a narrow specialist field of study, making it necessary to recruit more widely educated 'liberal thinkers'. A question in the Lawrence study on the determinants of career success in management invariably brought answers in terms of relevant training, qualifications and experience. Social background and personality factors were not often mentioned as of importance, a very different reaction from that common in Britain.

In a study conducted in 1958 in which the sample was made up of 646 managers in 28 small, medium and large private manufacturing firms in the Manchester area, Clements found that more than a third of the sample had left school at or before age 15 and had no formal qualifications whatever, 25 per cent of the sample had degrees, of which 10 per cent were in engineering and science, 26 per cent had attended fee-paying schools, 33 per cent had attended grammar school. Clements concluded that the advantages of a middle-class background were considerable, that industry had failed to provide an efficient ladder from the shop floor to management and that the educational system had been less successful than could be hoped in ensuring capable management (Clements, 1958).

Clements noted that trends in management recruitment were changing, a conclusion further investigated by Clark (1966). The sample, again in the Manchester area, was of 36 firms, public and privately owned, each with more than 600 employees. The responses of 818 managers were considered. Clark concluded that the greatest change among managers had been in their education. Over half the managers in the sample had attended grammar schools, twice as many as in the two previous studies. About one manager in three in the sample was a university graduate and the proportion of young managers with degrees was even higher. This also was greater than in previous studies.

Year of Sample Survey	*1956*	*1958*	*1966*
	Acton	*Clements*	*Clark*
% of graduate managers in the three main studies	19	25	35

The type of graduate had also changed. Over 80 per cent of the graduates in the 1966 sample had a degree in science or technology and less than 25 per cent were from Oxford or Cambridge, though it was still true that Oxbridge arts graduates attained the highest ranks. However, around a third of Clark's sample still had only elementary or non-grammar school secondary education. Many of these had gained some qualifications by evening classes, so the typically British pattern remained. Clark felt that this type of manager was giving way to the grammar school and university engineer, and that the trend would continue. Clark also suggested that changes in the British educational system and the increasing use of education as a channel to management success will, given the imperfections of the system, probably lead to a decline in the number of working-class managers, and an increase in the numbers from the middle class. This would occur because the educational system tends to favour its middle-class members and an increased supply of educated middle-class candidates would block the promotion channels from the shop-floor.

The British Institute of Management carried out a survey of 10,000 of their members in 1976. The response rate was 45 per cent. The report concluded that great changes had occurred in British managers' educational qualifications and social background. The evidence of the survey did not justify this conclusion. The sample of members of the BIM was not necessarily typical of managers in general. Even in their sample, less than one quarter had attended university full-time and part-time education was still very important. In terms of social background, the lack of change is shown by the high proportion who had attended fee-paying schools (23 per cent). Half had attended grammar schools and the rest had attended secondary modern and technical schools. This picture gives little reason for complancency. (Melrose-Woodman)

The social class of British managers, like their educational experience, makes them different from their colleagues in other countries. Granick discusses the anomaly that British management is easier to enter than management in most other countries, and points out that British industry has many managers who left school early and took up apprenticeships. In Britain, he says, unlike other countries

> the man without higher education or family connections is still not weeded out at the start of the managerial career race. Clearly this peculiarity of British industry is not due to the openness of British society as a whole. Rather, it is a reflection of the low social and economic status of industrial managerial careers in Britain. (Granick, 1971)

The typical German manager is middle-class or from an even more privileged background, and is Protestant even though the Catholic population is large. Those who reach the most important positions tend to be from the highest social background, and the importance of this background is greater in large firms. It must be remembered, however, that the social elite tend to take engineering degrees and enter industrial careers as a first choice of occupation, a startling contrast with the situation in Britain. Although it is possible in Germany to rise from the shop-floor, it is unlikely, and as in other countries, the expansion of educational opportunities is closing this route. The biggest recruitment pool is the lower middle class, who are well represented, although not so much in the top ranks.

The French top executive is upper middle-class, and is probably the most highly educated in the world. His career is highly regarded in society generally. Top executives form an élite group who have been educated for the most part in the Grandes Ecoles, the most prestigious educational institutions in the country, although outside the university system. These schools attract the best candidates available, who undergo a rigorously selective education.

A study by Granick showed that between two-thirds and three-quarters of top French executives in the companies surveyed had an education available to only a tiny percentage of their age group, an education which is both academically and socially exclusive. In the USA also: 'The men who hold the top positions in American business today are in most cases from the higher level of American society.' Between 16 and 32 per cent of top American executives who had attended college had been to Harvard, Princeton or Yale and between 30 and 53 per cent had attended one of only nine prestigious colleges (Granick, 1971). They tend as in Britain to have studied liberal arts subjects.

Many studies have confirmed the low position of management as a possible career choice for British graduates compared to journalism, academic life or the civil service. Kelsall, Poole and Kuhn comment that:

> . . . there was no question that in terms of preferences the professions, and perhaps most serious of all, management, appealed particularly to the academically less well-qualified man. . . . Key posts in the industrial sector are for one reason or another distinctly unattractive to those who have shown themselves most able to absorb an intellectual heritage. (Kelsall, Poole and Kuhn, 1972)

Table 5.1 summarises the major differences in the background and education of managers in various countries. As we have already said, Britain and the USA have much in common and differ considerably from the Continental model. The USA, however, has a much higher proportion of its population with a college education and a higher proportion of such college-educated personnel in management.

The major and significant difference between British managers and their rivals in most other countries are in their professionalism, in the number of engineers amongst them, and in their social class. The educational system in Britain is such that the most favoured subjects of study are not those most directly relevant to industry. It has been geared to non-industrial pursuits, and the pinnacle of achievement has been as far removed as possible from produc-

TABLE 5.1 Major differences in the background and education of managers in five countries

	Great Britain	*USA*	*Germany*	*France*	*USSR*
Social class background of managers	Mixed/low	Mixed/high	High/mixed	High	High
% of graduates in management	Low	High	High	High	High
% of graduates in population	Low	High	Low	Low	Medium
Main subjects of study (undergraduate)	Liberal arts Science Engineering	Liberal arts Engineering Science	Engineering Business Economics Law	Engineering	Engineering
Main subjects of study (postgraduate)	Management Engineering	Management Engineering	Engineering	Engineering	Engineering
Full-time versus part-time education	P-T high F-T low	P-T low F-T high	P-T low F-T high	P-T low F-T high	P-T low F-T high
Likelihood of having been promoted from the shop-floor	High	Medium	Low	Low	Low

SOURCE

All Chapter 5 references excluding Department of Employment Gazette (1976, 1977), and Mant (1977, 1978).

tion. Signs can still be seen in the unpopularity of industrial careers, with consequences for the quality of industrial entrants, for their competence and for their status. The vicious circle once established is difficult to change, although there is some suggestion that such changes are occurring.

The British manager is also different in other, less tangible, but perhaps not less significant, ways. Some writers suggest that British managers tend to over-emphasise the significance of personality in successful management, and of human relations-type approaches to management, with consequent under-estimation of the importance of the product (e.g. Lawrence, 1977; Mant, 1977 and 1978; Swords-Isherwood, 1977). Expertise is defined in terms of personal characteristics rather than technical competence, and the management function becomes one of leading or managing people and seeking promotion, rather than producing a product. Clearly this emphasis relates to the education managers have typically received, but seems to be so pervasive that it could well withstand educational changes and even undermine their effectiveness. The split between engineering and management (and perhaps even the idea of 'management' itself) is at the centre of the British sickness.

POSSIBILITIES OF CHANGE

There is fairly general agreement on what are the major problems of British management. There is less agreement on whether they are being solved, and if they are, how fast. One recent study 'into the involvement of line and staff managers in Britain in the conduct of workplace industrial relations' (Marsh, Gillies and Rush, 1976) has provided some interesting data on this point.

The managers studied came from the engineering, chemical, and print and publishing industries. The sample of 348 was further broken down by category of manager, and covered all age groups and all parts of the United Kingdom. Tables 5.2 and 5.3 give some of the results. Engineering and chemicals show a great majority of managers from state schools, printing and publishing (excluding production and maintenance functions) show a greater tendency to favour fee-paying schools.

> The most evident difference between the industries, however, is the outstandingly strong base of engineering on the technical college and the paucity of its university recruitment, the higher proportion of non 'extra-mural' background higher education managers in chemicals and their bias towards the universities, and the relatively low proportion of printing and publishing managers who fall within these same higher education limits. (Marsh, Gillies and Rush, 1976)

TABLE 5.2 Educational background of managers in the engineering, printing and publishing, and chemical industries (actual numbers, percentages in brackets)*

	Secondary School		*Public School*		*Technical College etc.*		*University*		*Extra mural*		*Total*
Research and Development	23	(82)	6	(21)	9	(32)	18	(64)	6	(21)	28
Professional engineers etc.	29	(80)	7	(20)	19	(52)	8	(22)	9	(25)	36
Technician	40	(89)	4	(9)	30	(67)	11	(24)	12	(27)	45
Administrative	38	(83)	8	(17)	12	(26)	6	(13)	21	(46)	46
Finance	32	(89)	4	(11)	9	(25)	4	(11)	11	(31)	36
Marketing	10	(59)	7	(41)	2	(12)	6	(35)	3	(18)	17
Sales	18	(82)	4	(18)	6	(27)	4	(18)	5	(23)	22
Production	76	(92)	6	(7)	20	(24)	24	(29)	22	(27)	83
Maintenance	34	(97)	1	(3)	26	(74)	6	(17)	12	(34)	35
All Categories	300	(87)	47	(13)	133	(38)	87	(25)	101	(29)	348

NOTE

* Percentages do not add up to 100 horizontally, since the categories are not mutually exclusive.

TABLE 5.3 Industry differences in education of management

	Engineering	*Printing and Publishing*	*Chemical Industry*
% graduates	13	14	50
% with fee-paying school education	6	20	15

SOURCE

Data from Marsh, Gillies and Rush (unpublished, 1976). Figures presented may be subject to some rounding errors.

The printing and publishing industry seems to be aberrant in the prior education of its managers and it is suggested by Marsh, Gillies and Rush that this might be a reflection of their social origins. Of the printing and publishing managers in the sample studied, 55 per cent came from families classified on the Census of Population's social class breakdown as 'professional' or 'intermediate'. The proportion of engineering managers with this background was 37 per cent and of chemists 39 per cent. The overwhelming majority of managers in all these industries were skilled working-class in origin and this together with their lack of formal full-time education confirms earlier findings and still sets them apart. The chemical industry might illustrate one possible future, in which the social class background of entrants has not changed significantly but the educational attainment has, 50 per cent being graduates. Significantly, these managers were also the youngest group in the study.

Within each industry there were differences in the social class origins of the various categories of managers, but with maintenance and production having the highest proportion of those who have risen from the shop-floor.

> It is evident . . . that the tradition that the skilled artisan becomes the manager in industry dies hard, even in so technological a situation as chemicals, or so 'polite' a productive industry as printing and publishing. In engineering it also provides an important supply, if not the most important supply, of research and development and professional engineering type management. (Marsh, Gillies and Rush, 1976)

CONCLUSIONS

The channels for recruiting managers in other countries have advantages and disadvantages. In France, managers are a highly educated group with a technical background, but the elitist basis of the recruitment pattern might ignore potentially talented groups from non-favoured social backgrounds who do not now enjoy an elite education. In Germany, too, industrial managers have a very high status and are members of an elite educational group. Any such problems are, however, negligible compared with those in Britain, where management as a career remains unattractive to the most educated group, and where many doubts are still expressed about the relevance of the educational provision for management roles. It is difficult to disentangle cause and effect where demand is low, and criticisms about the quality of supply are many.

The problem in Britain lies mainly in the anachronistic conflict between educational and industrial aims, and in a culture that is anti-industrial. Our system probably provides more channels than many other countries for able candidates from the shop-floor to reach management levels. It does not, however, ensure a supply of the most able people from the best or most prestigious educational institutions for management roles. The problem is compounded since our educational elite tend not to study subjects relevant to management. Such attempts as have been made to develop high-grade alternative technical institutions have failed because prevailing ideas on excellence require a non-technical bias, and attracting excellent students to such institutions has proved difficult.

The ideal might be to have a highly educated management group recruited from the widest possible base in society; no country achieves this. If there is to be an elite, it is clear that it must be relevantly educated and trained, and that social background is an insufficient qualification for excellent management performance. In Britain, management is not a coherent elite of any type, and it is certainly not a highly educated, technically competent group. It does provide channels of mobility from the shop-floor but this probably results more from the low status of the occupation than from any belief in the rightness or efficiency of such a recruitment pattern. The situation is changing but not fast enough or sufficiently radically. Substantial improvement will require tremendous changes in education and in industry. The first necessity is the will to change and this presupposes a recognition and acceptance of a problem. When and if this occurs, the future may look more hopeful.

REFERENCES

Acton Society Trust, *Management Succession* (Acton Society Trust, 1956).

W. G. Cables in Warner and Abegglen, *Big Business Leaders in America* (New York: Harper, 1955).

D. G. Clark, *The Industrial Manager: His Background and Career Pattern* (London: Business Publications, 1966).

R. V. Clements, *Managers: A Study of Their Careers in Industry* (London: Allen & Unwin, 1958).

G. Copeman, *The Chief Executive and Business Growth: A Comparative Study in the United States, Britain and Germany* (London: Leviathan House, 1971).

'Flow of New Graduates into Industry', *Department of Employment Gazette* (Oct. 1976).

'Early Careers of Graduate Survey', *Department of Employment Gazette*, (Sept. 1977).

Department of Industry, *Industry, Education and Management, A Discussion Paper* (London: Department of Industry, July 1977).

M. Fores and I. A. Glover, 'Engineers in France', *The Chartered Mechanical Engineer* (23 Apr. 1976).

I. A. Glover, 'Executive Career Patterns: Britain, France, Germany and Sweden', *Energy World* (Dec. 1976).

I. A. Glover, 'Professionalism and manufacturing industry', in *Manufacturing and Management* (London: HMSO, 1978).
D. Granick, *The European Executive* (London: Weidenfeld & Nicolson, 1962).
D. Granick, *Managerial Comparisons of Four Developed Countries: France, Britain, United States and Russia*, (Cambridge, Mass.: MIT Press, 1971).
D. Granick, *The Red Executive* (New York: Anchor Books, 1961).
D. Granick, *Management of the Industrial Firm in the USSR* (New York: Columbia University Press, 1954).
D. Hall, H. C. de Bettignies and G. Amado-Fischgrund, 'The European Business Elite', *European Business* (Oct. 1969).
S. P. Hutton, P. A. Lawrence and J. H. Smith, 'The recruitment, deployment and status of the mechanical engineer in the German Federal Republic', Department of Industry (unpublished, 1971).
R. K. Kelsall, A. Poole and A. Kuhn, *Graduates: the Sociology of an Elite* (Tavistock Publications with Methuen, 1972).
P. A. Lawrence, paper to Department of Industry (unpublished, 1977).
A. Mant, *The Rise and Fall of the British Manager* (Macmillan, 1977).
A. Mant, 'Authority and task in manufacturing operations of multinational firms', conference paper in *Manufacturing and Management* (London: HMSO, 1978).
A. Marsh, J. Gillies and M. Rush, 'The training of managers in industrial relations', Stage 1 Report, St Edmund Hall, Oxford (unpublished, 1976).
B. May, 'Social, Educational and Professional Background of German Management. A Review of the Literature', mimeo (Department of Industry, 1974).
J. Melrose-Woodman, 'Profile of the British Manager', Management Survey Report no. 38 (British Institute of Management, 1978).
M. Newcomer, *The Big Business Executive* (Columbia University Press, 1955).
R. B. Petersen, 'Chief Executives' Attitudes towards Education – An International Comparison', *Journal of Management Studies*, 9:1 (1972).
N. Swords-Isherwood, 'The reluctant manager', DPhil. thesis (University of Sussex, 1977).

6 Technical Change in the Defence Industry

Mary Kaldor[1]

The main arms-manufacturing sectors in Britain today are aircraft, shipbuilding, mechanical engineering, and electronics. Other industries, especially electrical engineering, instrument engineering and motor vehicles, are also engaged, to a lesser extent, in production for the military market. In the USA, the automobile industry plays a much more important role in the defence sector than in Britain. Table 6.1 shows the military share of output for each of these industries.

In 1977, defence production amounted to around £2800 million, about 7 per cent of manufacturing in general. The British military equipment programme generates directly about 200,000 jobs and overseas defence sales generate about 70,000 more. In addition, it is estimated that roughly the same number of jobs, around 270,000, are indirectly generated in support of the manufacture of military equipment. In the same year, £870 million was spent on R&D, of which around £600 million went to the arms manufacturers (some of which are Government-owned) as opposed to the Government establishments (UK Ministry of Defence, 1978). Some of the biggest manufacturing companies in Britain make arms, as can be seen from the list of top contractors provided in Table 6.2. Britain imports a very small share of its defence requirements.

British spending on military R&D is higher, both absolutely and in relation to GNP, than that of any other European country. The data in Chapter 3 show Britain's innovativeness in aircraft, missiles, and ordnance. Britain is the third, possibly fourth, largest exporter of arms in the world, after the United States and the Soviet Union and possibly France. In contrast to civilian products, British defence products tend to be more expensive, reflecting greater technical sophistication, than those of its main competitors. Hence the value per ton of the Chieftain tank is higher than the value per ton of equivalent battle tanks, and the same is probably true of warships.[2] The Lightning interceptor was more expensive than its nearest equivalents, the

TABLE 6.1 Military output as a share of industrial sectors, 1971

	Domestic military output (£m)	*Total final output* (£m)	*Total* domestic final output* (£m)	*Domestic military output as a share of total final output* (%)	*Domestic military output as a share of total domestic final output* (%)
Other mechanical engineering	112.8	1835.9	795.4	6.1	14.2
Instrument engineering	37.6	512.5	291.4	7.3	12.9
Electronics and telecommunications	202.1	1053.1	740.6	19.2	27.3
Electrical machinery, etc.	31.8	621.8	343.3	5.1	9.3
Shipbuilding	197.9	508.2	383.4	38.9	51.6
Motor vehicles	33.6	2059.9	1121.8	1.6	3.0
Aerospace equipment	301.8	647.8	401.9	46.6	75.1
Public administration, domestic service, rent	12,460.0	9506.0	9506.0	13.1	13.1

NOTE

* Total final output minus exports. This is because exports consist of both civil and military products. Domestic military output as a share of total final output understates the true impact of military spending on a sector. On the other hand, since the civilian sectors on average export more than the military sector, domestic military output as a share of total domestic final output probably overestimates the impact of military spending.

SOURCE

Business Monitor (1975).

TABLE 6.2 Defence expenditure with industry: UK-based MOD contractors paid £5m or more by MOD for equipment in 1976/77, together accounting for 90 per cent of domestic defence contracts

Over £100 million

British Aircraft Corporation Ltd[1]
General Electric Co. Ltd
Hawker Siddeley Group Ltd[1]
Rolls-Royce (1971) Ltd (now Rolls-Royce Ltd)
Royal Ordnance Factories

£50–£100 million

Plessey Co Ltd
Vickers Ltd[2]
Westland Aircraft Ltd

£25–50 million

British Leyland Motor Corporation Ltd
David Brown (Holdings) Ltd[2]
EMI Ltd
Ferranti Ltd
Hunting Associated Industries Ltd
Lucas Industries Ltd
Yarrow & Co Ltd[2]

£10–£25 million

Dowty Group Ltd
The Laird Group Ltd[1,2]
MEL Equipment Ltd (now a division of Philips Electronic and Associated Industries Ltd)
Racal Electronics Ltd
Scott Lithgow Ltd[2]
Short Bros & Harland Ltd (now Short Bros Ltd)
Smiths Industries Ltd
Sperry Rand Ltd
Swan Hunter Group Ltd[2]
Vauxhall Motors Ltd

£5–£10 million

Barr & Stroud Ltd (now part of Pilkington Bros Ltd)
Decca Ltd
Dunlop Holdings Ltd
Fodens Ltd
Marshall of Cambridge (Engineering) Ltd
Mullard Ltd
Northern Shipbuilding and Industrial Holdings Ltd[2]
The Rank Organisation Ltd
Standard Telephones & Cables Ltd

Thorn Electrical Industries Ltd
UKAEA
Ultra Electronic Holdings Ltd (now part of Dowty Group Ltd)
The Weir Group Ltd

NOTES

[1] Now partially or wholly vested in British Aerospace.
[2] Now partially or wholly vested in British Shipbuilders.

SOURCE

UK Ministry of Defence (1978)

French Mirage III, the American F-104 Starfighter, or the Soviet MIG-21. This might also be true of Britain's latest combat aircraft, the Multi Role Combat Aircraft, or Tornado.

The contrast between technical change in the military and civilian sectors in the UK is very long-standing. It can be traced back to the 1880s, the beginning of the Anglo-German naval arms race and the loss of Britain's industrial pre-eminence. Clive Trebilcock has extensively documented the contrast in the period before the First World War (Trebilcock, 1969 and 1977). Experiments by warship builders in the use of new alloys, like nickel, manganese or chrome, made an important contribution to the development of steel processes. Navies were among the first to adopt the turbine engine and later the diesel engine. The assembly line was invented for the manufacture of small arms. Trebilcock also shows how Britain managed to maintain a dominant role in the world market for arms.

This contrast between military and civilian sectors is not only to be observed historically. Since the Second World War it also bears international comparison. The relative decline in American productivity and productivity growth compared with Europe and Japan began around 1950, in the period when the United States was developing a peacetime arms industry (Melman, 1974). The most successful post-war capitalist economies, West Germany and Japan, are those with very small defence industries, although they are growing, Table 6.3 compares the share of GNP devoted to military spending ('military burden') with the share of GNP devoted to gross fixed capital investment. It can be seen that countries with high military burden tend to have low investment/GNP ratios and vice versa. By and large, countries with high investment/GNP ratios tend to enjoy relatively high rates of economic growth.

The persistence of the contrast between military sophistication and civilian stagnation, both historically and internationally, suggests the existence of

TABLE 6.3 Investment and military expenditure, Western countries, 1974

Country	*Military expenditure*[a] *(US$ x 10^6)*	*Military expenditure as percentage of GNP*[a]	*Investment as percentage of GDP*[b]	*Average annual growth rate in GNP 1963–73, per cent*[c]
United States	85900	6.15	18	3.9
United Kingdom	10100	5.24	20	2.7
France	10600	3.63	25	5.7
West Germany	13800	3.58	22	4.7
Netherlands	2320	3.45	22	5.4
Sweden	1780	3.10	22	3.4
Norway	671	3.13	32	4.7
Italy	4630	2.93	23	4.8
Belgium	1460	2.77	22	4.8
Denmark	728	2.37	22	4.5
Canada	2790	2.05	23	5.2
Switzerland	856	1.91	27	4.0
New Zealand	237	1.75	26	3.4
Finland	255	1.31	29	4.9
Austria	292	0.91	28	5.2
Luxembourg	18	0.87	26	3.4
Japan	3670	0.83	34	10.5

SOURCES

[a] US Arms Control and Disarmament Agency (1976).
[b] United Nations Department of Economic and Social Affairs Statistical Office (1976).
[c] US Arms Control and Disarmament Agency (1974).

some causal connection. The purpose of this chapter is to describe one possible explanation for the connection in Britain. It should be stressed that this explanation is specific to here and now. The first part of the chapter describes the characteristics of technical change in the defence sector. The second part attempts to explain these characteristics in terms of the structure of the defence market. The last part looks at the effect of technical change in the defence industry, and of its underlying institutional structure, on the civilian economy.

THE CHARACTERISTICS OF TECHNICAL CHANGE IN THE DEFENCE SECTOR

The military procurement budget is dominated by major weapon systems – warships, aircraft and armoured fighting vehicles. The Multi Role Combat Aircraft (MRCA) accounts for around 40 per cent of the Royal Air Force (RAF) budget; the three Anti-Submarine Warfare Cruisers, which are actually small aircraft carriers, with their associated escort and support ships, probably account for a fifth to a quarter of the naval procurement budget.

The form and function of the weapon system has not changed much since 1945. Technical change has largely consisted of improvements to a given set of performance characteristics, which are regarded as 'proxy indicator(s) of effectiveness' (Canby 1975). Submarines are faster, quieter, bigger and have longer ranges. Aircraft have greater speed, more powerful thrust and bigger payloads. All weapon systems have more destructive weapons, particularly missiles, and greatly improved capabilities for communication, navigation, detection, identification and weapon guidance. While the basic technology of the delivery system has not changed much, marginal improvements to performance characteristics have often entailed the incorporation of very advanced technology, e.g. radical electronic innovations such as micro-processors, or nuclear power for submarines, and this has greatly increased the complexity of the weapon system as a whole.

The cost of making incremental improvements to a given set of performance characteristics tends to increase over time. The technology of a weapon system eventually reaches a point of sharply diminishing returns, where marginal improvements entail disproportionate increases in cost, although this does not appear to have been documented publicly (Canby, 1975, and Carey, 1974). Tables 6.4 and 6.5 show the rapid increase in the cost of successive generations of aircraft and warships. The real cost of producing 385 Tornado aircraft, for example, will be slightly greater than the entire production costs of the Spitfire before and during the Second World War.

TABLE 6.4 British combat aircraft since the Second World War

Manufacturer	*Aircraft*	*Type*	*Weight* (lb)	*Max. Speed* (m.p.h.)	*Entered service*	*Number*	*Cost*[1] 1973 (dollars)
Fighters							
Supermarine	Spitfire	Fighter	L 5 000–9 000	370–440	1934	21 000	300 000
Gloster	Meteor	Jet fighter	E 10 600	592	1943	?	600 000
de Haviland	Vampire	Ground attack fighter	7 300	531	1946	≙2 250[2]	500 000
Hawker/ Armstrong Whitworth	Sea Hawk	Naval fighter	E 9 000	450	1953	(750)	600 000
Hawker	Hunter	Fighter	E 13 300	715	1954	2 000 +	600 000
English Electric	Lightning	supersonic all-weather interceptor		> Mach 2	1959	160+	2 000 000
Hawker Siddeley	Harrier	VTOL fighter	E 12 000	Trans-onic	1969	233	5 000 000
Sepcat	Jaguar	lightstrike/ fighter/trainer	E 15 400	Mach 1.1	1972	230[3]	4 000 000
Hawker Siddeley	Sea Harrier	naval version of Harrier	E 12 000	Trans-onic	(1979)	25+	5 000 000
Panavia	Tornado Adv	air defence variant of MRCA	E 22 000	≙ 1,000		165	(10 300 000)

Strike aircraft

English Electric	Canberra	medium bomber	E 21 700	541	1951	(1,300)[4]	600 000
A. V. Roe	Vulcan	jet bomber		Mach 0.94	1955	(80)	(3 000 000)
Vickers	Valiant	swept-wing bomber	E 75 900	Mach 0.82	1955	108	(2 000 000)
Handley Page	Victor	bomber		Mach 0.92	1957	(80+)	(2 500 000)
Blackburn	Buccaneer	naval strike	T.O. 56 000	Mach 0.85	1964	197	2 000 000
Panavia	Tornado IDS	multi-role combat aircraft	E 22,000	≙ 1,000	(1979)	220[5]	(8 700 000)

ABBREVIATIONS

≙ = approximately
? = not available
– = none

L = Landing
E = Empty
T.O. = Take off

NOTES

[1] Based on Stockholm International Peace Research Institute figures, used for calculating arms trade statistics. Bracketed items are estimates at Science Policy Research Unit, using the same method.
[2] In addition, Vampires were produced under licence in Australia, India, Italy, France and Sweden.
[3] France has jointly produced Jaguar and has purchased an additional 200 for the French services.
[4] In addition, Canberras were produced under licence in Australia and USA.
[5] Tornado is produced jointly with FRG and Italy.

SOURCE

Science Policy Research Unit arms production registers.

TABLE 6.5 Cost of battleships, cruisers, aircraft carriers and submarines

Name	*Type*	*Completed*	*Standard tons displacement*	*Official Estimated Building Cost* (£)	*Cost per ton* (£)
Battleships, etc.					
Vanguard	Battleship	1946	44,500	9,000,000	202.2
Eagle	Aircraft carrier	1951	44,100	16,335,000	370.4
Ark Royal	Aircraft carrier	1955	43,060	21,793,000	506.1
Blake	'Tiger' class cruiser	1961	9,500	14,940,000	1572.6
Antrim	'County' class cruiser	1970	5,440	16,740,000	3077.2
Bristol	Type 82 cruiser	1973	5,650	24,582,000	4350.8
Invincible	ASW cruiser	1978	≏20,000	≏100,000,000	≏5000
Submarines					
Ambush	'A' class submarine	1947	1,120	456,143	407.3
Porpoise	'Porpoise' class patrol submarine	1958	1,610	2,048,000	1272.0
Dreadnought	'Dreadnought' class fleet submarine	1963	3,000	18,455,000	6151.7
Warspite	'Valiant' class fleet submarine	1967	3,500	21,450,000	6128.6
Resolution	'Resolution' class nuclear-powered ballistic-missile submarine	1967	7,000	39,700,000	5671.4
Churchill	'Churchill' class fleet submarine	1970	3,500	24,661,000	7331.7
Swiftsure	'Swiftsure' class fleet submarine	1973	3,500	37,084,000	10595.4

Frigates					
Morecambe Bay	'Bay' class frigate	1949	1,600	500,000	312.5
Whitby	'Whitby' class frigate	1956	2,150	3,155,000	1467.4
Duncan	'Blackwood' type 14 frigate	1958	11,808	1,991,000	1687.1
Chichester	'Salisbury' type 61 frigate	1958	2,170	3,277,000	1487.1
Lynx	'Leopard' type 41 frigate	1957	2,800	2,885,000	1030.3
Ashanti	'Tribal' type 81 frigate	1961	2,300	5,220,000	2269.6
Dido	'Leander' class frigate	1963	2,450	4,600,000	1877.6
Ariadne	Broad-beamed 'Leander' class frigate	1973	2,500	7,403,000	2961.2
Amazon	Type 21 frigate	1973	2,500	17,161,000	6864.4
Destroyers					
Matapan	'Battle' class destroyer	1945	2,380	944,326	396.8
Battleaxe	'Weapon' class destroyer	1947	2,280	1,007,961	442.1
Diana	'Daring' class destroyer	1954	2,800	2,975,000	1062.5
Sheffield	Type 42 destroyer	1975	3,200	26,438,000	8261.9

The cost per ton of warships, not counting inflation, has increased since 1945 by anything from a factor of 10 (the difference between an early post-war 'Bay' class frigate and the last of a long series of 'Leander' class frigates) to a factor of 27 (the difference between an early post-war 'A' class submarine and a modern 'Swiftsure' class submarine).

If anything, these figures are understated because they refer only to production costs. Total life-cycle costs would be even more striking. It is estimated that the building costs of a ship account for 25 per cent of the total life-cycle costs (UK House of Commons, 1976). A study of the A-7D American combat aircraft shows that ownership costs, i.e. operation and maintenance, base support and training, are 30 per cent higher than acquisition costs – the cost of spares being included in the estimate for acquisition costs (Fiorello, 1975).

Technical improvements are likely to be more expensive the more quickly they are introduced into service. A study undertaken at the Rand Corporation (Perry *et al.*, 1971) has shown that the difference between original cost estimates and final costs is directly related to the degree of technical advance sought. By implication, this is also true of the increase in the cost of successive generations of military equipment, since cost estimates are based on knowledge of the previous generation. Technical advance was measured, crudely, through a system of subjective ratings ranging from one to twenty. The ratings were known as A-factors. It was found that programmes with A-factors less than 12 tended to be reasonably predictable, although outcomes tended to vary above eight.

Figure 6.1 reproduces the ratings for different programmes provided in the original study. All the British programmes had ratings above eight. Five British programmes had ratings above 12–Kestrel, P-1127, Lightning P-1 (which were all prototypes), Vulcan and Concorde. Concorde had the highest rating of any programme, British or American. MRCA was not included but it would probably have a rating above 12 since it is similar to the American plane, F-111.

In recent years, a number of strategic writers have come to question the utility of the criteria for technical improvements to weapon systems (Canby 1975, Augustine 1975, McGeogh, 1972). Many of the indicators of military effectiveness are thought to be no longer relevant to modern warfare. For example, the development of naval aircraft and submarines has meant that speed is no longer important for surface ships. Likewise, aircraft speed is only of advantage in air-superiority roles. Furthermore, the cost and complexity consequent upon improvements in individual performance characteristics may turn out to be a positive liability. Complexity greatly increases unreliability and reduces manoeuvreability and flexibility; it also entails considerable

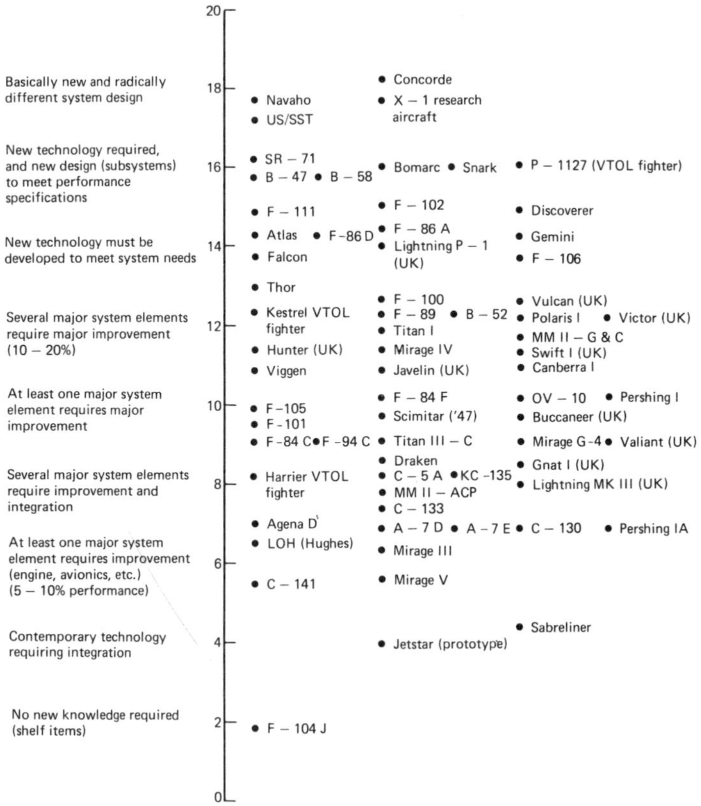

FIG. 6.1 Technological advance ratings

SOURCE
Perry *et al.* (1971).

logistic problems. High cost is a disadvantage because of the vulnerability of modern delivery systems, owing to improvements in the accuracy of guided munitions – the consequences of development in electronics. The new Precision Guided Munitions (PGMs) vastly improve the ability to identify and destroy targets. They are extremely cheap, although there is considerable debate about the cost of associated systems. A modern combat aircraft, for example, costs a thousand times more than a ground-based anti-aircraft missile.

The relative merits of alternative solutions to strategic problems, such as those put forward by Canby as well as others, are beyond the scope of this study. But their very existence suggests that the tendency to adopt sophisticated and expensive solutions cannot be explained entirely in terms of military effectiveness. In peacetime, notions of military effectiveness are necessarily subjective and are inevitably influenced by the past and by the environment in which they evolve. A more convincing explanation for increasing sophistication and experience would focus on the decision-making process and the structure of the institutions responsible for military technology.

THE STRUCTURE OF THE DEFENCE MARKET

The British manufacturers of major weapon systems are now largely nationalised. They include British Aerospace, British Shipbuilders, Rolls Royce Ltd, the Royal Dockyards and the Royal Ordnance Factories. In the private sector there are one tank manufacturer, two armoured car manufacturers, a major helicopter company, and a partially state-owned aircraft company. The electronics companies are all private and are much more numerous than the delivery system contractors. There are also thousands of smaller subcontractors, although information about them is extremely hard to obtain. Finally, there is a number of small companies specialising in particular types of military equipment, often for export. In particular, there is a number of boat-builders in the South of England, with a flourishing trade in small missile-firing patrol boats.

The main customer is the British Government, which buys over 70 per cent of total military output; it seems likely, although the information is not readily available, that this proportion is higher for the more sophisticated types of military equipment. Although there have been some significant foreign sales of major weapon systems (the Harriers sold to the United States, the Lightnings sold to Saudi Arabia, the Chieftains for Iran, and the submarines for Brazil and Israel), the staple exports are simple and refurbished aircraft, small patrol boats, helicopters and armoured cars. A growing proportion of military exports consists of services, like training, repair and maintenance, and construction (although the Government has never confirmed whether these services are included in the figure for defence sales which is published annually in the defence White Paper).

The Government is virtually the sole customer for research and development. Technical change is basically a product of the relationship between the Government and the contractors, although of course the Government does take into account foreign requirements and foreign technical developments, especially in the United States, when drawing up specifications.

Two characteristics of this relationship help explain the nature of technical change. The first is the *stability* of the industrial structure, and its relation to force structure. Firms have been amalgamated, taken over, or nationalised, but, basically, there has been very little rationalisation. The plants which receive prime contracts for major weapon systems have remained much the same, under different names, for 25 years. Obviously, there has been more specialisation and an increased amount of subcontract work both among the prime contractors and to outside firms, especially in the electronics industry. But there have been very few, if any, actual closures after the immediate post-war period. Equally, there have been no new entries into the major weapons markets. Even more important, perhaps, a major effort has been made to ensure continuity of design teams. The consequence is that a specific mix of skills and physical equipment amounting to a specific set of manufacturing capabilities has been preserved.

The stability of manufacturing capabilities is, moreover, only one side of the coin. The defence industry had developed alongside the armed forces. Like the defence industries, the armed forces have been pruned and centralised during the period since the war. But they remain functionally organised around particular weapon systems (Downey, 1977). The strategic doctrine of any particular military unit, expressed in the military specifications for a particular weapon system, is thus strongly identified with the performance characteristics of a particular weapon system which, in turn, is a product of the manufacturing capabilities of a particular contractor. The persistence of a particular set of performance characteristics is merely a reflection of the alliance between military specifications and manufacturing capability – in other words, the stability of force structure and industrial structure. Any new technology that threatened to change the organisation, as might simpler and cheaper weapons, is likely to be resisted.

The second characteristic of the defence market is the *technological competition* between the contractors. Historically the competition between the firms was the consequence of private enterprise. Individual firms had to maintain their independent viability, and since the Government was their main customer, and military orders tended to take the form of large and lumpy contracts, this resulted in intense competition to obtain any one order.[3] As the relationship with the Government has become secure, and as firms have been progressively nationalised, the historical competition between the firms has been translated into institutional rivalry, that takes the form of technological competition rather than price competition. Firms put more emphasis on the ability to offer improvements to the product than on the ability to reduce the cost of production. This is primarily because the Government is the customer and so long as the Government is committed to the survival of the contractors, price is fairly elastic. Were companies to offer cheap and simple solutions to military problems, this might reduce the total defence budget and hence the total market.

This tendency to what might be described as over-incremental technical change has been compounded by Government policy. Successive Governments have attempted to cope with the rising cost of weapon systems, combined with the limitation on peacetime military budgets, by narrowing the range of weapon systems produced, persuading different military units to share the same type, and through amalgamating the contractors, persuading one or more contractors to collaborate in development and production. This approach has consistently backfired. The consequence has been to increase the complexity of weapons systems, since it has led to an escalation in the number of performance characteristics specified for any one weapon system. Increased complexity has increased the cost of incremental improvements to any one performance characteristic because of the trade-off between different characteristics. And this appproach has also reinforced the underlying institutional structure.

Good examples of the way in which Government policies have exacerbated the tendency for cost and complexity are the TSR-2, the MRCA and the ASW Crusier. The TSR-2 followed a Government decision to phase out manned aircraft and to reorganise the aircraft industry. As the manufacturers of TSR-2 – and the design teams – were amalgamated but not rationalised, and as the services added to the military specifications roles that would formerly have been carried out by different aircraft, the cost and complexity of TSR-2 grew rapidly. (Williams *et al.*, 1972). The problems encountered with TSR-2 have been magnified in the case of MRCA, which is an attempt to amalgamate the manufacturing capabilities of several different countries and to reconcile the requirements of distinctly separate national armed forces – hence, its nickname, the 'egg-laying, wool-producing milk-giving sow'. (Albrecht, *et al.*, 1974). The ASW Cruiser, a small aircraft carrier, followed a decision to phase out aircraft carriers and to reorganise the shipbuilding industry. Like TSR-2, it has collected new roles and, along with other associated naval vessels, cost and complexity has escalated.

THE EFFECTS OF MILITARY TECHNICAL CHANGE ON THE CIVILIAN ECONOMY

The over-incremental nature of technical change in the defence industry, arising from the underlying institutional structure, suggests an explanation for the link between military spending and civilian stagnation that fits the analysis of Britain's economic decline put forward in Chapter 2. It is argued there that the institutional structure of production and demand, established in the First Industrial Revolution, centred around textiles and railways, hindered the adjustments that were necessary to adapt to the Second Industrial Revolution, centred around chemicals, electricity and eventually the automobile, which began in the last decades of the nineteenth century. David Landes talks about the 'burden of interrelatedness', the fact that 'no piece of equipment works in a void', and that any act of innovation calls forth a series of related acts in the industrial, technical and social environment (Landes, 1969).

This 'mummification', as Landes calls it, of the industrial structure pervaded all of human and social capital – the composition of skills, the style of living, education and transportation, and so on. Further, it can be argued (although Landes does not), that these obstacles to innovation set in motion a circular process of decline in which domestic investment was slowed down, thus reducing the possibilities for transforming the social and material infrastructure. At the same time, increasing overseas investment helped to increase the competitiveness of Britain's economic rivals, and further widen the gap in productivity growth, reducing the opportunities for profitable investment at home.

Military spending, it can be argued, played a role in this process. It enabled some of the most important companies of the period to grow and innovate within the confines of the established institutional structure. It reinforced the 'mummification' of British industry, and put off the day when the necessary structural adjustments would have to be made. It postponed the crisis of the First Industrial Revolution and, at the same time, prevented change. It contributed to the slow-down of investment by absorbing a growing share of the available surplus, and this is reflected in the inverse relation between military burden and investment as a share of GNP (Smith, 1977). And the failure to invest and to restructure civilian industry increased the tendency to seek military contracts. It absorbed some of the finest engineers and scientists and, although they were responsible for some of the most important inventions of the Second Industrial Revolution, it diverted their attention from commercial application and distorted their concepts of what constitutes technical advance. It channelled technical innovation, in other words, along a dead end, toward the grotesque combination of complexity, sophistication and conservatism that characterises much of modern military technology.

To put it more formally: by 1870, the technology that produced the mid-nineteenth century revolution in industry in Britain had reached the phase of diminishing returns, when investment no longer yielded the expected innovation, when every extra pound invested yielded a diminishing increase in productivity and hence in markets and profits. This reflected the growing rigidity of the industrial structure. Military spending helped to augment markets and, because of its form – the over-incremental characteristics of technical change, which reinforced the rigidity of the industrial structure – accentuated the tendency for diminishing returns. Military spending played a role in the cumulative causation of British decline in much the same way as overseas investment did.

A secular increase in such spending occurred in the 1880s, during the depression that marked the beginning of British decline. The reason was the developing imperial rivalry between Britain, France and Germany and, to a lesser extent, the United States. But the form of the increase, the emphasis on bigger and better and more expensive warships, is best explained by the underlying industrial structure.

During the 1880s, military contracts were first extended on a significant scale to private manufacturers. Some of the most dynamic companies of the period – the steel makers, Vickers, John Brown, Beardmore's, Cammells and Firths, the shipbuilders like Fairfields, J. & G. Thompson (later to become John Brown), Yarrow & Co. Ltd, and engineers like Armstrongs – turned to the military market as an alternative outlet to counterbalance the depression in trade and the effects of growing competition from Germany and the USA.

Over the next two decades, the new private contractors formed themselves into a formidable group of armament specialists and set in motion a technological competition, reflecting and reinforcing political competition, between Britain and Germany. That it was focused on warships was primarily a consequence of the force structure of the time. Although the late-nineteenth-century warship incorporated very sophisticated technology, in form and function it was not so very different from the capital ship of Nelson's day and, if anything, it merely gave prestige to navy traditions and doctrine. In contrast, the greater destructiveness and accuracy of guns and the introduction of automatic fire, which was used to great effect in Africa especially during the Boer War, did threaten to change the whole mode of land warfare, and with it the organisational structure of the army – the dominance of the cavalry, the importance of the individual marksman, for example.

The emphasis suited the manufacturers as well. Warships were the forerunner of the modern weapon system. They were much more lucrative than other kinds of military equipment; they combined the various capabilities of the armourer in a single hull; they required a long production period. In theory, readiness for war involved 'the annual accumulation of a few very capital-intensive units in a pre-war situation' (Trebilcock, 1975, p. 160) in contrast to the rapid industrial mobilisation, called forth by army requirements in wartime, which was quite unsuited to the industrial environment that created the specialist arms manufacturers. The competitive process that underlay the Anglo-German naval arms race was described by Engels in terms that anticipate post-1945 developments in weaponry:

> The modern warship is not only a product but also a specimen of modern large-scale industry, a floating factory – producing mainly, to be sure, a lavish waste of money . . . in this competitive struggle between armour-plating and guns, the warship is being developed to a pitch of perfection which is making it both outrageously costly and unusable in war. (Engels, 1894, pp. 238–9)

Military spending still remained a relatively small proportion of GNP up to 1914 (Mitchell and Deane, 1971; Mitchell and Jones, 1971). It reached a peak of 4 per cent during the Boer War in the early 1900s. It was concentrated on some of the largest companies in the country. In 1905, the arms companies represented 10 per cent of P. L. Payne's list of largest industrial contractors (Payne, 1967). They tended to dominate groups of smaller firms in related trades and particular regions, like North-east England, the West of Scotland, Northern Ireland and Sheffield, so that the effect of military contracts is likely to have been much more pervasive than the figures suggest. By 1914, most of the arms companies had become dependent on Government support. Vickers, Armstrongs and Beardmore's had become professional armourers, and although they continued to build merchant ships, their yards, like those of other shipbuilders, could not have survived without 'generously topping up the order book with naval contracts' (Moss and Hume, 1977, p. 129).

The military market diverted the attention of the companies from commercial application of their innovations. It was thus not simply a matter of postponing the kind of restructuring necessary for the survival of the old industries. It was also a matter of not entering the new ones. Armstrongs, for example, had a plan in 1906, two years before the Model T, to mass-produce 6000 cars. The proposal was rejected by the directors on the grounds that the profit would be less than on a single river gunboat (Trebilcock, 1969). Military spending represented an opportunity cost, for it absorbed resources that might otherwise have been used for investment and innovation in civilian sectors. It also reduced the incentive to use what resources were available for investment, by preserving outdated industrial structures.

The First World War involved an enormous expansion of defence industrial capacity and, although defence spending never fell to its pre-war level, arms manufacturers were deeply affected by the slump between the wars. But the belief that the capacity would be required again prevented permanent closure of many facilities which were outmoded and inappropriate to modern commercial practice. The Second World War, the Korean War, and the post-war boom in merchant shipbuilding and engineering which preceded the recovery of Britain's old and new competitors, staved off for another twenty years the challenge to Britain's 'mummified' industrial structure. It was not until the 1960s that the severe problems of the traditional industries became apparent. And this was when the policy of amalgamation, together with the escalation in the cost and complexity of naval vessels, really began. A history of the industries in the West of Scotland argues that 'the structural weaknesses of the [shipbuilding] industry' were 'disguised and reinforced' by naval construction before the First World War, by 'the artificial conditions' of war and by 'the 1950s boom, characterised by the absence of significant foreign competition and the temporary revival of the liner market' (Moss and Hume, 1977, pp. 102 and 104). A similar story can be told about Barrow-in-Furness, which is dominated by Vickers (Scott, 1962) and the North East of England, dominated by Vickers and by the companies, mostly warshipbuilders, which together form Swan Hunter.

The important role of naval construction and ordnance in simultaneously preserving and distorting the shipbuilding and engineering industries is indicated by the distribution of research activities. Other chapters stress the dearth of qualified scientists and engineers in the shipbuilding and engineering industries. Yet more than 3000 people are engaged in research and development in ship construction and underwater warfare and 5000 people are engaged in research and development on ordnance. The cost of naval R&D is £80 million and of R&D into ordnance is £67 million.

The modern sectors of the defence industry (aircraft and electronics) were grafted on to an existing institutional structure. Neither ever seems to have been able to break out of the military strait-jacket. Indeed, commercial technology, such as it is, seems to exhibit all the characteristics of military technology described above. Chapter 16 describes the failure of British electronics companies to escape the syndrome of low-volume, specialised military production, and the combination of 'technical virtuosity' and commercial mismanagement. The same is true of aircraft. The Vickers Viscount has been the only British civil aircraft to make a profit in the post-war period and Government attempts to help commercial aircraft led to Concorde, a superb example of cramming technical advance into an expensive aircraft, much like TSR-2, MRCA or the ASW Cruiser.

American aircraft and electronics companies have been more successful in breaking out of the military market, though, according to Miller and Sawers, only relatively so. They argue that, at least for aircraft, the success has been exaggerated, and that the US aircraft industry is stunted by its military history (Miller and Sawers, 1968). They argue that, if American firms have succeeded where European firms have failed, it is partly because of their pre-war commercial experience, and also because their disadvantages are offset by the sheer volume of the American market, both military and civil. This is probably also the explanation of the success of some, but not all,

American electronics companies (see Chapter 16). This suggests paradoxically that military spending in Britain is at once too large and too small. It fetters the civilian economy and preserves older, declining sectors, and at the same time, it is too small by comparison with the USA to provide a useful technical back-up for those industries that do have a dynamic commercial potential.

CONCLUSION

Sooner, rather than later, there is going to have to be a change in policy towards the defence sector. Already, the Government has decided to go ahead with a successor to the Chieftain tank and ideas are proliferating. A follow-up to the MRCA programme, known as Air Staff Target 403, is also under consideration. It is expected to replace the Harrier and Jaguar, and presumably a variety of planes operated by potential foreign partners, in 1990. Plans are said to centre on a supersonic multi-mission plane with a STOVL (short take-off and vertical landing) capability.

These programmes will be astronomically expensive. The current cost of MRCA and the cruiser has eaten into the procurement budget and resulted in a deterioration of conditions, as well as shortages of essential support equipment such as spares and ammunition. It is difficult to believe that the financial burden of over-sophistication can be borne for another generation of weapons.

Evidently, any change in policy would entail, first of all, a reassessment of strategic tasks – something which is outside the scope of this paper. But it is clear from the analysis above that the precondition for any new strategic thinking must be a reorganisation of the institutions in which ideas about defence are nurtured. And this, of course, would include the defence industry. The task of reorganisation would be both a contribution to and a part of the general problem of developing a flexible and imaginative strategy to overcome the structural weaknesses, the 'mummification' of British industry.

NOTES

1. The author is grateful to officials in the Ministry of Defence, who provided some very useful comments.
2. According to figures provided by the Stockholm International Peace Research Institute (SPIRI), the value per ton of the same generation of main battle tanks, as of 1973, was as follows: Chieftain (UK), \$7400; Leopard (Germany), \$8600; M-60 (US), \$6000; T-54 (Soviet Union), \$4600. Table 6.5 (pp.108–9) provides prices for warships. The price per ton of

British warships in 1973 was: cruiser, £4300; submarine, £10,600; frigate, £6900. The SIPRI figures for average international price per ton in the same year are: cruiser, £3800; submarine, £5000(?), frigate, £5000.
3. The 'do or die' mentality has been extensively documented in the United States (Fox, 1974; Peck and Scherer, 1962).

REFERENCES

U. Albrecht, Burkhard Luber and Peter Schlotter,'Das ende der MRCA?' in *Studiengruppe Militärpolitik, Ein Anti-Weisbuch*, Materialies für eine Alternative Militärpolik (Hamburg: Rowalt, 1974).
Normal R. Augustine, 'One Place, One Tank, One Ship: Trend for the Future', *Defense Management Journal*, USA (Apr. 1975).
Business Monitor, *Input-Output Tables for the United Kingdom*, 1971, PA10004 (London: HMSO, 1975).
Stephen Canby, 'The Alliance and Europe': Part IV, 'Military Doctrine and Technology', *Adelphi Paper No. 109* (London: International Institute for Strategic Studies, Winter 1974–5).
Sir Michael Carey, 'Military Procurement', *Royal United Services Institute Journal* (Mar. 1974).
John Downey, *Management in the Armed Forces. An Anatomy of the Military Profession* (London: McGraw-Hill, 1977).
F. Engels, 'The Force Theory', in *Anti-Duhring: Herr Eurgen Duhring's Revolution in Science*, translated from third German edition, 1894 (Moscow: Foreign Languages Publishing House, 1959).
Marco Fiorello, *Estimating Life-Cycle Costs: A Case Study of the A-7D*, Rand Corporation R-1518-PR (Santa Monica, California: Rand Corporation, Feb. 1975).
J. R. Fox, *Arming America: How the United States Buys its Weapons* (Cambridge, Mass.: Harvard University Press, 1974).
Jane's Fighting Ships (London, Jane's, Annual).
David Landes, *The Unbound Prometheus: Technical Change 1750 to the Present* (Cambridge: Cambridge University Press, 1969).
Sir Ean McGeogh, 'Command of the Sea in the Seventies', *The Waverly Papers,* Occasional Paper No. 1, series 4 (Edinburgh University, 1972).
Seymour Melman, *The Permanent War Economy: American Capitalism in Decline* (New York: Simon & Schuster, 1974).
Ronald Miller and David Sawers, *The Technical Development of Modern Aviation* (London: Routledge & Kegan Paul, 1968).
B. R. Mitchell and P. Deane, *Abstracts of British Historical Statistics*, University of Cambridge, Department of Applied Economics, Monograph 17 (1971).
B. R. Mitchell and H. G. Jones, *Second Abstract of Britain Historical Statistics*, University of Cambridge, Department of Applied Economics, Monograph 18 (1971).
Michael S. Moss and John R. Hume, *Workshop of the British Empire: Engineering and Shipbuilding in the West of Scotland* (London: Heinemann, 1977).

P. L. Payne, 'The Emergence of the Large Scale Company in Great Britain 1870–1914', *Economic History Review*, 20 (1967).

Merton J. Peck and Frederick T. Scherer, *The Weapons Acquisition Process: An Economic Analysis* (Cambridge, Mass.: Harvard University Press, 1962).

Robert Perry, Giles K. Smith, Alvin J. Harman and Susan Henrichsen, *System Acquisition Strategies*, Rand Corporation R-733-PR/ARPA (Santa Monica, California: Rand Corporation, June 1971).

Science Policy Research Unit arms production registers (Science Policy Research Unit, University of Sussex).

J. D. Scott, *Vickers. A History* (London: Weidenfeld & Nicolson, 1962).

Ron Smith, 'Military Expenditure and Capitalism', *Cambridge Journal of Economics* (Mar. 1977).

Clive Trebilcock, ' "Spin-off" in British Economic History: Armaments and Industry, 1760–1914', *Economic History Review*, second series, vol. XXII, no. 3 (Dec. 1969).

Clive Trebilcock, 'War and the Failure of Industrial Mobilisation', in J. M. Winter (ed.), *War and Economic Development* (London: Cambridge University Press, 1975).

Clive Trebilcock, *The Vickers Brothers: Armaments and Enterprise, 1854–1914* (London: Europa Publications Ltd, 1977).

UK House of Commons, Evidence of Vice-Admiral Clayton, *Fifth Report from the Committee on Public Accounts* (Session 1975–76, HCP 556 (London: HMSO, 1976).

UK House of Commons, *Appropriation Accounts* (London, Annual).

UK Ministry of Defence, *Statement on Defence Estimates, 1978*, Command 7099 (London: HMSO, Feb. 1978).

United Nations Department of Economic and Social Affairs Statistical Office, *Statistical Yearbook, 1975* (New York: United Nations, 1976).

United States Arms Control and Disarmament Agency, *World Military Expenditures and Arms Transfers 1963–1973* (Washington, D.C.: US Government Printing Office, 1974).

United States Arms Control and Disarmament Agency, *World Military Expenditures and Arms Transfers 1965–1974* (Washington, D.C.: US Government Printing Office, 1976).

Geoffrey Williams, Frank Gregory and John Simpson, *Crisis in Procurement: A Case Study of the TSR-2* (London: Royal United Services Institution, 1972).

Part II

7 Innovation in Textile Machinery

Roy Rothwell[1]

INTRODUCTION

Immediately after the Second World War much of the machinery manufactured in the UK was 'traditional', and the manufacturers had no strong commitment to technical development. A Board of Trade working party recorded in 1946:

> . . . in the last ten years textile machinery makers in other countries . . . have been spending money on research and development on a scale immensely greater than anything attempted in this country. (Cotton Industry Working Party, 1946)

The pressing need for textile machinery makers to establish research and development departments was further emphasised in the Evershed Report (Committee of Investigation into the Cotton Textile Machine Industry, 1947) with respect to both the cotton-spinning machinery and cotton-weaving machinery sectors. The spinning sector (in the form of Textile Machinery Makers Ltd. the forerunner of Platt Saco Lowell) responded well, and founded a strong central R&D facility at Helmshore. It also greatly increased its interaction with the Shirley Institute and others, and began to sponsor students to Manchester University. The weaving machinery sector, on the other hand, responded to a much lesser degree and subsequently failed to establish comprehensive R&D efforts.

Since 1945 the pace of technical change has accelerated greatly, and has become more radical in nature, often embodying techniques from other areas, such as electronics, aerodynamics, chemical technology (Rothwell 1976). The new growth sectors have generally been related to the enormous post-war advances made by the chemical firms in developing and marketing new synthetic yarns, such as nylon and polyester. The use of continuous filament yarns led to improvements in the precision of looms.[2] The developments in nylon yarns in the 1950s resulted in increases in the speed and use of warp knitting machines. The introduction of polyester yarns led to great improvements in the productivity and patterning ability of circular knitting machines. Improvements in yarn properties have facilitated the development of the tufted carpet industry. The use of synthetics has also led to the growth of a completely new machinery sector, that of texturising machines, where the natural-fibre-like properties of bulkiness and texture are imparted to the yarn. There have also been many associated developments in dyeing chemistry and technology, and many new machines are available for dyeing and printing both synthetics and synthetic/natural-fibre mixtures.

At the same time, many small increments of technical change have greatly improved the performance of all classes of textile machinery. In many cases, a radical change will trigger off an extended series of improvements; but without the initial breakthrough, these incremental changes could not have occured. Most of the technically more radical innovations since the Second World War, including those that have enjoyed the most marked commercial success (e.g. open-end spinning, shuttleless looms, electronically controlled knitting machines) were developed initially by manufacturers outside the UK.

THE UK INDUSTRY: STRUCTURE AND PERFORMANCE

In 1951 total employment in the UK textile machinery industry was 75,000; by 1973 it was 38,000. This employment is situated mainly in relatively poor areas. During the same period the total number of establishments declined, from 460 in 1951 to 177 in 1973. The total number of enterprises in the industry has remained at roughly the same level since the late 1950s, and nearly all of them are British-owned. In terms of net output per employee, firms employing fewer than 300 are considerably less efficient than their larger counterparts; and firms in the size range 300–1499 have gained an increased share of both net output and employment from larger firms (Department of Industry, 1977). Three firms dominate the industry today: Platt Saco Lowell (preparatory to spinning, texturising and twisting machinery), Bentley Engineering (knitting machinery) and James Mackie (jute and baste processing machinery). They account for nearly half the industry's output, and the top 25 firms account for about 80 per cent of total net output.

The market for textile machinery is very international, and the UK industry consistently exports about 75 per cent of its output. Table 7.1 lists the percentage of exports of the UK, West Germany and Switzerland to the nine

TABLE 7.1 Percentage of textile machinery exports to the EEC and developing countries from UK, West Germany, Switzerland

	Percentage of Exports		
Country	*1964*	*1969*	*1975*
United Kingdom			
EEC	23.5	26.7	19.6
Developing countries	32.6	29.7	35.7
West Germany			
EEC	37.1	32.0	24.2
Developing countries	22.4	26.7	34.1
Switzerland			
EEC	53.1	41.6	28.7
Developing countries	14.9	23.6	28.9

SOURCE

OECD Trade Statistics Series C, 1964, 1969, 1975.

TABLE 7.2 Sales per employee in nine countries in 1974 in textile machinery

Country	*Sales (£1,000)/Employee*
Switzerland	14.4
Japan	14.3
Netherlands	13.9
West Germany	11.8
Belgium	11.6
USA	11.5
France	11.2
Italy	7.1
UK	6.8

SOURCE

Department of Industry, information supplied to the author (1977).

countries of the EEC and to developing countries in 1964, 1969 and 1975. It shows the historical bias of UK exporters towards developing country markets. It also shows the recent trend of exports from all three countries towards developing country markets, and away from the EEC, which reflects the relative decline of the European textile industry, and the growth of textile industries in the low-wage developing countries. The traditional markets of British machinery suppliers are being penetrated by the major European competitors. In common with many other sectors of British industry, the UK textile machinery sector lags behind its major foreign competitors in labour productivity (see Table 7.2).

Figure 7.1 shows that the UK share of world trade fell from 30 per cent in 1954 to about 11 per cent in 1975, while the West German share has consistently been in the region of 30 per cent since the late 1950s, and the Swiss share reached 15 per cent in the 1970s. The UK industry had done reasonably well in 'spinning and extruding machinery' and in 'bleaching, washing and dressing machinery', but relatively badly in 'weaving and knitting machinery'. This reflects a continuation of the drastic decline, which began in the early 1960s, of the UK weaving machinery industry, and the demise between 1970 and 1975 of one of the UK's two major manufacturers of circular knitting machinery.

THE ROLE OF INNOVATION IN COMPETITIVE PERFORMANCE

A relatively low level of capital investment per worker, and a consequently low labour productivity, is often identified as the cause of lack of UK competitiveness in the textile machinery industry. The data presented below strongly indicate that low *technical* investment and poor *technical quality* are equally, if not more, important in explaining the post-war decline in competitiveness.

Without considering each machine type in great detail, it is difficult to obtain precise measures for technical sophistication, and to relate these to export competitiveness. Other measures can, however, be used as proxies for technical sophistication. One such proxy is export unit value (UV). Table 7.3 shows the unit value of UK and West Germany textile machinery exports, and the two countries' approximate shares in world trade in textile machinery for the years 1961/62, 1966/68 and 1971/73. It shows that the unit value of UK exports was consistently lower than that of West German exports, and while the UK share of world trade declined, the West German industry enjoyed an increase in world trade share.

A proxy for innovative activity is patent activity.[3] The data presented in

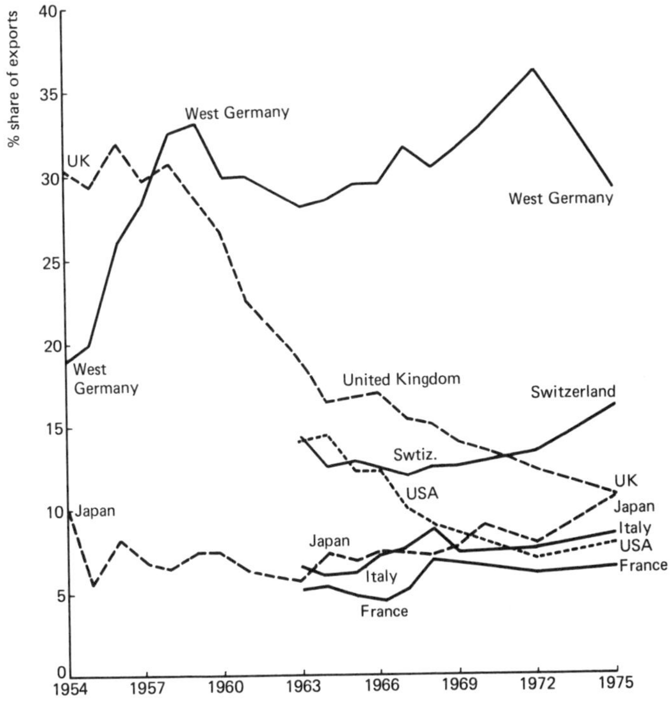

FIG. 7.1 Textile machinery: shares of world trade.

SOURCE
OECD.

Figure 7.2 attempt to relate country exports to the USA to country patent activity in the USA in textile technology. There are problems of causality in interpreting these data. However, taken together with a detailed knowledge of the industry (Rothwell, 1976a), they strongly suggest that trading success has depended to a considerable degree on technical leadership.

There is no doubt that machinery companies which have been 'technically progressive' have survived and prospered during the post-war years. According to one highly progressive managing director in the UK who has, during the past five years or so, been involved in winding up the activities of five former competitors:

> Most of these firms produced excellent machinery which was superbly well manufactured – often better than were my own machines – but the trouble with it was that it had changed little since the nineteen-thirties.

TABLE 7.3 Unit value and trading performance in textile machinery: UK and West Germany

	UK			West Germany			
	Export UV	*Import UV / Export UV*	*Approximate share of world trade (%)*	*Export UV*	*Import UV / Export UV*	*Approximate share of world trade (%)*	*UK Export UV / West Germany Export UV*
1961/62	2.24	1.43	21.5	2.82	0.95	29	0.79
1966/68	2.88	1.25	15	3.53	0.94	31	0.81
1971/73	4.76	1.19	12	6.31	0.73	33	0.75

NOTE

$$\text{UV} = \text{Unit Value} = \frac{\text{Value in thousand dollars}}{\text{Number of units}}$$

SOURCE

OECD Trade Statistics, Series C.

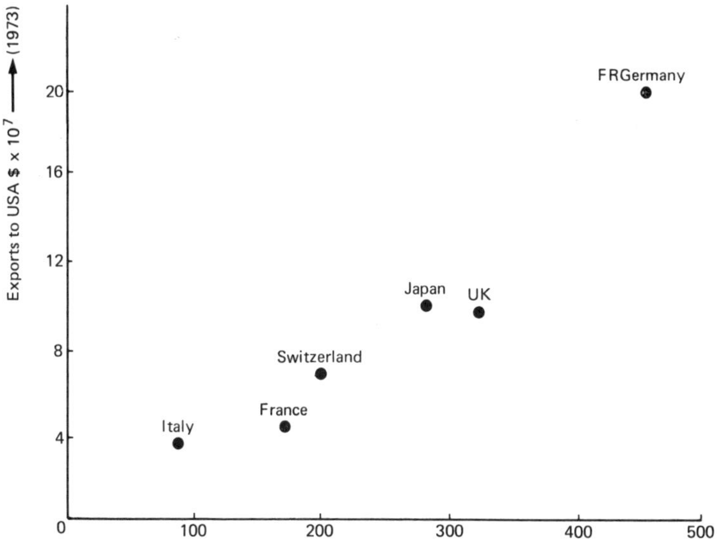

FIG. 7.2 Exports to USA and patents registered in USA in textile machinery

No. of Patents issued to country by US Patents Office in Textile Technology between 1970–1973

Textile technology is defined as the following US patent classes: 68 (fluid treatment apparatus), 19 (fibre preparation), 57 (spinning, twisting and twining), 28 (miscellaneous texturing, felting, warp), 26 (cloth finishing), 38 (ironing and smoothing), 66 (knitting), 139 (weaving).

SOURCES

Exports: OECD
Patents: Office of Technology Assessment and Forecast (1974).

Several instances can be quoted where firms have declined from positions of dominance twenty-five years ago to positions of near-oblivion today because they failed to update their machines sufficiently and to produce new models. British Northrop in the UK, for example, which was the first firm in Europe to produce the automatic loom in the 1930s, declined rapidly from the early 1960s onwards owing mainly to its lack of machinery development (Rothwell, 1975). A second company, Wilson & Longbottom, in contrast, pursued a vigorous innovation policy and is now technical and market leader in several specialist loom areas.

A third company, which had produced little real innovation since 1945, saw its traditional markets being eroded by its major competitor's more modern machines. In an attempt to protect its market share, the firm finally began a crash programme of technical development and, within a short time, was outselling its competitor, which had in turn become complacent. Five years after this turn-around, the firm was in such a strong position that its competitor was manufacturing 20 per cent of the firm's orders under licence.

Probably the person best qualified to determine the importance of technical sophistication in competition is the machinery *user*, who must make the decision whether or not to pay a premium for the more advanced models, or to purchase less sophisticated models more cheaply. A recent survey (Rothwell, 1977a) of more than one hundred textile companies in the UK set out to discover, among other things, the reasons why companies acquired foreign-built machines in preference to machines built by the home industry.[4]

TABLE 7.4 Reasons for UK textile companies purchasing foreign-built machinery, 1970–1975*

Reasons for Purchasing Decision	*Number†*	*Percentage*
Not available in UK	39	27
No suitable UK alternative	15	11
Superior overall performance and design of foreign machines (more reliable, more productive, greater operational efficiency)	45	32
Foreign machinery technically more advanced in design	19	13
Better service provided by foreign suppliers (i.e. spares and after-sales service)	8	5.5
Foreign-built machinery cheaper	6	4.0
Foreign manufacturers more aware of specific user requirements	5	3.5
Total	143	100

NOTES

* 89 per cent of the 107 companies completing the questionnaire bought foreign machinery during the period 1970–76.

† A number of respondents gave more than one reason for buying foreign.

SOURCE

Rothwell (1977a).

The results of this survey are shown in Table 7.4. The most frequently quoted reason for buying foreign (32 per cent of the total) was the superior performance of foreign-built machines: foreign machines were more reliable, more productive and offered greater operational efficiency. A related reason (13 per cent of the total) was that foreign-built machinery was technically more advanced in design. This means that, in those cases where UK machinery was available, 62 per cent of the reasons for buying foreign related to the performance or 'technical quality' of the machinery. Further, it was clear that, in most instances where companies bought foreign because there was 'no *suitable* UK alternative' (11 per cent of the total), 'unsuitable' meant machinery of poorer quality: foreign-built machines were 'generally better engineered' or 'worked better' than their UK counterparts. Since price-competitiveness appears in only 4 per cent of replies, this is a clear indication that textile companies (in the UK at least) are not willing to sacrifice quality in order to buy cheap.

FACTORS AFFECTING TECHNICO-ECONOMIC PERFORMANCE

The data presented in this section are taken from the results of a three-year study (Rothwell, 1976a) of some fifty innovations in more than twenty textile machinery companies in the UK and the rest of Europe. The sample included both successful and unsuccessful innovations, and both firms which continue to enjoy prosperity today and firms which, for various reasons, are no longer in existence. The period covered by the study was from 1945 to 1976. A number of factors significant in the technico-economic performance of firms emerged; the most significant of these are described below.

Qualified scientists and engineers in R&D

The increasing incidence and growing commercial importance of radical technical change has been reflected in an increased requirement for companies to employ graduate-level engineers and scientists, and to establish formal R&D departments. The most successful of the major post-war textile machinery innovations have been associated with the presence of one or more graduates in the firm, and with a formal, systematic R&D activity.

Table 7.5 shows that the more radical of the successful post-war textile machinery innovations introduced by UK companies were often associated with the presence of qualified scientists and engineers working in a formal R&D laboratory.[5] The 'incremental' innovations, on the other hand, were associated with non-graduates and a 'design and development' (D&D)

TABLE 7.5 Characteristics of the development department – radical and incremental innovators

Question	*Response*	*Classification*			
		Radical		*Incremental*	
			Concentration		*Concentration*
Does the firm have a formal R&D Department?	Yes	14		2	
	No	6		13	
If not, does the firm have a formal D&D department?	Yes	5		1	
	No	1		2	
Does the firm have:					
(*a*) Both?		6		1	
(*b*) Neither?		1		2	
How many non-graduate engincers were associated with development work at the time of the project (average no./firm)?		6	0.8%	3	1.3%
How many graduate engineers were associated with development work at the time of the project (average no./firm possessing graduates)?		3.4[a]	0.45%	1.7[a]	0.75%
How many graduate scientists were associated with development work at the time of the project (average no./firm possessing graduate scientists)?		2.2[b]	0.3%	2.0[b]	0.88%

NOTES

[a] These are the average number for firms that actually employed graduate engineers. *Two radical innovators and seven incremental innovators did not employ a single graduate engineer in development.*

[b] These are the average number for firms that actually employed graduate scientists. *Seven radical and thirteen incremental innovators did not employ a single graduate scientist in development.*

SOURCE:

department. The average size of the UK companies that produced the radical innovations was twice that of the companies producing incremental innovations.

The employment of technically skilled managers, particularly graduate-level managers, is also increasingly important. Out of a sample of 20 successful radical innovators and 15 successful incremental innovators, 55 per cent of chief executives were qualified to chartered engineer level (35 per cent graduates) whereas in the case of incremental innovators only 35 per cent were qualified to this level (26 per cent graduates).[6]

It is instructive to compare the levels of R&D expenditure and the employment of technical personnel in the industry in the UK and West Germany. In 1974, the average R&D expenditure as a percentage of sales in the UK was 1.4 per cent; in West Germany the corresponding figure was 2.05 per cent. In the same year, the percentage of scientific, technical and draughting personnel in total employment in the UK textile machinery industry was 5.6; in West Germany, 16.4 per cent of all employees were 'technical' employees, while 10 per cent of employees were occupied in R&D and construction. This goes some way towards explaining the higher level of technical sophistication of West German textile machines.

The home market

Since more than 70 per cent of UK textile machinery production is exported, the level of home demand might not appear to be critically important to the success of UK machinery suppliers. What is important for innovation, however, is the *attitude* of the home market towards the use of new machinery, particularly towards the testing of prototype machines. A conservative home industry (management and operatives) did little for many years following the Second World War to assist, or to stimulate, UK textile machinery manufacturers to innovate. This still persists, in some degree, in the wool and worsted part of the UK textile industry, particularly within smaller firms.

Textile machinery firms in West Germany and Belgium, for example, did not meet the same level of conservatism. The greater willingness of local customers to test prototypes and take up new manufacturing techniques aided and stimulated other Western European machinery producers in their efforts to innovate. The early involvement of textile mills in the development of novel textile-processing techniques also greatly assisted the innovative activities of textile companies and government institutes in Eastern Europe. However, with greatly increased levels of concentration and verticalisation in the UK textile industry during the last decade or so, this situation has changed dramatically. Large, go-ahead companies have proved their willingness to accept, and have even demanded, new and improved machinery.

Customer/producer interaction

The more successful textile machinery companies are, in general, considerably more market-orientated than are their less successful counterparts. A study of twenty-five successful UK textile machinery innovations (fifteen radical, ten incremental) looked at, among other things, the firms' motivation to innovate. (Rothwell, 1976c) In the case of radical innovations, 70 per cent arose in order to meet customers' needs as perceived by the innovating organisation; 18 per cent arose as a result of the innovators' desire to take advantage of a new technological capability; the remaining 12 per cent were initiated in order to strengthen the firm's market position compared to its competitors. For incremental innovations, 40 per cent arose in response to the perception of user needs, 40 per cent were the result of a customer's direct request, and the final two innovations were made to strengthen the firm's market position. For incremental innovations, market factors predominated and technological factors figured hardly at all.

While most textile machinery innovators established some contact with potential customers about new developments – where there were failures the amount of contact was often slight – the majority of *successful* innovators took this process one step further by actively collaborating with customers during the course of the development.

Many UK companies have suffered because of their unwillingness to provide an efficient after-sales maintenance service, to deliver spares on time, and to offer a comprehensive operative training service. The more successful machinery firms recognise the need to train users in the right uses and limitations of new equipment, and to teach them the appropriate trouble-shooting techniques. This requirement is particularly strong in the case of the more radical innovations.

The Empire

The complacency of many British firms after the Second World War was bred because of earlier lack of competition in protected Empire markets. Since these firms generally continued to enjoy high sales, mainly to developing countries (in 1963, 40 per cent of UK textile machinery exports still went to the Far East and Commonwealth countries), the consequences of this complacency went unnoticed, or ignored, for many years. By the time machinery manufacturers realised that they produced only obsolete machines, it was often too late for them to do anything about it.

In the new textile machinery areas, however – texturing, carpet tufting – where there was no tradition of sales to Empire markets, UK textile machinery firms have consistently been among the world's technical and market leaders. These companies appear to have been led by a new breed of manager, willing and able to face competition in the more sophisticated markets of the world, and unaffected by the traditional attitudes prevailing elsewhere in the industry.

Firm Size

The ability of firms to employ graduate engineers and scientists working in a formal R&D environment obviously depends in part on their financial resources and, indeed, the average size of UK companies producing radical innovations was twice that of firms producing incremental innovations. Lack of R&D resources is by no means that whole story; a radical new machine must be manufactured to the necessary high degree of precision, and in sufficiently large numbers to satisfy demand. This further imposes requirements on the innovator to establish a comprehensive distribution network and efficient after-sales servicing and operator training courses, all of which entail the expenditure of considerable resources beyond the capacity of small firms in most areas (in small specialist markets, however, small firms have proved able to cope with these factors). In addition, the sales team involved in selling a machine which embodies a high degree of technical novelty will often need to include technical specialists; this imposes further pressure on a company possessing only limited resources. Two non-UK companies did, in fact, experience great difficulty through lack of distribution and after-sales servicing facilities, when they produced technically advanced innovations destined for large markets. They both overcame their difficulties by reaching agreement with large, well-established companies, whereby the latter would handle sales and after-sales servicing.

One other advantage large companies have over their smaller counterparts is their ability to offer an integrated range of machines. At least one small (125 employees) innovative UK supplier in the highly fragmented finishing sector has suffered at the hands of foreign competitors, because of its inability to supply a related range of products.

Production efficiency

Foreign competitors have generally been more aware than their UK counterparts that careful design, linked to highly efficient production planning and control, can keep down the cost of machinery. For example, despite the fact that its production machinery was in the main twenty years older than that of its major UK competitor, one US company had higher labour productivity than the UK firm; this was achieved by more efficient production procedures linked to a smaller employment of indirect labour staff, and a much better linkage between design and production. (A comparison between similar machines built by the two firms showed that the American machine needed 50 per cent less labour input in its manufacture than did its UK equivalent.) A second foreign company, this time in continental Europe, linked its design so closely to its (highly efficient and modern) production procedures that seventeen separate models could be produced simultaneously on a single 17-station production line (Rothwell, 1976c). Its major UK competitor, on the other hand, said that it would sometimes hold up production of new machinery to produce an out-of-stock, and sometimes quite complex, spare part for a machine sold many years previously. While the non-UK company has thrived, the UK firm has undergone very marked decline. A third foreign company, again in continental Europe, through constantly improved production procedures linked to economies of scale, held the price of one key component constant for nearly a decade, which guaranteed the firm a very large share of the world market for that component.

The major UK textile machinery companies have recently become more aware of the importance of efficient production procedures linked to development and design. One company will, in the near future, be offering electronic in place of mechanical controls on one of its machines, primarily because of the relatively low labour content involved in the use of the former. A second major company has taken steps to integrate its R&D, prototype design and production efforts at an earlier stage in the development process. UK firms also appear to be using production engineers (either in-house or consultants) increasingly in planning and costing for production and in devising improved production techniques. A number of UK companies have complained of difficulty in attracting skilled production workers, and one or two have told of problems associated with shoddy workmanship during production. Several firms have suggested that the reluctance of production workers to accept new production machinery and techniques has placed UK machinery firms at a disadvantage compared to foreign competitors.

Management style

Those firms that have a horizontal, consultative management structure are generally the most successful innovators: this applied particularly to the R&D and marketing functions. Managers who consult at all levels within their organisations are also those who are readier to accept the need for innovation and change in their machinery. The UK textile machinery industry has suffered greatly from too many Dickensian firms, controlled by autocratic and often highly conservative managing directors.

There appears to be a growing professionalism among the more progressive UK textile machinery managers, with an increased use of formal corporate planning, and the formulation of explicit innovation and marketing policies, which they see as a valuable management tool in determining R and D expenditure, identifying new markets, and the forward planning of production runs.

Role of Government

The impact of the UK Government on innovation in the textile machinery industry has been significant. Seven out of fifteen radical innovations, and three out of ten incremental innovations, had direct Government support. In three of the radical innovations, the support was direct financial assistance (one from the National Research and Development Council; two from development grants); in one case the support involved technical assistance, while in two instances the nature of the support was unspecified. In one case of incremental innovation, Government support was obtained under the pre-production order scheme; for the other two incremental innovations the nature of the support was unspecified.

The R&D infrastructure

Although there is not a Government-supported research association (RA) devoted to the textile machinery industry, there are several textile industry RAs, which have made a valuable contribution to technical progress in textile machinery. Fundamental work by the Shirley Institute on the relationships between machine parameters and yarns and fabric properties has helped machinery manufacturers to design better machinery. The RAs have also made more direct contributions to machinery development through both technical problem-solving and direct machinery design. Perhaps one of the most valuable contributions by RAs has been the introduction, by the Shirley Institute, of the 'technical economy' technique to machinery producers. Several universities have also been used by textile machinery companies in the UK in the areas of technical problem-solving, new machinery design and improved production methods. These interactions have generally met with only limited success (Rothwell, 1978).

CONCLUSIONS

Technical innovation has been, and is, an extremely important determinant in the export competitiveness of textile machinery. Outside the 'new' machinery areas (texturising, carpet tufting, computerised control of knitting machines), the UK textile machinery industry has generally been less innovative than its main European rivals. *Radical* technical change has become increasingly significant during the post-war years. The fact that *successful* radical technical change has been associated with a formal R&D department staffed by qualified engineers, and sometimes scientists, has clear policy implications. Means must be found of injecting a higher level of technical expertise into those firms in the textile machinery industry which currently do not employ graduate-level engineers and/or scientists. The fact that the total number of scientists and technologists employed in the UK textile machinery industry fell by nearly 14 per cent between 1968 and 1973, and R&D expenditure fell by 30 per cent during the same period (the corresponding average drop in R&D expenditure for all mechanical engineering was 22 per cent), should be a cause for some concern on the part of both the industry and the UK Government, given that the major threat to the UK industry at present comes from companies in Western Europe producing technically sophisticated, high-quality textile machinery.

NOTES

1. This chapter draws heavily on information collected in an earlier and longer study (Rothwell, 1976).
2. While the total number of looms produced in the UK fell by 30 per cent between 1945 and 1968, the number of looms for weaving man-made fibres remained fairly constant.
3. For a fuller discussion of the uses and abuses of patent statistics, see Chapter 3.
4. As part of the same survey, UK textile machinery companies were asked to give their reasons for the UK textile machinery industry's drastic post-war decline in world trade share. 30 per cent of responses gave 'a general lack of development effort' as the prime reason.
5. These data were taken from a sample of 25 UK textile machinery firms.
6. The sample of 35 firms was taken from the UK, West Germany, Holland, Belgium and Switzerland.

REFERENCES

Cotton Industry Working Party Report (London: HMSO, 1946).

Committee of Investigation into the Cotton Textile Machinery Industry, Report (the Evershed Report) (London: HMSO, 1947).

Department of Trade and Industry, *Report on the Census of Production: Textile Machinery, 1963 and 1973* (London: HMSO, 1968 and 1977).

Department of Industry, information supplied to the author (1977).

Organization for Economic Cooperation and Development (OECD), *Commodity Trade Statistics*, series C (Paris: published annually).

Office of Technology Assessment and Forecast, *Technology Assessment and Forecast, Third Report*, US Department of Commerce (Washington DC: USGPO, 1974).

R. Rothwell, 'British Northrop: A Case of Decline and Renaissance', *Textile Institute and Industry* (Nov. 1975).

R. Rothwell, *Innovation in Textile Machinery: Some Significant Factors in Success and Failure*, Occasional Paper no. 2, Science Policy Research Unit (University of Sussex: SPRU, 1976a).

R. Rothwell, 'Picanol Weefautomaten: A Case Study of a Successful Machine Builder', *Textile Institute and Industry* (Mar. 1976b).

R. Rothwell, 'Innovation in Textile Machinery: The Results of a Postal Questionnaire Survey', *R&D Management*, vol. 6, no. 3 (June 1976c).

R. Rothwell, 'Technological Innovation in Textile Machinery: The Role of Radical and Incremental Technical Change', *Textile Institute and Industry* (Nov. 1976d).

R. Rothwell, 'Users' and Producers 'Perceptions of the Relative Importance of Various Textile Machinery Characteristics', *Textile Institute and Industry* (July 1977a).

R. Rothwell, 'Innovation in Textile Machinery: The Czechoslovak Experience', *Textile Institute and Industry* (Dec. 1977b).

R. Rothwell, 'Some Problems of Technology Transfer into Industry: Examples from the Textile Machinery Sector', *IEEE Transacting on Engineering Management* (Feb. 1978).

8 Innovation in Coal-mining Machinery: the Case of the Anderton Shearer Loader

Joe Townsend[1]

This chapter describes and analyses the introduction of the most important innovation since 1945 in the British coalmining industry – the Anderton Shearer Loader (ASL). The first section describes briefly the background to mechanisation in coal-mining; the second analyses the impact of the diffusion of the ASL on increased labour productivity in the 1950s and 1960s. The analyses are followed by assessments of the contributions of both the National Coal Board (NCB) and the machinery suppliers to the development and improvement of the ASL. The chapter ends with some policy conclusions about the coal industry's productivity, the machinery suppliers in international markets, and – more generally – the mechanical engineering industry.

THE BACKGROUND TO MECHANISATION

Until the Second World War diffusion of mechanisation within the industry was was slow. The percentage of total output cut by machine had taken 25 years to rise from 1.4 in 1900 to just under 20, and a further 13 years to reach 60 per cent in 1938.[2] The most significant advance towards mechanisation came with the publication of *Coal Mining*, the report of the Technical Advisory Committee to the Ministry of Fuel and Power (Ministry of Fuel and Power, 1945). The report envisaged a more flexible power loader as well as a special type of face conveyor, which could be moved bodily sideways by mechanical means several times in the course of a shift without any need for dismantling. It also recognised that the technique of the industry was inseparable from its organisation. Government handling of the industry after the war was vitally affected by these findings.

On nationalisation in 1947, the urgent need to satisfy an energy-starved industrial economy, in the face of a scarcity of technical and human resources, stimulated the initial drive to mechanise. The Coal Board embarked on two quite new policies for the industry: preparation of a fifteen-year plan of resource development and the establishment of a structure for the application of science in the industry. Increased coal production was considered the Board's primary task, and resulted in a concentration on the installation of machinery underground at the face.

Output per man-shift (OMS) increased from 20.6 cwt in 1946 to 24.5 cwt in 1951. However, the returns from underground mechanisation began to fall off in 1952. The new sinkings were planned to achieve OMS rates of up to 50 cwt in those collieries where conditions were favourable.

THE DIFFUSION OF THE ANDERTON SHEARER LOADER

New advances in technique could sustain further productivity increases. The period from 1947 to 1955 was one of intensive experimental development of new types of machine designed to solve the specific problems of completing the integrated mechanisations of cutting, loading and conveying at the British coal-faces. Many different machines were developed, tested and used, but ultimately the Anderton Shearer Loader (ASL) proved the most robust, versatile and productive in the conditions prevailing in most British mines.

Figure 8.1 shows the shearer's progress up to 1972 by comparison with all mechanisation. As shearer technology developed, many improvements were made on the prototype design, which enabled it to be applied on a still wider scale and with much greater effect. The technical basis had been laid for a sharp rise in productivity in the 1960s. However, there was a slowing down of diffusion of the ASL in the late 1950s, primarily because the first generation of machines tended to cut too much small coal for the market requirements of the time, and was not yet suited to the narrowest seams. Further technical improvements, discussed later, overcame the ASL's limitations in the 1960s.

Mechanisation 1955–65

Concurrently with the development and diffusion of the ASL the coal industry began to experience major competition from other sources of energy, with serious consequences for both its market and its mechanisation programme. Fuel oil from British based refineries had increased in price only half as much as coal from 1950 to 1960. In addition, technical changes in the capital equipment of the gas, rail and steel industries had made big changes in their fuel consumption, and in all three areas coal demand was to fall drastically by 1967/8. Coal prices generally had nearly doubled during the 1950s. However, from 1961 to 1966 several factors combined to hold them fairly steady. These were the early impact of the ASL-based mechanisation

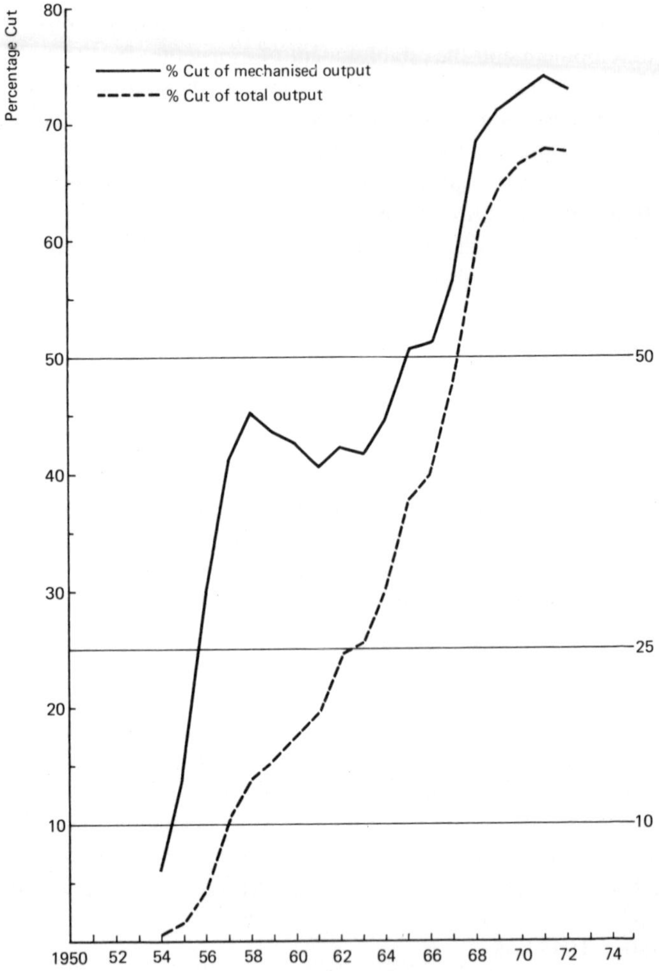

FIG. 8.1 Percentage of deep-mined coal cut and loaded in the UK 1953–1972

SOURCE
Townsend (1976) table 8 (based on data from NCB Statistics Dept.).

campaign and government measures to assist the industry. But prices were bound to rise again if productivity failed to keep pace with rising costs. Thus, with industry experiencing considerable pressure to contract its output, the impetus to mechanise the face assumed even greater urgency. Along with increased mechanisation, NCB's rationalisation plans included a programme of colliery closures and redeployment of a dwindling labour force.

Rationalisation 1965–75

From 1965 to 1974 the approach to mechanisation changed. The most important new direction was dictated by the decision to restrict the conveyor-mounted power loaders and self-advancing hydraulic props to the best faces, rather than applying mechanised methods to the widest possible range of coal-faces in the 500 or so remaining collieries. The *percentage* of mechanised longwall faces more than trebled during the period, although the total *number* of faces declined from 3603 in 1960 to 997 in 1971; of the 3603, 27 per cent (1973) were mechanised in 1960 and 89.1 per cent (888) were mechanised in 1971. The average number of mechanised faces per colliery dropped from 5.2 in 1960 to 3.4 in 1971, while OMS increased from 28.9 cwt in 1960/61 to 46.0 cwt in 1974/5 (see Figure 8.2). These figures reflect the triple impact of closures of uneconomic pits, increasing mechanisation, and concentration on high-producing faces. The proportion that each of these contributed to productivity increases is difficult to estimate. Posner (1973) calculated that about a quarter of the improvement in OMS from 1963 to 1970 could be attributed to colliery closures.

Comparison with technological diffusion processes in other manufacturing

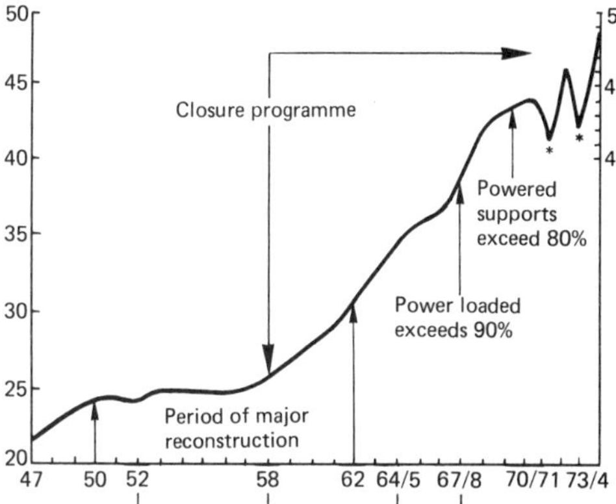

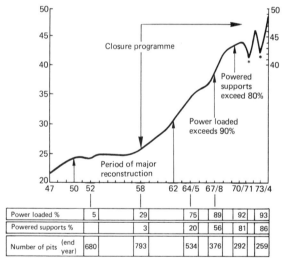

Power loaded %	5	29	75	89	92	93
Powered supports %		3	20	56	81	86
Number of pits (end year)	680	793	534	376	292	259

FIG. 8.2 Overall OMS (UK)

SOURCE
NCB Archives; from a paper prepared by T. R. Carr (MRDE)

* Industrial disputes

industries (Nabseth and Ray, 1974, Scott, 1975) shows that the ASL rapidly reached 25 per cent of its potential diffusion. The 'hiccough' in its advance from 1958 to 1962 meant that it achieved the 50 per cent benchmark a little more slowly than the average for six major manufacturing innovations analysed by Scott. If 75 per cent of total mechanised output is taken as the ceiling for ASL penetration, rather than 100 per cent, then the ASL diffusion was more rapid than average for the manufacturing innovations. At the same time, the overall rate of coal-face mechanisation was more than twice as fast as the diffusion of coalcutters in the pre-war industry.

A programme was begun in 1967 to establish a number of faces which could achieve 1000 tons per shift. Overall productivity was intended to rise to 75 cwt per manshift by the early 1970s. Unfortunately, the programme's efforts did not produce the expected results, and OMS showed no sign of reaching even 55 cwt by 1975. The causes of the setback are complex. Apart from the obvious impact of two major labour disputes in 1972 and 1974, there was the delayed impact of the drastic fall in investment in the coal industry. By 1968/69, colliery investment was (in real terms) running at less than half the expenditure of the 1950s, and the investment earmarked for major schemes declined from more than £50 million per annum in 1958/59 to £11 million (at current prices) in 1968/69. Related to this very sharp fall was the failure of OMS 'elsewhere underground' to keep up with coal-face productivity. While 'Face OMS' in 1972/73 was 148.8 cwt/per manshift, and had risen 44 per cent since 1965, 'elsewhere underground' it was 97.8 and had risen only 25 per cent.

The ASL alone could not solve the problems of raising productivity. Although it contributed a great deal, sustained high productivity growth required other complementary innovations, especially in underground haulage, and improvement in management and labour relations. However, the development of the ASL and its successful modification and improvement to cope with a great variety of geological conditions are extremely important in the history of the mining industry. The next section therefore examines in detail the contribution of the machinery-makers and the NCB to the continuous improvement of the ASL over a 20-year period.

THE ROLE OF MACHINERY SUPPLIERS

The principal firms

Before the Second World War, the only major new machine introduced was the Meco-Moore cutter-loader, launched by Anderson Boyes in 1938. The pre-war market provided little encouragement to innovative design and development, but Anderson Boyes had a particularly good record of technical advance, based in part on emphasis on good professional qualifications.[3] Mergers and growth subsequently made Anderson (Strathclyde) Limited the dominant British firm in the industry. British Jeffrey Diamond (BJD), the other major British firm, was taken over by a US mining and construction machinery firm in the late 1940s. By 1950, these firms were medium-sized engineering concerns employing about 1500–2000 men each. Anderson (Strathclyde) Limited employed about 5000 in 1975. The German firm of Eickhoff was established earlier than Anderson Boyes, but did not specialise in mining machinery until just before the First World War. It remained a family firm until the 1970s.

It was these firms – one British, one American-owned (but designing and manufacturing in Britain), and one German – which were to become the principal suppliers of the ASL. All had already made important contributions to mining technology, and their successful performance is evidenced by consistent application for and exploitation of patents, accumulation of registered designs, increased share of the expanding market for their products in the mechanisation of coalmining, concentration of effort, the continuous improvement of their standard products, and prompt incorporation of new ideas and materials into their technology.

The acute coal shortage all over Europe in the early post-war years created exceptionally favourable conditions for innovation in machinery. Anderson Boyes first introduced the drum-shearer principle, which was subsequently exploited in the ASL, in a comminuting machine for the French potash mines as early as 1946.

The origins of the Anderton Shearer Loader

The novelty of the ASL did not lie in any radically new engineering principles. It lay in the new combination of older devices to solve the peculiar problems of mechanising British coal-faces. The innovation can perhaps best be compared with the tank, which was simply a combination of an armoured, tracked vehicle with mounted weapons. None of the components was new, but the combination marked a radical innovation which transformed military technique. Like the tank, the ASL required a stream of adaptive follow-through improvements to allow it to be used in a variety of conditions, to improve its power and reliability, after the first radical breakthrough. The breakthrough did not come from any professional R&D group or establishment, but from what was essentially a group diverted from production and maintenance work in the National Coal Board. It was the result of work by a small team, authorised by J. Anderton, a General Manager, and led by

T. Lester, a mechanisation engineer, consisting of two fitters, a blacksmith and one draughtsman.

The Disc Shearer was put to work on 23 June, 1952. The first run of the machine was described by Lester as follows:

> It took the whole weekend to get it positioned on the 150 yard face; we had no idea how it would perform, so we switched on and hoped for the best. . . . we could not see what was happening because of the noise and dust; we knew it was advancing because the rope was winding, so we positioned ourselves . . . to see what was happening, and happening it was, spewing coal at a frantic rate, at least for them days. One of my apprentices remarked: 'By gum, Mr. Lester, I could watch that bloody thing doing that all day!' and that is precisely what we did.[4]

During the first few months of operation, fifty modifications were made to the machine. The prototype conversion, materials, time spent on design and development work covering work on the gearbox, deflector plough, plough connection, underframe, cable carrier, dust suppression devices and discs cost £2400 plus 98 per cent workshop overhead charges, totalling under £4800.[5]

Manufacture and licensing

By the middle of 1953 the disc shearer loader was beginning to assume an importance which could not be ignored by the suppliers. Its further development and manufacture were being pressed by the NCB, who saw not only the cutter loader gap being filled, but an opportunity to exploit an NCB innovation here and overseas.

From 1954, the suppliers in the UK embarked on fairly ambitious programmes of design and development, producing successful prototype shearers before the end of that year. The three companies had been negotiating licences with the NCB from 1953, although this did not immediately affect the UK companies because no licence was required for supply to the NCB. But licensing from the German company was very important. Eickhoff had supplied very little machinery to the NCB, but the German firm was among the first to recognise the importance of the shearer. From 1953 it began to convert its own standard coal cutters, and in 1954 produced a purpose-built 68 h.p. shearer exhibited at the Essen Trade Fair.

Further development

New models were introduced by all the three main suppliers. In each generation, regardless of the source of the solution to the problem, an accumulation of small or incremental changes usually followed its introduction. Such a new model might include one or several major (patented) innovations, or have been designed to have special application (e.g. thin seam shearers), but it also contained a substantial amount of incremental change accumulated since the preceding generation of shearers was introduced.

Over a 20-year period the machine became very much more powerful and productive, as a result of this process of continuous improvement and change. The early models were only 70 h.p., but by 1974 each of the three major manufacturers was producing 400 h.p. models. It also became much more robust and versatile. Almost every component of the machine underwent a series of changes and altogether nearly 1000 discrete technical improvements were identified from NCB archives, from manufacturers' records and from published sources.

Contributions to improvement and change

In addition to a large number of purely mechanical improvements, there was a continuous series of innovations affecting the electrical and hydraulic systems, and at a later stage the electronic steering systems. Dust suppression and safety were other major areas of technical advance. Between 80 and 90 per cent of the patents taken out by the machinery suppliers could be classified as essentially mechanical inventions or devices, and almost all the remainder as electrical, mainly to do with the motor and its control system. Only about two-thirds of the NCB's innovations, on the other hand, could be classified as mechanical. About a quarter were concerned with electronic control and sensing devices and steering systems, and the remainder (about 7 per cent) were concerned with dust suppression and safety. This suggests that the NCB, with its greater scientific and laboratory resources, took the lead in tackling the more complex problems of control systems. Their technical solutions were incorporated by the manufacturers in the later models of the 1960s and the 1970s.

The NCB must be credited with the original major innovative step, but the machinery manufacturers contributed a great deal to the improvement of the design. Both the NCB and the machinery firms thought it important to take out patents whenever they made a major technical advance. Consequently, our view is that the number of patents is an approximate measure of innovative effort.

Thus measured, all three principal suppliers contributed significant innovations to the ASL's further improvement. Their combined contribution was 44 per cent of all patents relevant to the ASL, whilst other manufacturers contributed a further 19.8 per cent, compared with 36.4 per cent from the

NCB. For innovations directly concerning the ASL, the figures were little different, with the NCB accounting for 38 per cent (Table 8.1).

On this basis, the manufacturers made a somewhat larger contribution on the ASL's improvement than the NCB itself. However, as we have seen, it was the NCB that accounted for a high proportion of the electronic and system innovations, which might perhaps be considered more important. To test this hypothesis, all the patented innovations were weighted on a scale from one to four, the most important innovations being given the highest weight. This weighting inevitably involved subjective judgements, but whenever possible independent evidence and assessments were used to supplement archives and interview information. The weighting made very little difference to the earlier conclusion that the machinery manufacturers contributed over 60 per cent

TABLE 8.1 Shares of NCB and suppliers in patented innovations, 1956–75.

Organisation	*Direct ASL Innovations*		*Indirect Innovations*		*Total Innovations*	
	Number	*%*	*Number*	*%*	*Number*	*%*
NCB	116	38.0	33	31.7	149	36.4
BJD	16	5.2	2	1.9	18	4.4
AB, M & C } AM	54	17.7	16	15.4	70	17.2
Hoy	20	6.5	12	11.5	32	7.8
Eickhoff	63	20.6	28	26.9	91	22.4
Other	36	11.8	13	12.5	49	12.0
Total	305	100	104	100	409	100

NOTES

BJD = British Jeffrey Diamond
AB = Anderson Boyes
M & C = Mavor and Coulson
AM = Anderson Mavor

SOURCE

NCB Archives and Patents Office.

of the significant innovations, after the NCB developed the first prototype. The NCB's 'weighted' contribution is almost the same as its 'unweighted' one.

The role of R&D

The earliest stages of inventive and development work on the ASL were initiated and implemented outside the NCB's formal R&D system. The supplier firms needed strong design and development facilities, and they all thought in those terms ('D&D') rather than in terms of Research and Development ('R&D'). This made sense in terms of the type of function they were performing in the 1950s and 1960s – mechanical inventions and their incorporation in successive new models of their machines. But it means that original work on new control systems or new materials was generally beyond their reach. A more formal R&D system was necessary for these types of development, and it was here that the NCB's much greater resources enabled it to make a major contribution in the 1960s. This was possible, however, only because the reorganisation of the NCB's R&D and engineering establishments brought the research into much more intimate contact with the design and development.

THE ROLE OF THE NATIONAL COAL BOARD

The NCB's R&D establishments

On nationalisation, the NCB set about establishing a more satisfactory and comprehensive R&D organisation. The first Coal Research Establishment (CRE) was created in 1948 and concentrated on the chemistry and processing of coal. A second establishment, the Mining Research Establishment (MRE), was set up at Isleworth, Middlesex, in 1952, to deal exclusively with problems connected with underground work. However, its location some hundred miles from the nearest coalfield meant that any prototype mechanical device had to travel that distance for field trials. The NCB therefore set up an engineering research facility closer to the scene of the action in 1954 – the Central Engineering Establishment (CEE) at Bretby near Burton-on-Trent. Until the CEE was established at Bretby most mechanical engineering development took place at divisional or colliery level.

The 1957/58 R&D programmes led to the first major new developments for the ASL. The MRE had begun instrumentation trials of the ASL, and research on the effects of power loading on the size and quality of coal produced. This research proved crucial in helping to solve the product degradation problems, which had arisen in the first five years of ASL use, and had slowed down its diffusion.

The combined total expenditure on coal-face mechanisation rose from 30 per cent of all R&D on mining technology in 1960 to 40 per cent in 1962, remaining between 40 per cent and 50 per cent of the total thereafter. The mining technology budget was usually about 60 per cent of the total NCB R&D expenditure,[6] which means that the work on coal-face mechanisation generally accounted for about a quarter of all the Coal Board's R&D. The proportion that has gone directly into ASL development has been diminishing as the wider problem of total underground development and automation has tended to subsume the work on any particular machine. In 1969 the CEE and the MRE were combined in one establishment – the Mining Research and Development Establishment. By 1971, when the MRDE was fully reorganised, there were still 35 projects affecting the ASL, out of a total of 124 projects. The number of projects directly concerned with the ASL had fallen from 21 to 14, whilst the number indirectly affecting it had increased. About two-thirds of the NCB's patented innovations related to the ASL came from the research establishments, but other sources (mainly the awards scheme, described below) were particularly important for the unpatented innovations.

Testing and appraisal

Between 1960 and 1972, an increasing amount of the Coal Board's R&D expenditure was allocated for testing and appraisal. With the development of major facilities for destructive and non-destructive testing of materials, manufacturers' equipment and prototypes, this area accounted for a quarter of all expenditure on applied technology by 1970. Simulations of underground conditions were built at the CEE and a test site established for use by the CEE and manufacturers' staff to test equipment. Many of the changes suggested by the CEE were incorporated into subsequent production models of manufacturers' equipment of components. 'Tested at Bretby' became an important feature in manufacturer's' publicity, and was often stamped on the equipment. The NCB was also able to develop prototypes and test these at its own experimental coal-faces, so that the machinery makers were able to benefit from a wide range of tested incremental design improvements with each new model that was introduced.

The incentive award scheme

With almost 1000 collieries and the engineering workshop facilities that went with them, the NCB inherited a large reservoir of un-coordinated expertise connected with the mining and processing of coal. In order to tap this source of knowledge, the NCB created an awards department, which offered cash incentives for ideas in technology. The Board's idea was not simply to mobilise the non-professional reservoir of experience, but to use the communication facility provided by the NCB's comprehensive information network to disseminate the ideas.

From an examination of records of awards made since inception, it has been possible to assess the contribution of the Award Scheme to shearer technology.[7] Between 1952 and 1974, more than 4500 individual awards were made. Of 634 with direct or indirect application to shearers, 45 won national awards, that is about one seventh of all the awards made under the scheme and one sixth of the national awards. Of the 634, about 40 were ultimately patented, representing about one third of all the ASL innovations patented by the NCB.

In coalmining, as in many other industries, local non-patentable adaptations of machinery and equipment are an extremely important part of the exploitation of innovations. Taking into account the variation in seams and coal-face conditions throughout the British coalfields, the awards scheme gives a fair indication of the scale and importance of this local adaptive learning process.

The number of awards rose rapidly in the 1950s and 1960s, and continued at a fairly high level in the 1970s, despite the sharp decline in the total number of men employed in the mines, and the increasing contribution from the NCB's professional R&D establishments. However, those applying to coal-face cutting and loading were diminishing, both absolutely and relatively. The increase in electronics awards indicates the shift of attention to steering control and other electrical systems.

Award winners have been divided into two groups: (A) professional or qualified, and (B) non-professional. (A) includes mechanical or mining engineers, electrical engineers, geologists, metallurgists, chemists, colliery managers, under-managers, etc. (B) includes fitters, blacksmiths, electricians, overmen, deputies, miners, machine operators, washery operators, foremen, supervisors, etc. Group B have consistently received a slightly higher proportion of the awards than Group A in the collieries and the workshops. Only at the Divisional level, as might be expected, do professionally qualified people contribute a higher proportion of award-winning innovations. The professionally qualified Group A contributed almost exactly the same total number of award-winning ideas as Group B for the years 1955/56 and 1967/68, but in 1973/74 Group B contributed a higher proportion of awards. This indicates the extent of user involvement in innovation at all levels. Even in the electronics area, awards were by no means monopolised by professionally qualified people. In general, about half of all the awards were won by men who, although they may have been craftsmen or other skilled tradesmen, did not possess the higher types of professional qualification.

Interchange of technical information and liaison within the industry

The discussion so far has shown that many different sources contributed to the incremental improvement of the ASL over a 20-year period. The complexity of the machines, the sheer number of components and modifications, and the variety of operating conditions, meant that there was an imperative and increasing need for good technical liaison, if all those affected were to be kept abreast of the rapid pace of technological change. The CEE and the MRDE at Bretby assumed an increasing responsibility for the dissemination of technical information and for liaison.

For the machinery manufacturers, an important contribution was made by the technical representatives of the companies in the field as well as links between their own R&D and that of the NCB.[8] The relationship of these companies with the NCB became particularly intimate in the 1960s. Most of the technical representatives or service engineers were former employees of the NCB. They are still quite numerous (one company has over 60) and are usually qualified mining or mechanical engineers. Most of the boards of the two UK companies, including the chairmen and managing directors, are ex-NCB, as are 75 per cent of upper and middle management. A substantial number of personnel on the workshop floor, in the drawing office and elsewhere also had experience within the NCB.

Another important factor has been the very liberal licensing policy followed by the NCB in relation to its original ASL patents, and the later ones. In effect, the NCB has made its technology available to the whole British mining machinery industry, in return for similar openness on their part. The comparatively small amount of cumulative royalties earned by the NCB over 21 years (£300,000) may have been well justified in terms of speedy dissemination of new technology. For similar reasons, the arrangement with Eickhoff seems to have been sensible and mutually beneficial. Eickhoff contributed at least as much as the other machinery suppliers to the improvement of the ASL, particularly in the development of models suitable for narrow seam working. The application of the machine in the German coalfields also had an important 'demonstration effect' for other markets for which Eickhoff were not licensed. The import of some machines by the NCB from Eickhoff seems to have been quite justified for three reasons. First, they increased supply at a time of acute shortage of machines and labour. Second, they provided an important competitive check on British suppliers for quality, price and delivery. Third, they made available some specialised machines and a feed-back of technical information, including that from Eickhoff's technical representatives in the field.

CONCLUSIONS

Future prospects

High and potentially increasing oil prices have made coal's future more buoyant than in the 1960s. In Britain, the long-term future for coal seems assured. Investment expenditures have increased and new pits will offer much greater possibilities for mechanisation and high OMS. Given the new interest in expanding world coal output, there will also be great possibilities for expanding exports of deep coalmining equipment to such regions as North and South America, China and India. By comparison with other sectors of engineering, the British industry has had an excellent export record. Between 1945 and 1970, Anderson Boyes exported about 42 per cent of its production of short-wall coal cutters. Table 8.2 shows that, from 1965 to 1977, British exports of underground coalmining machinery remained slightly ahead of those of Germany, whilst those of the machinery sector as a whole were diminishing from 65 [illegible] cent to 45 per cent of the German total.

Continued export success will depend on a number of new or additional elements: access to detailed, and regularly up-dated knowledge of developments in major export markets; a recognition that conditions in overseas markets, especially in the third world, require a very different approach from that normally practised in the past; in particular. The services offered by exporters are at least as important as the hardware. These could include training and consultancy, geological support services, equipment assessment and testing services, and financial provisions. The trend towards the development of complete mining systems by consortia has made joint research, design and development by the NCB and the machinery suppliers an essential aspect of technological innovation and competition on world markets. The establishment of Powell-Duffryn/NCB consultants (1973), and recent debates about the industry's strategy in NEDO and elsewhere, should increase British firms' awareness of potential export markets. The skills and know-how of the NCB and machinery suppliers must now be exploited on world markets, just as they have been in the past to increase the mechanisation of British coalmining.

TABLE 8.2 Exports of underground coalmining machinery: UK and Germany

	1965	*1966*	*1967*	*1968*	*1969*	*1970*	*1971*	*1972*	*1973*	*1974*	*1975*	*1976*	*1977*
Coalmining Machinery[a] Exports from UK (£m)[b]	–	19.6	20.6	22.5	28.4	29.6	36.8	39.2	45.4	68.9	83.1	96.4	89.6
Coalmining Machinery Exports[a] From FRG (£m)[b]	–	17.2	18.7	20.8	20.2	17.9	33.1	41.7	50.9	70.9	81.8	96.7	81.9
$\frac{UK}{FRG}$ for underground Coalmining Machinery	–	1.14	1.10	1.08	1.40	1.06	1.11	0.94	0.89	0.97	1.02	.997	1.09
$\frac{UK}{FRG}$ for all machinery[c]	0.65					0.50					0.45		

NOTES

[a] These tables are compiled from the UN 5 digit SITC which corresponds to the commodity sub-classes of the Brussels Tariff nomenclature 8-digit (UK) or, in the case of the FGR, the 6-digit Nimexe classification. There is some overlapping of commodities within each sub-class (e.g. some parts totals and some parts classes include machinery and spares for surface mining, some conveyors are for general mining), but where possible both sets have been made compatible and refer to underground coalmining and preparation machinery and process equipment. Included are: tunnelling, boring, cutting/loading machinery and parts, underground conveyors, haulage engines, winders and parts, sorting, washing and preparation machinery and parts, mining tools (interchangeable), various roof supports, strate control equipment and parts.

[b] Exports are measured in current prices.

[c] Machinery as Groups 71 and 72 in SITC.

SOURCES

UK: Overseas Trade Statistics of the United Kingdom, BOT/DM/DOT (1969–1977); H.M. Customs and Excise returns (1969–1977)
FRG: Aussenhandel Statistische Burdesaut, Series 2, 3 (1969–1977)

Policies for innovation

Although this chapter has concentrated on one machine, its conclusions have implications for industrial and Government policy. They show how much can be achieved if a powerful buyer of equipment interests itself strongly in the technical improvement of its machinery. The NCB was effective, not only because of this or because it held the original patents, but because it had the technical and scientific resources to talk with manufacturers at least on equal terms in relation to technical problems and their resolution.

The role of laboratories and establishments like those of the NCB is likely to become a more important focus of work in other mechanical engineering products. They will become increasingly concerned with whole systems, and collaboration between suppliers and between suppliers and users will become even more important. Although the incremental improvements in technology are still overwhelmingly mechanical in nature, the contribution of electronic, nucleonic and other more science-based engineering disciplines is growing. The experience of testing by the NCB confirms the experience of firms, such as IBM, which use their testing procedures as a major institutional screen to ensure high quality of development, and consistency with user requirements and with relevant Government policies and legislation.

In so far as it is possible to generalise from this case, one of the implications for the Research Requirements Boards, for NEDO and for industrial strategy is that in each sector of mechanical engineering the following questions should be among those asked:

In this sector, are there buyers (whether public or private) who use their procurement power to effect technical improvements?
Could this power be more effectively harnessed and expressed?
If not, what surrogate mechanism can be devised?
Is there in this sector a satisfactory institutional focus of user/innovator collaboration in technical development?
Are there in this sector R,D&D facilities, capable of relating mechanical engineering developments to new developments in science?
In what ways are inventive ideas from outside the formal R,D&D channels, solicited, stimulated, evaluated and disseminated?
Is there any scope for awards schemes or other institutional devices to galvanise this process?

NOTES

1. Much of this chapter is based on data from Townsend (1976).

2. Output cut by machine but hand loaded in a three shift system is different from mechanised output which refers to coal cut and loaded by power loaders in sequential or single operation.
3. One of the founders of the firm, Daniel Burns, studied at Coatbridge Technical College and Glasgow University and later held the Chair of Mining Engineering at the Royal Technical College in Glasgow. Alexander Anderson assisted Daniel Burns in his teaching after qualifying as a draughtsman through evening classes. His nephew, Forrest Anderson, who became the leading figure in the company from the 1930s to the 1970s, had degrees both in electrical and mining engineering, as well as a Mine Manager's Certificate.
4. Description given in a personal interview with T. Lester.
5. Letter from J. Anderton to I. Sclare, NCB Patents Office (22 April 1954) in NCB File no. AH 24080/1.
6. NCB Archives and Annual Reports.
7. NCB Award Scheme, File no. AB 17190, parts 1 to 13 1951/75, NCB Archives, Deneby Main, Hobart House, Anderton House.
8. In an interview with Mr Forrest Anderson of Anderson-Mavor Limited, in 1975, Mr Anderson suggested 'the main reason for our constant technical success is that from the beginning we were told to "keep our nose to the coal-face", as it's the only way to get to the problems, because that is where the problems are.'

REFERENCES

Ministry of Fuel and Power, *Coal Mining*, (the Reid Report), Report of Technical Advisory Committee, Ministry of Fuel and Power, Cmd 6610 (London: HMSO, Mar. 1945).

L. Nabseth and G. F. Ray, *The Diffusion of New Industrial Process: An International Study* (London: Cambridge University Press, 1974).

M. V. Posner, *Fuel Policy: A Study in Applied Economics* (London: Macmillan, 1973).

T. W. K. Scott, 'Diffusion of new technology in the British and West German carpet industries: The case of the tufting process', DPhil. thesis presented at University of Sussex 1975 (unpublished).

J. Townsend, *Innovation in Coal Mining Machinery: 'The Anderton Shearer Loader – the Role of the NCB and the Supply Industry in its Development.* Science Policy Research Unit, Occasional Paper 3 (University of Sussex: SPRU, Dec. 1976).

9 Forklift Trucks

Peter Senker[1]

INTRODUCTION

The UK forklift truck industry is a post-war industry. Between 1951 and 1961 production nearly trebled, as it did between 1961 and 1971; it reached 24,000 in 1974, but has declined sharply in the recent recession (Business Monitor, 1951–76).

THE NATURE OF THE INDUSTRY

The forklift truck industry consists of firms which design, assemble, market and distribute forklift trucks, and also supply spares and service necessary to keep those trucks in operation. Forklift trucks are assembled partly from components also used by the automotive industries (e.g. transmission components), and partly from more specialised components (e.g. hydraulics, forks, fork carriages). Bought-in components account for a substantial proportion of works-costs for all forklift truck manufacturers – as high as 85 per cent in some cases. Some firms manufacture somewhat higher proportions of their own components, or buy them from associated companies rather than on the open market.

Because of the relatively low proportion of value added accounted for by manufacturing activities, forklift truck manufacturers deploy a high proportion of their resources in such service functions as purchasing, stock control, kitting up, design, sales, marketing and after-sales service (including provision of spare parts). The principal production process is assembly in batches by conventional techniques, except that numerically controlled machining of batches of components is used increasingly.

Whilst the general-purpose truck still serves adequately as a mechanical handling workhorse, it has some disadvantages for some applications. Manufacturers have developed a large number of variants of forklift trucks, in order to mechanise a wider range of materials-handling operations. There has also been steady development of performance arising from the adoption of improved components: For example, electronic controls, principally based on thyristors, have been adopted widely on electric trucks (Senker *et al.*, 1977, pp. 9–22).

MARKET REQUIREMENTS

The market for forklift trucks is largely industrial and commercial, with growing agricultural and construction industry demand. The public sector market – principally nationalised industry (in particular the National Coal Board) – accounts for a very small proportion of total sales – perhaps 5–10 per cent. Hire to meet peak load problems has accounted for an increasingly important share of truck usage. About a quarter of the trucks bought in this country are for hire fleets, a substantial proportion being owned by subsidiaries of forklift truck manufacturing companies.

Users are concerned to acquire trucks well adapted to their materials-handling systems, and sufficiently strongly built to work reliably. A Dutch study on innovation in materials handling concluded that the usefulness of products rather than low initial cost was most important in determining the competitive performance of innovative products (TNO, no date, p. 41). Customers' satisfaction with forklift trucks depends on the efficiency and reliability with which their trucks perform their assigned tasks, and on the overall costs associated with operating them. These costs include not only the initial purchase costs and the costs incurred in operating them and keeping them in operation (drivers' wages, fuel, maintenance, etc.), but also costs imposed on customers' total materials-handling systems by forklift trucks' downtime. Customers especially those who use their forklift trucks intensively, have a great interest in ensuring that, when the trucks do break down, service and spares are readily available, so that expensive downtime is minimised.

THE NATURE OF COMPETITION IN THE INDUSTRY

There have been two basic routes towards success in the forklift truck business. One involves establishing market leads through product innovation and preparedness to modify trucks to meet varying customer needs. The other involves cost reduction through standardisation of components among different models of trucks and, in the case of multinationals, among countries, in order to reduce production and other costs (Senker *et al.*, 1977, pp. 48–9).

Even though this strategy has been the one favoured by the US multinationals who have been relatively successful, the US firms have not achieved sufficient competitive strength to impose standardisation on the market. The Dutch study (TNO, no date, p. 28) also found that new products were more important than new production processes in materials-handling markets.

The leading firms in the industry, both UK-owned and US-owned, have adopted, or are in the process of adopting, goals of long-term profitability, and formal procedures devised to achieve them (Senker *et al.*, 1977, pp. 43–8). The nature of the forklift truck business, in particular the key role played by parts and service in both profitability and market share, means that efficient planning and coordination are essential elements in firms' efforts to achieve their long-term goals. Many companies have attempted to increase their market share by promoting their trucks as more reliable than other manufacturers', but there is no evidence that any manufacturer has succeeded in convincing the market on any scale that any particular range of trucks is consistently superior in this respect.

Three UK-based firms have placed major emphasis on securing technical leads. However, only one succeeded in adopting coherent and effective policies based on using innovations as a means to secure leadership of major market segments. This firm coordinated all its policies, including marketing, sales promotion and pricing, to maximise the benefits from its innovations. At least two other UK-based firms have tried to be innovative. One used innovation as a basis for building up market share in one market segment, but much of the profits derived from this were dissipated in the attempt to build up market share where the firm had no significant competitive advantages. In another firm, research and development were not part of a coordinated strategy, and innovative products made little contribution to the firm's progress. Most of its profits were derived from selling standard trucks slightly below the market price set by major competitors.

The US owned multinationals with manufacturing facilities in the UK have aimed to offer adequate products to the major segments of the market, to standardise as much as possible, and to achieve economical production of trucks which meet the principal needs of most users (Senker *et al.*, 1977, pp. 92–104). Two UK firms also set up assembly lines for manufacturing standardised products: one very early in the industry's development, and the other in the early 1970s. Neither was successful, largely because neither planned the necessary marketing, financial and distributional support which success in such a project demanded. More recently, however, the Japanese have achieved some market success with standardised small to medium-capacity trucks produced in volume on assembly lines. These products have achieved some initial market penetration in the UK, especially as industrial workhorses for the short-term hire business (Senker *et al.*, 1977, p. 137). *All* firms attempt to some extent to achieve the advantages of standardisation, but some assign a greater relative priority than others to product innovation and to meeting customers' varying needs.

Most firms recognise that effective provision of parts and service is crucial to their success. Failure tend to lead to customer dissatisfaction with the forklift truck manufacturer concerned, and to loss of repeat sales. Firms vary considerably in their performance of after-sales service. Further, the provision of service and spares offers a significant source of potential profits to established forklift truck manufacturers. (Senker *et al.*, 1977, pp. 67–8).

WORLD TRADE AND MARKET SHARES

The UK accounted for about 7 per cent of world production of forklift trucks in 1974 (NEDO, 1977, p. 14). In recent years, there have been significant changes in the proportion of various countries' shares of total OECD exports. OECD countries account for the vast majority of world forklift truck exports, the only other significant exporter being Bulgaria.

From Table 9.1 it can be seen that there has been no significant decline in the UK's export share since 1970. The decline in the US share can be attributed largely to decisions by US multinationals to locate their production increasingly in the growing European market rather than in the US. Placing manufacturing facilities near to customers has obvious advantages for products as heavy and bulky to transport as forklift trucks.

TABLE 9.1 Major countries' shares of OECD world exports of forklift trucks, 1970–75

Country	*Export share (%)*					
	1970	1971	1972	1973	1974	1975
UK	15.9	18.7	17.3	15.7	14.7	15.9
West Germany	15.4	17.7	18.1	19.5	19.7	17.1
Japan	10.5	11.6	13.8	14.1	16.1	12.0
US	29.6	23.0	22.4	21.6	21.6	22.5

SOURCE

OECD, 1970–75.

TABLE 9.2 Proportion of imports in UK home consumption of forklift trucks trucks, 1970–5

	1970	*1972* (by value £m)	*1974*	*1975*
Imports	4.4	6.1	18.9	20.9
Home consumption	37.8	41.9	75.2	80.2
% of imports in home consumption	11.7	14.5	25.2	26.1

SOURCES

HM Customs and Excise, 1970–75; Business Monitor, 1970–75.

While the UK has maintained its share of world export markets in the last few years, the value of imports of forklift trucks to the UK increased very fast between 1970 and 1975 (see Table 9.2).

FACTORS AFFECTING COMPETITIVE PERFORMANCE

The US-owned multinationals are planned centrally from US headquarters. They all place strong emphasis on marketing and after-sales service, employing graduate engineers in marketing and sales far more than UK firms do. They all recognise the key importance of planning and coordinating marketing with the provision of parts and service to reduce costs and achieve long-term profitability. The US multinationals also gain advantages from their sheer size and overall profitability, the geographical spread of their operations, and the diversity of the products they make. Their size and financial strength, combined with better than average forward planning of their requirements, help them obtain better delivery and lower prices from component suppliers than their smaller competitors. Financial strength enables the multinationals to subsidise new ventures until they become self-sufficient, and to build up component and truck stocks in periods of recession, to meet anticipated upturns in demand. Geographical and product spread enables them to 'cushion' recessions in demand in some markets from other, less depressed, markets. The multinationals' geographical spread also helps them diversify their sources of component supply.

Component makers believe that British forklift truck manufacturers are generally slow to accept innovations (Senker *et al.*, 1977, pp. 126–7). For example, a battery manufacturer has claimed that forklift truck makers are slow to respond to innovations which enable batteries to operate longer without recharging, or to innovations making possible more rapid and safer battery changing. Similar suggestions were made by a manufacturer of hydraulic equipment, claiming that manufacturers' response to the availability of more efficient components, such as pumps which operate at higher pressures, is very slow compared to agricultural machinery manufacturers' response. The leading manufacturer of diesel engines claimed that forklift truck manufacturers were slow to accept cleaner engines. In the Dutch study on materials handling (TNO, no date, p. 26), co-operation with other firms, including suppliers, was found to be strongly correlated with innovativeness.

In general, the US-based multinationals were found to be more receptive to the need for component innovations than the larger UK owned firms. But the smaller UK-based firms, with smaller design teams, appear more receptive to new ideas, more inclined to see suppliers helping them with their problems (Senker *et al.*, 1977, pp. 125–7). Thus, the US-based firms appear to their suppliers to be more technically demanding and more professional in their approach to technical development than the UK-based firms. For example, UK firms are not prepared even to consider the adoption of less polluting engines before anti-pollution legislation is enacted. There have also been comments in European markets that UK firms have been slow to metricate.

FUTURE TRENDS

It seems likely that the successful marketing of forklift trucks will depend increasingly on the ability to design and market complete materials-handling systems (Senker *et al.*, 1977, pp. 84–5). In the European warehousing market, in particular, several large companies have already purchased total materials-handling systems, attracted by the possibility of enhancing the overall efficiency of their materials handling. The Dutch study also concluded that innovations involving integrated or turnkey supplies were very successful, most of these innovations being brought about by collaboration with complementary companies (TNO, no date, p. 41).

If large customers can be persuaded to buy complete materials-handling systems, this yields important advantages to suppliers. First, the supplier will naturally design his system around forklift trucks of his own manufacture. Second, a forklift truck manufacturer engaged in designing materials-handling systems as a whole will acquire a depth of understanding of customers' materials-handling needs which can provide a valuable input into development programmes. These may well achieve technical leads which contribute to increased competitiveness.

Manufacturers who market complete materials-handling systems need more complex design, marketing, purchasing and production operations. For example, they need deeper technical feedback from marketing staff; they also need more systematic, science-based research and development. These requirements are likely to increase the need for highly qualified staff, including qualified engineers and technologists at the highest levels in a company. Highly qualified staff, in particular engineers, would need to be spread across more functions than is typical of British-owned forklift firms at present. There would be increased needs for qualified engineers in marketing and sales, and for engineers, technologists and scientists in the design of materials-handling systems and forklift trucks.

Until recently, technological change in forklift trucks has been largely based on mechanical ingenuity rather than on formal science and technology. In these circumstances, British firms' relatively sparse resources of highly qualified manpower were probably not a serious disadvantage. However, in the likely future market and technological environment, UK-owned firms may have serious difficulties in maintaining their competitiveness in the absence of important changes in their recruitment and deployment of qualified manpower.

Another possible future trend is towards standardisation. Outside Japan, the US multinationals have adopted policies biased towards standardisation rather than innovation and diversity. But they have not standardised sufficiently to justify assembly line production. It is possible that Japanese firms will be able to increase their world market share on the basis of trucks manufactured relatively cheaply on assembly lines. But the trend towards the marketing of systems tailored towards customers' total materials-handling requirements may exert pressures on manufacturers that will prevent any substantial expansion in the use of assembly line techniques.

Increased domination of the UK forklift truck industry by US-owned multinationals is a possibility. Three have UK production facilities. In so far as these firms generally use one or two European production facilities as bases from which to export to the rest of Europe, this may have both employment and balance of payments advantages to the UK economy. But the benefits in terms of transfer of skills to local employees may be limited because the US multinationals tend to concentrate certain key functions in the US: in particular, research, development, design, corporate and marketing planning. To the extent that employment in the forklift truck industry relies on the decisions of US-owned multinationals, it is vulnerable to centralised decisions made in the US.

POLICY IMPLICATIONS

The UK has maintained a significant share of world exports of forklift trucks. The challenges posed by innovation based on formal science and technology are only now being felt. This contrasts with textile machinery, where such challenges have already led to a decline in international competitiveness (see Chapter 7).

Recently, there have been several mergers between UK-owned forklift truck companies. This has been partly the result of encouragement from the NEDC Industrial Truck Sector Working Party (NEDO, 1977, p. 1). The British-owned sector does not produce as much volume as some individual Japanese or US companies, and further concentration of the sector is recommended, possibly involving 'synergistic partnerships (not necessarily in equity terms) across EEC frontiers with national producers in France, West Germany and Italy' (NEDO, 1977, p. 3).

The findings of this chapter suggest that such a policy might not make a major contribution to the competitiveness of the British sector: since a high proportion of output is accounted for by bought-in components, production efficiency and economies of scale are not the main keys to success in this sector. Indeed, US multinationals each have production in several countries of the world to be near markets. Success appears to depend more on such factors as incremental innovation and the planning and co-ordination of sales, marketing and spare parts supply. Scale is important in some of these functions, particularly in distribution and service networks. But the key advantages of the multinationals may well reside in efficient centralised planning and control, and the general evidence in the UK that mergers lead to increased efficiency is not strong (Meeks, 1977).

The major problem likely to face the UK forklift truck sector over the next several years will be the maintenance of its generally good record in incremental product innovation in a changing market and technical environment. Innovation is likely to be based increasingly on formal research and development, and there is likely to be a need for more technical depth in the information feedback firms will need from markets. These trends suggest an increased need for centralised planning and control of all aspects of firms' policies. Technical capability in many functions, including design, marketing and top management will need improvement. Government encouragement to firms to employ more highly qualified people, to retrain their manpower in critical areas, and to adopt appropriate planning techniques, could be vital in maintaining the international competitiveness of this sector.

US-based multinationals undoubtedly have certain significant competitive advantages. But some UK companies have grown fast and been profitable.

Thus, one privately-owned UK firm has expanded relatively rapidly both by investment and acquisition, and has not been inhibited by capital shortage. This firm adopted coherent planning earlier than its major UK-based competitors, and was able to exploit its innovativeness to achieve market leadership which provided the basis for growing profits. Other UK firms, also highly innovative, have complained that capital shortage has restricted growth in their operations – particularly the development of overseas distribution networks – but these firms had not yet developed a consistent framework for their planning, nor exploited their innovativeness adequately. Problems of capital availability could well have been partly related to reservations by potential sources of finance about the ability of the managements of particular firms to deploy resources profitably. This chapter has indicated that, in order to be successful in a changing environment, UK-owned firms will need to enhance their planning capabilities and recruit and deploy more qualified people.

NOTES

1. Much of the information in this chapter is taken from Senker, Sciberras, Swords and Huggett (1977).

REFERENCES

Business Monitor, PQ 337, *Mechanical Handling Equipment*, Quarterly Statistics (HMSO, 1973–76).

Business Monitor, *Industrial Trucks and Tractors*, Production Series (HMSO, 1951–72).

HM Customs and Excise, *External Trade Statistics of the United Kingdom* (1970–75).

G. Meeks, *Disappointing Marriage: A Study of the Gains from Merger* (Cambridge: Cambridge University Press, 1977).

National Economic Development Office, *NEDC Industrial Strategy, Industrial trucks: Progress Report by the Industrial Trucks Sector Working Party* (London: National Economic Development Office, 1977).

Organisation for Economic Cooperation and Development, *OECD Statistics of Foreign Trade*, series C (Paris: OECD, 1970–75).

P. Senker, E. Sciberras, N. Swords, C. Huggett, *Forklift Trucks: A Study of a Sector of the UK Engineering Industry*, Report prepared for the Engineering Training Board by the Science Policy Research Unit, University of Sussex mimeo (1977).

TNO [The Industrial Research Organization], *Innovation Processes in Dutch Industry*, The Netherlands mimeo (n.d.).

10 Merchant Shipbuilding and Marine Engineering

Austen Albu

THE NATURE OF THE INDUSTRY

Shipbuilding is generally considered a medium-technology assembly industry, a combination of structural and mechanical engineering. Marine engineering is one of the branches of mechanical engineering, mainly producing power plants. In the past it was an industry steeped in tradition and employing large numbers of skilled men on the heavy work of construction. The myth grew up that apprenticeships and inherited skills were necessary for shipbuilding, but this has been destroyed by the rapid growth of new shipbuilding nations, especially Japan (Venus, 1972). In shipbuilding as in other branches of the engineering industry, the most successful countries in recent years have been those which have applied scientifically based innovations to design, particularly of components, and to production methods.

Most of these innovations have been incremental: for instance improved performance of propulsion machinery, increased size and speed of ships, improved navigational equipment based on the radical invention of radar. Radical changes in this century have included the introduction of steam turbine and immediately afterwards Diesel internal combustion machinery, all-welded hulls and, since the last war, automatic control of engine-rooms. Also, there has recently been a change in construction methods which, starting as a fairly radical innovation, has revolutionised the most important function in the building of the hull: the process by which a ship's plates are cut and formed prior to assembly and welding.

Less radical changes have included the design and building of standard, and increasingly specialised, ships from prefabricated components made and assembled on flow production lines; a system first used in the United States for the construction of Liberty ships during the war and introduced afterwards by the Japanese. Standard ships had been built on the Clyde in the 1890s and during the 1914–18 war (Moss and Hume, 1977). Although the covered berth was first introduced in British yards early in this century, the fully enclosed yard was a Swedish innovation. Most of these innovations have been easily transferable, sometimes under licence, but British yards were slow to adopt them. Very little in-house R&D is carried out by British shipbuilding firms; most by Government-supported research institutions, by Lloyds Register, by universities and by units of the Ministry of Defence.

ECONOMIC PERFORMANCE

The proportion of world shipping built in British yards declined concurrently with the decline in proportion of world shipping that was British-owned (from 49 per cent in 1900 to 11 per cent in 1970). The really drastic decline, however, took place in the 1950s with the phenomenal rise in Japanese output, while the Japanese merchant fleet was being built up from one of the smallest to one of the largest in the world (Table 10.1).

At present the British industry, in common with all others, is suffering from the world slump in shipbuilding orders, due mainly to the collapse of the tanker market. One effect of this has been to bring the Japanese, whose original extraordinary growth had been based on large tanker (very large crude carrier) construction, more into the market for special product and dry-cargo ships.

During the post-war period, British shipyards became less and less competitive and were unable to offset the decrease in the British-owned proportion of the world mercantile fleet, from which the bulk of their orders had come, by building for foreign owners. Even British owners began to place substantial orders abroad. British yards failed to take advantage of the enormous expansion of demand for ships after the war, reflected in an increased tonnage from 69 million gross registered tons in 1939 to 222 million tons by 1970, and were building less tonnage in 1970 than they had been in the 1920s and 1930s. Abroad, in contrast, shipbuilding capacity had increased to meet the demand, so that by 1960 West Germany had overtaken Britain in numbers of ships built and almost in tonnage, while Japan had jumped to top place in both. As can be seen from Table 10.1, Japan's growth was more in tonnage produced than in number of ships built, as was that of Sweden, which moved into second place in tonnage produced. By 1974, at the beginning of the shipbuilding slump, Britain's share of tonnage completed had fallen to 3.6 per cent, a figure it appears to be maintaining (Lloyds Register of Shipping).

Western European countries now face not only Japanese competition but also that of new nations developing shipbuilding capacity, among them Brazil, South Korea and Taiwan. In Eastern Europe, in addition to East Germany,

TABLE 10.1 Percentage of world shipbuilding output by leading countries by number and gross registered tons

	UK		*Japan*		*Sweden*		*Germany*		*France*		*Spain*	
	No.	*g.r.t.*	*No.*	*g.r.t.*	*No.*	*g.r.t.*	*No.*	*g.r.t.*	*No.*	*g.r.t.*	*No.*	*g.r.t.*
1900	57.1	62.6	0.2	0.2	0.9	0.3	5.4	8.9	4.8	5.1	0.1	0.1
1930	44.4	51.2	3.4	5.2	2.9	4.6	8.5	8.5	1.7	3.5	1.2	0.9
1950	27.1	38.0	9.6	10.0	6.2	10.0	17.1	4.4	5.1	5.2	2.5	0.8
1955	19.1	27.7	13.0	15.6	6.6	9.9	26.8	17.5	3.8	6.1	2.3	1.4
1960	12.5	15.9	32.1	20.7	4.3	8.5	12.6*	13.1*	2.7	7.1	3.7	1.9
1965	6.9	8.9	31.1	43.9	1.8	9.6	9.3*	8.4*	4.7	3.9	7.6	2.4
1970	4.8	6.3	36.8	48.3	1.4	7.9	6.5*	7.8*	4.7	4.4	4.6	4.3

NOTE

* West Germany only

SOURCE

Lloyds Register of Shipping

Poland has now entered world markets. World demand over the next few years is likely to be between 12 and 13 million gross registered tons annually, representing about one third of world output in 1976. Governments have increasingly turned to protective measures, including subsidies, extended credit terms, funds for reorganisation, grants for financing ships built on a speculative basis, naval orders and investment premiums on new ships built in home yards. Britain appears to have remained competitive for naval vessels, the proportion of tonnage of which rose from 10–12 per cent in the 1950s and 1960s to over 20 per cent by 1965 and over 30 per cent by 1970. In fact, British yards have become increasingly dependent on warship orders, whether for home or export (see Chapter 6). However, it is not conducive to efficiency to build both types of ship in the same yard.

During the 1960s anxieties about the performance of the British industry had already led to a plethora of enquiries, all of which emphasised the main causes of its decline as poor management and inflexible labour (DSIR, 1960; Shipbuilding Enquiry Committee, 1966; Patton, 1962; Booz, Allen and Hamilton, 1973). All reports drew attention to poor levels of productivity compared with competitors. The Department of Scientific and Industrial Research report of 1960 showed that no improvement had taken place in gross tonnage produced per person employed between 1946 and 1959. Average construction times in months during the period 1957–59 were: United Kingdom 19, Germany 10, Sweden 9 and Japan 8; these differences were too great to be explained entirely by differences in the types of ships constructed (DSIR, 1960, p. 7). Comparative studies underlined the effect of the unwillingness of workers to work on tasks outside their normal trade group (Patton, 1972; British Productivity Council, 1959). Industrial disputes caused delays and led to management being unwilling to accept penalty clauses for late delivery (Peat, Marwick, Mitchell and Co., 1961). Labour relations in the industry had been bad for at least a century, and demarcation disputes go back to the days of wooden ships (Webb and Webb, 1901). On the other hand, management had been traditionally authoritarian and working conditions poor. The main complaint of British shipowners had for some years been the excessive delays in completion; but lack of quality control has recently been frequently mentioned. A report written in 1972 pointed out the danger of the industry falling behind its competitors in terms of price, delivery, labour relations, technology, development and capital investment (Booz, Allen and Hamilton, 1973).

One of the advantages enjoyed by many foreign firms has been the use of modern yards built on green field sites. This has been difficult in Britain for social reasons and has added to the difficulties of modernising the layout of yards, often situated on congested sites. The one example of a brand-new, covered yard has been very successful; although only in building small and medium-sized ships.

THE INFLUENCE OF TECHNICAL CHANGE ON ECONOMIC PERFORMANCE

While most criticisms of the industry have concentrated on poor management, bad industrial relations and low productivity, there is little doubt that there has also been a serious decline in the relative technical competitiveness of the British industry. The nineteenth century was a period of radical innovation in the design of ships. Britain led in the introduction of iron hulls in the 1830s and steel hulls at the end of the century. Specialised construction of cargo carriers and passenger liners was a British innovation, and an important innovation in methods of ship design was the use of experiments on ship models begun by W. Froude in 1856 and taken up by the Admiralty.

In propulsion machinery, British reciprocating steam-engines led the way during the middle of the century, although they were falling behind at the end. The screw propeller, although probably first used in the USA, was first introduced generally in ocean-going ships by Britain. The Parsons steam turbine was a major British innovation, the internal combustion engine being introduced by licensees of the German Dr Diesel, of which Danish and Swiss firms took the lead. Both these new forms of propulsion were the products of university engineers. In the nineteenth century, British construction methods were the pattern copied in the countries building up a shipbuilding industry and in Germany, for instance, most of the special machines employed were of British make (Lehman-Felkowski, 1904).

Between the two world wars there were no radical changes in ship design or construction, with the important exception of the introduction of all-welded in place of riveted construction of the hull. Originally introduced in Britain, its rapid diffusion was delayed partly by the cautiousness of the Admiralty and the classification societies, but also by the difficulty during the economic depression of redeploying the large number of riveters employed in the yards. The Germans took advantage of the reduction in weight of welded ships to circumvent the London Naval Treaty of 1932.

It is not always possible to locate the source of a particular innovation and, in some cases, an invention will be made in one country and exploited in another (the double helical gear invented in Britain and exploited in the USA, and the welded hull are examples); however, some examples of technical innovation can be attributed with enough confidence to their sources to illustrate the decline of British technical competitiveness (Table 10.2). If a

TABLE 10.2 Main innovations and their origins

Period	*Innovation*	*Chief country of first general adoption*
Nineteenth century (first half)	Iron hull	Britain
	Separation of cargo carriers and passenger liners	Britain
	High-pressure steam-engine	USA
Nineteenth century (second half)	Steel hull	Britain
	Oil tanker	Britain
	Use of model tanks	Britain
	Sub-division of hull and cellular bottom	Britain
	Screw propeller	Britain and USA
	Compound engines	Britain
	Water-tube boiler	Britain and France
	Powered steering gear	Britain
Twentieth century (first half)	Steam turbine	Britain
	Geared steam turbine	Britain
	Diesel engine	Germany
	Longitudinal framing (the Isherwood system)	Britain
	All-welded hull	USA and Germany (first introduced in Britain)
	Tilting pad thrust block	Britain and USA
Twentieth century (second half)	Very large crude carrier	Japan
	Standard ship built in prefabricated units	USA and Japan
	Specialised ships	USA
	Electronically controlled and automatic engine-room	Japan and Sweden
	Advanced steam data for turbines – use of electrical plant manufacturers' designs	USA
	Very large single-shaft diesel engines	Denmark and Switzerland
	Stern oil seals	Germany
	Withdrawable stern gear	USA and Sweden (invented in Britain)
	Keyless propeller fitting	Britain
	Fully covered berth	Sweden
	Optical lofting	Sweden (invented in Germany)
	Photo-electric plate cutting	Sweden
	Numerically controlled cutting and fairing	Sweden, Norway and Britain. Now coming into general use with German and Norwegian equipment

willingness to generate and accept innovations is a prerequisite for maintaining a position in a highly competitive industry, this record of recent British performance compared with that of other countries could be a major explanation for the drastic decline in the relative position of Britain as a shipbuilding nation. Even when British yards had the advantage of building the first of a new type, they failed to maintain a lead. The first roll-on/roll-off ship seems to have been built in Britain for the cross-channel service, but other countries developed it for general use. Although the first ship built to satisfy the extreme conditions required to carry liquified natural gas was a cargo vessel converted at Harland and Wolff's, with American design assistance, by 1976 out of a total of 79 such ships built or on order only two had been built in British yards.

Very few other specialised types such as parcel tankers and chemical carriers, car transporters, large container ships, 'Lash' (lighter aboard ship) vessels, heavy-lift ships, large offshore pipelaying or crane ships have been built in British yards. If the hovercraft counts as a ship, it is certainly a British invention and innovation, but the hydrofoil has been developed in the USA, Italy and Russia. The Japanese lead in large tankers was due not only to far-sighted market research, but also to innovations in design and construction methods and the use of high-tensile steel plate leading to reductions in thickness, weight and cost. The first ship with a number of automated features, including the control of the main engine-room from the bridge and a large number of fully automatic systems was built, with Government support, in Japan in 1961 (Al-Timimi, 1975).

Although the first known experiments with one-tenth scale lofting are believed to have taken place in Britain in the 1920s, the system finally adopted was invented and developed in Germany in the 1950s (Hardy and Tyrrell, 1964). The next stage was the use of a plate cutter controlled by a photo-electric eye following the lines of the drawing. Although again this may originally have been a British invention, the Swedish yards took the lead in its diffusion. The final stage in the development of automatic plate cutting and fairing (fitting the plates to the hull) has been the use of numerically controlled machines leading to computer-controlled methods of design. The use of these machines was first developed by Swedish and Norwegian yards using Swiss, German and American machines in the early 1960s (Hardy and Tyrrell, 1964); but two examples of this system were built in Britain with DSIR support and installed in Britain in 1962. They were too complicated and in advance of their time. Although 'software' for this purpose has been developed by the British Ship Research Association, most of the machinery now in use is of foreign origin. By 1966, the share of steel cut by these new methods had reached 38 per cent in the UK, 48 per cent in Italy, 66 per cent in Germany, 68 per cent in France and 80 per cent in Sweden (National Institute Economic Review, 1969). In each case, although Britain was involved in the original invention, it was left to foreign shipyards and manufacturers to be the first to adopt and develop it.

British technical performance in propulsion machinery has been poor. By the time of the last war, Parsons designs had become conservative. The US Navy, which had depended on Parsons engineering, turned to the manufacturers of electrical plant, with their much higher annual throughput of machinery and extensive research and development, to produce turbines with much higher steam pressures and temperatures; so that the US Navy at the end of the war steamed all round British ships in the Far East (Albu, 1976). The anxiety of the Admiralty led to the setting up of the Parsons and Marine Turbine Research and Development Association (PAMATRADA) in 1944; but although it had a well-staffed research department the marine engine builders, most of which were adjacent to the shipyards, were too small to be able to support it, and lacked the level of technical management to be interested in the results of research. The Association declined into a licensing organisation for Parsons designs and the Admiralty tried again by asking the shipbuilders Yarrow to co-operate with the English Electric Company. This led to the formation of the Yarrow Admiralty Research Department. The original and unpublished version of the DSIR report of 1969 said that machinery built to PAMATRADA designs had poorer fuel consumption than other designs and that engines built in the small British works suffered more breakdowns than those built elsewhere. Today, turbines form only about a third of engines installed in large ships, and 5 per cent overall. The largest number recently installed in British-built ships has been of AEI/GEC design; but more than half of all those built in non-Japanese ships are being built to the design of the Swedish firm of Sta. Laval, while the Japanese design their own.

The trend in diesel engine development has been towards larger and larger engines operating on a single shaft. Only one British firm, Doxfords, has tried to design an engine of this scale and it has so far not been very successful. In the 1950s the English Electric Company (Napiers) developed an original but over-complicated design, the Deltic, which was used by the Navy for small ships. Between 1950 and 1959 the proportion of large marine diesels built to foreign design increased from 25 per cent to 46 per cent. Doxfords' position has been falling rapidly but they may be able to recover with their newly developed range of medium-size, medium-speed engines capable of using low-quality fuel. In the ten years to 1975 the percentage of types of Diesel engine of over 10,000 bhp installed in British ships was: Sulzer 40 per cent, Burmeister & Wain 36 per cent and Doxford 23 per cent (Lloyds Register of Shipping).

Moreover, there seems little evidence of British engine builders making significant innovations in the designs they build under licence. According to the original version of the DSIR report the failure rate of diesel engines, to whatever design, built in Britain engine-works was much higher than that of their competitors. Since that report there has been a concentration of engine-building into larger units.

FACTORS AFFECTING TECHNICAL COMPETITIVENESS

All reports have criticised the inadequacy of marketing management which led to investment decisions that had seldom been based on thorough assessment of their benefits in relation to the market to be served (Booz, Allen and Hamilton, 1973). The design efforts of the industry have tended to be dictated by the short-term demands of the customer rather than directed to longer-term developments for which separate facilities, not tied to the day-to-day work of the yards, were needed. For such longer-term developments, it has been suggested that a larger organisation than a single yard is required. One of the main post-war developments in the shipping industry has been a new 'systems' approach to ship design, intended to provide a streamlined flow of products from producer to importer. British shipbuilders suffered from being slower to develop the new techniques than shipbuilders in other countries; one of the reasons for this appears to have been the failure to develop a relationship between marketing and technology; a view supported by the Rochdale Committee (HMSO, Committee of Enquiry into Shipping, 1970). The owners were partly to blame, being unwilling to participate with the shipbuilders in joint programmes of research.

The failure to recognise the need for a related programme of marketing and technical development in specialised ships is illustrated by the story of the liquid natural gas (LNG) carriers. The attitude of the British shipbuilders of the original two ships has been that they would build more, if they were asked to, and that they could buy the necessary technology. Owners who wished to purchase carriers reported British builders lukewarm to their enquiries and unable to undertake the technical studies needed for the design and development of these very sophisticated ships.

Government support helped the French industry to take the lead in the design and building of LNG carriers, just as the Japanese Government helped their shipbuilders develop the automated engine-room (Yamashita, 1967). British Governments have made no attempt to support risky innovations, their main contribution to the industry being attempts to save failing yards.

When they did support the building of a single ship, it was the uneconomic and originally very conservatively designed *QE2*, fitted with Parsons-designed engines which failed on sea trials. The Shipbuilding Industry Board, established in 1966, was willing to give grants for the introduction of new ship designs, but these were only considered for proposed very large tankers.

Figures for the industry's expenditure on civil research and development are not easy to obtain, partly because several of the yards are naval as well as merchant shipbuilders and partly because some R&D is carried out by component manufacturers, and classified under various industrial headings.

Very little R&D is carried out by individual shipbuilders themselves. The main research organisations, apart from the Ministry of Defence, are the British Ship Research Association (BSRA), which absorbed PAMATRADA, the National Physical Laboratory Ship Division (now the National Maritime Institute) and the British Welding Research Association. In 1958, they spent between them just over a million pounds, of which a little more than a third came from Government (DSIR, 1960). By 1970, the total had risen to £2,540,000. Industry claimed to be spending another million pounds 'in-house' (Select Committee on Science and Technology, 1976), but most of this appears to have been spent on some form of market research or directed towards the operation of ships; only 10 per cent could be claimed as research with general shipbuilding application (Booz, Allen and Hamilton, 1973, p. 49). About £200,000 was spent by universities on contract research. The total represented about 1.7 per cent of the value of output. By comparison in 1972 the United States government provided $25,000,000 for maritime R&D and in 1970 the Japanese spent 9063 million yen (approximately £11 million), of which 20 per cent came from industry and 80 per cent from the proceeds of a special lottery (National Academy of Sciences, USA, 1972).

In 1971/72, the British industry reduced its contribution to BSRA from £500,000 to £400,000 and the Government contribution was reduced from 66.7 per cent of the industry contribution to 60 per cent, reducing the total to £2,350,000. It is a commentary on the industry's attitude to R&D that its reply to the Select Committee's question about investment by the industry in R&D consisted of a short and incomplete statement of the position in 1970. By 1975/76, when the industry's grant to BSRA had not changed, Government support under the new contractual relationships for work sponsored by the Ship and Marine Technology Requirements Board of the Department of Industry had risen to almost £650,000. The Association earned about £400,000 in other contract work and the percentage of this undertaken for foreign companies is now about 25 per cent. The annual expenditure in recent years by the Department of Industry on shipbuilding and marine R&D is illustrated in Table 10.3; but as these figures are at current prices they represent a real fall after the substantial increase of 1975/76.

It is difficult to assess the quality of this research work, or the degree to which it was applied in the industry's day-to-day design and production work. The research has been criticised for not being directed to areas which would have given UK shipbuilders particular competitive advantages and for the low priority given to shipbuilding methods. Since the nationalisation of the industry the Department of Industry's responsibility for R&D has passed to British Shipbuilders.

TABLE 10.3 Department of Industry Expenditure on R&D (£'000)

	1974/5	*1975/6*	*1976/7 (estimate)*
Ship operation	1024	1733	1775
Shipbuilding	240	495	475
Ship design	385	792	760
Marine engineering	433	892	856
	2082	3912	3866

SOURCE

Department of Industry (1977)

Defence expenditure on R&D in 1970 was £37,001,000 but much of this was concerned with nuclear propulsion for submarines, weapons and detection and surveillance systems. By 1977, when the figure had risen to £73,000,000 it was described as being for ship construction and underwater warfare. Some work is being done on propulsion systems and navigational aids; but the different requirements of naval and merchant ships in speed and fuel economy prevent the work on propulsion machinery being transferable (Ministry of Defence, Annual Statements on Defence).

QUALITY OF MANAGEMENT AND STAFF

Perhaps more important than the quality and quantity of R&D carried out by the industry has been the quality of managerial and technical staff on whom the application of its results and the efficiency of the industry has depended. All reports pointed to a low ratio of qualified staff, both in the design departments and in production, compared with that in Japanese and other European yards. This inadequacy became increasingly important as ship and shipbuilding technology advanced. Comparisons of numbers and quality of qualified staff in different countries are difficult to make, not least because, while most professional engineers in other countries have received full-time education in institutions of university level, this was not so in the UK. It had been reported during the last war that the establishment of the Royal Corps of Naval Constructors was inadequate and that in the private yards the numbers of qualified technical staff remained low compared with the engineering industry as a whole – not a very demanding comparison (Board of Education Papers, 1944).

The DSIR report of 1960, in its published version, gave the number of 'graduates or equivalent' in the shipbuilding and marine engineering industries as over 1200; but the vast majority were members of the Institute of Marine Engineers, the qualification for membership of which was a Ministry of Transport (originally Board of Trade) sea-going ticket. This was a qualification for operating machinery at sea, but hardly for designing and developing new machinery. In 1959, of 630 new corporate members of the Institute, only 40 were graduates, many of whom went to work for the classification societies or shipbrokers. At the time of the DSIR report, it was estimated that the total number of graduates in the British industry was 80, half of them employed in the Yarrow Admiralty Research Department. Since then, the number of graduates in the professional institutions has increased, to meet the requirements of the Council of Engineering Institutions.

In 1964, the Royal Institution of Naval Architects undertook an enquiry into the higher education and training of naval architects (RINA, 1966). Recommending a doubling of the number of graduate naval architects and those with Higher National Certificate qualifications employed in shipbuilding, the report drew attention to the fact that this could only take place as existing 'unqualified' staff retired. The number of qualified staff of all kinds (not only graduates and not only naval architects) as a proportion of all employees in shipbuilding and ship repairing had risen from 1:256 in 1949 (1:1687 graduates) to 1:52 in 1964 (1:232 graduates). Although there has been a steady increase in the ten years after the war, the major advance had been made after the changes made in the education system in the late 1950s. The Chapman Report (RINA, 1966) estimated that, (as far as comparisons were possible) for every 1000 shipyard workers, the number of graduates in naval architecture had been:

Japan	17
Sweden	7
Norway	8
West Germany	2
Denmark	7
UK	3 (plus one in another subject, mainly mechanical or electrical engineering)

The German figure seems low, but it appears to cover only Diplomates from the Technischen Hochschulen, whose course takes six years, and not the larger number who graduated from the Ingenieurschulen after a three-year full-time course. Nor does it include the Diplomates in Marine Engineering, who follow the same engineering course as the naval architects for their first two years. Significantly, the report stated that it was rare, if not impossible, for a man who was not academically qualified to rise to a senior technical position in Germany.

The number of naval architects per head of the population was lower than in the countries of our main competitors; in the years 1958–64 it was approximately 0.7 per million in the UK, 4.0 in Sweden, 1.7 in the Federal Republic of Germany (including Diplomates and Ingenieurschulen graduates) and 18.5 in Japan. Less than a third of the British graduates actually entered the shipbuilding and ship-repair industry. One source gave the figure in 1969 as 11 compared with 211 in Japan of whom about a third probably had qualifications equivalent to HNC. In addition, the Japanese recruited 352 graduates in other fields (Baxter, 1971).

By 1976, of 2193 executive directors and managers of British firms employing more than 100 workers, 1123 had technical qualifications but only 153 were graduates while 607 were qualified by reason of membership of a 'professional' body. In addition, there were 391 qualified scientists and engineers, most of whom would have had qualifications equivalent to a university degree (Shipbuilding Industry Training Board, 1977). The proportion of graduates to all employees had risen to 1:167. Obviously it will take some time for the influence of better-qualified entrants to have an effect on the industry's performance, although there are signs of it beginning to happen to some yards.

The industry's long record of bad industrial relations is well known and has led to low productivity and a decline in quality. Owners complain of long delays in delivery and lack of interest in quality control, a criticism confirmed by the classification societies; e.g. Lloyds Register. One of the most serious handicaps to increased productivity has been the rigidity, now somewhat reduced, of demarcation between trades.

The inflexibility of labour becomes an increasing handicap in a period of rapid technological change. No attempt was made by management during the prosperous time after the last war to come to an agreement with the unions to 'buy out' the practices, which often made the introduction of new processes unprofitable. A vicious circle has been created of initial management conservatism and resistance of workers to change, which in practice reinforces that conservatism. The end of the process has been the unwillingness of better-qualified and more entrepreneurial engineers to enter the industry or, if they do, to leave it for other employment, so reinforcing its decline.

CONCLUSIONS

The British shipbuilding industry is now under the control of the nationalised British Shipbuilders which has, at least in theory, responsibility for the structure, the management, the marketing and the R&D of the whole industry. Few can doubt that, in view of excess world shipbuilding capacity, the industry must be reduced in size by the closure of some yards (a difficult task in the face of overall unemployment). Much of the new world capacity is in yards built to the latest standards and employing low-wage and non-union labour. The overseas earnings of British shipping, still owning one of the largest fleets in the world, preclude any suggestion of forcing British owners to buy British ships if they cost more, take longer to deliver, or do not include important innovations compared with those from foreign yards.

As with other medium-technology products, in the production of relatively simple and especially standard ships, the new, low-cost yards will have the advantage. British yards and those of the older industrialised nations will, if they wish to maintain their high standards of living, have to concentrate, with ships as in other branches of engineering, on types with high added values based on R&D and design innovations. It has been suggested that the new shipbuilding nations will not for some time have the reserves of skill and technical knowledge needed to compete in the building of such sophisticated ships (Venus, 1972). For Britain this implies a continued improvement in the employment of highly qualified staff and an increase in R&D.

The current success of one or two standard British ship designs is likely to be short-lived, if they are not up-dated by innovations to suit a changing market. In 1977, there were available from British, Danish, German, Spanish and Japanese shipyards between twenty and thirty types of standard ship, excluding tankers (*Navires, Ports et Chantiers*, 1977, p. 585). Some of the Japanese types are roll-on/roll-off ships; but they are also developing other standard ships of more sophisticated design. In the design of these more sophisticated ships, the British Industry could take advantage of its new structure, which makes possible a central market development organisation with adequate R & D back-up.

This is not to imply that reduction of costs, through increasing productivity by using more advanced methods of building, is not necessary; more R&D should be directed to this end. That it should be long-term and imaginative is emphasised by the Japanese programme, which includes, for instance, work on the automatic welding of ships' plates, the extreme difficulties of which they seem to be overcoming. Of the greatest importance will be the quality and qualifications of managerial staff in the yards and their ability to persuade the various trades who contribute to the building of a ship and their trade unions to forget their past rivalries and to accept the introduction of new plant and new methods. That it can be done is shown by the acceptance by the shipwrights of the substitution of computer-controlled design and plate marking and cutting for the old template loft. In view of the importance of the introduction of new methods at a time when redundancy will become inevitable, the development of policies for reducing the human and social problems involved remains of the greatest urgency.

NOTE

1. I am indebted to a large number of people in the shipping, shipbuilding and related industries for information and help. I am particularly grateful to Mr Alfred Hill.

REFERENCES

A. H. Albu, 'Causes of Decline in British Shipbuilding and Marine Engineering', *Omega* 4: 5 (1976).

W. Al-Timimi, 'Innovation Led Expansion: the Shipbuilding Case', *Research Policy*, 4: 2 (May 1975).

B. Baxter, 'Qualifications for Shipbuilding', *Transactions of The Royal Institution of Naval Architects*, vol. 113, no. 1 (London: RINA, Jan. 1971).

Board of Education Papers, Interdepartmental Steering Committee on Further Education and Training, *Second Report,* PRO ED 46/295 (Dec. 1944).
Booz, Allen and Hamilton International, *British Shipbuilding 1972,* Department of Trade and Industry (London: HMSO, 1973).
British Productivity Council, *Shipbuilding in Sweden* (London: BPC, 1959).
Royal Institution of Naval Architects (the Chapman Report), *The Higher Education and Training of Naval Architects* (London: RINA, Feb. 1966).
Department of Industry, *Report on Research and Development, 1974–76* (London: HMSO, 1977).
DSIR, *Research and Development Requirements of Shipbuilding and Marine* Engineering (London: HMSO, 1960).
A. C. Hardy and E. Tyrrell, *Shipbuilding* (London: Pitman, 1964).
HMSO, Shipbuilding Enquiry Committee, *Report of the Shipbuilding Enquiry Committee, 1965–6,* (London: HMSO, 1966).
Committee of Enquiry into Shipping, *Report*, Command 4337 (London: HMSO, 1970).
Select Committee on Science and Technology (Science Sub-Committee: Industry and Scientific Research), Memorandum, Session 1975–6 (London: HMSO, 1976).
G. Lehman-Felkowski, *The Shipbuilding Industry of Germany* (London: Crosby Lockwood, 1904).
Lloyds Register of Shipping.
Ministry of Defence, Annual Statements on Defence (London: HMSO).
M. S. Moss and J. R. Hume, *Workshop of the British Empire, Engineering and Shipbuilding in the West of Scotland* (London: Heinemann, 1977).
National Academy of Sciences, Maritime Transportation Research Board *Shipbuilding Research and Development: A Recommended Programme* (Springfield, Virginia: NTIS, 1972).
Navires, Ports et Chantiers, 328, p. 585 (Sept. 1977).
National Institute Economic Review, 48, May 1969.
N. E. Coast Institution of Engineers and Shipbuilders, 1972.
J. Patton, *Productivity and Research in Shipbuilding, Report of Ad Hoc Committee* (Productivity and Research Organisation, 1962).
Peat, Marwick and Mitchell and Co., *Report to the Ministry of Transport on Shipbuilding Orders Placed Abroad by British Shipowners* (London: HMSO, 1961).
Shipbuilding Industry Training Board, information supplied to the author (1977).
J. Venus, *The Economics of Shipbuilding*, the 6th Blackadder Lecture delivered at the University of Newcastle upon Tyne, 1972.
S. Webb and B. Webb, *Industrial Democracy*, printed by the authors (1901).
L. Yamashita, 'Application of Technical Innovations and Automation to Ships Built in Japan', in C. J. Borwick (ed.), *Automation on Shipboard* (New York: Macmillan, 1967).

11 Innovation and Competitiveness in Portable Power Tools[1]

W. B. Walker and J. P. Gardiner

INTRODUCTION

Portable power tools make up one of the smallest sectors of the machine-building industry; worldwide, the sector employs fewer than 50,000 people. Nevertheless, it illustrates a number of features of wider significance: the process of mechanisation; the long-term economic significance of continuous, small-step improvements in technology based on a sustained commitment to design and development; a long-standing British backwardness in developing and adopting innovations.

A power tool may be loosely defined as any tool that contains a motor (rotary or reciprocating) and is capable of being guided and supported manually by the operator without undue strain. Most familiar of the industry's products is the household drill, but a wide range of other products is available for use in various markets, including hammer-drills, grinders and circular saws for use in the construction industry, jigsaws and routers in woodworking, shears and nibblers in sheetmetal-working, nutrunners and impact-wrenches in assembly line manufacture.

The power tool forms part of a range of production techniques, extending from the traditional hand-tool to the stationary machine-tool. Its attraction stems from its combination, within certain limits, of the flexibility and mobility of the hand tool with the power and precision of the stationary machine. Where it is in direct competition, the power tool is generally labour-saving relative to the hand-tool and capital-saving relative to the stationary machine. This chapter is concerned with electric and pneumatic (compressed air) power tools. Petrol-driven power tools (e.g. chain-saws) will not be considered.

The relative advantages of pneumatic and electric power tools in today's markets are shown in Table 11.1. Price is only one of the many factors that

TABLE 11.1 Relative advantages of electric and pneumatic power tools

	Capital Cost	*Energy cost (incl. cost of energy supply-system)*	*Reliability/ maintenance costs*	*Versatility of energy supply/ freedom of movement*	*Weight ergo-nomics*	*Noise vibration*	*Health/ accident risks*	*Risk of theft*
Electric								
– hf	2	2	1	3	3	2	2	1
– universal	1	1	3	1	2	2	2	3
Pneumatic	2	3	1	2	1	3	2	1

NOTE

1 = Good
2 = Moderate
3 = Poor

SOURCE

Walker & Gardiner (1978).

influence choice of energy type. Pneumatic tools are most frequently used in industrial settings where it is economical to supply compressed air for their superior safety and reliability, and for the unique technical performance of certain classes of tools. The wide availability of electrical energy, and the relatively low initial costs of universal electric tools make them appropriate for use in small workshops, in the building and construction industries, and in households. High frequency electric tools are only an economic proposition where the user has a large commitment to grinding, sanding or polishing.

HISTORY OF THE INDUSTRY, 1870–1945

The power tool was one of the many technologies made possible by the revolution in energy supply and materials technologies in the late nineteenth Century. In industry, as in mining and tunneling, the large-scale use of pneumatic power was pioneered in the USA. By the 1890s several companies were manufacturing pneumatic hammers, drills and riveters, and were exporting them to foreign markets. European manufacture was slow to develop, despite a market (especially shipbuilding) that quickly adopted the new technology. There is no record of a British firm manufacturing pneumatic tools for sale on the open market before 1900. A Swedish company, AB Atlas, later to become Atlas Copco, the largest European producer of pneumatic technologies, appears to have been the only European firm producing pneumatic tools on any scale before 1900.

The electric power tool was a German innovation, the credit going to the firm of C & E Fein of Stuttgart in 1895. This firm had been founded in 1867 by a characteristic German entrepreneur of the period with both scientific and industrial interests and appointments. While other firms in Germany and in the USA were quick to imitate and develop Fein's ideas, British manufacturers again showed little interest in the technology. Until the 1930s, the majority of electric tools sold in the British market were of US or German manufacture.

By the late 1920s, a wide range of electric and pneumatic power tools was available internationally. The technology in both sectors improved and became less expensive, and the industry remained oriented towards heavy engineering markets. The most important development between the Wars was the beginning of assembly-line manufacture (especially in the motor vehicle industry) which created demands for powered fastening tools to replace the traditional spanners, screwdrivers and drills. In the early 1930s a series of technical innovations led to a new range of light-weight power tools suited for use in the assembly industries.

British manufacture of power tools dates largely from the 1930s. Manufacture began in most cases as a consequence of the breakdown of open trading between the industrial economies and of opportunities within protected Commonwealth markets. Black & Decker, the largest US manufacture, set up production in the UK at this time for these reasons. Two firms entered as a result of technical innovations: Desoutter with miniature drills, Kango with a hammer drill. Most British firms gained their first taste of volume production during World War II when demand for power tools expanded considerably, especially in repair workshops and in aircraft manufacture. Thus, the UK power tool industry was a late arrival, developed when protected from foreign competition, and expanded under the influence of wartime demand.

EVOLUTION OF PORTABLE POWER TOOL MARKETS, 1945 TO THE PRESENT DAY

Since the Second World War, the power tool has found applications in a wide range of markets, the principal being:

- Manufacturing industries, in particular assembly-line manufacture, foundries, shipbuilding, engineering, woodworking and airframe assembly.
- Building and construction, whether undertaken by firms, professional tradesmen, or amateur householders (Do-It-Yourself).
- The garage trade.

As a result of the tremendous growth of demand in consumer markets, electric tools now account for between two-thirds and three-quarters of the world market for power tools. In 1976, the UK was the fifth largest Western market for power tools (£40–45 million), the largest being the USA (c.£300 million), equal second Japan and West Germany (c.£130 million), fourth France (c.£60 million).

It is useful to distinguish between the portable power tool markets in which products are manufactured or repaired in units or batches (most shipbuilding, airframe assembly, building and construction, various capital goods); and those in which products are mass-produced on assembly lines (motor vehicles, 'white' goods, electronic consumer goods).

In unit and batch production, there are factors that discourage intensive mechanisation. The product tends to be differentiated and is usually assembled *in situ* in distinct phases. As a consequence, capital equipment tends to be underused, and production requires a fluid, skilled work force.

Owing to its low-cost versatility and mobility (especially in relation to its ability to machine awkwardly-shaped workpieces), the power tool has found special favour in unit and batch production.

The diffusion of power tools into such markets has followed a distinct pattern. As tasks tend to be varied, the typical fitter in a shipyard, or tradesman on a building site uses a range of equipment. With rising labour costs, the tendency has been for a group of men first to share power tools, then for each to be allocated the tool for which he has the greatest need, and then for each to have a range of power tools at his disposal.

Because of the variability of tasks, the general-purpose tool is favoured in unit and batch production. However, with rising incomes and more exacting technical specifications, tooling has tended to become more specialised, and users have moved up-market to take advantage of higher performance tools. In DIY (Do-It-Yourself) markets, for example, there has been a trend away from the use of general purpose drills plus attachments towards 'integral units' for sawing, planing, routing, sanding and other tasks; and there has been a pronounced shift towards the use of sophisticated power tools in the aircraft industry. Saturation levels are not clear-cut. As demand for one type of tool falls off, demand for other – generally more sophisticated and expensive – tools may pick up, and multiple tool ownership tends to increase with rising incomes.

In mass production, power tools are used differently. At any one station on an assembly line, each worker has a fixed set of tasks to perform with tooling allocated accordingly. The number of tools he uses depends on the speed of the production line and on the complexity of tasks. It is usual for an assembly-line worker to operate between one and three tools. Saturation levels are here more distinct. Power tools used on assembly lines are normally highly specialised, tailored to perform a single task to a fixed specification of eight hours or more in the day. The volume and standardisation of assembly-line production invites greater mechanisation, both to reduce labour costs and to increase control over quality. In several assembly-line industries the number of power tools used is beginning to decline as more automated assembly techniques take over and new materials reduce the need for machinery and assembly.

Whatever the type of market, the degree of penetration of power tools varies widely from country to country. As one would expect, penetration is at its greatest in high labour-cost countries (USA, Germany, Sweden), at its least in the Third World. Compared with the high cost European and North American markets, the UK is backward in the use of power tools, although their use has increased considerably since the onset of serious wage inflation in the early 1970s. As we have seen, the German market was more than three times the size of the UK market. The difference in levels of tooling is less marked in manufacturing than it is in building and construction.

The discrepancy in the building and construction industry is explained partly by the higher quality of tools that is customarily used in Germany, as is described in the next section. It is tempting to put the rest down to different factor prices, but several UK manufacturers of portable power tools said that the low propensity of potential users to invest was more important (Walker & Gardiner, 1978). Indeed, some suggested that the earnings of tradesmen are low *because* so little is invested in labour-saving devices, not vice versa. It was argued that British tradesmen – and the managers of building firms – are more conservative than their Continental equivalents about the productive techniques they use. They are loath to use specialised equipment and to part with the traditional hand techniques that they have inherited from previous generations of craftsmen. This conservatism is part cause, part consequence of an educational system that is itself backward and beset with conservatism. The apprenticeship scheme perpetuates old working practices, and Technical Colleges are slow to introduce new ideas and practices into their curricula.

Another factor contributing towards the slow rate of diffusion of power tools in building and construction has been the Central Electricity Generating Board's slowness in connecting construction sites to the Grid. Only in the last few years has it become common practice to connect up sites at the start, rather than at the end, of construction. In Continental Europe and North America, this practice has a much longer history.

TECHNICAL INNOVATION

In the 100-year history of penumatic and electric tools, there have been surprisingly few technical landmarks, although those that are identifiable have been very important. They fall into two categories: those affecting whole ranges of tools; and those whose influence has been more localised, relevant to a particular class or type of tool. Included in the first category are the development and application of universal electric and rotary-vane motors, the double-insulation of electric tools, the welding of commutator connections, and tungsten-carbide coated tool-bits. Included in the second category are the early invention and development of the various classes of tools, torque-control mechanisms for impact-wrenches and nutrunners, variable-speed controls for electric power tools.

Such large technical advances have been comparatively rare. They have occurred against a more pervasive background of incremental changes which collectively have brought about major advances in performance and reductions in price. These have stemmed from improvements in materials and component parts (bearings, switches, plastics, lubricants, etc.) in production techniques (casting, gear-cutting, quality control, etc.) and in design configurations. Radical innovations have frequently been achieved only on the back of a host of minor ones, and have in turn set in motion new waves of incremental design changes, embodying new components, materials and design concepts.

The combined effect of major and minor changes can be illustrated by the development of pneumatic drills and grinders (Table 11.2). The transition from piston to rotary-vane motors accompanied by a range of improvements in design, materials, valves and other aspects of the technology, have resulted in marked improvements. The performance indicators cited in Table 11.2 capture only part of this improvement – they exclude the price-reductions and the improvements in reliability, safety and ease of use that have also occurred.

Very little of the technical development of power tools has been done outside the firms involved in their manufacture. Few firms have developed links with universities and government laboratories, and where there has been a contact it has been on an *ad hoc* consultancy basis – the contact being established usually in the event of a particular technical development being impeded by a lack of scientific or technical understanding.

There are four ways by which firms gain access to new technology in this industry: by in-house Design and Development; by imitation; by company acquisition; and by exchange agreements.

– *Design and Development*: although most innovative activity in the power tool industry is best classed as Design and Development, it may

TABLE 11.2 Performance of succeeding generations of Atlas Copco drills and grinders

Date of Introduction:	1915	1930	1940	1962	
Drills: Power-to-weight ratios (effective hp/grams)	67	166	276	358	
Date of Introduction:	1925	1935	1950	1960	1970
Grinders: Worked material (kilos per day)	1.4	1.8	2.7	4.5	9.0

SOURCE:

Gardland *et al.* (1974).

require scientific research aimed at improving understanding of the properties of materials, heat flows, motor losses, and so on. Technical development has tended to become more science-intensive in recent years. Although precise figures are not available, Design and Development expenditures range between 1.5 and 2.5% of annual sales, depending on the specialisation, resources and strategies of the firm in question. This level of spending is close to the average for the machine building industry as a whole.

- *Imitation*: as in other industries, the firms in this industry fall into two groups, the innovators and imitators, or leaders and followers. Imitation is not necessarily a cheap and risk-free means of acquiring new technologies. It requires considerable understanding of both technology and market, and usually involves borrowing ideas rather than attempting carbon copies. All firms imitate, even those that stand out as technical leaders, since resource constraints prevent companies with general product ranges from gaining technical leads in all product areas.
- *Mergers*: an important means of surmounting technical barriers to market entry has been company purchase. This has been one of the main reasons for increased concentration within the industry in recent years.
- *Exchange agreements*: licensing is rare in this industry, either between the major producers or between these producers and developing countries. More common are agreements between firms to market each others' products, or to exchange technical information.

Whether for pioneering new technologies, or learning from others, a strong in-house technical capability is an essential condition for competitiveness in this industry. Since 1945, the success of US and German firms in world markets has owed much to their innovativeness. As in earlier times, the US has remained the centre for the development of pneumatic technologies, while Germany and the USA have shared the honours in developing electric power tools and the processes required in their construction. The contributions of other countries (Sweden, Switzerland, the UK, etc.) have been marginal in comparison, although important in some specific instances. It is apparent from Table 11.3 that British electric power tool producers lag well behind their German and US competitors in patenting, even in the British market.

Since World War II, there has been a marked difference in the direction of technical change in the German and US electric power tool industries. In general, German (and Swiss) firms have devoted their innovative efforts to developing high quality and performance tools, while US firms have given greater priority to minimising prices. Although reinforced by the traditional US strength in volume production and mass marketing, and the German

TABLE 11.3 Electric power tool patents granted by the UK Patent Office, 1935–75

	1935–45	*46–55*	*56–60*	*61–65*	*66–70*	*71–75*	*Total*
F R Germany	6	4	3	13	18	65	109
UK	3	8	10	3	9	3	36
USA	7	3	1	24	25	25	85

strength in engineering and quality manufacture, the reasons for this contrasting behaviour lie also in different patterns of consumption in domestic markets. US purchasers tend to prefer using low price tools with short lifetimes (frequently throwing them away after breakdown), while German and most other European producers prefer to buy high quality tools and maintain them for several years.[2] The following factors influence quality preferences:

- *Resource Endowments*: the historic abundance of natural resources and their produce in the USA has led to a strong attachment to a high-consumption, high-waste way of life. In Europe, in contrast, periodic shortages of resources – and dependence on foreign supplies – have bred attitudes and practices that conserve material goods.
- *Market-Size*: the vast scale of the US market encourages the production of standardised goods for mass distribution. Such economies are more readily achieved with simple, low quality goods than with more complicated, highly engineered goods. Price differentials between the top and the bottom of the product range are considerably greater in the USA than in Europe, making the high quality good a less attractive investment.
- *Social Mobility*: in the USA it is customary to change jobs – and hence houses and localities – many times in one's working life, encouraging frequent turnover of household equipment. Lesser mobility in Germany (and other European countries) encourages populations to hang on to their possessions and to take a longer-term view of the accumulation of goods.
- *Cultural Attitudes*: there are various cultural features of European and North American societies – the roots of which are usually obscure – that have been cited as having a bearing on this issue. In particular, one

> hears talk of the North American's love of novelty, the German's obsession with 'Technik', his aesthetic appreciation of machinery and insistence on high standards of quality and workmanship, that influence both the choice of machine in the market place and the behaviour of firms.

The UK stands somewhere between Germany and the USA on this issue, probably with a leaning towards the latter. There has been a tendency to follow the North American pattern because of the dominance of US multinationals in the UK market, capital scarcity which has encouraged the purchase of cheap tooling, the absence of the German's appreciation of technical quality, and the dominance of chain-stores and mail-order firms in the retailing of these tools.

PRODUCTION

Power tools are generally mass-produced, although the extent of mechanisation varies widely with the volume of production, the nature of the product and the efficiency of the manufacturer. Power tool manufacture has become increasingly skill-intensive, in design and development, production, marketing, and the other facets of manufacture. This is as true of the low-value standard products, where special skills are required in gearing up for volume production and marketing, as it is of high-value specialised products, where the skill lies more in engineering and on the shop-floor. The combination of high capital-intensity and skill-intensity acts as a formidable barrier to aspiring new entrants to the industry.

It is usual for most of the value of the power tool to be added by the supplying firms; relatively little manufacture is subcontracted. However, power tool manufacture relies heavily on the external supply of high grade materials: plastics for housing, copper for motor windings, alloys for metal parts. The absence or unreliability of such supplies is a critical deterrent to setting up production in the Third World.

There are between 70 and 80 firms producing electric power tools in the Western World, of which 25+ are located in the USA, 20+ in F R Germany, 10+ in Japan, and 3 in the UK (Duplex, Kango and Wolf). There are closer to a hundred pneumatic tool producers, the greatest concentration being in the USA (50+). There are again 3 UK-owned producers of pneumatic power tools (Compair, Desoutter and McDonald). Few companies produce both electric and pneumatic tools. The rapid growth of demand for power tools notwithstanding, there have been few successful entrants since World War II. The successful entrants have all entered 'sideways', having previous experience in other areas of production.

Between half and two-thirds of OECD production of electric power tools is concentrated in the hands of six firms: Black & Decker, Skil and Rockwell (USA); AEG and Robert Bosch (F R Germany); Makita (Japan). There is similar concentration in the pneumatic sector, with Ingersoll-Rand, Chicago Pneumatic, Gardner-Denver (USA) and Atlas Copco (Sweden) dominant. The major US manufacturers are strongly multinational in their production policies, having plants in Europe, the USA and elsewhere in the West. The extent of diversification varies enormously from firm to firm. At one extreme are firms with turnover in excess of £1 billion, for which power tools account for less than 5 per cent of total production; at the other, firms with sales of less than £20 million, are totally committed to power tools.

INDUSTRIAL PERFORMANCE

A useful point of entry to a discussion of industrial performance is to consider international trade flows. Since comparable international trading statistics are not available for pneumatic power tools, we shall here be concerned with developments in electric power tool markets. However, it appears from interviews and other sources that post-War performance of the UK pneumatic tool industry in international markets has been very similar to that of the UK electric power tool industry.

In 1976, the value of OECD export trade in electric power tools was around $600 million. Between 1964 and 1976 it grew more than sevenfold in current prices, making it one of the fastest growing engineering sectors. Around a third of World sales are traded across international boundaries, mostly within the OECD area.

Table 11.4 shows the considerable shifts in shares of world trade in electric power tools since the early 1960s. The major change can be put simply: in 1963/64, the UK and USA together contributed 44 per cent of OECD export trade, as did Germany, Japan and Switzerland, taken together. By 1977, the UK/US contribution had fallen to 22 per cent, while the German/Japanese/Swiss contribution had risen to 64 per cent – a major change in such a brief period. For the UK, this trend reflects relatively slow growth rates of production, and declining competitiveness abroad. It also reflects the decision of the US-owned Black & Decker, the largest manufacturer of power tools in the UK, to feed the great expansion of demand in the EEC from plants located in France, Germany and Italy, rather than from the UK. Multinational behaviour of this type also explains a large part of the decline in US shares of international trade.

TABLE 11.4 Shares of OECD export trade, by country (percentages)

	*1963/64**	*1968/69*	*1972/73*	*1975/76*	*1977*
Germany	32.7	36.1	39.2	33.6	34.6
Switzerland	9.3	14.1	18.2	20.4	19.4
USA	27.8	16.2	13.1	14.5	9.5
Japan	1.6	6.1	7.0	7.2	9.5
UK	16.5	13.1	8.4	9.2	8.3
Italy	2.7	4.4	4.6	3.9	3.7
Netherlands	4.9	4.8	4.0	3.5	3.2
Canada	n.a.	2.1	2.5	2.6	2.7
France	3.1	1.7	1.6	2.0	2.3
Other	1.4	1.4	1.5	3.1	3.5
	100	100	100	100	100

SOURCE

OECD (1963–1976).

Table 11.5 shows that the OECD countries were the major consumers of power tools, and that most of the export trade was concentrated within Europe. The influence of geographical and political ties on trading patterns is also evident, the USA having strong ties with the Americas, the UK with former Imperial markets, Germany with Continental Europe, and Japan with countries bordering the Pacific Ocean. The most notable changes have occurred to the patterns of UK and Japanese trading. The proportion of UK trade destined for the former Dominions has fallen as sharply as Japanese exports to the same countries have risen. The importance of markets in the Developing Countries (especially the Middle East) for UK producers has also increased in recent years. The European market is still not as central to the fortunes of UK manufacturers as it is for other European producers.

In the decade following World War II, protection in Commonwealth markets, and the absence of European competition, led to a period of security and prosperity, but not modernisation, for UK power tool producers. Their difficulties began with the opening of international markets in the late 1950s and 1960s. Several producers disappeared at this time, and those that remained went through a difficult and painful period of adjustment. This often involved

TABLE 11.5 Destination of electric power tool exports, 1963/64 and 1975

	To / *From*	*Western Europe*	*Eastern Europe*	*USA Canada Japan*	*Australia N. Zealand S. Africa*	*Less Developed Countries*	*OECD*	*World*
1963/64	OECD	61.1	1.3	15.4	6.3	15.7	(82.3)	100
	Germany	80.9	2.9	3.3	2.5	10.7	(88.2)	100
	Japan	7.8	1.1	37.9	3.4	49.7	(48.3)	100
	Switzerland	83.5	1.0	4.2	2.8	6.1	(92.8)	100
	UK	55.6	0.2	4.6	18.8	20.7	(74.5)	100
	USA	28.8	0.1	44.8	6.8	19.5	(77.7)	100
1975	OECD	57.7	4.3	14.2	6.9	17.8	(79.7)	100
	Germany	73.9	4.7	6.6	4.8	11.1	(85.5)	100
	Japan	23.1	3.8	6.9	27.4	41.1	(57.4)	100
	Switzerland	78.6	4.9	11.1	3.1	7.6	(88.4)	100
	UK	46.0	7.0	5.6	12.2	30.8	(66.8)	100
	USA	23.1	0.2	41.6	7.8	28.2	(72.3)	100

SOURCE

OECD (1963–1976).

redirecting trade away from Commonwealth markets, rationalising production, adopting a new approach to marketing and modernising product-ranges.

In competing effectively with the US, German and Japanese firms that dominate world markets, the UK power tool industry continues to face three main problems, each of which reflects an underlying lack of innovativeness: small scale, relatively low productive efficiency, and concentration on low value products. These problems tend to reinforce each other. Small scale can be an advantage if a firm is producing specialised, high value products; it is a distinct disadvantage if a firm is concentrated on the low value product range. Regarding scale, British firms all have annual power tool sales of under £20 million. They are competing with foreign firms that are operating on an altogether larger scale, and more efficiently. Some of these firms are highly diversified and can call on substantial resources to increase their market competitiveness. They can afford to loss-lead to gain entry to markets.

The relatively low value per tonne of British exports of electric power tools is shown in Table 11.6. This is due partly to Black and Decker's specialisation in the sale of low-cost consumer goods, which it exports from the UK in large numbers, partly to British firms' failure to innovate and move up-market. Thus the UK industry is strong in the production of drills (Kango is an exception in producing high value hammer drills), but weak in the production of circular saws, percussion drills, grinders and jigsaws. A similar phenomenon holds for the UK pneumatic tool industry, which dominates the lower end of the British market, but gives way to foreign producers in more specialised and sophisticated technologies.

The familiar story emerges of British producers being squeezed by more efficient producers of the simpler types of power tool on the one hand, and manufacturers of high value products on the other. Some commentators have

TABLE 11.6 Value per tonne of exported electric power tools ($'000 per tonne)

	1963/64	*1968/69*	*1972/73*	*1975*
West Germany	7.6	8.0	11.7	14.3
Switzerland	7.4	9.0	13.5	20.7
Italy	5.3	4.5	6.4	8.4
UK	4.1	3.4	4.4	6.8

SOURCE:

OECD (1963–1976).

blamed the relatively slow growth and backwardness of the home market for the difficulties experienced in the 1960s and 1970s. Slow growth discourages investment in new plant, and the backwardness of the home market makes it risky and unprofitable for UK firms to develop new specialised tools, or tools with high launching costs, that have limited home market potential. Industrial drills, grinders and jigsaws with electronic speed control provide examples. While in fair demand in Germany and elsewhere in Europe, the market for these relatively sophisticated and expensive tools is non-existent in the UK, so that it is hardly surprising that British producers (Black and Decker included) have yet to add such tools to their product ranges.

There can be no doubt that the backwardness of the UK market has discouraged innovation and the growth of efficiency within the supplying industry. However, one can argue with equal conviction that the suppliers have lacked the capacity (in every sense) to manufacture the higher value types of equipment, and to encourage their use by effective marketing and instruction. In comparison with German and US firms, there is a lack of engineering ability in the UK industry, which has infected both UK-owned companies and multinational companies with subsidiaries in the UK.

The industry also appears to lack the capacity to embark on the high volume production of goods for the mass-market, requiring the application of advanced production and marketing techniques. In this respect, the Japanese and US power tool industries are formidable competitors. Japanese exports of electric power tools to the UK rose from £1.54 million in 1976 to £2.96 million in 1977 (around 8 per cent of the UK market), raising the spectre of destruction at the hands of Japanese firms as has happened in other industries in recent years. Makita, the main Japanese producer, now exports more to the UK than any other foreign firm.

The principal goal of the UK power tool industry in the coming years must therefore to be increase its productive efficiency and to move its product-ranges up-market; and generally to improve its capacity for making innovative responses to threats and opportunities. Given its advantage of relatively low labour costs and a favourable exchange rate in the last few years, though without wishing to diminish its real achievements in that time, one fears that unless the industry takes steps to modernise itself further it will have increasing difficulty in the medium- and long-term in coping with the superior scale, efficiency and technological dynamism of its foreign competitors. It may also have to cope with a less favourable exchange rate.

NOTES

1. This chapter is based on a longer and more detailed study by W. Walker and P. Gardiner (1978). Unless otherwise indicated, the information in it is

based on that collected from the industry during the course of the study, which involved discussions with the major companies in Europe and the USA.

2. In 1975, the unit value of electric power tools produced in F.R. Germany was 2.8 times that of those produced in the USA (Walker and Gardiner).

REFERENCES

T. Gardland, I. Janelid, H. Lindblad and D. Ramstram, *Atlas Copco 1873–1973, The Story of a Worldwide Compressed Air Company* (Sweden: Atlas Copco, 1974).

OECD, *Trade by Commodities, Series C*, Paris: OECD (1963–1976).

W. Walker and J. Gardiner, *The Portable Power Tool Industry: a Study of International Industrial Development* (mimeo, Science Policy Research Unit, University of Sussex, 1978).

12 Innovation in the British Steel Industry

Jonathan Aylen[1]

Until the 1880s Britain was the world's foremost producer of steel and a leading innovator, with developments such as Bessemer steelmaking to its credit (Dennis, 1967). But by 1890 Britain had been surpassed as a producer by the United States and by Germany, too, by 1900. Now Britain stands eighth in world steel output. In international trade Britain has performed badly compared to West Germany and Japan, a relative newcomer to world steel production. In 1965 Britain still had the fourth most favourable net balance among Western producers in direct steel trade; by 1974 she had become a net steel importer. The labour productivity of the British steel industry is now below that of all its major national European competitors, half that of the United States and almost a third that of Japan (American Iron and Steel Institute, 1975, table 4).

The slow pace of innovation in the British iron and steel industry is one explanation of the industry's relative decline. Temin (1966) attributes the low rate of innovation between 1880 and 1913 to a slow rate of growth of domestic demand. And as McCloskey (1968, p. 296) has emphasised, a low rate of expansion gave little incentive to recruit new human talent either. Others have treated the British steel industry's persistent technological lag behind America and Germany as a symptom of poor management. Burn (1940) and Erickson (1959) point to the unsuitable educational and social background of many steel managers, and emphasise how few were technically qualified to judge the worth of potential technological improvements. Our concern here is with recent technical innovation in the British steel industry.

THE STRUCTURE OF THE BRITISH STEEL INDUSTRY[2]

Internationally, the steel industry is highly competitive. Since steel is a fundamental material for both capital and consumer goods, most countries have a domestic steel industry of some sort. Firms are free to sell their homogeneous product in international markets. A distinction should be made between the relatively slow-growing international market for bulk, low-carbon steels, and the lower-volume, faster-growing market for special alloy and high-carbon steels. Special steel production is more limited: Britain, Italy, Sweden, West Germany, France, Japan and the USA are among the foremost producers.

Technically as well as administratively, the British steel industry is split into two sectors; nationalised and private. The nationalised sector, namely the British Steel Corporation, inherited the integrated works of the fourteen major domestic steel producers upon nationalisation in 1967 and thus became the world's third largest steel producer in terms of output by weight, though 57 per cent of its output was then produced using obsolete open hearth steelmaking. The bulk of the Corporation's ordinary steel is now produced by the blast furnace-BOS (basic oxygen steelmaking) route (Figure 12.1). No new integrated, green-field bulk steel works have been built. The Corporation has concentrated instead on rationalising its inheritance by 'rounding out' and removing bottlenecks at its larger works while closing the smaller, obsolete and poorly located plants, albeit more slowly than planned. The costs of adjusting to modern steelmaking technology have, however, been high. In 1976 steel accounted for 17 per cent of all the investment in UK manufacturing industry, nearly all of this being undertaken by the BSC.

The private sector is composed of the smallest firms not nationalised in 1967, many of which are special steel producers, plus new entrants to the bulk, low-carbon steel sector, who compete with the British Steel Corporation. Electric arc furnace melting from scrap – an alternative small-scale approach to steelmaking – predominates. Originally used for special steelmaking, this route has also been adopted by low-output 'mini-mills' for making general carbon steels suitable for continuous casting and subsequent rolling into light products such as bars or rods in low-output mills, or, more recently, for rolling into wide strip hitherto produced in integrated works.

Both sectors use electric arc furnaces for melting special steels. Here the private sector predominates in areas such as high-speed and tool steels while the BSC is the only integrated producer of stainless flat products. Otherwise both sectors compete across a wide range of alloy steels.

The private steel sector remains highly fragmented, which militates against any one producer securing the substantial economies of scale to be realised even in special steel production. Very few private producers are big enough to maintain an independent research and development capability, Johnson Firth Brown and GKN being exceptions. The former co-operative

R&D effort of the British Iron and Steel Research Association (BISRA) passed to the BSC on nationalisation, leaving most private sector producers in a technical limbo. Absence of research facilities is particularly crucial for the largely Sheffield-based private special steel producers.

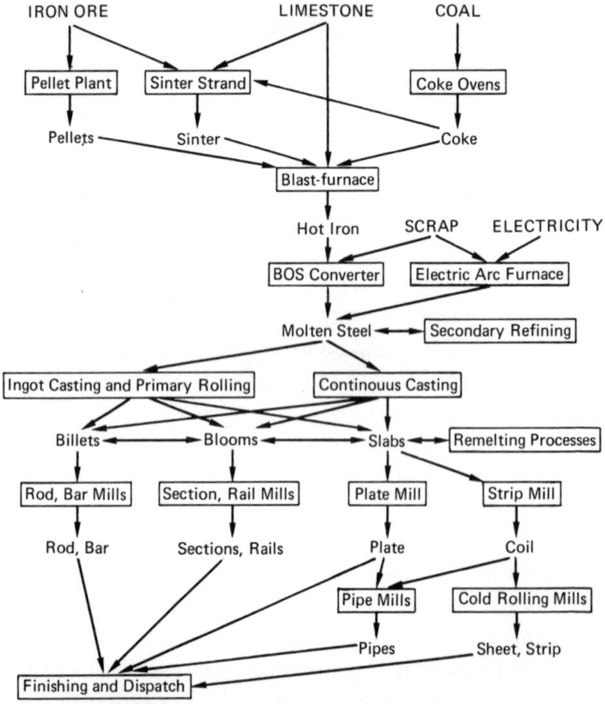

FIG. 12.1 Process routes to steel

Opinion in both sectors of the industry suggests that British Steel Corporation plant of recent construction tends to be more technically sophisticated, reliable and expensive than comparable plant in the private sector. To some extent, such a difference could reflect their differing product markets, since recent private-sector bulk steel plant was designed for the bottom end of the market. The high quality of BSC engineering is not just a question of managerial economies of scale, but also a result of the Corporation's management ethos.

INNOVATION IN THE STEEL INDUSTRY

The nature of innovation[3]

Process innovation in the steel industry over the past twenty-five years has gone mainly in two directions: the dominant trend has been towards unit cost reductions, often realised through output expansion; at the same time, there has been a move towards quality-enhancing innovation, particularly at the rolling and finishing stage. Developments such as oxygen steelmaking, continuous casting and better burden preparation for blast furnaces have also resulted in net energy savings within the industry. Most of the basic iron and steelmaking operations have not changed; they have just got faster and larger. Almost every single process for bulk and special steelmaking exhibits declining unit costs as outputs increase (Battelle, 1977). Although there are technical or market limits on the capacity of some types of plant, there is little evidence of diseconomies of scale, with the possible exception of large blast furnaces.

Technical economies of scale arise from a number of sources. Many items of steelmaking are vessels or furnaces of some sort. Owing to the familiar geometrical relationship between the surface area and volume of a container, capital and operating costs rise less than proportionately with plant size. (Leckie and Morris, 1968). Many costs such as plant manning, product handling or computer control have a large element of fixed cost which varies relatively little with the size of plant unit being handled. Similarly, an increase in processing speed brought by higher blast furnace top pressure, or faster mill rolling speeds, enables a workforce and their equipment to produce a higher output in a given time.

Some new techniques, notably continuous casting and direct reduction, have lowered the minimum efficient scale of operation. With the slowdown in growth of steel consumption in mature economies and the increasing market for plant suppliers in developing countries, there has been a discernible trend towards plant units with a lower initial capacity, such as ¾-continuous hot wide strip mills in place of fully continuous mills (Earnshaw, 1978). But the distinction is between the gigantic, and just the plain enormous. Even a plant unit or works below the theoretical minimum efficient size can be huge.

The predominant trend towards faster operation of larger bulk steel plants has been fostered by the adoption of basic oxygen steelmaking – the only recent 'revolutionary' bulk steelmaking innovation, in that it led to premature scrapping of existing plant and the rewriting of steelmaking textbooks. By drastically raising the minimum efficient scale of integrated steel plants, oxygen steelmaking reinforced the move towards higher outputs at other process stages. Secondary refining has had a similar 'revolutionary' impact on stainless steel manufacture, and may yet affect bulk steelmaking in the same way.

Other major innovations, such as continuous casting or direct reduction of iron, can be classified as evolutionary. They have taken time to develop technically and scale up to fully commercial operation. They only slowly supplant existing techniques as plant is extended or newly built. The prevalence of minor process innovations reflects the design and development emphasis in steel plant supply. Research may be commissioned to back-up design developments, but otherwise very little research is conducted on fundamentally new process routes.

As a result of innovation, the British steel industry has become more highly capital-intensive, much less labour-intensive and less energy-intensive (Shone, 1975, pp. 217–25). These trends are likely to continue in response to rising real energy prices and wages relative to the cost of capital, and are clearly reflected in recent plant design. Most innovations are embodied in new plant or new equipment added to old plant. The crucial role of investment in steel industry process innovation is illustrated by Meyer and Herregat (1974), who found that the investment rate, suitably lagged, was a major predictor of the rate of adoption of oxygen steelmaking both between countries and within a country over time. Minor capital expenditure usually continues after a new plant has been installed in order to up-rate it in the light of operating experience (Maxwell, 1976). However, interview evidence, visits to comparable plants and our detailed plant registers all suggest that there are marked differences in the way owners specify their plants and modify them after completion in order to improve their performance.

The role of plant suppliers

As a result of competition amongst plant suppliers, embodied process innovations are almost completely mobile throughout the world steel industry. Product quality and design experience are major features of competition between plant suppliers. New entrants to the industry have to offer substantial price discounts to overcome the barriers to entry posed by the accumulated technical reputation of existing equipment suppliers. To enter foreign markets, designers sell both technical developments and complete plant designs on licence to overseas plant makers and steelmakers. Mobility of innovations is reinforced by a comprehensive technical press with international coverage, by extensive publicity given to new plant and by informal word of mouth networks. Given the almost complete absence of multinational steel firms, operating experience is less mobile, although there are often informal links between steelmakers and there is some formal trade in know-how. On balance, innovation is more likely to be inhibited by the potential problems of financing and managing technical change and by constraints on market size than by the physical availability of new technology itself. Plant suppliers' product innovation is the steelmakers' process innovation. Problems of scaling up laboratory results and the high cost of pilot plants encourage plantmakers to undertake fundamental R&D on full-scale commercial plant in co-operation with a steelmaker.

TECHNICAL EFFORT AND THE DIFFUSION OF INNOVATION

Indicators of technical effort

To assess the British steel industry's performance as an innovator, we compare both its technical effort and its rate of adoption of new process innovations with that of major foreign competitors. The difficulties inherent in comparing indicators of technical effort such as R&D inputs or patent outputs are, of course, legion (see Chapter 3). We do not attempt to adjust exchange rates when comparing national R&D expenditures. Nor have we tried to weight patent outputs according to their relative importance. A further difficulty in the steel industry is that patents may not be attributed to their true country of origin. The major Austrian patents on oxygen steelmaking are registered with a subsidiary in Switzerland, for instance.

We also stress that much innovation originates from commercial design development rather than formal research, and is not reflected in measures of R&D inputs. Since design patents may be circumvented and imitated, plant builders may prefer cheaper and more secure ways of protecting design innovations. Measures of technical effort in steel will reflect an industry's bias towards areas of formal research and product development, notably in special steels.

Our evidence on inputs to formal research and development relates to levels of spending on R&D and qualified manpower employed in R&D (Table 12.1). In terms of manpower, Britain's effort is close to that of West Germany and well above that of France, though it is known to have declined markedly since 1974. With regard to R&D expenditure, the British steel industry is lower down the league, although this reflects a relative cost advantage in R&D activity. But even making major allowances for any non-comparability in Japanese figures, Japanese R&D appears to be well in the lead.

In terms of patent output, Britain again lags behind Japan and West Germany in numbers of patents registered in the USA and has a near average rate of growth (Table 12.2). We can tentatively conclude that while our

TABLE 12.1 Comparative research and development effort in ferrous metals, 1973

Country	*Level of intramural expenditure on R&D (million US dollars)*	*Total full-time equivalent natural scientists and engineers employed in R&D*	*Expenditure on R&D per tonne of crude steel (US dollars)*	*Scientists and engineers in R&D per thousand tonnes of crude steel*
Austria*	12.3	968	3.03	0.228
Belgium	22.3	1,040	1.44	0.067
Canada	8.5	252	0.64	0.019
France	29.9	1,215	1.18	0.048
West Germany	81.1	3,764	1.64	0.076
Italy	7.6	343	0.36	0.016
Japan	220.5	11,379	1.85	0.095
Luxembourg	n.a.	n.a.	n.a.	n.a.
Netherlands	n.a.	n.a.	n.a.	n.a.
Sweden	35.7	1,660	6.30	0.293
United Kingdom*	34.6	3,519	1.37	0.139
United States	147.0	n.a.	1.07	n.a.

NOTES

* 1972 figures.
Expenditure converted from domestic currency at average spot rates.
UK figure not full-time equivalent manpower units.

SOURCE

OECD (1977) (Ferrous Metals is equivalent to ISIC 371).

TABLE 12.2 Number and rate of growth of patents recorded in the USA for primary ferrous products, 1963–76

Country	*Total Number of Patents*	*Constant Annual Rate of Growth of Patents (%)*	*Patents per million Tonnes of Crude Steel*	*Constant Annual Rate of Growth of Patents per Tonne of Steel (%)*
Austria	83	9.7	1.55	6.2
Belgium	44	10.4	0.25	6.4^{ns}
Canada	205	9.3	1.33	4.8
France	314	5.7	1.02	3.4
West Germany	609	7.8	1.05	5.3
Italy	80	8.1^{ns}	0.04	1.6^{ns}
Japan	578	17.0	0.49	7.1
Luxembourg	12	no trend	0.17	no trend
Netherlands	60	14.8	0.90	9.4^{ns}
Sweden	173	10.6	2.37	8.4
United Kingdom	381	8.0	1.11	9.0
United States	8721	1.7	3.46	1.3^{ns}

NOTE

^{ns} = upward slope of regression equasion not significant at the 5 per cent level.

SOURCE

OTAF (1977).

technical effort is not outstanding and could be improved relative to that of West Germany, it stands comparison with the admittedly low effort of other major European steel producers, notably France and Belgium. Both the R&D inputs and patent outputs show a high relative technical effort in Sweden, and to a lesser extent Austria, reflecting their emphasis on special steels and their conscious commitment to innovation as a way of overcoming other competitive handicaps such as small domestic market size and high unit labour costs. These findings on technical effort correspond quite closely with our findings on national rates of adoption of new innovations. However, Britain does not do as well at innovation as her technical effort might indicate, which accords with interview evidence of difficulties in getting successful developments transferred into commercial operation.

The adoption of process innovations

A major disadvantage of using national diffusion rates as an innovation yardstick is that the range of cost-effective innovations and their optimal rate of adoption depends upon domestic factor prices, which may differ between countries. This is not as serious as it seems because many factor inputs such as iron ore, coking coal and steel plant are traded internationally. But labour costs do differ markedly, even within OECD countries, with the United Kingdom having one of the lowest total labour costs per worker of any major Western steel producer, though this is entirely offset by low labour productivity. Empirical work by Ault (1972) concludes that export performance can be explained in terms of differences in wage costs and adoption of new steelmaking techniques. Those countries which lag behind in imitating significant process innovations are likely to suffer a declining world trade share, particularly if innovation tends to be quality-enhancing as well as cost-reducing. Yet despite relatively low employment costs per worker, the export trade share of the British steel industry has declined in recent years, a fact consistent with a low rate of innovation and consequently low labour productivity.

Not that it is necessarily desirable to be the leading innovator. A world leader like Japan bears the cost of innovation, yet the resulting benefits are only partially internalised in the form of licence fees or additional sales and profits for plantmakers. Latecomers are able to learn cheaply from these and similar mistakes.

Oxygen steelmaking[4]

Oxygen steelmaking is currently the best practice and the most widely used method of bulk steelmaking. There are two major alternative techniques: basic oxygen steelmaking (BOS) in a top-blown LD converter and a more recent development, bottom-blown oxygen steelmaking, known variously as the Q-BOP, OBM or LWS process. Because of its high speed of working, BOS or Q-BOP steelmaking is both capital and labour saving as compared with open hearth steelmaking. In the British Steel Corporation BOS has a labour productivity more than double that of open hearth, while the best BOS shop has an average labour productivity some nine times higher than that of the worst open hearth plant (Aylen, 1978). Because oxygen steelmaking is exothermic, there are substantial savings in energy too. The process was scaled up rapidly and easily (Friedl and Schmidt, 1972, Figure 1) to bring very substantial economies of scale at the steelmaking stage (Cockerill, 1974, Table 33).

The United Kingdom has one of the lowest shares of oxygen steel output as a proportion of crude steel output among the major steel producing nations (Figure 12.2), principally due to retention of obsolete open hearth steelmaking

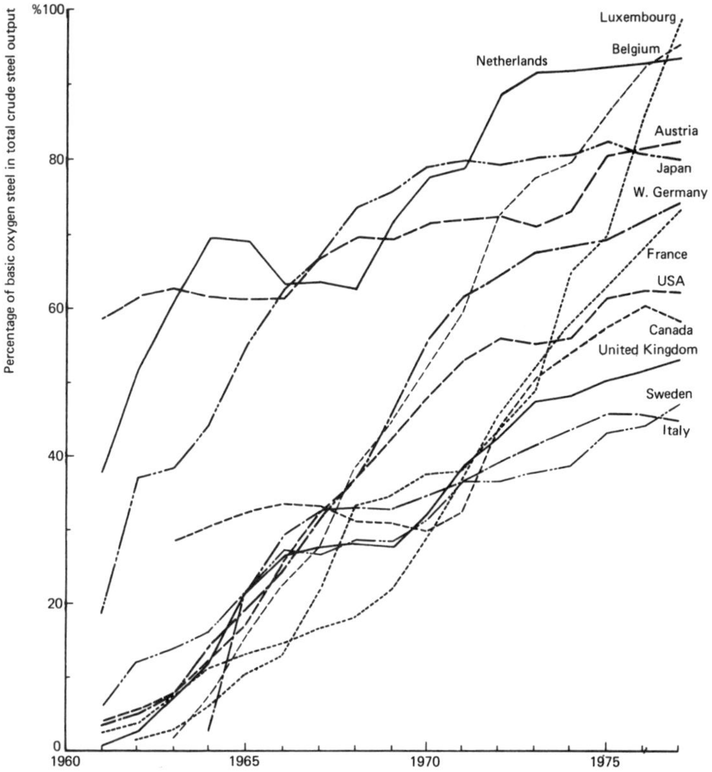

FIG. 12.2 The diffusion of oxygen steelmaking

SOURCES
OECD, IISI.

facilities. The United Kingdom has one of the lowest rates of diffusion of oxygen steelmaking, regardless of whether the diffusion ceiling is assumed to include or exclude electric arc steelmaking as an alternative best practice technique.[5]

Yet, while the UK has been slow to adopt oxygen steelmaking, BOS shops that have been built, particularly since nationalisation, are comparable both in terms of vessel size and plant output with those of leading innovators, notably Japan (Table 12.3). Attainment of economies of scale at the oxygen steelmaking stage should not, however, be unduly emphasised, because the loss of economies of scale at the steelmaking stage may be outweighed by gains in operating efficiency of continuous casting machines.

Continuous casting[6]

Continuous casting machines solidify liquid steel directly into semi-finished products by continuously pouring molten metal into an open-ended reciprocating water-cooled mould. It brings a number of major gains compared to ingot casting and rolling, notably a higher yield of steel, savings in energy, a net saving of capital, and higher quality.

In contrast to oxygen steelmaking, techniques of continuous casting evolved slowly over time. During the early stages, Britain had a lead both in technical developments and commercial application of continuous casting. Output of continuously cast steel then remained stagnant in Britain until both British Steel Corporation bulk steel slab casters and bloom casters began to come on stream in the early 1970s and the mini-mill boom got under way (Figure 12.3). There is a close association here between the slow diffusion of oxygen steelmaking and the delayed adoption of continuous casting. Parallel diffusion of the two processes reflects the need to invest in new casting facilities for new oxygen shops, especially those feeding wide hot strip mills and plate mills. Yet neither strip or plate mills were built here during the late 1960s or early 1970 – in contrast to, say, Germany or Japan, who were leading adopters of BOS and continuous casting over this period. The low rate of growth of UK steel demand, and adequate primary mill capacity, also reduced the need to adopt continuous casting in order to provide extra steelmaking capacity, while the cost reductions and yield gains brought by continuous casting were insufficient to justify replacement of existing primary mills. As a result, Britain has one of the lowest levels of diffusion among those Western steelmakers who have adopted continuous casting.

As with oxygen steelmaking, being a latecomer gives access to plant designs improved in the light of earlier adopters' experience. One constraint on the adoption of continuous casting has been the restricted throughput of

TABLE 12.3 Number and size of BOS steelmaking shops, June 1977

	Total annual rated capacity ('000 tonnes)	*Number of shops*	*Average annual shop capacity ('000 tonnes)*	*Average number of converters per shop*	*Capacity weighted average converter size (tonnes)*	*Capacity weighted average start-up date*
Austria	5 200	4	1 300	2.75	90	1966.6
Belgium	15 150	8	1 890	2.12	180	1967.7
Canada	9 195	4	2 300	2.75	158	1966.8
France	17 400	12	1 450	1.83	194	1969.3
W. Germany	45 520	14	3 250	2.50	217	1967.5
Italy	14 620	5	2 920	2.80	274	1968.3
Japan	122 780	39	3 150	2.51	198	1968.7
Luxembourg	6 140	5	1 230	1.20	129	1972.6
Netherlands	7 150	2	3 580	3.00	231	1967.7
Sweden	1 970	2	990	2.00	99	1972.8
UK	17 910	8	2 240	2.50	227	1968.2
USA	81 050	37	2 190	2.19	204	1966.3

NOTES

Top-blown LD converters only.

Data for USA converted from American short tons and subject to rounding error. Where a shop has been developed by staged expansion a median start-up date has been taken as the usual addition of a third converter doubles steelmaking capacity.

SOURCE

Stone (1977), with corrections.

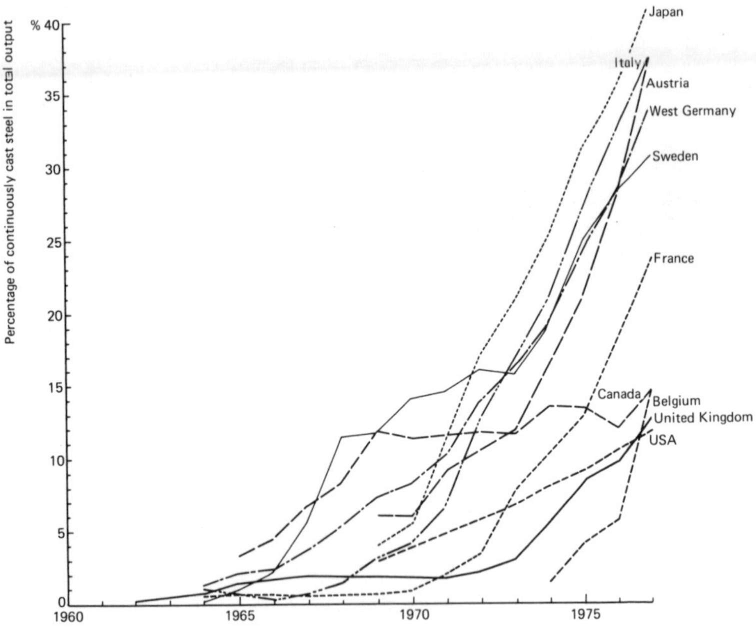

FIG. 12.3 The diffusion of continuous casting

SOURCES
OECD, IISI.

machines, particularly bloom and slab casters, relative to the output of the oxygen steel-making shop they serve. Comparing the strand area of British machines with those of other national producers suggests that delayed adoption has enabled the British steel industry to install larger and later designs (Table 12.4). These machines have usually been built in Britain either to West German or Concast design.[7] So here again, the UK steel industry has been slow to adopt a new process innovation, although plants that have been built are of adequate size and quality.

Blast furnace design and performance[8]

A blast furnace is a pressure vessel in which iron-bearing material is heated and chemically reduced to molten iron. The technical and economic performance of blast furnaces is broadly determined by two aspects of their technology: their design, and the choice of ore and fuel burden charged to the furnace.

Increases in furnace size have been paralleled by improvements in furnace operating conditions (Aylen, 1978), and so furnace size is a good summary measure for many other aspects of furnace technology. Table 12.5 shows

TABLE 12.4 Number and capacity of continuous casting machines, January 1977

	Slab Casters		*Bloom Casters*		*Billet Casters*	
	Number of machines	*Ladle size weighted average strand area × average no. of strands (cm^2)*	*Number of machines*	*Ladle size weighted average strand area × average no. of strands (cm^2)*	*Number of machines*	*Ladle size weighted average strand area × average no. of strands (cm^2)*
Austria	6	4420	no bloom casters		4	230
Belgium	4	4320	1	800	1	700
Canada	3	3600	4	1890	13	670
France	6	5230	1	1410	7	570
W. Germany	20	5600	6	2560	12	490
Italy	6	6270	6	1700	85	470
Japan	39	6110	19	2160	69	500
Luxembourg		no continuous casting machines of any kind in operation				
Netherlands		no continuous casting machines of any kind in operation				
Sweden	5	3040	2	2540	5	690
UK	7	5590	5	3310	8	490
USA	19	5370	4	1860	48	510

NOTES

Continuous billet casters defined as machines with an average section size not exceeding 150 mm × 150 mm.
Continuous slab casters defined as those which produce products whose width is at least twice their thickness.

SOURCE

Concast (1977).

TABLE 12.5 Adoption of large blast furnaces

Country	*Number 2000–3000 m^3 volume*	*Number 3001–4000 m^3 volume*	*Number over 4001 m^3 volume*	*Total*	*Percentage of furnaces over 2000 m^3 volume*
Austria				0	
Belgium				0	
Canada	1			1	8%
France	3		1	4	6%
West Germany	4	1	1	6	8%
Italy	4		1	5	25%
Japan	17	7	6	30	42%
Luxembourg				0	
Netherlands	1		1	2	29%
Sweden				0	
UK	1			1	2%
USA	5			5	3%

NOTES

Status mid-1975, except Japan as of end of 1974.
Due to differing definitions of volume, some entries may be slightly mis-classified. Inner volume is used as the basis for classification wherever possible.

SOURCE

Blast-furnace survey derived from Cordero and Serjeantson (1974) and other sources.

national adoption rates for large blast furnaces, all blown in since 1964. Even allowing for diseconomies in operating efficiency above a hearth diameter of 12 metres (3000 m^3 volume), all these furnaces are likely to be within a couple of per cent of the minimum efficient cost. Furnaces below this size are likely to experience higher unit costs, not only because they are smaller, but because they are probably of older design. By implication, the United Kingdom has a higher share of less efficient ironmaking capacity than most of its major competitors. Given the low rate of growth of UK steel output, existing blast furnaces have adequately met increased demand for iron.

High top pressure is a major advantage for blast furnace operation. Here we look at just one important patented innovation: the bell-less furnace top designed by Paul Wurth of Luxembourg. Rates of adoption are given in Table 12.6. Britain lags behind European competitors. As original innovators, the West German rate of adoption has been high. Despite their early commitment to other 'false start' high-pressure top designs, Japan too has a high rate of adoption of bell-less tops, which does suggest that good innovators are also good imitators.

The other important aspect of blast furnace technology is the quality of inputs into the blast furnace. Improvements in burdening practice are reflected in blast furnace fuel rates – the amount of fuel added to the blast

TABLE 12.6 Adoption of bell-less tops on blast furnaces, early 1978

Country	*Blown in on rebuilt furnaces*	*Blown in on new furnaces*	*Percentage of furnaces fitted*
Austria	1		10
Belgium	1	1	4
Canada		2	14
France	2	1	4
West Germany	5	1	8
Italy	3	1	19
Japan	5	1	8
Luxembourg	1		4
Netherlands	–	–	0
Sweden	–	–	0
UK	1	–	2
USA		1	0.5

SOURCE

Paul Wurth, Luxembourg, Reference List as at June 1977.

furnace to heat and reduce the burden per tonne of hot iron produced. Fuel rates also fall with higher operating temperatures and higher blast furnace top pressures. What fuel rates do *not* show is the effect of increasing furnace size, as there is no evidence of economies of scale with respect to fuel use; if anything there is evidence of slight diseconomies. So fuel rates are a reasonably reliable measure of the composite effects of good design, a good burden and good operating practice. Our comparison suggests (Table 12.7) that the UK has one of the worst fuel rates among Western producers

Assuming our limited evidence on blast furnace design and performance is symptomatic, we must conclude that Britain has lagged behind in adopting new blast furnace technology, both in construction of new large furnaces and in adoption of improved burden preparation, design, and working practice at existing furnaces.

Developments in rolling mill design[9]

Rolling mills, like blast furnaces, have improved over time due to the gradual accumulation of a number of small innovations. Many of these have been directed towards improved product quality as well as lowering unit costs. The pace of innovation has varied between different types of mill, but here we look at rates of innovation in two areas of rapid design improvement, hot wide strip mills and plate mills.

Hot wide strip mills

Our survey of hot strip mills rolling products over one metre wide covers two types of mill: fully continuous and semi-continuous. The difference between the two types of mill is in the initial preparation of the breakdown strip from slabs, continuous mills having a higher capacity than equivalent width semi-continuous mills. The minimum efficient scale of strip mills increased markedly with the advent of the computer-controlled Generation II strip mills of the 1960s (Ess, 1970). Economies of scale are now realisable up to at least 5.5 million tonnes a year for a continuous 90-inch mill, and up to 3.5 million tonnes for a 66-inch $\frac{3}{4}$-continuous mill, assuming a typical range of products (Battelle, 1977). No mill in Britain and very few mills outside Japan have even three-quarters of the current optimum capacity, though a number of mills are designed for eventual extension to these levels of output. Average national mill outputs are about half the minimum efficient capacity, with Britain at the lower end of the scale (Table 12.8). Britain is certainly not getting the economies of scale in strip production realised by Germany, France and Italy.

The disparity between British and West German strip mill capacity, design and performance is most striking. Britain has only one recent, very small

	Coke Rate *kg/tonne*	*Liquid Fuel Rate* *kg/tonne*	*Natural Gas Rate* *m^3/tonne*	*Overall Fuel Rate* *kg/tonne*
Belgium	559	20	0.19	579
Canada	476	24	–	500
France	551	58	n.a.	609+
West Germany	517	56	–	573
Japan	442	38	–	480
Sweden	540	39[a]	–	579
UK	606	18	1.00[b]	625
USA	596	17	9.56	623

NOTES

[a] 1973 figure
[b] estimate

Conversion Rates

1 kg of coke = 1 kg of oil or tar = 0.95 m^3 of natural gas.

SOURCES

Belgium	Groupement des Hauts Fourneaux et Aciéries Belges
Canada	OECD
France	Chambre Syndicale de la Sidérurgie Français
West Germany	Herausgegeben von der Wirtschaftsvereinigung Eisen und Stahlindustrie
Japan	Japanese Iron and Steel Federation
Sweden	OECD and Carlsson (1975)
UK	British Steel Corporation
USA	American Iron and Steel Institute

TABLE 12.8 Hot Wide Strip Mills – fully continuous and semi-continuous rolling products over 1 metre wide

	Number of fully continuous mills	*Number of semi-continuous and ¾-continuous mills*	*Arithmetic mean start-up date*	*Average current rated capacity (m. tonnes p.a.)*
Austria		1*	1955	2.2
Belgium		5	1965	1.8
Canada		3*	1954	1.2
France	4		1960	3.3
West Germany	1	5*	1965	3.5
Italy	2	2	1964	2.7
Japan	8	9	1963	2.9
Luxembourg		Steckel strip mill only		
Netherlands	1	1	1962	2.3
Sweden		1	1962	1.2
UK	2	3	1958	1.8
USA	23	14*	1952	2.1

NOTES

Status at January 1979.
* includes mill with combination roughing stand/plate mill.
Coil plate mills excluded.

SOURCE

Strip mill survey.

private-sector mill of conservative design, Alphasteel at Newport, less than fifteen years old; Port Talbot is thirty years old, Shotton forty years old. West Germany has two substantially rebuilt twenty-year-old mills, the remaining four being of more recent construction. Klöckner Werke at Bremen replaced an 80-inch hot strip mill in April 1974 after operating it for fifteen years, as it was unable to meet production and quality requirements. And, unlike many American mills, none of the British mills have been extensively rebuilt. As a result, British strip mills have a lower rate of adoption of both quality-enhancing innovations, such as walking beam slab reheating furnaces, and output-enhancing innovations, such as higher slab and coil weights, higher rolling speeds, more powerful mill drives, computer control and fast roll changing devices. Quality also depends upon the preceding casting and steelmaking stages and subsequent cold rolling. The only British strip mill comparable in design with the best in Europe, Llanwern at Newport, is handicapped, at least on quality grounds, by not being fed with continuously cast slabs. It is reasonable to conclude that the relatively inadequate size, older age and lower technical sophistication of British strip mills goes some way to help explain recent import penetration for coil, strip and sheet products.

Plate mills

Plate mills illustrate in acute form the dilemmas posed by the British steel industry's failure to innovate. During the 1960s, when the industry was under private ownership, there was a boom in heavy and medium plate mill construction for the shipbuilding market. Four mills were installed, all with capacity in the range of 0.3 to 0.6 million tonnes a year and a maximum width of about 3.5 metres. With the decline of the domestic shipbuilding market and world overcapacity for heavy plate rolling, there has been no further investment in heavy plate mills, except for a sophisticated but low-output 4-metre stand, fitted to an existing mill at Dalzell by the British Steel Corporation.

With the development of wider, high-output, high-power mills, this capacity is now obsolescent. None of the mills is wide enough to roll plate for making large-diameter welded tubes, with the result that most of the North Sea oil pipeline has been imported. Apart from considerations of quality and product range, the operating costs of these older mills are high compared with a fully loaded modern mill. It is apparent from Table 12.9 that the British steel industry has not realised economies of scale in plate rolling which are enjoyed by some of its competitors.

The table also shows that considerable wide-plate capacity has already been installed elsewhere, notably in Japan and Italy. Even by steel industry

TABLE 12.9 Heavy and medium plate mills

	Number of mills	*Arithmetic mean start-up date*	*Average current rated capacity (m. tonnes p.a.)*	*Plate width from widest mill (metres)*
Austria	1	1958	0.35	4.00
Belgium	3	1966	0.44	4.20
Canada	3*	1965	0.50	3.90
France	4	n.a.	0.34	4.40
West Germany	8	1963	0.68	4.80
Italy	7*	1963	0.80	4.50
Japan	16*	1968	1.54	5.30
Luxembourg		no reversing plate mills		
Netherlands	1	1947	0.50	3.05
Sweden	3*	1962	0.39	3.40
UK	9	1963	0.44	3.96
USA	20*	1953	0.64	5.23

NOTES

Status at January 1979.
Excludes 2 and 3-high reversing mills.
n.a. = information available on less than 80 per cent of mills.
* includes combination roughing stand/plate mill

SOURCE

Plate mill survey.

standards a plate mill is a very capital-intensive unit, with two-thirds of the total cost per year being accounted for by capital charges. So a mill will only be profitable if fully utilised. Faced with a highly competitive market, the British Steel Corporation is left with the choice of either innovating by replacing existing capacity with a high-output mill of doubtful viability or losing the plate market to imports. The dilemma of importing or competing is common to a wide range of bulk steel products. The problem arises partly because the expansion of world steelmaking capacity in the 1960s and early 1970s has depressed world prices below the anticipated long-run marginal cost of future developments, and partly through Britain's declining competitiveness in world markets compared with other major producers, notably Japan. The British Steel Corporation lacks any wide-plate capacity for the foreseeable future, the proposed Redcar mill having been turned down by the sponsoring Government department.

Secondary refining for stainless steelmaking[10]

Secondary refining has revolutionised the manufacture of stainless steel within a decade. Stainless steel is an alloy of chrome and, often, nickel, with a very low carbon content. Secondary refining enables carbon to be removed in a separate refining vessel following initial melting in an arc furnace, without simultaneous loss of the valuable chrome content. At present, there are three secondary refining techniques available: the predominant process, Argon-Oxygen Decarburisation (AOD), a variant of AOD known as CLU, which partially replaces argon with steam, and the earliest process, Vacuum-Oxygen Decarburisation (VOD), which may yet prove to be a false start (Leach, 1977).

West Germany pioneered secondary refining with the VOD process, but Britain was one of the earliest adopters of AOD, which originated in the American nickel industry. The British Steel Corporation has since scaled up Arc-AOD melting with considerable success and married it to continuous casting in order to secure the economies of scale inherent in special steel melting. Swift diffusion of secondary refining was helped by the substantial capital and raw material cost savings realised by its adoption. The high rate of growth of stainless steel consumption also encouraged adoption of the process, since melting shop capacity could be effectively doubled by addition of a separate refining vessel at only a quarter of the cost of a second arc furnace. In Britain difficulties over joint public and private ownership of one of the main flat stainless works at Sheffield inhibited capacity expansion and delayed the adoption of secondary refining until the British Steel Corporation obtained full ownership in May 1972. Being a latecomer, the British Steel

Corporation was able to benefit from its own AOD experience, and US and Japanese success at continuously casting stainless steel on curved mould machines, to develop one of the world's largest arc-AOD melting shops for stainless steels at Shepcote Works, Sheffield.

No direct evidence is available on the share of stainless steel output produced by secondary refining processes. Instead, we impute the share of output made via this route on the basis of the known standing capacity of secondary refining vessels installed in each country in each year relative to their stainless steel production for that year. The unknown link between capacity and output is the number of heats produced by each refining vessel per year. In practice, the true constraint on output is likely to be the associated electric arc melting capacity cycle time. So we take a figure of 2400 heats a year. On this evidence (Table 12.10) the UK has a very high rate of adoption of AOD steelmaking, matched only by the USA, who initiated the technique. The lead is less marked when other processes are taken into account. Nevertheless, it reflects considerable credit on those who identified its potential and scaled up its operation, and offsets the poor commercial record of the UK stainless steel sector throughout the 1960s and early 1970s (Houghton, 1975).

Adoption of innovations: the overall picture

Our overall conclusion must be that the British steel industry has been slow in adopting new process innovations as compared with its major overseas competitors, notably West Germany and Japan. However, such new plant as has been built by the British Steel Corporation is technically sophisticated and sufficiently large to secure most of the technical economies of scale available in steelmaking. One notable exception in the picture of slow innovation is AOD secondary refining for stainless steelmaking. During interviews, British Steel Corporation Stainless emerged as a textbook example of an ideal innovator, relying both on its own developments and the best overseas practice as the basis for scaling up and swiftly adopting new technology with the support of considerable investment. It is possible that similar successes are to be observed in other areas we have not examined in detail, such as rod and bar mill technology and electric arc furnaces, where the BSC has achieved some remarkable performances.

THE DETERMINANTS OF INNOVATION

The investment record

To isolate any single factor as the sole cause of the British steel industry's

TABLE 12.10 The diffusion of secondary refining for stainless steelmaking

	Imputed Gini coefficient of diffusion for AOD refining, 1968–76	*Imputed Gini coefficient of diffusion for AOD and VOD refining, 1968–76*
Austria	VOD refining only	0.563
Belgium	No data on stainless steel output	
Canada	No data on stainless steel output	
France	0.132	0.272
West Germany	0.243	0.844
Italy	0.420	0.420
Japan	0.179	0.453
Sweden	0.239	0.688
UK	0.618	0.688
USA	0.616	0.713

NOTES

Assumes 2400 heats per vessel per year.
These diffusion coefficients assume full utilisation of installed capacity. Because of work-up difficulties, competition between producers, the cyclical nature of stainless steel production and the use of refining units for producing other alloy grades, the true rate of diffusion is likely to be below the hypothetical rate imputed here.

SOURCE

Plant survey based on Leach (1977) and output data from Inco Europe.

relatively poor innovative performance would be misleading. Yet given that most new techniques in the steel industry can only be introduced through capital spending on new plant and equipment, the cumulative effect of low investment in steel must bear a large part of the responsibility for the slow adoption of new innovations. In addition, a high rate of investment would provide a profit incentive for domestic plant manufacturers to develop high-quality capital goods while also enabling them to secure unit cost reductions through economies of scale in plant design and construction. By and large, British plant manufacturers have not had this incentive. For in terms of dollars spent per tonne of crude steel produced, the British steel industry's investment rate was well below that of major competitors throughout the innovatory period of the 1960s (Figure 12.4). It was not until British Steel Corporation investment schemes came to fruition that British investment rates

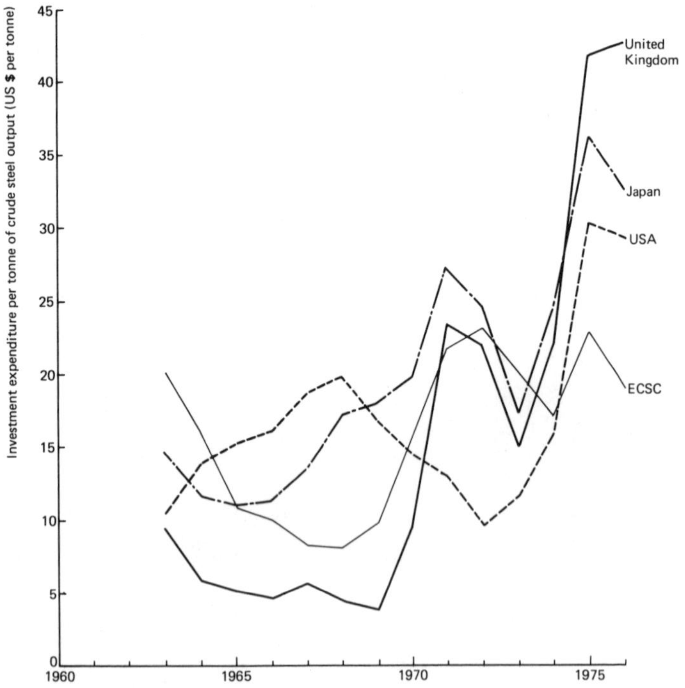

FIG. 12.4 Rates of investment in the world steel industry

NOTES
ECSC is former six members only.

SOURCE
OECD.

rose to match and then exceed world levels. No doubt Britain's relatively low rate of investment must go some way to explain the correspondingly low rate of embodied technical progress in many areas, particularly in rolling mills, blast furnaces and continuous casting.

Some crude but useful econometric evidence from Meyer and Herregat (1974) suggests steel industry investment can be readily explained in terms of two variables: profits and the pressure of demand as measured, say, by capacity utilisation. Britain does particularly badly in both these variables, steel industry profitability and the rate of growth of demand having been strikingly low as compared with other Western steel producers (Tables 12.11 and 12.12).

The slow rise in apparent steel consumption in Britain is attributable to a low rate of growth of national income and population, the maturity of the economy and the relative decline of the heavy steel-using industries such as shipbuilding and railway equipment (International Iron and Steel Institute 1972, 1974a). The industry has also faced declining international competitiveness in overseas steel markets and a loss of home markets to imports. A slow rate of growth of demand not only fails to provide an incentive to invest in

TABLE 12.11 National profit rates: operating profits as a percentage of capital employed

Country	*1961–71 Average Return on Capital (%)*
UK (fourteen major companies or BSC after 1967)	3.4
ECSC (including UK but excluding Italy)	13.3
Japan	19.2
USA and Canada	18.4

SOURCES

International Iron and Steel Institute (1974b); Shone (1975).

TABLE 12.12 National rates of growth of apparent steel consumption

Country	*1955–70 Rate of Growth (%)*
UK	2.1
ECSC	5.3
Japan	15.2
USA	3.2
Canada	5.1
World average	5.7

NOTE

Apparent Steel Consumption = Domestic Production + Imports – Exports

SOURCE

International Iron and Steel Institute (1972).

new plant to meet market expansion, but there is little impetus to replace existing plant either, since investment to meet market growth is often lumped together with replacement investment. We have already shown, for instance, how adoption of continuous casting and recent blast furnace technology was inhibited because existing capacity was adequate to meet the low rate of growth of derived demand for ironmaking and steelmaking.

Again, profits for the British steel industry were well below those of European, Japanese or North American producers throughout the 1960s (Table 12.11). Declining profitability has been attributed, with some force, to price control by the Iron and Steel Board and later by Government, coupled with a drop in capacity utilisation, and a world steel surplus which reduced the rate of return on export sales.[11] The period also saw the rise of Japan as a major steel exporter and competitor, helped by her lead in adopting new technology. So it might be argued that the British steel industry had neither the cash flow nor the market incentive to invest in new process technology.

In the 1960s some of the new plants that were built adopted technology that was inferior by world standards of the time. Both in terms of size of plant and choice of process, various firms made decisions which appear, with hindsight, either to be mistaken or, at least, sub-optimal from the point of view of the industry as a whole. In the case of oxygen steelmaking, firms were of insufficient size to exploit fully the economies of scale. A number of oxygen steelmaking plants adopted 'false start' technologies which were soon to prove inferior to BOS steelmaking. A Rotor plant was built at Redbourn, VLN converters installed at Port Talbot and three Kaldo plants completed at Shelton, Parkgate and Consett (Allen, 1967). All these plants were scrapped soon after nationalisation, apart from Shelton which was temporarily reprieved by Government intervention on closures. Few other countries made such bad judgements in their choice of oxygen steelmaking process, most world steelmakers adopting the now prevalent LD process at the outset. One explanation is that British steelmakers were reluctant to incur the upheaval and marked change in operating practice brought by LD steelmaking, and preferred processes which were closer in cycle time and chemistry to traditional open hearth steelmaking. Apart from a few firms, such as Richard Thomas & Baldwins and United Steel, the industry was technically conservative in its investment decisions while under private ownership.

Ownership and intervention

Nationalisation has been a unique influence on the investment performance of the British steel industry. Before nationalisation, the major private-sector firms lost their incentive to invest, a problem accentuated by uncertainty as to the likely date of nationalisation and difficulties in raising finance. After nationalisation, the industry took a breathing-space to sort out its future, with the result that investment spending did not rise until 1970. It is difficult to assess the true significance of nationalisation since we cannot know what would have happened during the period 1965–70 if the industry had not been taken into public ownership. Its impact on adoption of oxygen steelmaking is evident as a hiccup in the diffusion curve for Britain (Figure 12.2), and may also help explain Britain's lost lead in continuous casting (Figure 12.3).

Public ownership enabled the British Steel Corporation to sustain an internationally high level of capital spending during the 1970s through access to Government capital. As a result, within a decade of nationalisation all the major integrated works apart from Shotton were based on large-scale oxygen steelmaking. The switch to imported ores was complete, wherever relative prices favoured their use. Obsolete works were closed, though not as quickly as might have been hoped given that 17 per cent of BSC output was still produced via the open hearth route in 1977.

But otherwise nationalisation has proved a mixed blessing. For although the strategic decision to nationalise the industry may have been conducive to innovation in the long run, tactical Government intervention over particular schemes has been, by all accounts, disastrous. It is not necessarily that the British Government intervenes more often in the steel industry than Governments elsewhere, for intervention is widespread throughout the world steel industry (Federal Trade Commission, 1977, Chapters 5 and 6); rather that it intervenes less successfully. Steel's political importance is summed up by the fact that fourteen ministers represented steel constituencies threatened by plant closure in the 1976 Labour Government. The regional concentration of British Steel Corporation plants in Wales and Scotland adds devolutionary tensions. Such political pressures have led to decisions on the industry being taken at Cabinet and ministerial level without regard to technological and commercial considerations.

Government intervention has held back innovation by the British Steel Corporation in two ways: through delaying completion of new capacity and by withholding permission for closures of obsolete plant. These decisions have repercussions which spread far wider than the particular plant at issue as plants which are directly affected in this way usually form part of an inter-related system of production units.

As a result of constraints on plant closure and delays in sanctioning new schemes, the Corporation has been unable to adjust its capacity in line with demand. The combined effects of retaining plants beyond their optimal replacement date and maintaining surplus capacity, coupled with Government price control, severely limited the Corporation's ability to finance investment from its own internally generated funds. The Corporation relied instead on Government finance and consequently accumulated substantial liabilities in interest payments on uncompleted or under-utilised capital schemes. The resulting financial crisis, which became apparent in 1977, then had to be resolved partially by cutting back the investment programme. So Government intervention has, both directly and indirectly, held back innovation. There has also been widespread criticism of the technical competence and skills of civil servants charged with affecting Government policy towards the industry (e.g. Turner, 1977). Specific criticisms have been directed at the high rate of turnover of civil servants and their consequent lack of familiarity with the steel industry, and the sponsoring department's inability either to appraise the Corporation's investment proposals, or assess the efficiency of their eventual implementation.[12]

Labour and managerial problems of technical change

During interviews, the labour problems posed by technical change were also said to be a constraint on innovation. Apart from redundancy as a result of plant closures, difficulties have also arisen over manning, working practices and pay rates for new plants. The British Steel Corporation had particular difficulties over commissioning and working up a series of new, large plant units in the early 1970s, when handicapped by a shortage of management skills and the absence of recent experience of plant commissioning. However, generalisations are dangerous, since marked differences in approach can be observed between technically similar works. Nor are problems confined to the public sector. Difficulties of negotiating 21-shift manning for new plant units in Sheffield special steelworks were volunteered by both the public and private sector during successive interviews. The more successful commissioning seems to have been achieved at plant units where the management of innovation is recognised to be not only a question of excellent engineering, but also of good labour relations and training, and where manning and pay rates have been satisfactorily negotiated before plants were completed.

Labour problems have also arisen at steel plant construction sites, with labour productivity declining since 1970. The consequent delays in completion, and escalation of labour costs have outweighed any learning effects from repeat programmes. As a result, the British steel industry now has higher capital costs for equivalent new plant than Japan or Western Europe.

Shortage of skilled labour at prevailing wages was often mentioned as a further difficulty when commissioning new and sophisticated plant. The shortages seem to correspond with labour shortages elsewhere in the economy, notably of electricians for maintenance of new electronic control technology and, in the plant supply industry, of draughtsmen.

CONCLUSION

By and large, the British steel industry has adopted process innovations more slowly than its major Western competitors. Where modern steelmaking technology has been adopted in the industry, the new plants are comparable, at least in terms of capacity, with plants of leading steelmakers overseas. But unlike Japan and West Germany, the British steel industry has not innovated right across the board at all stages of production. British iron and steelmaking plant, especially blast furnaces and rolling mills, are older, smaller and less well equipped than those of our major OECD competitors. Although the steel industry's technical effort at R&D is comparatively strong, it is behind that of West Germany and Japan, largely confined to the public sector of the industry, and now declining.

Given the link between choice of technology, size, design and plant performance, and also the link between costs, quality and competitiveness, the relatively slow rate of adoption of innovations in the British steel industry is cause for concern. Unless the industry is to continue to rely on a relatively low level of real wages to maintain competitiveness, the level of adoption of new process innovations will have to rise in order to secure markets for the complete range of steel products in the face of even greater world competition in both bulk and special steels.

A faster rate of adoption of recent process developments could be readily achieved through a higher rate of investment. There are no significant supply constraints on the availability of best-practice technology and no construction or commissioning difficulties that could not be solved by good management. The success of the stainless steel sector in adopting AOD secondary refining demonstrates that none of the problems of innovation are insuperable. An innovation policy for British steelmakers is also an innovation policy for plant suppliers. The higher rate of learning and economies of scale inherent in designing and constructing steel plant at a faster rate should help both their own domestic innovative effort and, through provision of reference designs, their export performance.

NOTES

1. I owe an enormous debt to many British and German steelmakers and plantmakers for their time, advice and hospitality between 1976 and 1978. Although much of the material in the chapter was obtained from these interviews and visits, no unpublished items of information have been attributed, in order to protect confidentiality of sources. Any merit this paper might have is attributable to their help and to the comments of Mike Brown, Ian Christmas and Bernard Keeling. Christine Fielding and Bob Ward provided research assistance. But I alone must take the blame for errors, omissions and misinterpretations which remain.
2. For an analysis of the influence of steel industry structure on industry performance see Cockerill (1974).
3. Maxwell (1976) is a major contribution on the nature of innovation in the steel industry. An indication of the scope of world steelmaking innovations from an American viewpoint is provided by Pitler (1977).
4. The literature on oxygen steelmaking innovation includes an excellent study by Meyer and Herregat (1974).
5. See Meyer and Herregat (1974, p. 198–9) for the derivation of this Gini coefficient of diffusion. Briefly, the relative coefficient of diffusion for each country is given by:

$$\tfrac{1}{2} \sum_{t=1}^{n} (p_t + p_{t-1})/(n-1)$$

where p_t is the proportion of output produced by the new technique in each of the n years of diffusion.

6. A dated but still useful assessment of continuous casting is United Nations Economic Commission for Europe (1968). Also see Schenk (1974).
7. Concast is a multinational design organisation based in Switzerland but partly owned by the British Steel Corporation.
8. Useful discussions of blast furnace innovations are provided by Lenger (1972) and Iron and Steel Institute (1973).
9. Lederer (1973) is useful for plate mills, Lederer (1975) and Ess (1970) discuss strip mills.
10. For an introduction to secondary refining, see Leach (1977).
11. See British Iron and Steel Federation (1966, Chapter 6). Shone (1975) disputes the significance of price control.
12. See, for instance, National Economic Development Office (1976), Select Committee on Nationalised Industries (1973, p. 102, 163) and Select Committee on Nationalised Industries (1978, vol. 1).

REFERENCES

(i) *Books and Articles*

J. A. Allen, *Studies in Innovation in the Steel and Chemical Industries* (Manchester: Manchester University Press, 1967).

American Iron and Steel Institute, *Steel Industry Economics and Federal Income Tax Policy* (Washington, D.C.: AISI, June 1975).

D. Ault, 'The Determinants of World Steel Exports: an Empirical Study', *Review of Economics and Statistics*, 54 (Feb. 1972) 1, 38–46.

J. Aylen, 'The British Steel Corporation and Technical Change', appendix 23 of Select Committee on Nationalised Industries, vol. 3 (1978) .

Battelle-Institut, 'Scale Advantages of Equipment in the Iron and Steel Industry' Bilaga 6 of *Handelsstålsutredningen* (1977).

British Iron and Steel Federation, *The Steel Industry, Stage I Report of the Development Coordinating Committee* (Benson Report) (London: BISF, 1966).

D. L. Burn, *Economic History of Steelmaking 1870–1939* (Cambridge: Cambridge University Press, 1940).

D. L. Burn, *The Steel Industry 1939–59* (Cambridge: Cambridge University Press, 1961).

B. Carlsson, *Scale and Performance of Blast Furnaces in Five Countries – a Study of Best Practice Technology* (paper presented at the Second Conference on Economics of Industrial Structure, Nijenrode, Netherlands: Apr. 1–3, 1975) mimeo.

A. Cockerill with A. Silberston, *The Steel Industry* (Cambridge: Cambridge University Press, 1974).

CONCAST Documentation Center, *World Survey of Continuous Casting Machines for Steel (Situation 1.1.1977)* (Zurich: Concast AG, March 1977).

R. Cordero and R. Serjeantson, *Iron and Steel Works of the World* (Worcester Park, Surrey: Metal Bulletin Books, 6th edn., 1974).

Council on Wage and Price Stability, *Report to the President on Prices and*

Costs in the United States Steel Industry (Washington D.C.: US Government Printing Office, Oct. 1977).

W. H. Dennis, *Foundations of Iron and Steel Metallurgy* (Amsterdam: Elsevier, 1967).

E. Earnshaw, 'Notes on the Layout of Wide Hot Strip Mills', *Steel Times* (Apr. 1978) 303–16.

C. Erickson, *British Industrialists: Steel and Hosiery 1850–1950* (Cambridge: Cambridge University Press, 1959).

T. Ess, *The Hot Strip Mill Generation II* (Pittsburgh: American Association of Iron and Steel Engineers, 1970).

Federal Trade Commission, *Staff Report on the United States Steel Industry and its International Rivals: Trends and Factors Determining International Competitiveness* (Washington, D.C.: US Government Printing Office, Nov. 1977).

E. Friedl and C. Schmidt, 'Dimensioning of LD converters', in Iron and Steel Institute (1972) 78–94.

Handelsstålsutredningen, Handelsstålsindustrin inför 1980 – (Nabseth Report) 2 vols (Stockholm: Statens Offentliga utredningar, 1977).

G. Heynert and E. Legille, 'Bell-less Top for High Top Pressure Furnaces', in Iron and Steel Institute (1973) 109–30.

D. Houghton, 'Planning for a Stainless Future', *British Steel* (Winter/Spring 1975) 8–15.

International Iron and Steel Institute, *Projection '85: World Steel Demand* (Brussels: IISI, 1972).

International Iron and Steel Institute, *Steel Intensity and GNP Structure* (Brussels: IISI, 1974a).

International Iron and Steel Institute, *Financing Steel Investment in Certain Major Steel Producing Countries 1961–1971* (Brussels: IISI, 1974b).

Iron and Steel Institute, *Operation of Large BOF's* (London: ISI, 1972)

Iron and Steel Institute, *Developments in Ironmaking Practice* (London: ISI, 1973), special report.

J. C. C. Leach, 'Secondary Refining for Electric Steelmaking', *Ironmaking and Steelmaking*, 4 (1977) 2, 58–65.

A. H. Leckie and A. J. Morris, 'Effect of Plant and Works Scale on Costs in the Iron and Steel Industry', *Journal of the Iron and Steel Institute*, 206 (May 1968) 442–52.

A. Lederer, 'The Plate Mill of Today', *Iron and Steel Engineer*, 50 (Jan. 1973) 1, 41–52.

A. Lederer, 'Zum Entwicklungsstand von Warmbreitbandstrassen', *Bänder Bleche Rohre*, 6 (1975) available in revised form as *State of Development of Wide Hot Strip Mills* (Düsseldorf: Sack, 1978).

F. Lenger, 'Modern Blastfurnace Design in Germany', in J. Szekely (ed.), *Blast Furnace Technology* (New York: Marcel Dekker, 1972).

P. Maxwell, *Learning and Technical Change in the Steelplant of Acindar SA in Rosario, Argentina* (Buenos Aires: United Nations Commission for Latin America, Monografia de Trabajo, 4, 1976).

D. N. McCloskey, 'Productivity Change in British Pig Iron, 1870–1939' *Quarterly Journal of Economics*, 82 (1968) pp. 281–96.

J. R. Meyer and G. Herregat, 'The Basic Oxygen Steel Process' (1974), in L. Nabseth and G. F. Ray (1974) 146–199.

L. Nabseth and G. F. Ray (eds), *The Diffusion of New Industrial Processes* (Cambridge: Cambridge University Press, 1974).

National Economic Development Office, *A Study of UK Nationalised Industries* (London: NEDO, 1976).

Office of Technology Assessment and Forecast, *US Patent Activity in Thirty Nine Standard Industrial Classification Categories*, information supplied to the Science Policy Research Unit by OTAF, US Department of Commerce (Washington: 1977).

Organisation for Economic Cooperation and Development, *International Statistical Year 1973, Survey of the Resources Devoted to R-D by OECD Member Countries, Vol. 1, Business Enterprise Sector* (Paris: OECD Directorate for Science Technology and Industry, 1977).

R. Pitler, *World Technological Developments and their Adoption by the Steel Industry in the United States* (paper presented at annual meeting of American Iron and Steel Institute, 1977) mimeo.

W. Schenk, 'Continuous Casting of Steel', in L. Nabseth and G. F. Ray (1974) 232–50.

Select Committee on Nationalised Industries, *First Report from the Select Committee, Session 1972–3, British Steel Corporation* (London: HMSO, 1973).

Select Committee on Nationalised Industries, *First Report from the Select Committee on Nationalised Industries, Session 1977–8, British Steel Corporation*, 3 vols (London: HMSO, 1978).

Sir R. Shone, *Price and Investment Relationships: a Study in Applied Economics* (London: Elek, 1975).

J. K. Stone, *L-D Process Newsletter No. 69* (Zurich: Brassert Oxygen Technik AG, June 1977).

Statistical Office of the European Communities, *Quarterly Iron and Steel Statistical Bulletin* (Brussels: Statistical Office, 4th quarter 1976).

P. Témin, The Relative Decline of the British Steel Industry' in H. Rosovsky (ed.) *Industrialization in Two Systems* (New York: Wiley, 1966).

G. Turner, 'Do We Get the Right Chaps?' *Sunday Telegraph* (8 May 1977) 6–7.

United Nations Economic Commission for Europe, *Economic Aspects of Continuous Casting of Steel* (New York: UN, 1968).

J. Vaizey, *The History of British Steel* (London: Weidenfeld & Nicolson, 1974).

(ii) *Statistical Series*

American Iron and Steel Institute, *Annual Statistical Report* (Washington, D.C.: AISI.)

British Steel Corporation, *Iron and Steel Industry: Annual Statistics for the United Kingdom* (Croydon: BSC.)

Chambre Syndicale de la Siderurgie Française, *La Siderurgie Française en 19–: Rapport d'Activité* (Paris: CSSF, annual).

Groupement des Hauts Fourneaux et Aciéries Belges, *La Sidérurgie Belge en 19–* (Brussels: GHFAB, annual).

Herausgegeben von der Wirtschaftsvereinigung Eisen und Stahlindustrie *Statistisches Jahrbuch 19– der Eisen und Stahlindustrie* (Düsseldorf: Verlag Stahleisen, annual).

Inco Europe, *World Stainless Steel Statistics 19–* (Worcester Park, Surrey: Metal Bulletin Books, annual).

International Iron and Steel Institute, *World Steel in Figures 19–* (Brussels: IISI, annual).

Japanese Iron and Steel Federation, *Book of Iron and Steel Monthly Statistics* (Tokyo: JISF, monthly, in Japanese).

Organisation for Economic Cooperation and Development, *The Iron and Steel Industry in 19–* (Paris: OECD, annual).

13 Heavy Electrical Plant

A. J. Surrey, C. M. Buckley and M. J. Robson

In the 1950s, the UK industry – which included Metropolitan Vickers, British Thomson-Houston, English Electric, Brush, Parsons, Reyrolle, GEC, Ferranti, Crompton Parkinson, and Richardsons Westgarth – had a healthy flow of home orders and a large share of world trade in electrical generating plant and transmission equipment. The 1960s saw a large peak in home orders and a wave of takeovers that left GEC and Reyrolle Parsons as the only UK suppliers offering a full product range, including large steam-turbine generators, power transformers and switchgear. The 1970s have been a lean period for the UK industry, with few home orders and lingering uncertainty about the future. This chapter examines the industry's recent performance and its prospects. First, we explain the technical and market framework in which it operates.

THE COMPETITIVE FRAMEWORK

The main features to be highlighted are the importance of product reliability, increasing unit size, fluctuations in ordering, specialist engineering and know-how, a high degree of concentration, and non-tariff-barrier protection of domestic markets.

Proven reliability is of crucial importance to utilities, given their public service obligations to meet demand and avoid supply interruptions, and high additional fuel and repair costs imposed by late completion or breakdown. If, for example, a 500 MW steam-turbine generator, operating at 75 per cent annual load factor and 35 per cent thermal efficiency, breaks down and remains out of service for six months, and if its output has to be replaced by older plant with a thermal efficiency of only 25 per cent, the result is an extra consumption of about 250,000 tons of coal equivalent. If the fuel price is £20 a ton, the utility will face an additional fuel bill of about £5 million. Additional fuel costs and repair costs are high in relation to the initial cost of the turbine generator. While price, credit terms and customer-supplier preferences are often the deciding factors between bids of approximately equal technical merit and reliability, a supplier that can demonstrate greater manufacturing experience and product reliability is usually at a considerable advantage compared with one that is competing primarily on price.

Technical progress, largely incremental in nature, has been a marked and continuous feature of the industry since its inception around 1900. It has been reflected in a worldwide trend towards larger turbine generators and higher-voltage transmission equipment. The typical size of steam-turbine generators being installed in the industrialised countries rose from 30–150 MW in the mid-fifties to 500–1200 MW in the mid-seventies. The promise of lower capital and operating costs is the reason that utilities with sufficiently large integrated transmission systems have installed successive vintages of bigger, more fuel-efficient plants. The aim has been to minimise total system costs by operating modern plants with relatively low running costs at base load, and by demoting less efficient plant to successively lower load factors.

Since it typically takes five to eight years to build new conventional thermal power stations (and eight to fourteen years for nuclear stations), quite small changes in the forecast growth rate of demand for electricity induce pronounced fluctuations in ordering. Bigger fluctuations, induced by longer lead times and increased size of units, have aggravated the difficulties of the suppliers, who need to achieve high use of their development, design, and manufacturing resources to recoup overhead costs and remain profitable. Long lead times also lengthen the process of incorporating operating experience into equipment design.

Continuous improvement in product design and performance requires experienced design and development teams, highly specific test facilities, precision engineering and know-how, acquired over years of continuous design and manufacture, and a variety of technical support services. A further prerequisite for survival is the financial resilience to weather-lean periods and teething troubles with new designs. Both requirements tend to confer advantage on the large supplier, and are reflected in the high degree of concentration and stiff barriers to new entrants, especially at the advanced-technology end of the product range. The dozen full-line suppliers that dominate the world industry today are major groups that are highly diversified, often in mutually reinforcing areas of technology such as nuclear power, gas turbines, aerospace, computers, and other electronic capital goods, and a variety of consumer appliances.

Domestic markets are generally highly protected, especially by nationalistic procurement policies and customer preferences based upon technical and personal familiarity with particular suppliers. Informal barriers, such as a utility's dependence upon the supplier for technical support services, fear of being kept at the back of the queue when orders bunch, and the odium surrounding foreign procurement when local jobs are at stake (especially for publicly owned or regulated utilities) are often more important than formal protection. For some utilities, a further important consideration is the fear of being left at the mercy of a monopoly supplier.

Dependence on a safe home market is common throughout the world. It is true even of Brown Boveri, the Swiss-based group which, through its many foreign subsidiaries and licensees, has access to many protected home markets. Even in the large US market, where there are approximately 200 utilities, General Electric and Westinghouse have retained the dominant share. Foreign supply has been mainly confined to a few big utilities that have sufficient technical resources to be independent of domestic suppliers and which regard importing as a means of increasing competition.

Within the industry, a profitable base of home orders is widely held to be the *sine qua non* of long-term survival. This is necessary to enable manufacturers to sustain high overhead costs, to acquire the experience in manufacturing their latest designs needed to descend the 'learning curve' (thereby reducing variable costs), and to obtain a 'shop window' to display their technical merits to overseas customers. A supplier is generally unlikely to be able to export more technologically-advanced designs than those embodied in its domestic orders, or survive for a long period on export business alone.

Closely associated with the protection of national companies and markets is the extent of know-how licensing, both among the major groups and among them and their foreign subsidiaries and associated companies. Besides generating direct income, which helps to sustain a broad-based development and design effort, licensing often yields major orders for components that are beyond the licensee's technical capability. Export restriction clauses and the possibility that technical support may be withdrawn also tend to inhibit the licensee's freedom outside his domestic market. Licensing and the use of tied aid are important ways by which the major groups seek to maintain and extend their share of overseas markets.

International competition is further regulated through the International Electrical Association, which imposes financial penalties upon its members who undercut recommended prices in export markets (Newfarmer, 1978; Epstein and Mirow, 1977).

PREVIOUS DIAGNOSES

By the 1970s, the situation in the UK industry was very different from that of ten years earlier. The forecasts of demand that had caused the boom in home ordering in the early sixties were too high, with the result that home ordering diminished because electricity demand had not caught up with generating capacity. According to the CPRS (Central Policy Review Staff, 1976), the UK plant supply industry had an output capacity of 8-10 GW a year.[1] In the most pessimistic case, home orders would consist entirely of replacement demand (2 GW a year) and only one-third of the industry's capacity would be utilised throughout the eighties.

In addition, severe delays and teething difficulties had beset the introduction of the 500 MW high-speed, tandem-compound steam-turbine generators and the subsequent 660 MW version. Series ordering of 500 MW units began in 1960, without prototype experience or standardisation.[2] By 1968, 10,705 MW of CEGB (Central Electricity Generating Board) plant were subject to delay, 30 out of the 70 units affected by at least 12 months (UK Government, 1968). Lead times and operating performance of new plant have continued to cause concern.

It will be difficult for UK suppliers to regain export markets lost in the sixties, since competition has intensified from established European and American groups, from emerging Japanese suppliers, from local firms with domestic preferences in former export markets, and from the Communist countries. Having acquired American technology under licence, the Japanese industry has been competing since 1970 on the world market across the full range of heavy electrical equipment; it has been especially successful in Far Eastern markets and has made inroads elsewhere.

Few export markets are sufficiently large to provide a *flow* of orders. Foreign and local suppliers have made considerable inroads in Britain's major traditional markets (Canada, South Africa and Australia). The principal export markets offering a flow of orders have been the USA in particular and the more developed countries of Latin America; but UK suppliers had not previously obtained significant business there (Surrey and Chesshire, 1972). UK suppliers can offer neither an exportable nuclear reactor design nor the 'systems' capability needed to design and build complete power stations in some of the less developed countries (CPRS, 1976). Increased unit scale has also accentuated the problem of over-capacity in Continental Europe. It has been recognised that nationalistic procurement has contravened the spirit of the Treaty of Rome, and that two or three groups could supply the whole of Western Europe; nevertheless, rationalisation in Europe has everywhere taken place along national lines and home markets have stayed protected. The EEC hoped to bring about an eventual rationalisation of the European industry; but, as in several other key industries such as computers, aerospace and nuclear power, it has bowed to the pressures of technological nationalism. American light water reactor technologies have been firmly established throughout Europe since 1970 (except in the UK).

According to the CPRS, 33,000 jobs were held to be at risk in the UK power plant manufacturing industry (including turbine generators, boilers and major component suppliers). Unemployment and social security payments for 33,000 redundant workers would be £110 million in the first year alone. If the industry collapsed, the annual balance of payments cost in the eighties would be around £350 million (£250 million in lost exports plus £200 million in imports, minus £100 million for workers re-employed in other export industries). The redundancies would aggravate regional unemployment, especially in the North East, Strathclyde, Northern Ireland, Rugby and Stafford.

The studies by the CPRS and by Surrey and Chesshire concluded that a strong UK capability in this skill-intensive, high value-added industry was essential for the balance of payments, regional policy, the Government's over overall industrial strategy, and related activities such as nuclear reactors and gas turbines, which need a strong base in power engineering.

THE UK INDUSTRY IN CONTEXT

How has the UK industry performed compared to that in other countries? This is difficult to answer concisely, except in terms of broad market shares, given the heterogeneous output of the industry, and changes in classification in the official trade statistics. However, both the USA and the UK, the largest exporters of generating and transmission equipment in the fifties, suffered a contraction in market share in the sixties (see Table 13.1). In both cases, however, the decline seems to have been arrested in the seventies. The opposite was true for Japan and France, whose shares increased significantly in the sixties. It is clear also that Germany has established itself as the leading exporter.

To give a clearer picture of the international standing of the UK industry with regard to turbine generators, we present the findings of a survey we conducted in 1977, which covers units of 30 MW and above for nuclear, fossil fuel and hydro-electric power stations commissioned since January 1970, and those due to be commissioned by December 1985.[3] Our survey covered 58 countries (all the non-Communist industrialised countries and the larger developing countries); it thus includes almost all plants of 30 MW and above installed since 1970 and on order outside the Communist countries.

As in the fifties and sixties, manufacturers' home markets today generally remain tightly closed to outsiders. Domestic suppliers account for all the plant installed and on order in the UK, France, Germany and Italy and around

TABLE 13.1 Shares of world exports of electric power equipment, 1955–75

			percentages			
	1955	*1959*	*1964*	*1969*	*1972*	*1975*
UK	22.2	19.0	13.2	9.4	8.9	8.8
France	6.0	6.1	9.1	9.3	10.3	11.6
Germany	18.5	22.8	22.6	23.7	21.9	21.6
Italy	1.9	1.8	4.6	5.4	4.9	4.3
Sweden	2.5	2.5	4.7	2.7	3.3	3.4
Switzerland	n.a.	n.a.	5.1	5.3	4.8	4.9
USA	31.9	26.2	22.8	20.3	17.2	18.0
Japan	1.3	5.8	3.8	8.5	10.2	8.5
Main exporters	84.3	84.2	85.9	92.6	81.5	81.1
Others	15.7	15.8	14.1	7.4	18.5	18.9

SOURCE

United Nations Commodity Trade Statistics, SITC 722.1 and 722.2.

90 per cent in Sweden, Switzerland, Japan and the USA. Japan's imports are confined to large units for nuclear and oil-fired plants, in keeping with the tradition of importing the first unit of a new design and manufacturing domestically under licence all subsequent units. The USA is the only home market where foreign supply has increased (11 per cent in 1970–85 compared with 6 per cent in 1955–70). Nevertheless, the 89 per cent retained by the US industry represented a far bigger home market than that available to any of its competitors. Excluding plants for which the manufacturers were unknown when the survey was made, exports formed around 26 per cent of the world market; but the true proportion is likely to be lower, given that many of the units for which the manufacturer was unknown are being installed in largely closed markets.

In orders obtained for installation in the period 1970–81, the British suppliers each appear to be on a par with Alsthom (France) and the three Japanese suppliers, but only half the size of Kraftwerk Union and Brown Boveri, and only a quarter the size of General Electric and Westinghouse (see Table 13.2). This comparison excludes ancillary work (major overhauls, sub-contract work and hydro-electric generators) which uses some of the technology and resources involved in the manufacture of steam-turbine generators.

TABLE 13.2 Installation of steam-turbine generators by principal manufacturers, 1970–81

		GW			
		1970–3	*1974–7*	*1978–81*	*1970–81*
General Electric	(United States)	47.3	60.4	45.7	153.4
Westinghouse	(United States)	53.1	30.9	40.5	124.5
KWU	(F R Germany)	14.7	18.2	19.8	52.7
Brown Boveri	(*)	18.4	24.6	18.0	61.0
GEC	(UK)	13.4	5.9	15.9	35.2
Parsons	(UK)	11.8	12.4	9.8	34.0
Toshiba	(Japan)	12.2	10.7	8.2	31.1
Mitsubishi	(Japan)	10.0	11.1	10.3	31.4
Hitachi	(Japan)	9.5	9.7	7.2	26.4
Alsthom	(France)	5.1	6.9	14.6	30.6

NOTE

* Includes works in Switzerland, F R Germany, and France.

SOURCE

Survey by authors in 1977.

In exports of steam-turbine generators, Germany and Japan have gained strength, whilst the shares of world exports of the USA, UK and Switzerland have shrunk (see Table 13.3). However, the trade performance of the US and Swiss industries is understated in Table 13.3, since they both supply major components to foreign subsidiaries with whom the main orders are placed. In many cases the utilities that supplied the data attributed the orders to the domestic subsidiary rather than the parent group.

The regional distribution of exports varies considerably amongst countries (see Table 13.4). Those from Britain strongly reflect old Imperial ties, whilst those from Germany and Switzerland are concentrated on Europe and the USA. French exports are concentrated on Europe, whilst Japan and the USA depend more on South East Asian and Latin American markets. Canada, Australia, South Africa and Hong Kong account for three-quarters of UK exports, but in each case the UK share has contracted. The flow of UK exports to Canada is largely due to Parsons' link with James Howden, a domestic parts-manufacturer, which enabled Parsons to obtain a series of orders for Ontario Hydro. Unlike its major competitors, the UK industry has obtained very few orders from the non-producing countries in Europe and

TABLE 13.3 Production and exports of steam-turbine generators by the principal manufacturing countries, 1970–85*

	Total production GW	*Exports GW*	*% Share of World Exports 1970–85*	*(1955–75)*
Germany	103.3	55.2	27.4	(16.8)
Japan	94.5	30.6	15.2	(4.6)
France	48.0	19.1	9.5	(8.1)
UK	71.8	34.4	17.1	(26.8)
Switzerland	32.6	31.9	15.9	(20.5)
USA	352.4	20.9	10.0	(20.1)

NOTE

* Excludes Sweden, Italy, and Eastern bloc; their exports formed 4.9 per cent of total exports in the survey period.

SOURCE

Survey by authors in 1977.

Latin America. Brown Boveri has consolidated its position as the leading foreign supplier in the US market, and Kraftwerk Union – with the aid of the link it formed in 1970 with Allis Chalmers – has become the second.[4] These two account for 86 per cent of US imports of steam-turbine generators in the survey, both having established a reputable position among some of the major US utilities. The British industry obtained only three out of the 51 US orders placed with foreign suppliers all with GEC (or its pre-merger companies) in the late sixties, before Kraftwerk Union became the second preferred foreign supplier.

Exports of steam turbine generators are analysed by unit size in Table 13.5. Care is needed in interpreting the data, given technical differences amongst the various types of unit; technical difficulty tends to increase not only with size but, among other things, with the rotating speed of the low-pressure turbine and the generator. Of the 629 units exported in the survey period, 545 were under 600 MW and 289 were under 200 MW. Of the 84 units above 600 MW that were exported, 61 were for nuclear plant. Of those, six were for heavy water reactor and 55 for light water reactor nuclear plants. Despite having no home market for such machines, Parsons has obtained orders for five units for nuclear power stations in Canada, and GEC are supplying three units above 1000 MW for light water reactor plants in the USA. Kraftwerk

TABLE 13.4 Principal export markets of the six largest countries which make steam-turbine generators, 1970–85

	GW (no. of units) exported from					
Where installed	*USA*	*UK*	*France*	*Germany*	*Switz.*	*Japan*
USA		3.3(3)	1.0(2)	18.5(28)	19.3(18)	
Canada		14.8(34)		0.8(4)	0.3(2)	2.3(10)
EEC*		0.1(1)	8.9(23)	4.2(8)	5.0(16)	
Other European†	1.0(2)	1.0(5)	2.4(11)	9.5(33)	4.8(17)	4.2(18)
Japan	5.8(7)			0.4(1)		
Australia and New Zealand		7.9(34)		2.1(10)	1.0(2)	4.5(11)
S.E. Asia	7.8(13)	4.3(18)	1.8(7)	3.2(12)		7.9(42)
Latin America	1.8(8)			4.9(12)	0.3(6)	8.7(34)
South Africa		1.8(3)	4.3(9)	4.6(17)	1.1(5)	0.1(2)
Iran	0.7(4)	0.1(1)	0.2(5)	6.7(8)		0.7(2)
Other	3.2(11)	1.4(4)	0.5(9)	0.5(3)	0.1(4)	2.7(17)
Total	20.3(45)	34.7(103)	19.1(66)	55.4(136)	31.9(70)	31.1(136)

NOTES

* Predominantly Belgium, Netherlands and Denmark.
† Predominantly Spain, Turkey and Finland.

This table excludes other exports, chiefly from Sweden, Italy and the Eastern bloc; these form 5.5% of total exports.

SOURCE

Survey by authors in 1977.

TABLE 13.5 Manufacturers' export performance by size of unit, 1970–85

	Largest set for installation in home market		*30–200*		*201–400*		*401–600*		*601–800*		*801–1000*		*1001–1200*		*1201*	
	CONV	*NUC*	*CONV*	*NUC*	*CONV*	*NUC*	*CONV*	*NUC*	*CONV*	*NUC*	*CONV*	*NUC*	*CONV*	*NUC*	*CONV*	*NUC*
	MW		*Number of units installed in export markets*													
General Electric	884	1260	12		8	1		1		1	2	4		2		
Westinghouse	1080	1358	2		4		1			6		3				
Brown Boveri	707	1295	27		45	1	19		2			1		3	5	8
KWU	740	1300	38		26	1	4		12	1		1		7		6
Alsthom	585	925	11		17	2	3					4				
GEC	660	660	13		10	2	10							3		
Parsons	660	660	35		8		11	8		6						
Toshiba	1000	1100	18		8		4									
Mitsubishi	1000	1175	39		25		2			2						
Hitachi	1000	1000	23	1	17											
Others	640	1000	70		6	6	5	1	2	2		1				
			288	1	174	13	59	10	16	18	2	14		15	5	14

SOURCE

Survey by authors in 1977.

Union are exporting 14 units above 1000 MW for light water reactor plants and Brown Boveri are exporting nine. At the time of the survey, the Japanese suppliers had not exported units above 800 MW, although they had made them for their home market.

TOWARDS A SOLUTION

We conclude that the UK industry today faces problems which are similar to, but more severe (because of the downturn in international ordering) than those portrayed in the earlier diagnoses. The problems are partly cyclical (few current orders owing to low growth of electricity demand at home and overseas) and partly structural (too much manufacturing capacity distributed among too many locations to permit efficient production in the future). During the 1970s, these problems have led to two broad types of Government and CEGB assistance to the industry.

First, at Government instigation and with Government compensation, the CEGB placed an advance order in 1972 with Parsons for two 500 MW units for the Ince B oil-fired power station. A year later, three 660 MW units for the Littlebrook D oil-fired power station were ordered from GEC. But for the situation facing the plant supply industry, it would be difficult to understand why the order was not cancelled when oil prices quadrupled a few months later.

All electric utilities try to keep enough spare capacity (plant margin) to insure against unexpectedly high levels of demand or plant breakdown. Until 1968 (when it was raised to 20 per cent), the CEGB thought that 17 per cent was the required plant margin. In 1977 the desired plant margin was raised to 28 per cent, partly because of the uncertain performance of the largest units. The 28 per cent plant margin, together with accelerated scrapping and lengthening lead times, served also to bring forward the date that could justify the placing of new orders. The situation of the plant supply industry (including the reactor design teams and nuclear component suppliers) was also a factor in the 1974 decision to build steam-generating heavy water reactors, which was later rescinded when the technical difficulties came to light (see Chapter 14).

The decision in 1977 to build Drax B coal-fired station was also an 'advance' order – the CEGB is to receive up to £50 million compensation. After long, sometimes acrimonious negotiations, Parsons was promised the order without the prior agreement on rationalisation that was recommended by the CPRS, the CEGB and the National Enterprise Board. In 1978 the Government authorised two further AGR (Advanced Gas-cooled Reactor) power stations, resulting in orders for four 660 MW steam-turbine generators.

Other assistance to the industry has included the bringing forward of major overhauls, payments by the CEGB for R&D (through the Power Engineering Research Committee), and the co-operation of the electricity supply industry in setting up British Electricity International to provide technical advice to home and especially overseas clients. This assistance falls a long way short of a strategy to solve the underlying problem (see Surrey and Chesshire, 1972 and CPRS, 1976). Such a strategy must have four components:

1. *Rationalisation and modernisation*. However efficient an individual works may be, the overall efficiency of the industry will be impaired as long as the orders available are spread between the four works of GEC and the one owned by Parsons. Rationalisation and modernisation are essential if an efficient UK capability in heavy electrical engineering is to be achieved. World over-capacity means that transnational mergers, as contemplated in the early seventies, will probably not be possible in the foreseeable future on acceptable terms regarding management control, redundancies, and development and design work. The UK industry is unlikely to have sufficient orders and financial strength to offer a full product range embodying the latest technology while it retains its present structure. A more viable basis would be one turbine generator supplier with rationalised production facilities. Rationalisation will need to be preceded by a detailed investigation to identify the resources and skills worth preserving and building upon. It must be followed by investment in modern manufacturing and test facilities.
2. *Domestic ordering.* Especially if electricity growth remains low, further advance orders will be out of the question. Unless exports increase, a new crisis will be likely when current home orders are completed. At worst, further home orders might consist of only 2 GW a year of 'replacement' demand (CPRS, 1976). As far as possible, the CEGB should try to smooth its orders. If electricity demand grows faster than we think likely, the CEGB should try to avoid an excessive bunching of orders.
3. *Exports.* It will not be easy to increase UK exports, especially if international ordering remains low and if UK efforts remain concentrated on increasingly competitive Commonwealth markets to the exclusion of other opportunities. If the industry is to obtain business in the Third World, it will need a turnkey or systems capability for orders arising from the less developed countries. It will need to co-operate with those industrialising countries that want to increase domestic content and require access to a comprehensive range of technical services, including know-how for manufacturing components, civil engineering, and training.

Even Canada must be considered a vulnerable market now that James

Howden has changed its technological affiliation from Parsons to Brown Boveri. Parsons can no longer count upon a customer-supplier preference from Ontario Hydro, the biggest Canadian utility. Thanks mainly to currency movements, Britain does not seem badly placed in international price competition. In the period 1970–76 labour costs (measured in 1970 US dollars) rose by only 85 per cent in the UK, compared with 214 per cent in Japan, 176 per cent in France, 173 per cent in Switzerland, and 145 per cent in Germany. Another factor is that, since 1975, many foreign suppliers have received few home orders. While this situation lasts they cannot spread their overhead costs over a significantly larger volume of domestic orders than UK suppliers. Unless sterling appreciates further, UK suppliers should not be at a price disadvantage, provided that they manufacture as efficiently as their foreign competitors. GEC's success in obtaining orders in South Korea seems to bear this out.

4. *Technology.* The UK industry will remain technologically competitive only if it maintains sufficient development and design effort to stay at the forefront of technological advance *and* if it obtains sufficient experience in manufacturing new designs. Design contracts help to retain experienced teams and are cheap compared with placing 'advance' orders for plant. Prototypes are necessary before a new design is ready for series ordering. Neither prototypes nor design contracts, however, are a substitute for experience gained in manufacturing current designs.

We have no evidence that UK designs have generally been more prone to difficulties than foreign designs, but there have been difficulties with 500 MW and 660 MW units, due initially to problems with the generators and recently with the low-pressure turbine blades (Fryer and Rogers, 1978). International comparisons of operating performance are difficult because of differences in reporting procedures (for example, forced outages due to operating errors are sometimes included as well as outages due to design defects), and because basic differences in design mean that the comparisons are not strictly like-with-like.

Table 13.6 suggests that forced outage has been higher in the UK than the USA, but the evidence is not conclusive owing to differences in types of unit, the possibility that units of a comparable size and design had been in operation longer in the USA, and the different time-periods involved. Units of 1000 MW and above in the USA appear to have experienced turbine-blade failures at least as serious as those in the UK with the 500 MW and 660 MW high-speed units. Failure of low-pressure turbine blades is also a problem in France, with high-speed units no bigger than current UK designs and with the larger, slow-speed units for nuclear plants. The problems experienced in the

TABLE 13.6 Forced outage rates for turbines and generators for conventional steam power stations in the USA and UK

USA (1967–76)			*UK (1972–73 only)*		
Unit size (MW)	*Turbine (%)*	*Generator (%)*	*Unit size (MW)*	*Turbine (%)*	*Generator (%)*
100–299	1.0	0.2	200	1.7	0.2
300–599	2.2	0.5	275–300	6.4	2.0
600+	3.4	2.1	500	5.0	7.7

SOURCES

US data: Edison Electric Institute (1977).
UK data: Barden (1976).

UK therefore seem not untypical of foreign experience with large units.

If export demand developed for units significantly larger than the biggest currently installed on the CEGB system, UK suppliers would be at a disadvantage; but we do not think this gives cause for concern at present. The majority of units exported by all manufacturers are below the maximum size that UK suppliers currently make for the CEGB. Neither Brown Boveri nor GEC were prevented from obtaining export orders for very large, slow-speed machines, although neither had previously built them for their home markets. No foreign supplier is currently supplying high-speed tandem-compound machines significantly larger than the 660 MW machines made in Britain; and the lower operating availability of large units has made utilities reluctant to order bigger and more technically advanced designs.

We therefore disagree with the CPRS suggestion that the UK industry should be encouraged (i.e. subsidised) to develop, design and build a prototype 1300 MW high-speed turbine generator. The CPRS did not examine the probability of a flow of orders for such machines from markets where the UK could hope to compete. Given the experience with earlier technical jumps, the CEGB is unlikely to take the risk unless the Government meets the costs (estimated unofficially at £70m and consisting chiefly of development work on the generator).

CONCLUSION

The heavy electrical industry and related areas of power plant engineering present some of the most intractable problems in industrial policy. The objective is to create an internationally competitive industry, but the means of doing so are unclear and errors are all too likely to lead to a rundown of the industry with severe costs in terms of unemployment and the balance of payments. Barring further 'advance' orders, the choice will be between the so-called 'market' solution in which one supplier goes out of business or is taken over by the other, and a 'hybrid' solution requiring more active involvement by the Government and the CEGB. The distinction, however, is by no means black and white and the CEGB as the major domestic customer is bound to be involved in a greater or lesser degree. Both solutions involve streamlining the industry and the emergence of a monopoly domestic supplier.

The 'market' solution is favoured by those who place more emphasis upon the survival of the stronger, who think that rationalisation problems should be left to the industry, and who would prefer a solution involving neither Government 'interference' in planned closures nor CEGB 'interference' in design matters. But several points must be remembered here. Firstly, the takeovers of the sixties did not produce the required rationalisation of manufacture; secondly, neither politicians nor workers are likely to remain passive bystanders in decisions on the phasing and location of major redundancies; and, thirdly, the urgent need for restructuring concerns only one part of the industry's product range – very large steam-turbine generators – and it is not evident that merging *all* the interests of the two companies concerned is necessary or desirable.

Before the 'market' solution becomes unavoidable, careful consideration must be given to a 'hybrid' solution, with the view to creating a single group containing the turbine-generator manufacturing facilities of GEC and Parsons, the reactor design interests of the National Nuclear Corporation and the relevant R&D and design resources of the CEGB. If a practical 'hybrid' arrangement can be devised, the resulting group could offer architect-engineering services, conventional plant and equipment, and nuclear reactors – in short, a turnkey capability. Its practicability would depend upon reaching agreement upon unified management control and design philosophy, and upon plans for rationalisation and the phasing of redundancies. Positive involvement, perhaps through capital participation, by the Government and CEGB would be necessary – the Government because of its overall responsibility for the economy and industrial policy and because the taxpayer will have to foot the bill for the resulting unemployment; and the CEGB because of its interest as the major customer.

Restructuring is, admittedly, something of a panacea among those considering industrial problems in the UK. Very probably a merger of the large steam-turbine generator interests of GEC and Parsons, whether of the 'market' or 'hybrid' variety, will bring managerial difficulties. Inescapable though the need for restructuring is in this instance, it is important that the need for high-calibre technical and commercial managers, for investment in modern equipment and R&D, and for success in export markets are not overlooked. These, too, are essential components of a longer-term solution.

NOTES

1. This was thought to be 8 per cent of the capacity of the world industry. Note that output capacity in this industry is elastic. It is affected by the size and composition of orders, the amount of repair work (in 1978 this represented 20–25 per cent of the UK industry's earnings) and sub-contract work from other firms and industries.
2. Four separate 500 MW unit designs and two 660 MW designs were developed and built (a close parallel to the AGR experience – see Chapter 14).
3. Data for our survey were collected from official reports, technical journals and manufacturers' supply lists, sent to utilities to be verified and amplified, and then analysed by computer. The survey covered 3409 units (1174 GW). The method was the same as that used by Surrey and Chesshire in their survey of the period 1955–75, which covered 5088 units (852 GW). Note that the dates in the tables refer to the year of first commercial operation, not the year the order was received or completed.
4. According to industry sources, Siemens is contemplating building a turbine generator works in Florida (with Allis Chalmers having a 15 per cent holding) to enable Kraftwerk Union to be a 'domestic' supplier in the USA and to reduce the financial risks of exchange rate movements. If the plant is built, the high-technology components, such as the rotors and turbine blading, would continue to be made at Mulheim in Germany.

REFERENCES

S. E. Barden, 'Turbine Generators – Management for Reliable Operation and High Availability', *Electronics and Power*, 17 Oct. 1976), pp. 834–7.

Central Policy Review Staff, *The Future of the United Kingdom Power Plant Manufacturing Industry* (London: HMSO, 1976).

Edison Electric Institute, *Report on Equipment Availability for the Ten Year Period 1967–76*, Equipment Availability Task Force of the Prime Movers Committee (New York: EEI, 1977).

B. Epstein and R. K. U. Mirow, *Impact on Developing Countries of Restrictive Business Practices of Transnational Corporations in the Electrical Equipment Industry. A Case Study of Brazil* (Geneva: UNCTAD, 1977).

J. Fryer and P. Rogers, 'Why Ince B is three years late already', *Sunday Times* (18 June 1977).

R. S. Newfarmer, *The International Market Power of Transnational Corporations. A Case Study of the Electrical Industry* (Geneva: UNCTAD, 1978).

A. J. Surrey and J. H. Chesshire, *The World Market for Electric Power Equipment: Rationalisation and Technical Change* (University of Sussex: Science Policy Research Unit, 1972).
UK Government, *Wilson Committee, Report of the Committee of Enquiry into Delays in Commissioning CEGB Power Stations*, Cmnd., 3960 (London: HMSO, 1968).
United Nations, *Commodity Trade Statistics* (New York: United Nations).

14 Nuclear Reactor Development in Britain

C. M. Buckley and R. Day

The British nuclear power industry dates from the Second World War. Britain has developed an expertise which promises a continuing share in the growing world fuel cycle market. Its performance in developing commercially feasible nuclear reactor technology has been less satisfactory. Although large resources of finance and manpower have been poured into R&D on indigenous reactor technology, and into large commercial nuclear programmes, Britain still lacks a proven reactor design which can reliably supply home and export markets.

The nuclear industry is characterised by a highly complex technology requiring stringent quality control and is based on large requirements for R&D. In all countries, the nuclear industry must still be regarded as an infant industry, heavily subsidised by Government in a variety of ways, including R&D, export credits, the construction of prototypes, and some areas of fuel-cycle supply. The world market is largely dominated by American light-water technologies, licences for which are held by a number of countries. The only other thermal reactor technologies in commercial service are the heavy-water technology (e.g. the Canadian 'Candu' reactors) and the gas-graphite technologies produced in Britain and France. It is doubtful that any nuclear plant manufacturer finds its investment in nuclear power profitable. Indeed, since 1976 there have been recurrent rumours that one US supplier, General Electric, was intending to pull out of reactor construction.

Past forecasts of nuclear power growth have been wildly optimistic. The uncertain impact of economic recession, escalating costs, and widespread opposition to nuclear power make it difficult to forecast future levels of growth. The expected scale economies potentially to be gained by increasing reactor size are as yet unrealised. In Britain the discovery of offshore hydrocarbons, the high margin of electricity generating capacity surplus to current requirements, and the restricted potential for electricity growth, point to the need for a reassessment of the prospects for the growth of the British nuclear industry.

THE INITIAL PHASE OF NUCLEAR POWER DEVELOPMENT

Military preoccupations dictated the development of the British technology in the early post-war years, because plutonium was needed for the bomb programme (Gowing, 1974). A natural uranium reactor was constructed at Harwell for this purpose in 1947, followed by another in 1948. In important respects, these reactors laid the foundation for later programmes. They were fuelled by natural uranium, moderated by graphite, and relied on air cooling. They differed from the initial experimental reactors in the USA, where water was chosen as coolant. Since water absorbs more neutrons than gas, enriched uranium is required rather than the natural uranium used by the first reactors in the UK. Britain had no enrichment capacity at the time, and gas-graphite reactors were efficient in their production of plutonium. The greater cost of gas-cooled technology, and its poor fuel economy, were important factors in the American rejection of the gas-graphite route. Meanwhile, however, the decision was taken in Britain to construct two plutonium piles at Windscale, on the basis of the existing technology. The first went critical in October 1950, the second in June 1951. In October 1952, Britain exploded its first atomic bomb.

THE FIRST CIVIL NUCLEAR PROGRAMME: THE DEVELOPMENT OF THE MAGNOX REACTOR

By 1953, demand for plutonium had risen sharply. For some time the possibility of generating electricity along with plutonium had been in the air. Four reactors were built at Calder Hall, the first feeding electricity to the grid in 1956, and four at Chapelcross. Their primary function was to produce plutonium. They were owned by the Atomic Energy Authority (AEA) and later by British Nuclear Fuels Limited (BNFL). Natural uranium was used as fuel, graphite as the moderator and carbon dioxide as coolant.

Interest in the electricity-generating potential of nuclear reactors stemmed partly from the UK's energy situation. The potential inadequacy of the UK coal industry to meet demand became apparent, while the offsetting major role of oil in the future was not recognised. Government plans were announced in 1955 to develop the coal industry, and for the first civil nuclear programme. Such plans were given added emphasis by the Suez crisis of 1956.

In the period up to 1954 the major emphasis had been on the development of the technology embodied in the Calder Hall reactors, but the ultimate objective was seen as the development of the fast breeder reactor (FBR), also the priority in the United States. In fact, R&D on the breeder has proceeded in parallel with the commercialisation of gas-graphite reactors. There was little enthusiasm for pressurised water-cooled reactors in Britain. It was thought that performance in terms of temperature would be poor and that the system would be a cul-de-sac development (Gowing, 1974, p. 277). Water-cooling would involve a major, unwarranted change in the development programme. A design study for a pressurised-water reactor was abandoned in 1956 as a consequence of the Strath Committee's Report on the Reactor Programme, which argued that resources were spread much too thinly over too many projects.

Britain became involved in work on the High Temperature Gas-cooled Reactor (HTGR) in the mid-fifties, and on the Steam Generating Heavy Water Reactor (SGHWR) in the early 1960s. Nevertheless, the major proportion of resources was committed to developing the Magnox reactor and its successor in the thermal line, the Advanced Gas-cooled Reactor (AGR), and to developing the FBR as an advanced reactor type. This concentration of resources is demonstrated in Table 14.1 for the period 1965–76; the costs considered were incurred by the Atomic Energy Authority, and do not reflect the full costs of nuclear power development resulting from commercialisation of prototype designs.

It is important to note the difference in organisation of the nuclear effort between the United Kingdom and the United States (Allen, 1977). From the outset in the UK, there was a monopoly of technical information, initially through the Ministry of Supply, and then through the Atomic Energy Authority. Companies were involved in supplying items for the reactor developments, but at no stage were they involved in R&D activities. In contrast, in the United States, although information and nuclear research were initially channelled through the Atomic Energy Commission (AEC), commercial companies were brought into the R&D effort at the prototype stage, and a variety of different reactor designs was built and assessed before the choice was made to pursue commercial light-water technology. The approach followed by Britain was inherently more risky. At the time, the views of future power needs supported centralisation and early commitment to the first nuclear power programme. However, there were some who argued that there was no urgency and that centralisation ought to be avoided (Burn, 1967).

In all, nine Magnox stations, each with two identical reactors, were built in the UK, all using on-load refuelling. They were constructed by consortia of companies, four of which were formed in 1955 and a fifth in 1957. The number of consortia may have led to a semblance of competition, but this was never real. Orders were placed by rotation and the available qualified manpower was spread thinly over the consortia and AEA (Pocock, 1977).

TABLE 14.1 UKAEA expenditure and employment on civilian nuclear R&D, 1965–76

	1965	*1969*	*1973*[c]	*1976*
EXPENDITURE (£m)				
Power Programme				
(i) Gas-cooled reactors	14.8	4.7	4.7	6.6
(ii) High temp. reactors	a	3.3	2.7	b
(iii) Water mod. systems	12.7	7.1	4.2	8.7
(iv) Fast systems	16.4	26.7	31.9	53.2
Total Reactor Development	43.9	41.8	43.5	68.5
Total Nuclear R&D (including reactor development)	68.3	56.4	57.6	107.5
EMPLOYMENT (number of qualified scientists and engineers)				
Power Programme				
(i) Gas-cooled reactors	425	225	130	110
(ii) High temp. reactors	a	275	160	b
(iii) Water mod. systems	410	245	145	185
(iv) Fast systems	670	735	750	650
Total Reactor development	1505	1480	1185	945
Total QSEs on nuclear R&D	2645	2460	2100	2275

NOTES

[a] Published sources do not distinguish between R&D on the HTGR and support work until 1967.

[b] Not separately identified after 1974.

[c] Expenditures on the nuclear programme after 1973 are not directly comparable with previous years.

SOURCE

UKAEA Reports and Accounts.

The Magnox programme was characterised by several incremental innovations. Reactor size increased steadily. The cores of the earlier reactors were contained in steel pressure vessels, but a major step forward in engineering design was achieved at Oldbury with the use of a pre-stressed concrete pressure vessel containing boilers, gas-coolant circulators and steam generators, as well as the reactor core. This led to a more compact design which allowed Oldbury and Wylfa to operate at higher coolant pressures and temperatures, improving overall reactor efficiency. It also led to greater inherent safety. However, the move to larger reactor sizes and higher temperatures and pressures has been accompanied by a deterioration in performance (Burn, 1978, p. 184).

Even with the benefit of hindsight it is difficult to evaluate the conflicting evidence on the merits of the Magnox programme. On the one hand, official estimates of the overall cost escalation for the programme, at 16 per cent (Department of Energy, 1975, p. 53), seemed modest by the standards of the later AGR and LWR programmes, although it is unlikely that interest charges were included in these figures. The estimate included, however, much higher than anticipated costs for earlier plants. The SSEB's (South of Scotland Electricity Board) Hunterston plant incurred cost escalation from £37½ million to £60 million between 1957 and 1962 (Pocock, 1977, p. 110). According to Burn (1978, p. 12) 'the first Magnox plant, finished in 1962, cost 80 per cent more than the 1957 estimate'. The costs of the first commercial light-water reactors in the United States were also higher than expected, although built, as loss leaders, on a turnkey basis. Fuel supply security was the main policy concern in the UK in the mid-1950s and '. . . cost was a secondary matter' (House of Commons Select Committee on Science and Technology (SCST), 1967, p. xxxiii). However, policy-makers were impressed by the promises of low-cost electricity made by the proponents of nuclear power in the mid-fifties. There was confidence that the high capital costs would be offset by low operating costs, making Magnox power competitive.

In operation, Magnox reactors have been relatively trouble-free, although corrosion difficulties have caused all but one to be down-rated. The earlier sets have achieved cumulative lifetime load factors (Howles, 1978, p. 26) which compare favourably with the other reactor types, although their operating conditions (e.g. steam pressures and temperatures) are low. It is difficult to assess the Magnox reactors' costs per unit of electricity compared with other reactor types operating abroad, and with the costs of fossil-fuelled plants. Given historic cost depreciation, and the low fuel cost characteristic of nuclear plants, they are bound to be producing electricity cheaper than base-load fossil-fuelled plants.[1]

It was principally as a result of high capital costs that the export sales of Magnox reactors were disappointing. Only two reactors were sold early in the programme, to Italy and Japan. These represent the only exports of any British reactor systems.

THE SECOND CIVIL NUCLEAR PROGRAMME – THE ADVANCED GAS-COOLED REACTOR (AGR)

The Magnox reactors were completed in the period 1962–71, but well before the first station entered service the structure of the consortia was reorganised. The initial plan for 12 Magnox stations was adjusted to nine. Since the size of reactors and turbine-generators was increasing with experience fewer were needed, and this trend could be expected to increase in the future. Furthermore, oil was in more plentiful supply and cheaper, and the demand for nuclear power, which was turning out to be more expensive than planned, had diminished. The five consortia were reduced to three in 1959/60, and this was the organisational structure which was in being when the decision was faced on the second nuclear power programme.

Even in the early years of the programme, the Atomic Energy Authority was developing the successor to Magnox – the Advanced Gas-cooled Reactor (AGR). The 30-MW(e) prototype was built at Windscale. As in Magnox, carbon dioxide was used as coolant rather than water, which was in wide use elsewhere. The AGR broke away from the Magnox design in using ceramic uranium dioxide fuel rather than metallic uranium, permitting higher gas temperatures. Stainless steel rather than magnesium alloy cans were required, to withstand the higher temperatures. Fuel enriched in uranium-235 was needed to counter the higher absorption by neutrons by the steel canning.

The move to enriched uranium represented an important turning-point. Some in the British nuclear establishment felt that, given enriched uranium, it was preferable to move to light-water technology (Burn, 1978, p. 118). It is significant that the French, who had also been developing gas-graphite technology, later in 1969 shifted to light-water technology.

The AGR was chosen on grounds that gave cause for concern. Some argued that the evaluation of the competing bids was heavily biased against the American Boiling Water Reactor (BWR) and the decision was made on the basis of figures which were uncertain, and within the margin of likely statistical error.[2] In all, five plants were ordered from 1965 onwards, four by the CEGB and one by the SSEB. They were due to enter service from 1970 onwards. The first went critical in 1976. The whole programme encountered important technical difficulties relating to corrosion and insulation, which became evident before the orders for the final plants in the programme were placed. These difficulties were exacerbated by managerial problems; site labour relations contributed to construction delays. The programme was subject to significant cost escalation, as Table 14.2 shows for the CEGB stations. Indeed, as Dungeness B, Heysham and Hartlepool have still to enter service, these figures may not yet reflect the

TABLE 13.2 Cost escalation for the CEGB AGR stations

Date of original estimate	*Dungeness 'B' 31 Mar. 1965*	*Hinkley Point 'B' 31 Mar. 1966*	*Hartlepool 31 Oct. 1968*	*Heysham 30 Nov. 1970*
Originally expected date of completion of commissioning	1971	1973	1974	1976
Assumed commercial operation date of No. 1 reactor	Early 1980	Operating	Early 1981	Early 1981
Original estimate at prices at dates given above (£m.)	89	95	92	142
Estimate of final cost (1978 prices, £m.)	367	158	328	344

SOURCE

CEGB cost figures, *Daily Telegraph* (31 Oct. 1978).

final cost. In any event, they do not represent the full resource costs of the AGR programme. Burn and Henderson have made estimates that suggest that these could be considerably greater than the final costs shown in Table 14.2. (Burn, 1978; Henderson, 1976).

A number of factors have contributed to this disappointing experience, many of which had their roots in the Magnox programme and before. The AEA had developed the AGR and was the predominant source of top-level advice to the Government. Sir Stanley Brown, the then Chairman of the CEGB, stressed that there was no 'court of appeal' from the AEA's technical judgement.

Atomic Power Construction (APC), the weakest of the three consortia, was invited by the AEA to help prepare a priced design study for the AGR, which incorporated a 36-rod core cluster rather than the 18-rod arrangement of the Windscale prototype. This was used at the last minute as APC's bid for the Dungeness B contract.[3] APC won the contract to build Dungeness B, and the second nuclear power programme was firmly based on AGRs.[4]

Several questions arise about the AGR programme:

Was it a sensible programme when a commercial AGR involved a 20-fold scaling up on the Windscale prototype, when the fuel system to be used at Dungeness B had never been tested in the prototype, when the steam temperature and pressure were to be much higher, and when a mass of detailed design work remained to be done?

Was it sensible to maintain three consortia with separate technical and design staffs, working on three essentially different reactor designs of the same basic, unproven, technology?

Was the size of the programme too large, a result in part of the need to provide orders for the three consortia, as well as a reflection of the optimism associated with the National Plan?

The decisions on the AGR programme demonstrated the importance of ensuring that the nuclear plant supplying firms had the managerial, financial and technical capabilities to do the job properly. If the capabilities of Atomic Power Construction had been assessed in 1965, the firm is unlikely to have been awarded the Dungeness B contract.

THE PROPOSED THIRD CIVIL NUCLEAR PROGRAMME

The 1974 Choice of the Steam Generating Heavy Water Reactor

The AEA had, since 1959 been involved in R&D on water-moderated technology, though it was always regarded as secondary to the gas-cooled technology. A 100-MW(e) demonstration plant of the Steam Generating Heavy Water Reactor type was operating at Winfrith in 1966. It resembled the Candu reactor in using heavy water for the moderator and pressure tubes to contain the coolant, and the BWR in providing steam directly to drive the turbines. Once the SGHWR was operating, R&D expenditures tailed off, and by 1974 the annual expenditure on this type was of the order of £3.5 million (see Table 13.1 above).

In 1972/3 a further restructuring of the nuclear industry took place. As in the previous reorganisations, it was aimed at solving, once and for all, the problems of the nuclear supply industry. There would be one single British reactor design and construction organisation, which would operate commercially and have the General Electric Company (GEC) as a majority shareholder. The main holding company was to be called the National Nuclear Corporation. The implementation of NNC's policies was to be through the Nuclear Power Company – a design and construction group with no manufacturing facilities of its own. All components were to be bought from other engineering companies. The initial structure of the NNC was:

GEC	50%
UKAEA	15%
British Nuclear Associates	35%

While the reorganisation was being considered, discussions were under way on the choice of reactor for the next programme. The CEGB announced in December 1973 that it wished to order 18 American-designed Pressurised Water Reactors (PRW) before 1979, and perhaps an additional 18 in the following five years. Sir Arnold Weinstock of GEC also endorsed this move for the PWR, which would have totalled 41,000 MW had the full programme been implemented.

Prolonged public debate and Government deliberation took place on reactor choice, one of the main concerns being safety, in particular the structural integrity of the PWR's pressure vessel, and the high power density of the core. It was resolved, in July 1974, when the Government decided that the Electricity Boards should adopt the SGHWR for their next nuclear power programme and announced a programme of six reactors in two power stations amounting to 4000 MW(e) over four years, one tenth of the size of the CEGB's desired programme.

The commercial design of the SGHWR turned out to be not much closer to its 100-MW(e) Winfrith prototype than the AGRs were to the 33-MW(e) prototype at Windscale. The technical risks and the costs of a nuclear programme based on SGHWRs would in fact have been those of launching a new thermal reactor system. The designs of the complicated steam drums and of the fuel cluster were considerably modified. The delay in ordering SGHWR plants was in marked contrast to the claim given in the Secretary of State's Report to Parliament (July 1974) that '. . . we can proceed to order quickly'.

The debate in 1974 over the choice of reactor system (for the third nuclear power programme) differed in two important respects from that in 1965:

- there were greater differences between the views of the interested institutions, thus neutralising their powerful but individual influences, and forcing the Government to make and follow its own judgement;
- the House of Commons Select Committee on Science and Technology played a crucial role in calling upon the interested parties to justify their cases, in opening the debate to public scrutiny, and in stimulating debate.

The divergence of opinions of the 'experts' was particularly noticeable (*Atom*, 1974, pp. 134–44). Mr Hawkins, Chairman of the CEGB, told the Select Committee that the SGHWR was '. . . an out-of-date technology', whilst Mr Tombs, Chairman of the SSEB, thought it suitable for commercial operation since it was a '. . . tested and proven system'. Sir John Hill, Chairman of the AEA, told the Committee that, though it was sad that so many years had been lost in not adopting the SGHWR, it was not out of date.

As a result of the SGHWR decision, GEC indicated its wish to reduce its shareholding in NNC. This was achieved by increasing the UKAEA share to 50 per cent and reducing GEC's share to 30 per cent. GEC retained the management contract in NPC.

The 1976 Choice of Reactor Type

By 1976, the continued low growth of demand for electricity made a third nuclear programme less urgent than had been suggested by the forecasts put forward by the CEGB in 1974. In addition, greater optimism over the possible performance of the AGR system, further study on the characteristics of the PWR pressure vessel, and the growing realisation of the changes and expense involved in scaling up the SGHWR design and constructing the early plants, resulted in doubts about the wisdom of the choice of the SGHWR.

In early 1976 Mr Wedgwood Benn accepted a proposal from the National Nuclear Corporation to study the merits of the three nuclear systems: SGHWR, PWR and AGR. The review (NNC, 1977) compared the estimated costs of the three systems, as well as technical qualities, safety and export potential. All three systems were judged capable of meeting UK safety requirements. The expected availability of the three systems could not be predicted accurately because of lack of data. It was assessed that the capital cost of the PWR would be about 15 per cent lower than the AGR and 25 per cent lower than the SGHWR. The final generation cost advantage to the PWR would be about 10–15 per cent compared with the AGR and more than 20 per cent compared with the SGHWR. The larger unit size of the PWR accounted for about half the advantage over the AGR. Significantly, before the report the NNC favoured the PWR, the only 'known' reactor system. It is significant, also, that more was known on PWR costs than on the costs of the other types.

On 26 January 1978 it was announced that early orders for two new nuclear power stations, based on the AGR design and costing an estimated £650 million each, were to be placed by the electricity supply industry. The new stations, totalling about 2600 MW, will be modified versions of the stations at Hinkley Point and Hunterston, redesigned to facilitate maintenance and inspection.[5] The Government also approved a CEGB proposal to develop the PWR to the stage of being a valid option over the next four years. This would involve obtaining the necessary safety approvals and planning consent to order a PWR station of about 1300 MW not earlier than 1982.

The decision did, however, leave questions relating to the PWR unresolved. There appeared to be no guarantee that the CEGB would be able to order a commercial PWR station in the 1980s, without ministerial decision, an issue that needed clarification before CEGB committed any resources to the design work. Furthermore, considerable doubts existed as to the capacity of a monopoly supplier to maintain two supply options effectively. The half-hearted commitment to the PWR also seemed to be a contributory factor in GEC's announcement that it wished to reduce its shareholding in the NNC and give up its supervisory management contract. Furthermore, the NNC/NPC structure had not worked as well as had been hoped in 1973. The utilities had been frustrated by the three-tier structure of the NNC, and there were signs of resentment of the dominant role of GEC by other members of the NNC. It would also be necessary to clarify the exact role of the new organisation and in particular its relationship to the CEGB's own nuclear expertise, centred on Barnwood. The uncertainty regarding structure seemed likely to delay the schedule for the necessary design work on the AGRs.

CONCLUSIONS AND POLICY IMPLICATIONS

Both nuclear programmes undertaken so far in the UK, particularly the AGR programme, have encountered delays and cost escalation. Such difficulties have not been restricted to Britain. Nevertheless, the USA, Federal Republic of Germany, France, and Canada have established reactor designs capable of supplying home and export markets.

The difficulties of establishing a workable and efficient structure for the industry are obviously at the heart of Britain's disappointing performance. These stem from a small home market, limited engineering resources and an indigenous reactor technology which has not been accepted in world markets, conditions not anticipated in the early years of reactor development.

The UKAEA, with its dual role as an R&D organisation developing nuclear technologies, but also the main adviser to Government on nuclear matters, has been the predominant influence on the choice of reactor and the scale of the first two nuclear programmes. There was no satisfactory mechanism for involving the utilities (CEGB and SSEB) and plant manufacturers in decision-making, nor in nuclear development work. It is inherently difficult for the Government to balance conflicting views and interests, particularly when there is disagreement between the electricity supply industry, plant supply industry, and the UKAEA, on reactor choice. The only alternative is to leave decision-making to the utility–manufacturer axis.

Britain concentrated on a 'narrow front' of reactor development, focusing on gas-cooled thermal reactors, and the liquid metal fast-breeder reactor. Involvement in developing to prototype stage the Steam Generating Heavy Water Reactor and the collaborative High Temperature Reactor was not regarded as in the mainstream of technology development. An early commitment to the Magnox reactor for the first nuclear programme reinforced the tendency to a 'narrow front', justified on the ground that resources would not be too thinly spread over a number of options. The UK's main competitor at that time, the USA, was allocating R&D funds more broadly on a diverse range of reactor types, with the aim of evaluating them all before choosing a suitable one on which to base commercial development. Premature commitment also took place on the AGR programme – since dogged by technical and managerial problems – which involved a programme commitment of 6600 MW(e) in 660-MW(e) units, on the basis of one 30-MW(e) prototype. Fortunately, this mistake was not repeated with the putative SGHWR programme, owing to the sensible precaution of undertaking further development and design work, which revealed the difficulties in scaling up to commercial size. But for the pressing problems of the nuclear plant supply industry, it would probably have been less risky to delay the ordering of the two AGRs in 1978, until adequate periods of commercial operation had been achieved with the first plants constructed.

The UK's experience demonstrates the importance of broad-based R&D on alternative technical options before commercialisation; the problems which may be encountered in undertaking large increases in scale, both from prototype to commercial plant, and within programmes; and the need for detailed design work before construction.[6]

The AGR and SGHWR designs were highly complex when compared with the Magnox and LWR types, and this contributed to the problems encountered in converting both to commercial designs. This may reflect a lack of balance between pure and applied science in the development programme, and the inadequate attention paid to engineering (and commercial) feasibility. Construction delays were all the more likely with the AGR programme, given that the AGR involved proportionally more on-site engineering than the LWRs, and given also deficiencies in project management and labour relations. Underlying the decisions on reactor choice was the pervasive belief in British leadership in this particular area of high technology. This belief led to premature commitment to commercial reactor development, and to a very costly 'go-it-alone' philosophy.

The existence of worldwide manufacturing over-capacity, together with the lack of an established and exportable reactor technology, raises questions on the viability of an independent nuclear industry. It is important to designate precisely what is to be included within the 'nuclear industry'. Research and development work has been the responsibility of the UKAEA, although the CEGB maintains R&D establishments to ensure an understanding of reactor technologies; to undertake detailed design work relating to proven technologies; and to permit limited work on their operating reactors. The National Nuclear Corporation, and its operating arm, the Nuclear Power Company, is at present responsible for building power stations. The actual construction of component parts is sub-contracted, in large part to constituent companies of NNC. British Nuclear Fuels Ltd advises on UK acquisition of nuclear fuels, and provides fuel-cycle services, such as enrichment, fuel element fabrication and reprocessing. A strong British nuclear programme is obviously valuable in ensuring BNFL's own future, but BNFL is able to operate in the world market even though the UK has been unsuccessful in reactor sales. The UKAEA undertakes R&D on reactor technology (as well as in other areas broadly related to the nuclear programme). This has been central to the Authority's work in the past, but is the area of greatest uncertainty in the future. Any further design work for the thermal programme – specifically for the new AGRs and any PWR that might be ordered – will probably be undertaken by the generating boards and the NPC (or any successor). A redirection of AEA activity would be necessary if the decision is against building a commercial demonstration fast breeder reactor (CDFR) in the UK, or if the main involvement is in international collaboration, where it is unlikely that Britain would be the major partner (e.g. possible collaboration in the French or German FBR programmes).

A restructuring of the NNC seems inevitable, given GEC's lack of commitment to the AGR. It is difficult to envisage NNC having the requisite resources to organise and control design and construction work simultaneously on two competing reactor types – the AGR and PWR (should the CEGB decide to proceed with a PWR order). If the CDFR is ordered then this might even involve a third reactor for indigenous construction.

Within the constituent companies of NNC/NPC it might be difficult to identify facilities and capacity solely required for continued participation in the nuclear industry. The major 'nuclear' resource in these companies will be the skilled manpower, and experience established through participation in nuclear orders, although the recent uncertainties regarding the future development of nuclear power in the UK may well have been reflected in staff wastage, and an erosion of expertise. In the final analysis, the capability of UK manufacturers to build nuclear plants depends on the health and efficiency of the individual firms in their particular specialisations.

The final structure and corporate involvement may well revolve on reactor choice, and the magnitude of likely future orders. But it is important, in the meantime, to identify the specialised resources involved in the 'nuclear industry' which would need to be retained and developed, if a nuclear capability is to be maintained.

NOTES

1. 1971 was the first year in which Magnox stations produced the cheapest electricity on the CEGB system – Dungeness A producing at 0.31p per KWh., the same as the oil-fired Kingsnorth station. However, many would argue that calculations mixing both historic and current costs are unsuitable for judging past investments.
2. The CEGB and AEA together conducted an appraisal of the tenders and reported to the Minister of Power on the relative technical and economic merits of the competing systems. This seemed to show that, in UK conditions, AGRs would produce electricity at 0.457d/kWh, 7 per cent more cheaply than the BWR cost of 0.489d/kWh (see CEGB, 1965). For accounts of the AGR decision, see Burn (1967) and Rush *et al.* (1977).
3. The Nuclear Power Group (TNPG) had proposed a 36-rod cluster as early as 1961. The AEA at this time was not convinced of the value of going to the larger cluster.
4. GEC–Simon-Carves, who in 1960 had joined with APC to form the United Power Company (UPC) did not support the APC bid, and withdrew from UPC. By 1969, APC had collapsed and the English Electric Group (reconstituted as British Nuclear Design and Construction) took over the management of the Dungeness project.
5. The relative inaccessibility of major components for routine maintenance has been regarded as a defect in the initial design. There are still problems of insulation and corrosion, the on-load fuel system cannot be worked yet, and there is a carbon deposit problem not yet fully assessed.
6. In the view of Mr R. Peddie, a board member of the CEGB, every £10,000 not spent at the beginning of the project in reducing the technical risks might well incur costs one hundred times greater in modifications and delays.

REFERENCES

W. Allen, *Nuclear Reactors for Generating Electricity: US Development from 1946 to 1963* (Santa Monica, California: Rand, 1977) R-2116-NSF.

Atom, 212 (June 1974), 'Nuclear Reactors', pp. 121–52.

Atom, 239 (Sept. 1976), letter by Sir John Hill to the Secretary of State for Energy, pp. 231–5.

Atom, 257 (Mar. 1978), 'Thermal Reactor Policy', pp. 56–62.

D. Burn, *The Political Economy of Nuclear Energy* (London: The Institute of Economic Affairs, 1967).

D. Burn, *Nuclear Power and the Energy Crisis* (London: Macmillan, 1978).

CEGB, *An Appraisal of the Technical and Economic Aspects of Dungeness B Nuclear Power Station* (London: HMSO, July 1965).

Department of Energy, *Energy Paper Number 7, North Sea Costs Escalation Study* (London: HMSO, Dec. 1975).

M. Gowing, *Independence and Deterrence: Britain and Atomic Energy 1945–1952*, vol. 1: Policy Making, vol. 2: *Policy Execution* (London: Macmillan, 1974).

P. D. Henderson, *Two British Errors: Their Probable Size and Some Possible Lessons*, Inaugural Lecture, University College, London (24 May 1976).

House of Commons Select Committss on Science and Technology, *UK Nuclear Reactor Programme, Report: Minutes of Evidence and Appendices* (London: HMSO, 1967).

L. R. Howles, 'Review of nuclear power station achievement – 1977' *Nuclear Engineering International*, 23 (Apr. 1978) pp. 25–8.

National Nuclear Corporation Ltd, *The Choice of Thermal Reactor Systems* (London: HMSO, 1977).

R. F. Pocock, *Nuclear Power: Its Development in the United Kingdom* (Old Woking: Unwin Brothers and the Institute of Nuclear Engineers, 1977).

H. J. Rush, G. MacKerron, J. Surrey, 'The Advanced Gas-cooled Reactor', *Energy Policy*, 5, 2 (June 1977) pp. 95–105.

15 The Broad Base of Technical Change in the Gas Industry

Howard J. Rush[1]

The past two decades have seen the British gas industry evolve from a minor position as a manufacturer of gas into a major nationwide distributor with a significant share of the energy market. The success of what is arguably the most rapidly growing industry in Britain rests substantially on the development of several alternatives to the traditional coal carbonisation process, the mainstay of the gas industry from the late eighteenth century until the mid-1960s.

A cursory review might credit the industry's recent success solely to the windfall of natural gas reserves found in the North Sea. Indeed, the shift to a role of distributor of gas is marked by a dramatic increase in sales, as illustrated in Table 15.1, and an increase in length of mains pipeline. More thorough analyses, however, particularly those of Ray and Jones (1974 and 1975) and Harlow (1977), note the importance of the R&D strategy followed by the industry since nationalisation in 1949, and an organisational structure which allowed this strategy to succeed. The conclusions of a Science Policy Research Unit study (Rush, Mackerron and Surrey, 1976) of the nationalised energy industries support this argument. Whereas the 'luck' of discovering natural gas at one's doorstep has assured the current position of the gas industry, the broad base of R&D activity, quite unlike the 'narrow front' of the UK Atomic Energy Authority's nuclear programme (Rush, Mackerron and Surrey, 1977) has enabled the gas industry to capitalise rapidly on new technological advances and unexpected reserves, because of experience gained in previous developments. The ability of the industry to maintain this position after its current reserves are depleted will depend heavily on the continuation of the R&D strategy.

TABLE 15.1 Historical development of the gas industry

	1885	*1920*	*1945*	*1950*	*1960*	*1968*	*1970*	*1973*	*1976/77*	*1977/78*
Gas sold (000m. cubic ft.)										
Town gas	75	235	386	489	551	873	832	352	n.a*	n.a.
Natural gas	–	–	–	–	–	110	1639	8956	13837	15172
Consumers (million)	2	7.5	11.5	11.9	12.5	13.3	13.4	13.6	14.2	14.5
Mains (000 miles)	18	39	68	78	97	118	124	129	134	136

NOTE

* Gas available in 1976/77 totalled 14,694 million therms. Of this total 129.2 million therms was manufactured town gas.

SOURCES

Mitchell and Jones (1971); British Gas Corporation and Gas Council, *Annual Reports* (1950 – 1977), Ministry of Fuel and Power (1978). National Institute for Economic and Social Research estimates, in Ray and Jones (1975).

TECHNOLOGICAL NATURE OF THE INDUSTRY

The industry's predominant technology when nationalised was coal carbonisation, a process which produces coke as a by-product. Within the gasworks, coke was then used in the production of 'water gas', a low-quality energy product requiring enrichment. For a decade after 1949, the industry relied almost exclusively on these two processes for manufactured gas. It did also buy gas, mainly from coke ovens and oil refineries, and almost invariably at lower cost per therm than manufactured gas. The industry played a minor role in the UK's total energy consumption, as compared with such primary fuels as coal or oil. The principal disadvantage of the process was high costs, both in feedstock and maintenance, and inflexibility of output (failing to meet peak loads at a reasonable cost). Restructuring of the industry (primarily by closing the smaller carbonisation plants) (Ray and Jones, 1975) marginally improved overall technical efficiency.

Technical policy in the first decade after nationalisation concentrated on rationalising the industry's production and distribution capacity, to improve technical efficiency. Although considerable R&D effort went into coal and oil gasification from the early 1950s, the absence of any significant technical change meant that the competitive position of gas deteriorated in both domestic and industrial markets. Between 1950 and 1960, gas prices rose by 64 per cent, whereas those of electricity and oil increased by 24 per cent and 40 per cent respectively (Reid, Allen and Harris, 1973).

In the early 1960s, however, three new technologies reached potential commercial-scale production. The first was the Lurgi process, a modification of the German process for gasifying brown coal, with considerable advantages over traditional coal carbonisation, including the use of less expensive coal and higher thermal efficiency. Initially, the prospect led the gas industry to plan for large Lurgi plants to be constructed in coalmining areas. In 1958 the first coal-gasification plant was ordered, and by the early 1960s two Lurgi-type plants were in commercial operation. However, construction delays seriously hampered any major contribution from the Lurgi process in the early 1960s.[2] While the Lurgi process operated at considerable economies of scale compared with coal-carbonisation plants, the concurrent development of facilities to import natural gas from the huge Algerian fields and of a cheaper petroleum feedstock process for gasification prevented subsequent expansion of Lurgi plant.

Although the first oil-gasification plant was built in 1958, it was not until 1962, when ICI announced a new process which produced a lean gas from steam reforming of naphtha, that oil as a feedstock became commercially viable. This technology was rapidly adopted by the industry as an alternative to coal carbonisation for base-load supplies. Within a year 12 plants had been ordered representing one-third (400m cubic feet per day) of the total capacity of the then operational coal-carbonisation plants (Harlow, 1977). However, the ICI plants required expensive enrichment with liquid petroleum gas, and by 1965 a cheaper Gas Council gasification process was being adopted by the Area Boards. The Catalytic Rich Gas process quickly reached a capacity of nearly 800 million cubic feet per day (Harlow, 1977).

The decision between the coal (Lurgi) and oil-based gasification proved a sound one. Large-scale coal-based plants would (it was estimated in the 1960s) have produced gas at 3.2–3.5p per therm, compared with 2.7–3.1p per therm from oil-gasification. The latter plants had lower capital costs, and proved more responsive to short-term changes in demand. Furthermore, with oil-gasification there was no need to restrict plants to a specific geographical location, nor was there as great an effluent problem.[3] With these advantages, oil-gasification helped re-establish the competitiveness of gas and by 1968 (the peak year for oil gas as a proportion of total gas availability) total gas sales had risen considerably.

The shift of feedstock raw materials from coal to oil led to significant economies of scale, and a reduction in plant numbers and labour. It also entailed transmission of large quantities of gas greater distances under pressure, requiring the introduction of a national grid. These technological and structural changes required greater centralisation of decision-making within the industry, and can be seen as important preparation for further changes that the industry would undergo in the shift from manufacturer of gas to distributor (Political and Economic Planning, *A Fuel Policy for Britain* (1966), referred to in Ray and Jones (1975)).

During the same period, the Government announced the approval of Gas Council plans for importing Algerian natural gas, and the experimental work begun in the late 1950s quickly led to the construction of storage tanks, evaporators and a distribution system. By 1964 liquid natural gas (LNG) imports distributed by high-pressure gas to seven Area Boards had become economic (see Table 15.2), and by 1966 accounted for 10 per cent of the UK's gas supplies.

Although the proportion of imported LNG was to decline with the discovery of North Sea gas, it served as an important source of methane used in the enrichment of lean gas, and was cheaper than most of the manufactured gas (Ray and Jones, 1975). Perhaps of greater importance to the industry was the experience gained in the handling of natural gas, the further development of storage facilities, and the grid system which was to prove invaluable in the exploitation of North Sea gas.

With the discovery of North Sea natural gas in 1965, the industry was

TABLE 15.2 Breakdown of gas availability by source (%)

Gas made	*1960*	*1965*	*1970*	*1976–77*
Coal Gas	59.0	33.0	3.5	n.a.
Lurgi Gas	0.001	1.8	0.4	n.a.
Water Gas	14.4	9.9	0.02	n.a.
Oil Gas	2.2	18.0	17.9	n.a.
Total made	76.5	62.9	21.9	3
NCB Coke Ovens	9.2	5.7	4.1	Neg
Other Coke Ovens	8.4	5.6		
Oil Refinery Gas	4.6	7.9	2.0	Neg
Liquid Petroleum Gas	0.8	9.7	3.1	Neg
Natural Gas (for enrichment)	0.5	8.2	36.9	Neg
Total bought	23.5	37.0	46.0	Neg
Natural Gas – direct	0	0	32.0	97
Total	100	100	100	100

SOURCES

British Gas Corporation and Gas Council *Annual Reports* (1950–77).

faced with further technical and economic decisions. To a large extent, however, the know-how acquired during previous developments allowed for the choice of a rapid exploitation rate. This was based on the belief that the more rapid the rate of depletion the lower would be the beach price of natural gas, on the prospect of foreign exchange savings, and on the assumption that contracts with supplying firms for large amounts of gas would provide incentives for further exploitation (UK Government, 1967). Furthermore, it was hoped that technological advances in processes for making Substitute Natural Gas (SNG) would be able to supply cheaper fuel by the time the North Sea reserves were depleted (Posner, 1975).

It was also necessary to choose between diluting the gas, which has twice the calorific value of manufactured gas, or to convert appliances and distribute the gas directly to the consumer. It was estimated as less expensive to build a direct distribution network from the North Sea landing points, and convert the appliances (nearly 40 million) of 13 million consumers over a ten-year period, than to build new reforming plants. The cost remains considerable. With the change of the source of gas from local manufacturing plants to wells in the North Sea, it was necessary to lay a large mileage of new pipeline transmission system, so that the natural gas could be fed to as many consumers as possible. However, the Gas Council has estimated the savings through conversion (as opposed to building reforming plants) as likely to reach £1400 million over a thirty-year period (UK Government, 1967).[4]

As a result of the transition to the high-calorific North Sea natural gas, which was available to the industry at a landed price of 1.20p per therm, gas became much more competitive. This is clearly borne out by the later rapid expansion in gas sales in the early 1970s (Table 15.1 above), resulting from the inroads made into domestic and industrial markets. Although the actual number of consumers did not rise dramatically, the amount of gas sold rose substantially. A sectoral analysis by Chesshire and Buckley (see Table 15.3) shows that, in terms of percentage of heat supplied, 1960–75, the gas industry's share rose by 31 per cent in the domestic market, and by 23 per cent in industry (excluding iron and steel).

TABLE 15.3 Sectoral demand for gas 1960–75 (per cent share on heat supplied basis)

	1960	*1965*	*1970*	*1972*	*1973*	*1974*	*1975*
Iron and steel	9	9	10	13	13	13	15
Other industries	5	5	7	18	22	26	28
Domestic	9	13	24	31	32	36	40
Public services	6	5	6	10	14	16	18
Miscellaneous	12	13	17	21	19	24	25
All classes of consumer	6	7	11	17	18	24	23

SOURCE

Derived from Chesshire and Buckley (1976; pp. 237–54).

ECONOMIC AND TECHNICAL PERFORMANCE

The use by Government of price control in the nationalised energy industries as a means of fighting inflation, makes most financial analysis of the gas industry relatively meaningless as an indicator of economic performance. Comparatively favourable prices however, have obviously played an important role in the increased share of the energy market now occupied by gas. Using 1970 as the base year (100), retail prices of gas rose to 161 in 1975 compared to 197 for coal, and 253 for electricity (Chesshire and Buckley, 1976). This competitive advantage helped the gas industry's share of the energy market to rise from 6.3 per cent in 1960, to 10.7 in 1970, and again to 24.1 per cent in 1976 (UK Government, 1960–1976).

In the absence of a more satisfactory indicator, one measure of technical performance in the gas industry is the rate of diffusion of new technology, compared to rates of diffusion in manufacturing industry in general. Table 15.4 shows a comparison of the major gas innovations with a wide range of innovations in manufacturing.[5] There are fundamental differences between innovations in natural gas (extraction and distribution rather than a manufacturing technology) and innovations in manufacturing technology (including oil-gasification). However, the switch to natural gas involved technical and organisational problems (i.e. storage, transmission, and

TABLE 15.4 Rates of diffusion of innovations

Benchmark (% of total output or sales using innovation	*Mean number of years to reach benchmark*			*Dispersal around benchmark = standard deviation (years) for six manufacturing studies*
	Average of six manufacturing studies	*Oil gasification**	*Natural gas – direct use**	
10	4.93	4¼	2¼	3.55
25	7.60	6	3¼	3.98
50	10.73	–	4¼	6.13

NOTE

* Estimated to nearest quarter year.

SOURCES

Scott (1975); British Gas Corp. and Gas Council (1950–77).

conversion of appliances) greater or at least similar in scale to those encountered in introducing new manufacturing technology.[6]

Oil-gasification never achieved 50 per cent of gas sales because it was rapidly superseded by North Sea natural gas, but the 40 per cent mark was reached after roughly eight years. Diffusion proceeded at a rate slightly faster than that of the manufacturing innovations.[7] The diffusion of natural gas (for direct use) proceeded at a more rapid rate than virtually all the manufacturing innovations that have been studied. The experience gained in the use of earlier technologies is partially responsible (see next section).

FACTORS AFFECTING TECHNO-ECONOMIC PERFORMANCE

While money spent on R&D is not necessarily synonymous with research results, nor research results with successful innovation, examination of both the organisation and level of R&D expenditure is none the less useful in assessing the reasons behind the rapid diffusion of technology in the gas industry. Under the 1948 Gas Act, research was one of the specific duties to be carried out by the Gas Council. To a certain extent, this was facilitated by the inheritance of a wealth of R&D experience and personnel, a consequence of several larger firms having operated R&D facilities before nationalisation. In addition, the industry had since the 1930s been funding a fellowship programme at Leeds University, which eventually led to the formation of the Gas Research Board (1944), whose function was to initiate and co-ordinate research.

The direction of the R&D effort in the years following nationalisation was determined by a Research Committee composed of scientists and engineers.[8] Three research stations were opened during the early 1950s, incorporating facilities dating back to the 1920s. This effort to establish an effective organisation required a level of expenditure previously not available to any individual firm; an amount which would continue to increase, in real terms, throughout the 1960s and 1970s. Table 15.5 shows that even in a time of extremely depressed market performance such as the late 1950s, the proportion of turnover devoted to Gas Council R&D rose.

The doubling of expenditure in the six years to 1960/1 corresponds to the development of steam re-formers, using light petroleum distillate, and the Lurgi process. Although initial research on both coal and oil gasification had begun in the early 1950s, the shift in emphasis towards a process suited to base-load operations bore results in the early 1960s, which were to help revitalise the industry. Throughout the 1950s, however, relatively little R&D indigenous to the Gas Council was adopted by the Area Boards, in spite of the increases in both expenditure and qualified personnel.[9]

TABLE 15.5 Research and development expenditure of the gas industry

	1954/55	*1960/61*	*1968/69*	*1973/74*
Expenditure* at 1960/61 prices				
£ thousand	1064	2278	4758	4768
Index, 1954/55 = 100	100	214	447	448
Expenditure* as percentage of turnover	0.3	0.6	0.9	0.9

NOTE

* North Sea explorations costs, etc., are excluded.

SOURCES

British Gas Corporation and Gas Council, Annual Reports (1950–77); Ray and Jones (1975, data from NIESR estimates).

During the 1950s and early 1960s, the decentralised structure of the industry allowed each Area Board considerable autonomy over the purchase of technology, and individual R&D programmes. Since each Area Board was economically responsible for its activities, a policy of waiting for a proven technology, which could provide high cost savings, was the general rule. As a result, most of the new production capacity built up until the mid-1960s employed processes originating either from individual Area Boards[10] or from private industry, much of which was of foreign design.

The flexibility allowed by the industry's structure, and the resulting broad base of technological experience, were to some extent dictated by the individual needs of each Area Board and the shifting cost of feedstock supply. For example, the German-designed Lurgi process (with Gas Council modifications) was attractive to the Scottish and the West Midlands Boards, because of their proximity to coalfields and the favourable prices offered by the NCB. Although only two Lurgi plants were made operational in the UK, the R&D into the handling of gas under pressure was valuable for the industry's eventual transition from production to distribution.

Of even greater importance in the step towards low-cost, high-pressure transmission was the development and diffusion of the oil-gasification process, and the subsequent introduction of the national grid. Originally, R&D on oil gasification, begun in the 1950s, had been aimed at finding a process with the capacity to supply peak loads economically. During the 1950s, over 25 plants were in operation using technology produced locally from Area Boards, or purchased from France, Italy and the US. Although production capacity from these pilot plants may have been small, they gave the Area Boards the necessary experience in which to operate the high-pressure processes which were soon to become commercially viable (Harlow, 1977).

As the price of oil fell, the emphasis on research shifted towards the use of light distillate fuels as a base-load supplier. It has been estimated that a total of £1,140,000 had been spent on oil gasification between nationalisation and 1961. The shift in relative feedstock prices is reflected in increased expenditure on oil gasification from £199,000 in 1957/58 to £298,000 in 1960/61 (UK Government, 1961).

As we have already seen, with the development of new oil-gasification technologies, there was a good case for a more centralised industry. An argument not officially aired at the time, but one to which the Gas Council's R&D establishment was no doubt sensitive, was the value in centralisation for the diffusion of indigenous technology. This is underscored by the situation in which increases in expenditure and a dedicated team of research personnel had significantly advanced the Gas Council's own oil-gasification technology, only to find the Area Boards selecting from private industry for the first commercial process.

The ICI process, initially designed as part of a fertiliser production process, was based on a catalyst originally developed by Dr F. J. Dent, the Director of the Gas Council's Midlands Research Station. However, by the mid-1960s the Gas Council's Catalytic Rich Gas (CRG) process had become accepted by the Area Boards as the best available technology, and soon replaced both the ICI and Gas Recycle Hydrogenator (GRH) as the principal producer of gas (Ray and Jones, 1975). Credit for the development of the CRG process must also be accorded to the vision and dedication of Dr Dent and his research development team. Research for this process dates back to the 1940s, although it was not until 1958 that the first pilot plant was built (1 million cubic feet/day). By 1962 a second, slightly larger, plant (4 mcf/d) had been built, in which the problems of impurities were resolved. The task of convincing the Area Boards, who had no experience with a catalyst process, to accept a commercially unproven technology delayed construction of a commercial-sized plant until 1964.

While only on a minor scale as compared with the transmission network required for North Sea gas, the industry began in the mid-1960s to supply markets further from the source of gas production. As essential as knowledge gained with coal and oil gasification was the research and development work into technologies of storage and pipeline maintenance necessary for the use of Algerian methane.

The flexibility of the industry's research and development policy allowed for joint ventures between the industry and private enterprise. In the late 1950s, the R&D for the transporting and storage of liquid natural gas was undertaken by the Gas Council and an American firm, with seven shipments by 1961 demonstrating the viability of the project. By 1964 when imported natural gas had grown to commercial scale (see Table 15.2 above), landing and storage facilities had been developed for evaporating the gas. High-pressure mains, later to be used in distributing the first of the North Sea reserves, were constructed to control the flow of gas to seven Area Boards. This operation, which required considerable managerial and technological skill, instigated R&D into control and detection of leaks, line packing and welding, etc. Thus, to a significant degree, experience (and training) had been gained on a large-scale 'grid' distribution system, both storing and transmitting natural gas under pressure, well before the extent of North Sea gas reserves was realised. This undoubtedly played a major part in the rapid and successful diffusion of North Sea supplies.

With the advent of North Sea gas, R&D and expenditure rose in 1968/69 to £4,758,000, double the expenditure of the early 1960s. Reflecting the different needs of conversion to a high-Btu natural gas, to be transmitted at high pressure, the focus of R&D was redirected from production to transmission, storage, distribution and use. Expenditure in these areas rose from £0.39 million in 1966 (from a total R&D budget of £3.66 million) to £5.20 million in 1973 (out of a total of £8.12 million). Over the same period, expenditure on production and treatment rose only slightly from £0.96 million to £1.14 million, having dipped to £0.23 million in 1970. By 1968, transformation of the industry from one of declining output 'based upon localised gasmaking and distribution into a high-growth industry supplying "premium" fuel through a national transmission network' was virtually complete (Ray and Jones, 1975).

POLICY IMPLICATIONS

A broad base of R&D activity has clearly played an important part in smoothing the successive adjustments of the gas industry to the use of progressively cheaper primary fuels. The experience accumulated through each stage of development, from pilot to commercial scale, permitted technological change to take place rapidly, thus contributing to the growth made possible by the more economic feedstocks. These conclusions do not exclude the recognition that other variables have played a significant role in the industry's resurgence. However, the ability of the industry to respond in a competitive manner has rested with the ability to introduce and rapidly diffuse new technologies – once they had been proven commercially.

The demand for proven technology has at times been viewed as an overly defensive policy. With hindsight, the conservatism of individual Area Boards can be seen to have delayed the diffusion of what would become best-practice technology. This same autonomy, however, which in a number of cases proved a temporary frustration to the introduction of indigenous R&D, also provided a flexibility and balance which added a wealth of experience on pilot plants of varying foreign and private design. Much of the success of this strategy rests with the high value placed on pilot plant development; the working out of technical problems before the introduction on a commercial scale; and the experience gained in judging the technical merits of new technology. This can be contrasted with the strategy of the UK nuclear industry, and the difficulties with AGR technology resulting from the ordering of three different designs simultaneously, before adequate prototype development (see Chapter 14).

The combination of a shift from manufacturing to distribution with the maturing of indigenous R&D capabilities brought the usefulness of a decentralised structure to an end. However, a look at recent levels of R&D expenditure indicates that what may have begun as economic expediency in view of shifting feedstock prices has continued as deliberate policy. While a heavy emphasis remains on those areas necessary for the handling of natural gas, substantial R&D has continued on substitute natural gas (SNG), using oil feedstocks, as well as on advanced coal-gasification processes.

Overall R&D expenditure for the past three years has been £11.7 million in 1974/75, £16.1 million in 1975/76 and £18.2 million during 1976/77. Of this, nearly £2½ million, financed by oil companies in the United States, has been for co-operative R&D at the Westfield Development Centre, the site of the first Lurgi-style process in the UK. British Gas with the German Lurgi companies have here developed a high-pressure coal gasifier, operating under slagging conditions, whose commercial viability has already been demonstrated at outputs 'several times greater than that of a conventional Lurgi fixed-bed gasifier' (British Gas Corporation, *Annual Report and Record of Accounts*, 1975/76).

Building on the experience gained during the development of the Catalytic Rich Gas (CRG) and Gas Recycle Hydrogenator (GRH) processes during the 1960s, the British Gas Corporation, as well as operating a number of SNG plants in the UK, also provides technical support for the 14 commercial SNG plants operating overseas.[11] Although future oil prices might restrict these processes in favour of a coal feedstock, continued R&D expenditure of over

£1 million per year (through 1974–77) has resulted in improved catalysts which maintain the CRG's commercial potential.

The success in overseas licensing, unusual for a nationalised industry, demonstrates the current strength of the British Gas Corporation's R&D base. More important than the prestige that international co-operation accords is the opportunity to keep abreast of technological developments elsewhere. As the UK is unlikely to be the first to introduce SNG commercially, it can keep its options open by maintaining direct contact with development of this technology abroad.

With the continued need for peak load supplies, as well as insurance against the depletion of North Sea reserves, the ability of the industry to maintain its current R&D strength will be especially important in determining the future of the industry. In case premium demand exceeds natural gas availability (owing either to controlled depletion policy or to the approaching exhaustion of reserves), and as a means of retaining non-premium sales in the industrial market, the industry must be prepared to revert to its role as a manufacturer of gas by the 1990s. The need for manufactured gas may arise suddenly and on a large scale. The timing and scale of that demand is likely to depend partly on factors outside the industry's control (e.g. Government depletion policy and the price of alternative sources). This uncertainty places a premium on the industry keeping its options open. This will most likely be achieved through continued investment in a broad base of R&D, closer collaboration with the National Coal Board on gasification technology, and the continued licensing of its own know-how abroad, while also remaining open to technology developed abroad.

NOTES

1. The author would like to thank John Surrey, Gordon MacKerron and Graeme Madeley for their comments on earlier drafts of this chapter.
2. The West Midlands Board decided to build a Lurgi plant as early as November 1952. However, difficulties in receiving planning permission from local government delayed completion of the plant until 1963 (UK Government, 1961; British Gas Corporation, Annual Report, 1964.
3. Various authors place the capital costs of the ICI process at anywhere from one-third to one-eighth that of a comparable coal carbonisation plant.
4. The cost of conversion, estimated at £400m in 1966, ran to a total of £600m.
5. The innovations included cover a wide range of industries (i.e. steel, textiles, shipbuilding, brewing, etc.) with differing ownership patterns and engineering complexity.

6. A comparison of expenditure on plant per employee from Census of Production data shows the high cost of innovation in the gas industry as compared with manufacturing in general, or individual sectors such as chemicals.
7. The degree of dispersal around the mean for the manufacturing innovations is considerable. Even if it is true that oil gasification proceeded slightly faster than the manufacturing average, there was a substantial number of manufacturing innovations that reached the 10 per cent and 25 per cent benchmarks more quickly than did oil gasification.
8. Harlow (1977) notes that in selecting, in addition to the directors of each research station, three professors of chemistry, the Liversey Professor of Coal Gas, the President of the Institute of Gas Engineers and five members of the Gas Council, the Committee achieved a good balance between scientific and practical orientation.
9. The Gas Industry's First Annual Report in 1950 recorded a total of 341 scientific personnel engaged in research and development, the majority of which were employed by the Area Boards. According to evidence presented to the Select Committee in 1961 (UK Government, 1961) this figure had by then doubled.
10. The most successful innovation to come from an Area Board was Segas, a process for producing gas from heavy fuel oil, developed by the South Eastern Gas Board.
11. It is likely that, without the research contracts from the USA to test coals at the Westfield plant, R&D into gasification would have ceased in the UK (British Gas Corporation and Gas Council, *Annual Report*, 1976/7).

REFERENCES

British Gas Corporation and Gas Council, *Annual Reports* (1950–1977).

J. Chesshire and C. Buckley, 'Energy use in UK industry', *Energy Policy* (Sept. 1976).

C. Harlow, *Innovation and Productivity and Nationalisation: The First Thirty Years*, Political and Economic Planning, (London: Allen & Unwin, 1977).

Ministry of Fuel and Power, *Digest of UK Energy Statistics* (London: HMSO, 1978).

B. R. Mitchell and H. G. Jones, *Second Abstract of British Historical Statistics* (Cambridge: Cambridge University Press, 1971).

Political and Economic Planning, *A Fuel Policy for Britain*, No. 51, 1966 (quoted in Ray and Jones, 1975).

M. Posner, *Fuel Policy: A Study in Applied Economics* (London: Macmillan, 1973).

G. F. Ray and D. T. Jones, *Innovations in the British Gas Industry*, National Institute of Economic and Social Research (London: NIESR, July 1974) mimeo.

G. F. Ray and D. T. Jones, 'The innovation process in the gas industry', *National Institute Economic Review*, 73 (Aug. 1975) pp. 47–60.

G. Reid and K. Allen, *Nationalised Industry* (London: Penguin, 1970).

G. Reid, K. Allen and D. J. Harris, *The Nationalised Fuel Industries* (London: Heinemann, 1973).

H. J. Rush, G. MacKerron and J. Surrey, 'The advanced gas-cooled reactor: a case study in reactor choice', *Energy Policy*, (June 1977) pp. 95–105.

H. J. Rush, G. MacKerron and J. Surrey, *The Impact of Government on Technical Performance in the UK Nationalised Energy Industries,* A Report to the National Economic Development Office (London: NEDO, June 1976) mimeo.

T. W. K. Scott, 'Diffusion of new technology in the British and West German manufacturing industries: the case of the tufting process' (University of Sussex: unpublished PhD thesis, 1975).

UK Government, *Fuel Policy White Paper*, Cmnd., 3438 (London: HMSO, 1967).

UK Government, *Report from the Select Committee on Nationalised Industry, The Gas Industry,* vol. 1; *Report and Proceedings* (London: HMSO, July 1961).

UK Government, *UK Digest of Energy Statistics* 1960–1976 (Dept. of Energy).

T. C. B. Watson, 'The role of the gas industry in the British energy markets in the 1970s', in D. Forsyth and D. Kelly (eds.), *Studies in the British Coal Industry* (Oxford: Pergamon, 1969).

16 The UK Semiconductor Industry

E. Sciberras[1]

INTRODUCTION

The significance of the electronics components industry worldwide can be understood both by its phenomenal growth and by its pervasiveness. Growth was over five times that of US GNP for the ten years to 1973 in the semiconductor industry. In qualitative terms, new areas of application, from watches to microwave ovens to electronic mail, computing and telecommunications, have mushroomed. An understanding of the pattern of industrial innovation and economic performance of the still small UK semiconductor industry is a key to understanding the development and future competitiveness of a much wider range of advanced industrial sectors in the UK economy.

The semiconductor industry is part of the electronic components industry, which provides devices for the systems and sub-systems of electronic end-equipment users in the state, industrial and consumer sectors (see Figure 16.1). The components industry consists of passive (and electro-mechanical) devices and active devices. Active devices are electron valves or tubes and semiconductor devices.[2] Semiconductors can be discrete devices, integrated circuits, opto-electronic devices and microprocessors.[3] The integrated circuit combines up to thousands of discrete components in a single chip, so that they perform as an electronic circuit or even as a complete system. The most recent technical development is the microprocessor – MPU.[4] Although still only a relatively small section of the total semiconductor market, MPUs are the fastest growing product group.

The semiconductor industry has expanded in three main directions: first, traditional areas (brown goods, computers, etc.); second, technological substitution, where semiconductors have replaced electro-mechanical devices, such as telephone switching; and third, technological pervasiveness, where radically new areas of application have emerged, such as pocket calculators.

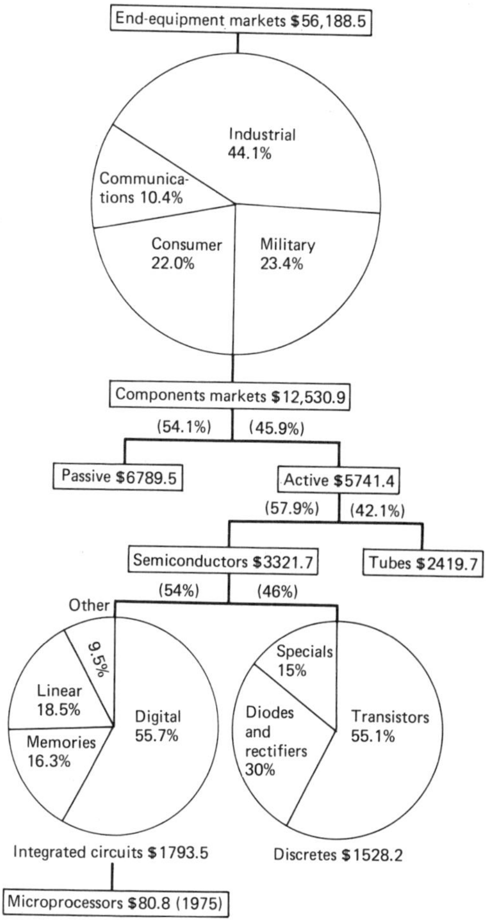

FIG. 16.1 Major elements of the electronics industry in the USA and W. Europe, 1974

SOURCE
Sciberras (1977, p. 45).

Hogan (1974) predicted that traditional fields of application, which now account for around 55 per cent of the market, will fall to around 25 per cent by 1980, with new applications increasing from around 5 per cent to around 40 per cent, including such areas as consumer, entertainment, health, security, transport, communications and domestic equipment.

COMPETITIVE PERFORMANCE

The industry in the UK

In 1971, the UK electronics industries accounted for 3 to 4 per cent of new output. Their R&D expenditure was more significant, accounting for almost 20 per cent of total R&D in manufacturing in 1971. About one third of the R&D funds were provided by the Government (Maddock, 1974). In value terms, the semiconductor market in the UK (production plus imports minus exports) was £62 million in 1971, £120 million in 1973 and £180 million in 1976. Forecasts have been made of a market of £350 million in 1979. This market growth was, however, accompanied by the poor competitive performance of the UK industry. While exports grew faster than imports, the trade deficit worsened from £17 million in 1971 to £60 million in 1976. The US trade balance, although fluctuating, was positive, and increased from $58 million to $229 million between 1965 and 1973.

As Table 16.1 shows, foreign multinationals account for about 85 per cent of UK sales of semiconductors. The leading position is shared by the subsidiary of the world's largest producer – the US Texas Instruments Inc., and the subsidiary (Mullard) of the largest European producer – Philips. The leading UK manufacturers – Ferranti, Plessey, Lucas and GEC – account for only 16 per cent of the UK industry. They are themselves multinationals, with Plessey's operations abroad accounting for around a quarter and Ferranti's for around one-fifth. These operations are, however, marketing and sales and not semiconductor manufacture.

The relative positions of the firms have not been stable. New entrants (domestic and overseas), drop-outs, and mergers have meant that, of the 17 firms listed as active in the UK semiconductor industry in 1961, only 11 remained in 1968, and six new competitors entered the industry. By 1974, only 10 of the 17 remained as major competitors. New entrants from overseas – Motorola, Fairchild and General Instruments – now occupy major shares of the UK market. Previous market leaders SGS and GEC (through ASM) have fallen to occupy minor shares. The two leading positions, however, have been with Mullard and Texas Instruments since 1962. The changes since 1962 for the leading six manufacturing firms are shown in Table 16.2.

The international industry

In 1977, the US market accounted for 47 per cent of the total world market for semiconductors of $6844 million, Western Europe for 24 per cent, and

TABLE 1 .1 Major semiconductor firms in UK, 1977

Firm	*Estimated UK turnover 1977* ($ million)	*Market share %* (approx.)	*Ownership*
Texas Instruments	54	21.1	T.I. Inc., US
Mullard Ltd	46	18.0	Philips, Netherlands
Motorola Ltd	26	10.2	Motorola Inc., US
ITT Semiconductors	20	7.8	ITT Corp., US
Intel	20	7.8	Intel Inc., US
Fairchild Ltd	14	5.5	US
National Semiconductor	13	5.1	National Semiconductors Inc., US
Lucas Ltd	12	4.7	UK
GEC†			
GEC Semiconductors	6	2.4	General Electric, UK
AEI Semiconductors	8	3.1	
RCA	8	3.1	RCA Inc., US
Plessey Ltd	6	2.4	UK
General Instruments†	6	2.4	G.I. Microelectronics, US
SGS Ltd†	6	2.4	S.G.S., Italy
Mostek	5	1.9	Mostek Inc., US
Ferranti Ltd	3	1.1	UK
Hughes Microelectronics Ltd	1	0.4	Hughes Aircraft Corp., US
NEC†	1	0.4	Nippon Electric Co., Japan
	255	100	

NOTES

† These firms have not been included in the study. It was not possible to arrange an interview with General Instruments in the time available. SGS Ltd has fallen considerably in market share in the UK since its break with Fairchild in 1968. It had been the third-ranking semiconductor firm in the UK, with 14 per cent of the market. GEC largely pulled out of semiconductor manufacture in 1969, when it reduced its share in the Associated Semiconductor Manufacturers (ASM) (owned two-thirds by Mullard and one-third by GEC) to a nominal holding. It has only recently made moves through its two semiconductor operations to re-establish itself.

SOURCE

Industry estimates.

Japan 29 per cent. The US share is expected to fall from 48 per cent in 1974 to 42 per cent in 1980. The Japanese share is expected to stay at about 28 per cent, and Western Europe's to rise from 23 to 28 per cent. In integrated circuits, the USA accounted for 53 per cent of a total world market in 1977 of $3633 million, Western Europe for 21 per cent, and Japan for 27 per cent.

A recent analysis of *firm* performance predicts that the increase in the Western European market will be satisfied by the subsidiaries of US-owned firms. US-owned production will rise from 62 per cent to 64 per cent in the world semiconductor industry between 1974 and 1980, whilst the share of world production by Western European firms will fall from 14 per cent to 10 per cent.

Until recently, the five leading manufacturers of the most rapidly growing segment of the semiconductor industry (microcircuits) were all US firms. The only European entrant is the Dutch firm Philips, following the outright purchase in 1976 of the US Signetics Corporation. The top 15 manufacturers are shown in Table 16.3. Four are Japanese. Only four European firms are in this group. None are UK firms.

TABLE 16.2 Relative market positions of six leading manufacturing firms in the UK semiconductor industry, 1962–77 (% = market share)

1962		*1967*		*1968*		*1973*		*1977*	*%*
ASM	49	ASM	23	T.I. Ltd.	23	T.I. Ltd.	18	T.I. Ltd.	21
T.I. Ltd.	13	T.I. Ltd.	22	ASM	22	Mullard	17	Mullard	18
Ferranti	10	S.G.S. Fairchild	16	S.G.S. Fairchild	14	Motorola	14.4	Motorola	10
A.E.I.	7	S.T.C.	7	S.T.C.	7	ITT	13.5	ITT	8
West. Brake	5	Ferranti	5	Motorola	6	Ferranti	4.5	GEC	6
S.T.C.	2	West. Brake	5	Ferranti	5	Plessey	4.0	National Semi-conductors	5
Other	14	Other	22	Other	23	Other	28.6	Other	32
	100		100		100		100		100

SOURCE

Golding (1971, p. 179), interviews, and industry estimates (1977).

US domination of the industry's technology was apparent from its early years. US firms developed 14 of the 15 first major product innovations, and nine of the 10 first major process innovations between 1950 and 1964 (Tilton, 1971, Table 3.1). This domination has continued since with few notable exceptions. The only technological contributions made by the UK were the Collector Diffusion Isolation (CDI) process of Ferranti, which Bell Laboratories failed to develop successfully, and Plessey's very high speed Process III integrated circuits. GEC Semiconductors also developed the first European Charge-Coupled Device (CCD) following US pioneers Fairchild, RCA and Bell, for use in miniature TV cameras. US dominance continued for the most recent technology – Large Scale Integration (LSI) where only two major non-US breakthroughs have been recorded, one by the Japanese and one European. This is shown in Table 16.4 The only UK development which

TABLE 16.3 The world microcircuit leaders (1975)

	Sales including in-house sales ($m)
Texas Instruments (US)	300
National Semiconductor (US)	168
Philips (Holland)	160*
Fairchild (US)	153
Motorola (US)	120
Intel (US)	111
Rockwell (US)	75
RCA (US)	73
Nippon Electric (Japan)	60
Hitachi (Japan)	56
ITT (US)†	46
Siemens (Germany)	33*
Toshiba (Japan)	29
Sgs-Ates (Italy)	23
Thomson (France)	20

NOTES

Main base in brackets.
This excludes production of IBM and Western Electric, who although major manufacturers produce semiconductors for in-house only.
* Philips $200 in 1976; Siemens $60m.
† Much of ITT's production is in Europe.

SOURCE

Financial Times (1977a).

possibly may justify inclusion in this category is an LSI version of the CDI process announced in 1973 by Ferranti.

Another indicator of relative technological performance may be obtained from corporate patenting activity. A total of 109,743 patent grants by the US Patent Office were made between 1963 and 1976 for the Electronics Components Industry. Patents of US origin accounted for 75 per cent of the total. The leading foreign patenting activity was by Japan with 6 per cent,

TABLE 16.4 Major product and process innovations and firms responsible 1970–78

PROCESS INNOVATIONS	*Firm Responsible*	*Country*	*Year*
Ion implantation	Mostek	US	1970
Self-aligned silicon gate	Intel	US	1972
Integrated injection logic	Philips	Holland	1973
Vertically oriented transistor (VMOS)	AMI	US	1975
Double polysilicon process	Mostek	US	1976
Automatic bonding on "exotic" (35 mil. film) substrate	Sharp	Japan	1977
Vertical injection logic (VIL)	Mitsubishi	Japan	1978
PRODUCT INNOVATIONS			
Static RAM (256 bits)	Intel	US	1969
Calculator circuit	Mostek	US	1970
3 transistor cell dynamic RAM (1K bits)	Intel	US	1971
Microprocessor (4004)	Intel	US	1972
1 transistor cell dynamic RAM (4K bits)	Intel	US	1974
Microcomputer (8048)	Intel	US	1977

SOURCES

Iann Barron (Industry consultant) and Mick McLean (Science Policy Research Unit).

followed by Germany with 5 per cent and the UK with 4 per cent. The rapid annual growth rates from 1963 to 1976 of German (16 per cent) and especially Japanese (145 per cent) patenting activity contrasts with the UK (6 per cent).

The role of state and military markets

The US end-equipment markets for semiconductors in defence sectors are five times larger than those of Western Europe. Government contracts of $40 million awarded to twelve US transistor manufacturers in 1956 made possible scales of operation which resulted in far larger yield[5] increases than otherwise would have been possible at the time. A year after the introduction of the first i.c. by Texas Instruments in 1961, contracts for three hundred thousand i.c. devices were awarded for application in the new Minuteman II missile project.

This pattern had already begun to change during the early 1960s. The widespread application of integrated circuits became feasible following the development of the planar process of manufacture by Fairchild, without Government funds and without military market objectives. The most important recent technological development, the microprocessor, was developed entirely for commercial application, by the US Intel in 1972 after a request by one of its Japanese customers for an advanced circuit for its calculator family (see Kleiman, 1975.)

The industry leaders also first introduced MPUs for commercial markets. The Fairchild F8 and the Texas Instruments TMS 9900 were followed only later by military devices, such as the Texas SBP 9900. This changing pattern shows that the most important recent technical innovations found their stimulus in requirements for standard devices for consumer markets, rather than in those for custom devices in military markets. A recent survey for the OECD by McLean found that the leading firms argued that state markets had ceased to be the major source of new technical developments in the US (McLean, 1978).

State and military markets still account for a substantial share of UK firms' sales. The Ferranti microprocessor was developed for the UK Ministry of Defence, and has found few commercial uses. This focus on specialised devices for custom markets, where Government is a major customer, will further entrench UK firms in market areas which are a diminishing stimulus for technical innovations with widespread applications.

THE INFLUENCE OF INNOVATION ON ECONOMIC PERFORMANCE

Successful innovation is crucial to competition in the industry. The UK has had firms which have demonstrated technical virtuosity, by being able to introduce products rapidly, closely following their US competitors. Ferranti introduced the first European microprocessor – the F-100L – while US leaders, Texas Instruments and Fairchild, were still getting the bugs out of their developments. The Ferranti product was even based upon their new process, Collector Diffusion Isolation. GEC and Plessey quickly produced microprocessors under licence from US firms, Intel and National Semiconductor. The UK firms, however, failed to innovate successfully, since the products were not developed into commercial successes. This weakness in follow-up development has resulted in poor competitive performance by the UK firms.

The *pattern* of diffusion of innovations has in the past reflected the price-elasticities of demand of various applications, from the price-insensitive military market, to the highly price-conscious consumer market. The *pace* of diffusion is linked to the process of steep cost reduction through cumulative production volume and experience which pervades the industry. This process is described by the learning curve, and is made up of a technological and a manufacturing element. For the semiconductor industry, it was found that the doubling of output volume reduced manufacturing costs by 27–30 per cent (Clough, 1974).

The rapidly falling costs of componentry are passed on as lower costs for the sub-systems and systems of end-equipment manufacturers. Such reductions encourage the wider use of end-equipment, and applications in areas previously excluded for reasons of cost. This increased end-use demand further stimulates semiconductor production, and a further round of cost falls, and so on.

FACTORS AFFECTING COMPETITIVE PERFORMANCE

Competition among firms within the UK semiconductor industry takes two distinct forms: one for the worldwide industry leaders, and the other for the smaller firms. The different types of behaviour stem from the approaches to the two types of markets within the industry – the mass, standard product markets which have become the preserve of the industry leaders, and the generally smaller, custom products markets which are left to the smaller firms. Table 16.5 shows the relative market sizes for particular areas of application in which the little league firms are concentrated.[6]

In the UK, the indigenous firms have avoided markets outside custom products, thereby staying in the 'little league'. Together these firms, Ferranti, Plessey, GEC and Lucas, account for only about 10 per cent of the UK market. The 'big league' firms are the world leaders, Texas Instruments, Fairchild, Motorola, National Semiconductor and Philips/Mullard. They pre-empt markets by the cost and price reductions that follow volume production. Custom volume markets and specific applications force the little league firms into a different competitive dynamic of high price, low volume. In the case of Plessey and Ferranti, the 1971 price war – which established the industry leaders – forced them out of the mass, standard-device market. Within the custom-device market, the firms have followed a strategy of hiving off for each other specialised 'niches', either with particular markets, or with particular technologies. The near-monopoly positions thus created are exploited through profit margins higher than for mass-produced standard products.

TABLE 16.5 UK semiconductor market distribution: 1972/3 by shares, and totals 1972/3–1977

	Standard		*Custom*		*Totals* *1972/3*	*1977*
	%	£m.	%	£m.	£m.	£m.
Data processing	34.8	(5.9)	1.9	(0.3)	6.2	28–30
Industrial control	19.9	(3.4)	.8	(0.1)	3.5	38–40
Consumer products	8.6	(1.5)	2.1	(0.4)	1.9	15–17
Communications	6.2	(1.1)	1.5	(0.3)	1.4	7–9
Motor vehicles	–		–			
Defence/Aerospace	16.6	(2.8)	4.1	(0.7)	3.5	18–20
Other	3.2	(0.6)	0.4	(0.1)	0.7	
	89.3	(15.3)	10.8	(1.9)	17.2	106–116

A new entrant cannot obtain large volume without low price and cannot obtain low price without low cost, unless it is prepared to sustain losses. For microprocessor devices, the cost of establishing a production line for an established manufacturer has been estimated at £2 million. The marketing costs of entry would be additional and possibly substantially higher in the (very likely) event of aggressive reaction by the leaders. For potential, aspiring entrants from the little league, in the UK, this cost would be totally prohibitive. A further barrier is that entry into the big league poses serious problems of adjusting to a totally new competitive dynamic. These adjustments are not only of size but also of new production, technology, management and corporate decision-making and behaviour. For the little league firms in the UK industry, these changes would necessitate complete transformation.

The UK firms' experience in competition and the focus of their management has encouraged short-term competitive strategies and perspectives. *The Economist* (13 May 1978) has argued that:

> In Britain shareholders have often seemed to look for high short-term profit rates, geared to dividends rather than long-term growth with or without dividends. Plessey, for example, is under pressure from its institutional shareholders to improve on pre-tax profits . . . but major

continental competitors earn less and the US Intel pays no dividends, just grows.

Ferranti, owing to its recent financial crisis, has pursued similar short-term profit objectives and Arnold Weinstock of GEC is renowned for his concern for short-term returns (Turner, 1978; *Electrical and Radio Trading*, 1978). Their custom-device orientation is reinforced by this focus and experience. The US competitors have planned and pursued essentially long-term strategies, which recognise the standard device manufacturing scale economies and massive long-term profit opportunities through the learning curve. UK managements have not been prepared to undertake this risk.

POLICY IMPLICATIONS FOR FIRMS AND GOVERNMENT

A wide range of policy options has been discussed in the UK industry, from opting out of hardware manufacture altogether, and concentrating on design or on custom products only, through to full, mass, standard product manufacture. Leading consultants and Government policy-making bodies, such as the DoI and NEDO, have indicated preference for one or other option. Sweden, France, Germany and Japan are evaluating various policies within this range. It is not possible here to review in detail the policies of Japan or of other European countries. But we shall assess briefly the options in the light of the preceding analysis.

Withdrawal from component manufacture altogether

In this option it is acknowledged that the UK must introduce microelectronics into its end-products to take advantage of the improvement in quality, performance and price-competitiveness that the technology will allow. However, it is far more important that the UK *use* the technology than it is for the UK to supply it. The supply industry is after all only 1–2 per cent of the economy.

This argument assumes that productivity and competitiveness of end-equipment is independent of learning in the process of design and manufacture of componentry. Componentry, however, accounts for an increasingly large share of the *hardware* cost and therefore the competitiveness of end-products. If the UK virtually ceased to manufacture advanced components, its end-user industries would become reliant upon US and Japanese component development. The principal competitive disadvantage would stem from the loss of opportunities to design end-equipment in parallel with component developments, and in turn to influence component development in the light of end-equipment market needs. This integration has been a major factor in the competitiveness of Japanese products. Also, the dangers of time-lag in the event of dependency on supply from abroad have been recognised by the NEDC in the UK (*The Times*, 1977a).

Maintenance of design capability only (with possible future specialist device manufacture)

It has also been suggested that a joint laboratory sponsored by the Department of Industry should be set up to undertake basic research in the field. This might eventually lead to manufacture of specialised devices. Some smaller European countries such as Sweden have also found this option attractive. The assumption is that knowledge from such research and design efforts can be quickly and effectively translated into useful and cost-competitive products for end-users. The evidence is strongly against such an assumption.

In the mid-1960s the US firm, Fairchild, was a clear technical leader in the sense that it developed highly sophisticated products of advanced design and introduced them quickly into production. But the firm was failing in competition because it could not translate technical virtuosity into effective manufacture and marketing. These are complex 'skills' in their own right, and expensive and difficult to acquire. Only after major strategy and management changes did Fairchild improve these skills and regain a competitive position in the industry (Sciberras, 1977, p. 135).

The attraction to the UK industry of the design option is obvious given the technical virtuosity of UK firms. Such a policy, however, would reinforce their innovative weakness. It could deny the UK industry the major source of benefit of a local component industry – the learning experience and economies of manufacture. This experience may itself be very important in the pace at which new component developments can be incorporated into new commercial end-products.

Manufacture of specialised devices only (with possible entry into mass devices if a successful 'special' is developed)

The option has been considered in French policy thinking of a joint venture of the 'national champion', Sescosem, with the US leader, Fairchild (*Guardian*, 1978). The Government funding of the German semiconductor industry has also had this policy basis. The arguments against such an approach are based upon the consequences of staying in the little league. In summary, they are:

1. The small scale of production of such devices denies access to the cost-

competitiveness of learning curve-based economies realised by mass standard-device manufacturers.

2. In terms of technical innovation, the stimulus for advanced developments has come increasingly from commercial application in large markets, such as calculators. In practice, the custom-device orientation of the UK firms has meant focusing on declining markets – particularly the military.

3. Overall competitiveness of the UK firms in the industry will depend upon competitive strategy changes by management, involving marketing, production, pricing and goals. In the light of the past orientation of the UK firms, a policy based upon custom-device manufacture will serve to discourage these necessary changes by reinforcing strategies and practices that evolved within the little league.

Manufacture of mass, standard devices

This option has been adopted by the Japanese industry. A four-year project began in 1976 with the Japanese Ministry of Trade and Industry and the leading five Japanese semiconductor and computer manufacturers. The aim is to develop VLSI technology for the next-generation computers by 1980. A total of $250 million is being provided – three-fifths by industry and two-fifths by Government. This has made Japan the only effective challenger to the US industry. The difficulties and objections to this policy option in the UK are numerous.

The first is the enormous cost for a firm, for the industry, and for Government, through subsidies, loans, etc., of entry into mainstream semi-conductor competition. The heavy financial burden comes with the decision to manufacture and market. For the UK as a whole it has been estimated that the cost of full entry into mass standard-device manufacture would be around £400 million.

The second is the questionable ability of UK management to adopt the commercial strategy necessary for success. The existing firms have not provided the opportunity to acquire this commercial production and marketing experience. The subsidiaries of the US firms do not formulate such policies in the UK; they are the responsibility of corporate management in the USA.

Plans to set up an entirely new semiconductor firm with returning UK engineers now in 'Silicon Valley' in the US, and backed by NEB venture funds, go some way toward circumventing existing management attitudes in the UK industry (*Sunday Times*, 1978). However, these fail to obtain the advantages of the opportunity for integrated design and development of components and end-equipment which the existing multi-divisional firms in the UK industry offer. If the benefits of integrated design and production enjoyed by the US competitors are to be realised, the future strategy for the industry will have to incorporate the multi-divisional firms as well. This is all the more necessary, given the present British weakness in the design and development of durable consumers' goods (McLean and Rush, 1978; Murphy, 1978; see also Chapter 3).

Some European firms have begun to acquire the requisite technological and managerial skills through acquiring technically strong US firms. The Dutch Philips began this trend with the acquisition of the US industry 'number 5', Signetics, in 1975. Bosch followed with the acquisition of 25 per cent of AMI in June 1977 and Siemens with 17 per cent of Advanced Micro Devices (AMD) in October 1977. The beginning of a UK approach to this strategy emerged with GEC's announcement that it had been searching for an acceptable US acquisition having looked at 50 companies since 1975 (*Financial Times*, 1977b). Unlike Siemens, GEC has not shown itself committed to mass component manufacture which may account for its delay relative to the German firms in finding a suitable 'mate'. Ferranti has also adopted this strategy, announcing the purchase in 1978 of the small US firm Interdesign, which manufacturers customer design logic arrays. Acquisitions aimed at providing the technological, managerial and market bases for firms' entry into standard market competition, along the lines of the Dutch and German firms' strategy, could prove a means to successful entry for the UK industry, but only if they are accompanied by changes in management attitudes and strategies.

NOTES

1. This chapter is based upon evidence from a study by the author of the UK semiconductor industry, *Multinational Electronic Companies and National Economic Policies* (JAI Press, Connecticut, 1977). More recent technical and competitive developments in the industry have been analysed in the chapter.
2. Semiconductor devices operate by '. . . a group of mobile easily controllable electrons in the solid (germanium or silicon). The motions of these electrons, in response to applied electric fields and signals, constitute the action of the various kinds of devices.' The inherent properties of semiconductor devices overcome the major two limiting features of electron tubes – reliability and efficiency (Brophy, 1966).
3. The major discrete devices are transistors, diodes and rectifiers. A transistor is a 'tiny chip of crystalline material, usually silicon, that amplifies or switches electrical current' (Brophy, 1966).
4. The device, which performs arithmetic and logic like a computer, but on a single integrated chip, becomes a true microcomputer, when combined

with a memory device. MPUs which contain all these functions on a single chip are already available.

5. This is the proportion of total output accounted for by devices of acceptable quality.
6. Integrated circuits may be developed for markets which have either requirements for standard devices or for custom or 'special' devices.

REFERENCES

I. Barron, *Report to the Computer Systems and Electronics Requirements Board of the UK Department of Industry* mimeo (Science Policy Research Unit, University of Sussex, 1977).

J. J. Brophy, *Semiconductor Devices* (London: Allen & Unwin, 1966).

C. Clough in 'Boom times again for semiconductors', *Business Week* (20 Apr. 1974).

Economist, 'Circuits Crossed' (13 May 1978).

Electrical and Radio Trading (8 June 1978).

Financial Times (20 June 1976).

Financial Times, 'Independent Market Estimates' (17 Jan. 1977a).

Financial Times (6 June 1977b).

Financial Times (9 Dec. 1977c).

A. Golding, *The Semiconductor Industry in Britain and the United States*, (DPhil thesis, University of Sussex, 1971).

R. R. Heikes, 'Role of an American Multinational in Europe', paper to conference, 'Tomorrow in World Electronics', London, 14–15 May 1974.

C. Lester Hogan, 'Prospects for Semiconductors', paper to conference, 'Tomorrow in World Electronics', London, 14–15 May 1974.

H. S. Kleiman, *Working Paper on the Microprocessor*, Research Report, Battelle, Columbus Laboratories (Battelle, 16 Dec. 1975).

I. Maddock, 'The Commercial Exploitation of Electronics Research', paper to conference, 'Tomorrow in World Electronics', London, 14–15 May 1974.

M. MacLean, unpublished survey for the current OECD study, *Science and Technology in the New Socio-Economic Context* (1978).

M. MacLean and H. Rush, *The Impact of Microelectronics on the UK: A Suggested Classification and Illustrative Case Studies*, Occasional Paper No. 7, Science Policy Research Unit (University of Sussex, 1978).

J. Murphy, 'Crisis for UK Consumer Electronics Industry', *Electronics Times* (19 Oct. 1978).

National Economic Development Organisation, *The UK Microelectronics Industry – the manufacturers' view*, Economic Committee for the Electronics Industry (London: NEDO, 12 March 1973).

E. Sciberras, *Multinational Electronics Companies and National Economic Policies* (Connecticut: JAI Press, 1977).

Sunday Times, 'State puts £m50 in electronics' (28 May 1978).

The Times (27 August 1977a).

J. E. Tilton, *International Diffusion of Technology – the case of semiconductors* (Brookings Institution, 1971).

G. Turner, *Sunday Telegraph* (4 June 1978).

Part III

17 Policies in Industry

Roy Rothwell

INTRODUCTION

The previous chapters of this book confirmed that a major reason for the long-term decline in Britain's competitiveness in manufactured goods has been an inability to compete in innovative products and processes. The purpose of this chapter is to discuss the performance of British management in the light of current knowledge about the successful management of innovative firms. The discussion will concentrate on British weaknesses in managing innovation, because Britain's economic performance in general suggests that the weaknesses highlighted here are widespread. This book, however, also reveals some strengths, such as the steady commitment of the chemical industry to innovative activities, and the considerable British achievement in technical innovation and international competitiveness in coalmining machinery. There are also examples of retrenchment and recovery, for example, in textile machinery. The British weaknesses are neither universal, nor irremediable. We discuss them here in the hope of stimulating action that will eventually eliminate them.

Over the past fifteen years several studies have tried to identify the features associated with successful innovators and technically progressive firms. Table 17.1 tries to present the main results that emerge from these studies. There is considerable agreement amongst them on the importance of a number of key features, each of which we shall now discuss.

CORPORATE COMMITMENT TO INNOVATION

The first and obvious requirement for successful innovation is the recognition of its importance in international competition, and the commitment of sufficient resources to innovative activities. Pavitt and Soete have shown in Chapter 3 that, particularly in the mechanical engineering industry, the British commitment to innovative activities has been declining rapidly

TABLE 17.1 Characteristics of successful innovators and technically progressive firms*

1. *Commitment to Innovation*

Innovative capacity is associated with an active policy of finding and developing new products. Successful innovators undertook a deliberate search for innovation. Successful projects are initiated by the firm's top management.

Success is promoted by enthusiastic and committed top management. The executive in charge of success has more involvement with, and enthusiasm for, the project; he has more status, power and authority. The clear will of management to innovate is essential to achieve successful innovation.

2. *Innovation as a Corporate-wide Task*

Innovation is a corporate task, not R&D in isolation; it cannot be left to one functional department. The balance of functions of production, marketing and R&D is important to success: it is a question of qualitative as well as quantitative balance. Successful firms, on average, out-perform failures in *all* the areas of competence encompassed by the innovation process.

Harmonious co-operation among research, development, production and financial departments contributed to the project's success and was an important characteristic of the technically progressive firm. Successful firms took steps to co-ordinate the efforts of the various functional departments.

3. *Attention to Marketing, User Needs and After-sales Servicing*

Successful innovators understand user needs better and pay more attention to marketing and sales; successful innovations arise in response to a market need. Technically progressive firms also adopt an effective selling policy. Knowledge of demand is an important factor in success. Successful firms have a formal marketing policy.

Technically progressive firms offered good technical service to customers. Successful firms provide an efficient and reliable after-sales maintenance and spares supply service. Successful firms paid more attention to user education and to adequate preparation of customers.

4. *Efficient Design and Development Work*

Successful innovators perform their development work more efficiently than failures. Successful innovators eliminate technical defects before commercial launch. A characteristic of technically progressive firms is conscientiousness in R&D.

Success was considerably facilitated if the enterprise succeeded in overcoming operational problems before commercial launch, and by adequate preparation of facilities for solving emergencies during the course of pilot production. Successful innovations suffer from fewer after-sales problems.

5. *Good Internal and External Communication*	
Good internal communication is associated with success, as is good intra-firm co-operation. Successful innovators had better contacts with the scientific and technical community in the specific area associated with the innovation. Technically progressive firms enjoyed better contacts with outside technical establishments and a higher quality of incoming information.	Successful innovators collaborated with potential suppliers and customers during development, and maintained frequent contac with customers thereafter. Technically progressive firms showed a willingness to share knowledge and to co-operate with outside agencies.
6. *Management Skills and Professionalism*	
A characteristic of technically progressive firms is the good use of management techniques. In the cases of successful innovations, planning was more highly structured and sophisticated. Most successful innovators formulate explicit innovation policies. Characteristics of technically progressive firms are: good recruitment and training policies and good-quality – and enough – intermediate managers.	Technically progressive firms possess an open-minded, high-quality chief executive. Senior staff are often engineers, but other graduates are included. Successful firms have an ability t attract talented and qualified people and provide ample scope for management training

NOTE

* This table is based on the main results of nine major empirical researches which together represent the study of over one thousand industrial innovations: Carter and Williams (1957); Hayvaert (1973); Langrish, *et al.* (1972); Myers and Marquis (1969); Rothwell *et al.* (1974); Rothwell (1976); Schock (1974); Szakasits (1974); Utterback *et al.* (1975). For a more comprehensive listing and discussion of success factors, see reference Rothwell (1977).

compared to that of our main competitors; and that most of this decline cannot be explained away as an inevitable and automatic consequence of slower rates of growth in Britain.

A recent survey by Rubenstein (1977) of management attitudes towards innovation and competition in four countries showed some significant differences between British managers and those of the other countries:

> Respondents in Germany and Japan were obviously the most receptive to competition. German respondents stressed the close links between competition and pressure for effective research, development and innovation. But, they seemed to feel that such competition was a positive factor in industrial development and for this reason were positively disposed toward it. . . . The Japanese managers also welcomed the opportunity to compete internationally, as this is where the real payoff to R&D and innovation exists in terms of market expansion. . . . In France, the larger

> firms seemed positively disposed towards competition, again for the market opportunities available. British respondents seemed far less anxious for competition in that they seemed less confident of meeting it successfully. (Rubenstein, 1977)

There is also evidence that, in a number of areas, British management has sacrificed long-term viability for short-term profits. Pratten (1976) found that Swedish industrialists gave greater priority to long-term growth and investment than their UK counterparts. More specifically, the major UK weaving machinery manufacturer consistently failed to produce new generations of machinery during the 1950s while enjoying market success and high profits. Subsequently the firm has declined catastrophically. The major UK spinning machinery manufacturer, in contrast, maintained a comprehensive and costly central R&D facility and is now among the world's technical and market leaders (see Chapter 7).

A report of the Boston Consulting Group (1975) on the failure of the British motor-cycle industry also found an emphasis on short-term profitability at the expense of longer-term aims:

> Prices are set at the levels necessary to achieve profitability – and will be raised higher if possible. . . .
>
> The cost of an effective marketing system is only acceptable . . . where the British are already established and hence profitable. New markets will only be opened up to the extent that their development will not mean significant front-end expensive investment in establishing D&D systems ahead of sales.
>
> Plans and objectives are primarily oriented to earning a profit on the existing business and facilities of the company, rather than on the development of a long-term position of strength in the industry.

As a consequence:

> . . . profitability, the central short-term objective to which these policies have been directed, has in fact deteriorated in the longer term to levels that now call into question the whole viability of the industry. (Boston Consulting Group Ltd, 1975)

Another recent report, this time on the British machine tool industry, reached similar conclusions:

> The UK industry's failure to supply British firms with the NC machine tools they have increasingly been wanting to install, is a direct consequence

> of the short-term strategies the machine tool firms pursued in the sixties. British machine tool firms were most vulnerable to major trade recessions because they were, comparatively, technically backward – both in terms of the designs of the machine tools they produced, and of the processes by which they produced them . . . They were, therefore, unable to compete effectively against their chief international rivals . . .
>
> This technical 'inefficiency' can be accounted for by the failure to invest in research and development or in new machinery. . . . ('Coventry Workshop': draft report commissioned by the Coventry Machine Tool Workers Committee, 1978).

There are, of course, notable examples of British firms sacrificing short-term profits in order to ensure long-term viability. For example, when in 1973, with the change from purchase tax to VAT, Lotus car manufacturers found a major portion of their UK market – the kit car – eliminated, management's response was to quadruple R&D, and to produce a new range of advanced cars. It does, of course, help firms faced with such drastic changes to have corporate and product development strategies that deliberately explore future opportunities and threats and outline the firm's response to them. Evidence from the UK textile machinery sector suggests that only a few of the larger firms formulate in writing explicit product development strategies. In the UK forklift truck sector Senker found that only one firm – the market leader – had an explicit innovation policy (Chapter 9). Current research indicates that it is mainly Continental European firms that possess carefully worked out long-term development plans in textile machinery and agricultural implements.

INNOVATION AS A CORPORATE-WIDE TASK: THE NEED FOR BALANCE

Innovation is a corporate-wide task that involves a balance amongst all those corporate functions that together, constitute the process of innovation. Successful innovating firms in general out-perform unsuccessful ones in *all* functions. Success generally does not depend on doing one or two things brilliantly, but on doing everything competently and in a properly balanced and co-ordinated manner.

In the UK, there has been a failure to achieve a balance amongst the different corporate functions, which may explain in part the relatively low productivity in British R&D activities discussed in Chapter 3. In the high-technology sectors, there has often been too much emphasis on 'technology push', to the neglect of production and marketing. In Chapter 6, M. Kaldor argues that, in both civil and military aircraft, there has often been much technological embellishment irrespective of users' needs, and similar features are identified in nuclear energy by Buckley and Day (Chapter 14) and in electronics and by Sciberras (Chapter 16).

In contrast, the British mechanical engineering industry has neglected R&D by comparison with other corporate functions. This emerges clearly in Chapter 3 and in the chapters on sectors of mechanical engineering (Chapters 7 to 11). It has often been assumed that 'British is Best', and that old designs, coupled with incremental change, are good enough. There has been a failure to respond to major technical advances made by foreign competitors. Technology-push has been weak, a phenomenon closely related to the small number of well-qualified engineers in the British engineering industries, in comparison with those of other countries (Albu, Chapter 4).

EFFICIENT DESIGN AND DEVELOPMENT WORK

Successful innovation requires efficient development work and, in particular, the elimination of technical defects preferably by the prototype or pilot stage, and certainly before commercial launch. Evidence elsewhere in this book suggests that such efficiency may be impaired in the UK as a consequence of the same duality between what might be described as the scientifically and technically over-endowed high-technology sectors, on the one hand, and the technically starved sectors of mechanical engineering, on the other. In the high-technology sectors, 'technology push' could sometimes be more accurately described as 'science push', to the neglect of normal engineering principles. Witness, for example, the description in Chapter 14 of the decision to build a commercial-scale Advanced Gas-cooled Reactor on the basis of a prototype an order of magnitude smaller. In textile machinery, on the other hand, many British firms had considerable difficulties because their traditionally trained mechanical engineers could not cope with the aerodynamics and the electronics that were essential features of radical and highly competitive innovations.

MARKETING AND USER NEEDS

The marketing function and close contacts with users are critical to successful innovation. Innovative firms must obtain regular information about changing users' requirements. They must be ready to translate these into design. They must also educate and train users in the proper operation, and in the limitations, of the equipment and the products that they make; this is particularly important for radical new products or processes, and for new customers for complex goods. It is also necessary to offer good technical service to customers, in terms of speedy response to breakdowns and of fast and efficient supply of spares.

There may have been a general failure in British industry to understand users' needs in the sense that great emphasis has been placed on the *price* of British goods, whereas *quality* is important in determining competitiveness. For example, British textile machinery producers ranked sales price of greater importance than did the machinery users; machinery users, on the other hand, ranked overall running costs of greater importance than did machinery producers. Overall running costs are clearly related to reliability and to performance – in other words to technical quality.

In addition, there has sometimes been a failure to establish comprehensive marketing networks and to back up products with a high standard of technical service (parts, spares, etc.). This has certainly been evident in forklift trucks and some areas of textile machinery. The British motor-cycle industry also failed to offer satisfactory after-sales support for its products.

By no means all of British industry has found itself unable or unwilling to adapt to changing market and economic circumstances. Some textile machinery firms have vigorously and successfully innovated to meet new user requirements; coalmining machinery manufacturers have consistently updated the design and performance of their machinery to meet the requirements of the National Coal Board; the gas industry, using its considerable technical capability, showed itself capable of reacting quickly to adapt successfully to changed circumstances (Rothwell, Chapter 7; Townsend, Chapter 8; Rush, Chapter 15).

One reason for the failure of British management to recognise the need to update products, and to make strenuous efforts to detect and meet changing user needs, is a heavy reliance on sales to the old Empire markets. Walker has shown in Chapter 2 the marked historical bias of British exporters towards these markets. As a result of fairly easy sales in these once protected markets, UK management has often failed to see, or to detect, the need to update products and to produce new generations of products. UK trade has suffered not only in the advanced economies, but more recently in traditional British markets as well, in the face of strong competition, based on technically superior products, from other advanced nations. This was clearly the case in the weaving sector of the UK textile machinery industry, and it is mainly in the new areas of textile machinery (tufting, texturising), where there was no tradition of sales to the Empire markets, that UK firms have performed best. The UK forklift truck industry is similar. It is a post-war industry, which operates in a diversity of markets. In both cases, management has generally been aware of the need to produce goods of high technical quality, to provide customers with the goods *they* wanted, and to mount the right sort of technical back-up operation.

GOOD COMMUNICATION

Successful innovation needs good internal and external communication: efficient communication links must be established between the functionally separate departments within the firm, between the firm and outside sources of science and technology, and between the firm and customers. This requires an open-minded, consultative and outward-looking style of management.

Within British firms, one important problem is the lack of communication between design and production. It is well known that productivity in UK manufacturing industry is lower than in major competitor countries. This is related not only to the relatively low level of adoption and use of modern production machinery in the UK, but also to an inability of British management to link R&D and design to production. In the textile machinery industry, for example, one major UK firm discovered that one of its products contained 50 per cent more labour input than the same product made by a major US company. In contrast to the American machine, the UK machine had not been designed with efficient series production in mind.

In the forklift truck sector, Senker found that the 'makeability' of US trucks was greater than that of their UK equivalents, because the US firms linked design much more closely with production (Chapter 9). The US firms were also more successful in incorporating a level of flexibility into the mass-production sequences through some modularisation in production; they thus succeeded in obtaining the maximum variety in output with the minimum of components. Inflexible production sequences can pose a serious barrier to the incorporation of technical innovations; there is some evidence of this happening in the UK tractor industry (Coombs *et al.*, 1978).

MANAGEMENT: SKILLS AND PROFESSIONALISM

The establishment in a firm of all the above features of successful innovation cannot be divorced from general management skills, from the existence of technically qualified managers at all levels of the firm, or from a deliberate policy of management recruitment and training.

As Albu and Swords-Isherwood point out in Chapters 4 and 5, British management is, on the whole, a long way from meeting this specification by comparison with other countries in Western Europe. The proportion of graduates in managerial and technical functions is lower, as are the status of engineers and the level of technical qualifications of graduate managers. One sector stands out in contrast to this general picture: the British chemical industry, where a high percentage of managers are graduate scientists or engineers. This is consistent with the relatively strong commitment of the British chemical industry to innovative activities over the past ten years (Chapter 3). These factors are much more widespread in Germany (and neighbouring countries with similar traditions) where graduate engineering training and technical excellence are given much greater weight by management than in the UK.

WHAT CHANGES MUST BE MADE?

If British industry is to become more innovative, there must exist the *will* on the part of top management to innovate; and British managers must recognise that in an increasing number of industries British goods have fallen behind those of our major foreign competitors in technical sophistication and design. This means that managers will be required to lengthen their time horizons, balancing immediate profit against long-term viability.

There also needs to be more balance in top management skills. For example, in the textile industry, a growing number of accountants in top-level decision-making has in some cases resulted in a neglect of investment in technical development. In the mini-computer industry, a preponderance of engineers in top-level decision making has led to over-engineering. A balance in top management skills is most likely to lead to a balance of functions, mentioned earlier, the achievement of which is so crucial to the firm's long-term success. More qualified engineers are needed in the British engineering industry, especially – as in West Germany and Sweden – in positions of management responsibility. There is a concurrent need for more management training to produce qualified managers with a high general level of competence.

In many instances, the 'makeability' of British goods seems to be dismally poor. This is probably related to the relatively low level of qualifications of British production engineers, and to poor communication between R&D and design, on the one hand, and production on the other.

Probably because of an historical bias towards once-captive Empire markets, many British firms have failed to establish marketing networks to discover users' needs and have instead clung to a traditional 'we know best' attitude towards the market. They have thus failed to detect often obvious demand shifts. The organisation of effective marketing, selling, distribution and after-sales service networks in carefully selected areas will be crucial to the future success of those parts of British industry which currently lack them.

The root of many of the problems of British management is lack of professionalism. While chance and uncertainty can upset even the best-laid schemes, and while no firm is immune from major changes in the economic environment, the success or failure of innovations and of firms rests squarely on the shoulders of the firms' management. The factors associated with the successful management of innovation are in no way unique. They are all general management skills – holding a balance and achieving co-operation between the different corporate functions, proper management of people, proper management of resources, etc. The point about the management of innovation is that it places *greater demands* on the application of these skills, since it involves the management of *change*, and change in *all* the functions of the firm, from R&D right through to marketing and sales and beyond.

The need for these skills is not restricted to high-technology industries, chemicals, machinery and durable consumer goods, from which most of the examples cited in this chapter have been taken. The capacity for traditional industries to survive, in the face of competition from the newly industrialising countries, will depend on their ability to adapt and to develop more sophisticated design, production and marketing skills. A recent report on the British footwear industry by the UK Government (Footwear Industry Study Group, 1977) concludes that the industry has weaknesses in:

> . . . marketing and product strategy, design and design management, exporting, financial control, production planning and control. . . . The areas listed are all ultimately the responsibility of company managements, and . . . the solution . . . lies in strengthening of management generally.

While much of British industry has been run by managers possessing few, if any, formal technical or managerial skills, our major competitors' industries have been controlled more often by trained managers possessing a range of such skills. It might be that, as in English cricket, in British industry the days of the amateur are numbered.

REFERENCES

Boston Consulting Group Ltd, *Strategy Alternatives for the British Motorcycle Industry*, a report prepared for the Secretary of State for Industry (London: HMSO, 1975).

C. F. Carter and B. R. Williams, *Industry and Technical Progress* (Oxford: Oxford University Press, 1957).
R. Coombs, P. Gardiner, M. Gibbons and R. Johnstone, *Technology Change and the UK Tractor Industry*, Interim Report for the Department of Industry, Department of Liberal Studies, Manchester University, July (unpublished, 1978).
'Coventry Workshop', draft report commissioned by the Coventry Machine Tool Workers Committee (Coventry: 1978).
Footwear Industry Study Group, *Report* (London: HMSO, April 1977).
C. H. Hayvaert, *Innovation Research and Product Policy: Clinical Research in 12 Belgian Industrial Enterprises*, Catholic University of Louvain, Belgium (unpublished, 1973).
J. Langrish *et al.*, *Wealth with Knowledge* (London: Macmillan, 1972).
S. Myers and D. G. Marquis, 'Successful Industrial Innovation', National Science Foundation (Washington, D.C.: NSF 69–17, 1969).
C. F. Pratten, *A Comparison of the Performance of Swedish and UK Companies*, Department of Applied Economics, Occasional Paper no. 47 (Cambridge: Cambridge University Press, 1976).
R. Rothwell *et al.*, 'SAPPHO Updated: Project SAPPHO Phase II', *Research Policy*, 3 (1974).
R. Rothwell, *Innovation in Textile Machinery: Some Significant Factors in Success and Failure*, Science Policy Research Unit, Occasional Paper Series no. 2 (University of Sussex, Science Policy Research Unit, June 1976).
R. Rothwell, 'The Characteristics of Successful Innovators and Technically Progressive Firms (with some comments on innovation research), *R and D Management*, 7:3 (June 1977).
A. Rubenstein *et al.*, 'Management Perceptions of Government Inventives to Technological Innovation in England, France, West Germany and Japan', *Research Policy* 6 (1977).
G. Schock, *Innovation Processes in Dutch Industry*, TNO Industrial Research Organisation (Apeldoorn, The Netherlands: TNO, 1974).
G. D. Szakasits, 'The Adoption of the SAPPHO method in the Hungarian Electronics Industry', *Research Policy* 3 (1974).
J. M. Utterback, T. Allen and J. H. Holloman, *The Progress of Innovation in Five Five Industries in Europe and Japan*, Centre for Policy Alternatives, MIT (Cambridge, Mass.: MIT Press, 1975).

18 Government Policy

C. Freeman

This book is intended as a contribution to the wider debate on the post-war performance of the British economy. Unlike most of the other contributions, it emphasises certain long-term weaknesses on the *supply* side, which have in our judgement seriously impaired the competitive efficiency of the British economy. It has attempted to show that the efficient management of technical change is central to both price and non-price competition; the former through cost reduction and the latter through product design and improvement. It has also attempted to demonstrate that the poor British performance relative to other countries in both these types of change is related to under-investment and to misdirected investment in the activities that promote such change.

To remedy this situation will require changes throughout British society by no means easy to accomplish. Somehow or other we have to improve simultaneously the quality of Government and industrial management, and to raise the level of skill and its application throughout the economy. This chapter deals with the changes needed in Government policy and argues for an active interventionist strategy on the part of Government to deal with our structural weaknesses. The objective should be to close the gap in productivity between the UK and other members of the EEC by the end of the century. The strategy to achieve these objectives should include the provision of more and better education and training for managers, engineers and other workers; and the mobilisation of a battery of policy instruments to raise the technical level and competitiveness over a wide range of British industry and services. Such a strategy must inevitably be of a long-term nature. The micro-electronic revolution will be both a threat and an opportunity. A considerable reorientation will be required in the objectives of British R&D activities, as well as other activities concerned with technical change.

WHY A GOVERNMENT POLICY?

Formulating and implementing an effective Government policy will not be easy. Earlier chapters of this book illustrate clearly some past shortcomings.

But we believe that Government must inevitably play a major role in improving British economic performance. Unless one argues that Government is inherently incapable of any improvement, or by its very nature is incapable of useful intervention in economic and industrial life, the potential exists for much more effective Government action. We believe that the effectiveness of Government policy and the quality of the decision-makers can and must be improved. Indeed we believe that this has to some extent already happened. But the whole of British society, including Government itself, will inevitably be involved in pulling itself up by its own boot-straps for a generation or more, if we are to reverse our long-term relative decline.

It is rare in our experience for economists, businessmen, technologists or civil servants to deny outright the importance of the factors stressed in this book. The theory of economic growth has always given strong and explicit emphasis to the role of technical change, and all recent research has served to confirm this. The theory of international trade and the theory of the firm have also given increasing emphasis to the crucial importance of technical innovation in competition. All schools of economic thought are agreed that Government must bear a major responsibility for the infrastructure which facilitates and promotes technical change.

Nevertheless, this formal recognition still falls a long way short of the formulation and implementation of an effective industrial policy. There have been some important cultural and structural impediments to the development of such policy in the UK. Most economists are still uncomfortable in dealing with *supply* management, even if they recognise the importance of technical change. They have a tendency to treat it as exogenous and outside their terms of reference. Whilst certainly accepting the responsibility of Government for the performance of the economy, Keynesian economics has in practice interpreted this responsibility predominantly in terms of *demand* management.

Until recently the civil service was also reluctant to accept a role for Government in developing a long-term strategy for industry. Interventions were usually treated as exceptional responses to a particular crisis or collapse. This of course sometimes contributed to their ineptitude, since they were not grounded in a thorough knowledge of the circumstances and the long-term possibilities. The 'sponsoring' divisions in Government departments sometimes tended to see their role as spokesmen and advocates for existing industrial interests and grievances rather than as long-term strategic planners for each sector. The most authoritative recent study of British economic policy since the war concluded unequivocally that industrial policies were 'limited to a peripheral role of tidying up at the edges of the economy, rather than providing any central thrust to alter and improve industry's performance and that of the economy as a whole' (Blackaby, 1978).

The combination of these mutually reinforcing attitudes and structures has tended to frustrate the various attempts to cope with the deeper long-term problems of the British economy. Such attempts have been made with increasing frequency during the 1960s and 1970s because the problems simply would not go away. The fluctuating fortunes of NEDO bear witness to the way in which successive British Governments have been groping with increasing anxiety for an appropriate way to cope with the structural weaknesses of British industry.

The past failures of Government would not have been so serious if British industrial management had been as strong and efficient as German industrial management in coping with the problems of international competition and the associated technical change. But this is manifestly not the case. In sector after sector serious long-term weaknesses have become apparent which require a concerted long-term strategy to rectify. The advent of the microprocessor revolution will exacerbate these problems in many sectors and, whilst North Sea oil provides a unique opportunity to develop a long-term techno-economic strategy, it is no panacea. It can provide some respite from the immediate pressures on the balance of payments, and some additional resources to undertake much-needed long-term investment and so ease the pangs of structural change. But the Dutch experience shows that it would be dangerous to be complacent. Such a temporary resource advantage could in fact aggravate our long-term problems if it is used as an excuse to postpone or avoid necessary changes.

All of this is not to deny the importance of exchange rates, financial instruments and demand management, but to make the simple point that *none* of these policies will be effective unless the long-term structural and infrastructural problems are tackled on the supply side. Technology policy and economic policy must be integrated to be effective, and failure to achieve this integration has been the chief weakness of industrial policy. For a while in the 1970s, The Department of Industry began to accept this approach. But previously 'technology' policy had often been thought of as something concerned mainly with rather esoteric and very expensive nuclear and aircraft projects, rather than with measures designed to promote efficient technical change throughout the economy, and there is now the danger of relapse.

We are only too well aware that it is extremely difficult for Britain to develop and implement such policies. Many of the problems and shortcomings listed above are themselves the manifestations of deeply rooted historical trends (see Chapter 2). The contrast with Japan is illuminating. Whereas Britain achieved her pioneering success in industrialisation partly as a result of abolishing corrupt and inefficient mechanisms of Government regulation and intervention, Japan achieved her much later success by very deliberate long-term Government policies for industry and trade (Oshima, 1978). Obviously a completely different set of attitudes and unwritten 'rules of the game' for relationships between Government, industry and the banks has grown up as a result of these differing historical experiences. Both the banks and the Government in Britain have eschewed responsibilities for long-term industrial investment and marketing plans which were readily accepted in Japan. In the past, British industry was often content to rest on the laurels of past achievements and the apparent security of Empire markets and investments. Attitudes to management, marketing, Government intervention and long-term planning have all reflected these socio-cultural factors.

POLICY OBJECTIVES

One reaction to these difficulties is to conclude that the British decline is irreversible because these problems are so deep-rooted. Another is to conclude that only a long period of strong protection for British industry can provide the climate for convalescence. These counsels of despair are not the conclusions of this book. Our belief is that once the diagnosis is correctly made and *widely understood at all levels in British society*, the great resilience in the British economic and political system will afford every possibility of a greatly improved relative performance. This resilience made possible national survival in the Second World War and it can do so again in our changed circumstances today. This book does not deal with trade union attitudes and industrial relations, but we do not think that those problems invalidate this general point. The participation of workers at all levels is increasingly necessary for technical change to be implemented efficiently.

There is, however, one sense in which the *relative* position of the British economy may continue to decline in common with that of other industrial countries, namely, in comparison with some of the developing economies of the third world. The prospect, even though still fairly remote, that some countries in Asia, Latin America and Africa may catch up with the USA, the EEC, the Soviet Union and Japan in standards of living is very welcome. Indeed it has been and should remain a major objective of the UN, the OECD and of British foreign and economic policy to facilitate the evolution of the world economy in this direction. An expansion of the world economy and of world trade is in any case a necessary condition for an improved British economic performance. A rapidly growing world economy in which the poorer countries steadily catch up with the richer ones is both a desirable and feasible global scenario for the next half-century, and we do not accept the view that physical resource constraints will prevent its attainment (Freeman and Jahoda, 1978). Such growth in the poor countries will, however, be an additional pressure on British industry to compete in sectors where technical quality, rather than cheap labour and resources, is the critical factor.

The *relative* decline that concerns us is different. It is the decline in productivity and trade performance by comparison with our partners in the EEC. We see no reason to resign ourselves to the prospect of being one of the poorest regions of the EEC indefinitely with per capita income less than half that of our immediate neighbours.

We are a little sceptical about the merits of quantitative targets in a market economy, open to the fluctuations of international trade and investment. However, in so far as an objective does need to be specified, we would suggest that the long-term aim of British economic policy for the next 20 years should be to catch up with the average levels of productivity prevailing elsewhere in the EEC by the end of this century, whilst maintaining long-term equilibrium in the balance of payments.

Some economists believe that this objective can be attained only by a British withdrawal from the EEC. Whilst accepting that there are serious problems of adjustment for the British economy, and that there is a need for some major changes within the EEC, particularly with respect to agriculture, we nevertheless believe that, following the referendum decision in 1973 and the the reorientation of the British economy and trade that has already taken place, it would be folly to reverse this process. It would tend to reinforce some of the very deep-rooted cultural obstacles to an earlier and more effective response to the poor British performance in the past 30 years – narrow-minded complacent insularity, reflected in an unwillingness to learn from others. For similar reasons we are doubtful about the desirability of a long period of general trade protection for British industry, quite apart from the difficulties of negotiating such arrangements internationally.

Protectionist strategies would in our view be justified only if in the 1980s it became apparent that the EEC rate of growth was so slow and the structural unemployment in the UK so high that this was the only way back to full employment. A much more desirable scenario would be a high EEC rate of growth in the 1980s, with an improving relative UK position within the EEC. This does not necessarily rule out selective controls to deal with the structural problems of particular sectors or firms.

Everything that has been said in this book indicates that such a scenario cannot be realised unless there are major changes in the UK. These will not in our view occur spontaneously, simply by virtue of our continued EEC membership. On the contrary, they will only occur as a result of specific UK policies within the EEC. It is for this reason that we have not directed our attention to what *European* institutions might be doing, important though this undoubtedly is. We certainly hope that EEC growth and industrial policies will increasingly concern themselves with the problems of management of technical change that are our central concern. This will indeed be essential for the competitive survival of the EEC itself in relation to Japan, the USA and the emergent industrialising countries. But our preoccupation here is with the *specific relative* weakness of the UK *within* the EEC. Only British policies can remedy these deficiencies, although the EEC can provide a secure and helpful framework, provided that expansionary economic and regional policies are maintained over the next two decades. If we fail to make some drastic improvements, then protection may be the only alternative.

POLICY STRATEGIES

A reversal of British decline relative to other EEC countries will require a considerable relative improvement in the technical quality and competitiveness of manufacturing industry. Strategies to achieve these objectives must inevitably be long-term. Changes in the education and skills of managers, engineers and other workers take a long time to make themselves felt in industry. Building up industrial skills and R&D capabilities also takes time, as does the design, development, commercialisation and marketing of new products. Fortunately some of the changes we advocate have already been initiated, but the consequences of today's decisions in these areas will often be felt only well into the future. Rothwell shows in Chapter 7 that decisions taken by British weaving machinery firms in the late 1940s led to their virtual disappearance twenty years later. Putting things right means thinking about the next twenty years.

The reader might expect a fairly detailed blueprint outlining the changes that should be made in the structure of Government and the precise instruments of Government intervention that should be mobilised. We do not provide this, for several reasons.

First of all, both politics and industry have a high rate of change. It is impossible for us to foresee all the twists and turns in British national life and the world economy that will occur before this book appears and is read. Secondly, we do not have the detailed first-hand acquaintance with the machinery of Government to make a 'blueprint' for reorganisation. Thirdly, and more important, we do not in fact believe that this is the principal requirement. There have been a great many reorganisations of the machinery of Government, both for industry and for science and technology, in the last fifteen years. We would say there have been too many, and that the main problem has been the lack of a wholehearted, long-term and consistent commitment on the part of Government, such as has been a continuous feature of Japanese policy. The choice of policy instruments is secondary to this commitment, and there is much to be said for using a great variety of instruments to achieve the long-term goals.

Such a commitment by Government will of course be effective only if it finds widespread understanding and support throughout industry and the community generally, and this too has been lacking. The main thing is to try and change the entire climate of opinion in the country, in order to create conditions in which the adverse long-term trends can be reversed. We hope that our book will make a small contribution to the achievement of this purpose.

EDUCATION AND SKILLS

We believe that the inadequacies of skilled manpower have been the most crucial British weakness on the supply side, and the one where Government clearly has great responsibility and power to act. Much as already been done; there has been a bewildering succession of enquiries, committees and recommendations about the education and training of engineers for more than thirty years. So much so that some observers have become irritated by the way this problem keeps coming back to the surface, and others dismiss it as the creation of a pressure group of scientists and engineers, and suggest that there is in fact an over-supply of engineers. It is of course true that supply has increased considerably since the 1950s, when the purely *quantitative* shortage was most evident.

However the problem of *quality* remains, and so too does the problem of status, misallocation of resources, and balance between various types of engineer. Many of the best engineers in the country were deployed in the nuclear and aircraft industries when similar individuals in Germany and Japan were much more widely distributed throughout the economy. The opportunity costs of this allocation of scarce resources have been very high. The shortage of electronic engineers is perhaps the most serious immediate problem, but a more general problem is the continuing lack of sufficient breadth in engineering education to embrace the systems approach to industrial and technical problems and to develop understanding of the economic and social problems involved. Finally, there is the deep cultural problem of the undervaluation of engineering as a function.

Albu has shown in Chapter 4 that over a century the quality and numbers of engineers and technicians in the UK changed only slowly in response to obvious shortcomings, and usually as a result of national emergencies. The Japanese, on the other hand, carefully studied various systems of training engineers and chose what they considered to be the best in the world at that time as a model for their own development. As a result of this very deliberate long-term approach, Japan and Germany (and other countries which imitated the German system) now have an enormous source of strength in the quality and attitudes of skilled manpower available to industry. This is perhaps the most decisive advantage a country can have on the supply side, as it affects the quality of decision-making and of production and marketing throughout the economy. Despite the already great relative strength of the German economy, as recently as 1976 the Vocational Training Act was approved which made several further major reforms, including provision for regular research and statistical work on future needs for vocational training.

We have to keep on looking in the same sort of deliberate way at all aspects of educating and training skilled workers, managers and engineers. Important steps have already been taken and others may be taken as a result of the work of the Finniston Committee. Although there seems to be a strong case for an extended first-degree course for some engineers along the lines now being supported by the University Grants Committee, there is probably also a need for a larger number of more practical engineers to be trained in a full-time course similar to those of the German Ingenieurschulen. But this is only one step in what must be a sustained unremitting effort to improve quality of skilled manpower.

Clearly the quality of university and polytechnic-educated engineers is fundamental, and industrial experience is vital for both students and teachers. The same principle of industrial and/or Government experience should also be applied in the education of economists and other social scientists to overcome the 'academic' bias (in the bad sense of the word) which is otherwise almost inevitable. As much as Government or industry, the higher-education sector has to examine and improve its own performance.

There are some signs of the demand for better-qualified engineers spreading in industry, but it is far from universal. The vicious circle of low remuneration, low status and inadequate quality will never be broken unless there is both the industrial demand for and the academic supply of more first-class engineers. This involves not only better and more attractive courses linked to industrial experience; it also involves raising the quality of the intake from schools and from mature students.

The micro-electronic revolution provides a unique opportunity to awaken enthusiasm, interest, new attitudes and new courses in schools. In purely quantitative terms the main expansion needs to be in the supply of electronic and systems engineers, and these aspects of engineering must also affect the curriculum for all other engineers. So, too, must the economic and social aspects of technical change. The micro-electronic revolution provides the possibility for Britain to tackle the supply of engineers and other skilled workers in such a way that the supply side is no longer a major constraint, but a major new opportunity for establishing a strong international position in a technology in which we do have some comparative advantages. The opportunity needs to be grasped at the level of higher education and at all other levels.

The education system can provide a broad basis of high quality, but it must be complemented by intensive and varied forms of training. The establishment of the Industry Training Boards and the Manpower Services Commission (MSC) provide a framework in which it is now possible for Britain to tackle the problem of industrial training and retraining imaginatively and effectively. But, again, comparison with Germany and Sweden suggests that we are still not thinking and acting in a sufficiently ambitious way and will have to devote even greater resources to this work. It is a matter of urgency to relate future skill requirements arising from the micro-electronic revolution to the training plans of the Boards, the MSC, and to the curricula of all types of educational institution. This is a case where it need not be 'too little and too late' if there is sufficient stimulus now.

There seems little doubt that, even after the achievements of the Engineering Industry Training Board before the levy/grant system was abolished, our craftsmen and technicians are, for the most part, less well educated and trained than those in other countries. This problem needs attention but, in the meantime, Government could resuscitate two ideas half-heartedly attempted in the past.

The first is compulsory day release from industry for all up to 18 years of age. The second is the revival of the technical secondary school or an explicitly technical stream in the comprehensive school, not as a poor relation but as an equal educational opportunity.

INTERVENTION IN INDUSTRY

Although industry also has an important role in training, the provision of more and better education for the workforce at all levels, and for frequent refresher, retraining and post-experience education is the major single responsibility of Government in relation to industrial efficiency. The Government at one time accepted some responsibility for an adequate level and direction of investment in most if not all sectors of the economy, and this went far beyond purely financial measures. This is a hard pill to swallow for the more extreme advocates of free enterprise. But there are so many areas of structural weakness in the British economy that for the Government to wash its hands of responsibility for sectoral policies could be a recipe for total industrial disaster. British problems in motor-cycles, typewriters, shipbuilding, cars and machine tools are all familiar. No UK Government could permit the wholesale collapse of large sectors of the vehicles, mechanical and electrical engineering industries, with all the associated consequences in employment and the balance of payments.

As we have already emphasised, the question of policy instruments is in our view secondary to the wholehearted acceptance of the commitment to 'supply management', not just on a fire-brigade or first-aid temporary basis, but also as a continuing long-term responsibility. A wide range of instruments is already available, including the National Enterprise Board, the National Research Development Corporation, the National Economic Development Office, the Monopolies Commission, various forms of public or hybrid ownership, regional policies, fiscal policies, and the various powers of intervention that the Government has under the Industry Acts. All these instruments are interrelated. Just as a good military commander will vary his combination of infantry, artillery, tanks, engineers, aircraft and so forth in different campaigns and climatic conditions, so Government industrial strategy must be capable of a flexible and varied response in specific sectors. The great diversity of circumstances preclude a single recipe or procedure.

The Department of Industry has in fact already used a wide variety of instruments, and several valuable new initiatives have been launched, such as the various special schemes to encourage new investment, particularly where this embodies new technology. Such schemes have been operating in the textile machinery, printing machinery, machine tools, paper and board and electronic components industries, and there are also a series of special measures affecting new applications of micro-electronics. These schemes, as well as the work of the National Enterprise Board, all illustrate the point that it is not enough simply to promote and steer R&D through the Research Requirements Boards, but that policy for technical change must also concern itself with the level and direction of investment and the structure of industry. All this already represents a first attempt to influence the supply side of the economy. But much more remains to be done, and quite new requirements will inevitably arise.

One of the most notable characteristics of the Japanese Ministry of Trade and Industry's industrial strategy has been its electicism in its choice of policy instruments (Oshima, 1978). It has not been inhibited by doctrinal purity or by tradition from using any combination of private and public investment and management which it thought appropriate to the situation. Nor has it hesitated to use the powers of Government licensing, procurement, financial aid and taxation to achieve its objectives, which have always been the long-term strengthening of Japanese competitive technical and economic performance in every sector. It is notable that for many 'traditional' sectors of industry these instruments operate mainly at the regional level and include what amounts to continuous technical and managerial consultancy.

The Department of Industry in this country had also increasingly recognised the importance of management consultancy and advisory services in relation to technical change. The Manufacturing Advisory Service was an indication of this, but it must also be remembered that the Research Associations have a well-established and extremely important capacity for providing technical advisory and information services. Many of the RAs now have an all-round capacity for the promotion of technical change in the industries which they serve, which goes well beyond the old co-operative R&D function. This role could be further enhanced and strengthened as another important policy instrument.

In discussing various policy instruments that are available we start from a position of eclectic agnosticism. In our view rigid general doctrinal positions are of little help in the development of British industrial policy. We start from the assumption that circumstances are very varied in different sectors of the economy and that, as Chapters 7 to 16 have shown, an appropriate strategy in one sector may have no relevance for another. This is of course the strength of the pure 'free enterprise' argument – that only the managers of the firms in each sector have enough detailed knowledge and experience to make good decisions. The argument for the flexibility, speed and initiative of decentralised enterpreneurship remains extremely strong whether in private, public or mixed enterprises. No one should underestimate the dangers of bureaucratic delay and bungling often associated with over-centralisation. But in our view this does not absolve Government from some responsibility for long-term strategy for investment and technology in each sector of the economy. Central overall responsibility needs to be combined with decentralised initiative in all mature industrial societies, whether capitalist or socialist, and we have to find a practical solution, not one based on doctrinaire positions.

The argument for decentralised initiative is at its strongest in relation to new small firms, which have an extremely important role in relation to the development of new technologies. At present, small firms have a less important role in the British economy than in the German, Japanese or American. They need special ground rules to help the innovative firm through the early stages of production and marketing of new products. The role of large firms and even Government laboratories acting as umbrella organisations for 'spin-off' small firms is also one to be developed and encouraged.

However, it would be illusory to imagine that a 'small is beautiful' policy could by itself be the cornerstone of British industrial policy. Going back today to Adam Smith will not help. There is no way in which the British steel, chemical or aircraft industries can go back to the nineteenth century, and there is no Government in the world that follows the rules of small-firm perfect competition. A policy of encouragement of small innovative firms is no panacea in relation to the massive problems of British Leyland, British Steel, the Post Office, British Rail, and so forth. Sometimes large is beautiful, sometimes small is beautiful, and sometimes both for different parts of the same industry. This is uncomfortable for those in search of tidy overall prescriptions or of political campaign rhetoric.

Nor in our view is a Government strategy of 'picking winners' viable. Almost all sectors of the British economy have shown some competitive weakness, and improvements are needed across the board. To this extent general arguments for protection or competitive devaluation have some validity. However, experience has shown that these strategies have not solved the more fundamental long-term supply problems affecting all sectors of British industry. The foundation of a good long-term techno-economic strategy must affect the entire economy, with a whole battery of specific instruments designed to cope with the individual problems of each specific sector. Just as the Japanese accepted that they had to learn from us, we have now to learn this from them.

The House of Commons Select Committed on Science and Technology (UK Government, 1978) in its report on the factors leading to Japanese success in science-based industries emphasised that these factors are all interconnected and related to a national consensus on the importance of science and technology for economic survival. Whilst it rejected the simplistic view that one culture can be transplanted to another, it nevertheless emphasised how much we can learn from their experience, particularly with respect to technically qualified people. We should also, not forget that Britain has many long-term social, cultural and political advantages in adapting to periods of change and conflict.

MICRO-ELECTRONICS

This applies above all during the next two decades when, on the one hand we shall enjoy the unique opportunity afforded by North Sea oil, and on the other we shall be confronting all the turbulence brought about in every sector by the micro-electronic revolution. The importance of this technological revolution is still under-estimated in Britain in terms of its overall economic consequences. The early computers were huge, expensive, clumsy, unfamiliar and often unwelcome. It is remarkable that they were adopted in the 1950s and 1960s as rapidly as they were. Microprocessors are extremely small, extremely reliable and extraordinarily cheap. Moreover they are becoming available at a time when a fairly large pool of skilled people exists (although not nearly large enough) already familiar with electronic computer technology and systems analysis. We have dealt in Chapter 16 with some of the policy issues relating to micro-electronics, but make no apology for returning to these issues in this chapter.

The micro-electronic revolution is not just 'one more' step in the process of technical change or one more new product. It is far more significant for the entire British economy than aircraft development or nuclear power, which at present constitute the largest part of Government-financed R&D activities. It affects both the design and the production process for an enormous range of goods. It will also revolutionise many of the service sectors, both private and public. We need to improve economic performance in almost all branches of the economy, but to achieve such an improvement throughout the economy we need to recognise which are the 'heartland' technologies – those that can give leverage over the whole system and raise its level of performance. Steam power and electric power were such key technologies in their time. Today, electronic information technology represents this 'heartland' technology critical for our entire future. The capacity to handle, process, store and transmit information is now the critical technology for advanced industrial countries in both industry and services. Although a great deal has been done, this technology still finds inadequate recognition in our Government structures, in our R&D priorities, in our investment priorities, in our industrial strategy, in our education system and in our national thinking. It must find such recognition. To achieve the necessary rate and type of technical change in this and other respects requires, on the one hand, careful programming of public and private R&D and, on the other, effective mechanisms for rapid and efficient embodiment of the technology throughout industry.

R&D ACTIVITIES

The previous Chief Scientist at the Department of Industry, Sir Ieuan Maddock, recognised repeatedly that the major problem of British industrial R&D strategy over the past 25 years has been the complete mis-match between the pattern of our Government and industrial R&D expenditures and the pattern of manufacturing exports. Despite his exhortations, the pattern has changed only slowly. We continue to spend far more on defence and prestige-type projects than on the technologies which matter most for industrial competitiveness. Not only is the scale of German and Japanese industrial R&D now twice as great as our own in absolute terms, it is also directed far more to those industries which matter most in terms of world trade: machinery, electrical goods, electronics, instruments, chemicals. Several chapters in this book have emphasised our relative weakness in mechanical engineering: the new electronic technologies could be one means of helping to overcome these weaknesses.

It is quite possible to change this situation. The establishment of the various Research Requirements Boards within the Department of Industry has introduced an element of long term strategic thinking and planning where it is most needed. We now for the first time have the basis for a deliberate long-term strategy for R&D which combines Government and industrial resources. A gap still remains in the support of 'fundamental' or 'enabling' technologies. These are not promoted on a sufficient scale by Rothschild methods or by the market, or by the universities. However, the Advisory Council for Applied Research and Development has shown the type of awareness and initiative that suggests that it may play an important role in the determination and coordination of strategic R&D policy.

Most of the required R&D can and should be performed in industry with appropriate stimuli where needed; but the major Government laboratories and the smaller Government laboratories have together great scientific and technical resources, including considerable computing facilities and skills and a great deal of expertise generally in electronics. If these resource could be deployed effectively they could greatly assist the development and application of micro-processor and other fundamental technology throughout the economy.

Many people are highly sceptical about the ability of Government laboratories to make this type of contribution to industrial and service technology. But there is a precedent. By all accounts the achievements of British radar R&D were one of the great success stories of the Second World War, and several historians have suggested that it was decisive for our national survival. The whole of this effort was spearheaded by the TRE, which developed a wide range of new equipment that was technically ahead of Germany and all other countries at that time. This was a model of good technology. Good decisions were made about the allocation of resources to the right policy priorities in R&D, because the R&D decisions were related all the time to scientific advances and the needs of the users – in this case the armed forces. There was an intimate dialogue all the time between the TRE industry and the ultimate users.

However, it would be wrong to overemphasise the role of Government research establishments. It is the performance of industry and the services that matters most. In this book we have been dealing almost entirely with manufacturing, but this should not be taken in any way as implying that we belittle or underestimate the present and future importance of both private and public sector service activities for the UK, especially communications and information. Public investment and a clear long-term strategy are essential here, particularly in relation to telecommunications, where the Post office is a major influence on the rate and direction of innovative and investment activities.

CONCLUSIONS

Getting the right national priorities in R&D is only one step, although a very important one. The promotion of technical change on the requisite scale means much more. Government must also concern itself with the improvement of technical quality throughout the economy. Much of this will depend on the behaviour and decisions of management at all levels. But Government economic and technological policies can create a climate which makes it easier for managers and workers to become aware of, to develop and to use new technologies efficiently. In the specific case of the microprocessor revolution, information, advisory and consultancy services to potential users of of microprocessors are extremely important, and the Government research establishments, the Research Associations, the Department of Industry and the higher education sector all have an important part to play, as well as specialist organisations, such as the National Computing Centre: it would be wrong to concentrate Government support solely on the supply industry.

Finally, some of our critics would maintain that this book is purely 'technocratic' and that it ignores on the one hand the whole issue of 'quality of life' and on the other the issue of fundamental changes in the social and political system, whether in the direction of a pure free-market economy, of full-blooded socialism, or some other ideal. We would fully accept that the only justification for the types of change we are advocating is to improve the quality of life for the people of this and other countries. But we do not believe that it will be possible to make such improvements, under whatever social or political system, unless the problems we have described are tackled. Moreover, we believe that unless they are dealt with, there is a serious possibility of relative and absolute deterioration in the quality of life in the next next twenty years.

We would fully accept that there are many other issues, such as environmental protection, civil liberties, urban renewal, the future of the arts and so forth, which are extremely important for the future quality of life. We are not competent to deal with all these issues but we do not take the philistine position that none of them matter by comparison with economic efficiency. However, we do take the view that improvements in all these areas do in part depend on some improvement in the performance of the economy. That is the rationale for our choice of theme.

REFERENCES

F. T. Blackaby (ed.), *British Economic Policy 1960–1974* (London: Cambridge University Press and National Institute of Economic and Social Research, 1978).

K. Oshima, *The Role of Technology in the Change of Industrial Structure* (Japan: Industrial Research Institute (IRI), 1978).

C. Freeman and M. Jahoda (eds), *World Futures: The Great Debate* (London: Martin Robertson, 1978).

UK Government, Select Committee on Science and Technology, *Innovation in Research and Development in Japanese-based Industry*, vol. 1: *Report* (London: HMSO, 1978).

Author Index

Subject Index